The Political Economy of China's Provinces

The Political Economy of China's Provinces challenges the notion of a centralised and unified China, and outlines how provinces are taking on new economic and political roles, forced upon them by decentralisation. Although central leadership in Beijing retains the overall initiative, decision-making powers for major policies are shifting to the provinces. The provinces are becoming economic and political agents with their own economic/social agendas, and distinct political and cultural identities.

One of the main tenets of this volume is that Chinese provinces in reform cannot be easily subsumed under larger policy frameworks such as the coastal–inland dichotomy or major economic regions. Instead, in this groundbreaking volume, the provinces have been analysed with a view to their variations in terms of geography, competitive advantage, economic priority, demand from the centre, political ideology and cultural policy as determinants of emerging provincial identities. These determinants provide more subtle insights into the development of individual provinces as well as their potential for interregional interaction and inter-provincial competition. The issue of provincial identities, as it emerges from this approach, is a complex one which includes economic strategies, political ideology, social policies, cultural elements, and can be closely linked with local tradition stretching back decades or even centuries.

On the basis of seven provincial case-studies, the book charts different provincial paths of economic and political development, and analyses how individual provinces use their comparative and competitive advantage to formulate strategies in inter-provincial competition. This is a radical new approach which contests the idea that it is safe to regard what happens in one province as representative for the whole country.

Hans Hendrischke is Head of the Department of Chinese and Indonesian Studies at the University of New South Wales. **Feng Chongyi** is Senior Lecturer in Chinese Studies at the University of Technology, Sydney.

The Political Economy of China's Provinces

Comparative and competitive advantage

Edited by Hans Hendrischke and Feng Chongyi

London and New York

First published 1999
by Routledge
11 New Fetter Lane, London EC4P 4EE

Simultaneously published in the USA and Canada
by Routledge
29 West 35th Street, New York, NY 10001

Routledge is an imprint of the Taylor & Francis Group

Typeset in Times by Keystroke, Jacaranda Lodge, Wolverhampton
Printed and bound in Great Britain by Creative Print & Design
(Wales), Ebbw Vale

British Library Cataloguing in Publication Data
A catalogue record for this book is available from the British Library

Library of Congress Cataloging in Publication Data
The Political Economy of China's Provinces: Comparative and
    competitive advantage / edited by Hans Hendrischke and Feng Chongyi.
        p.   cm.
    Includes bibliographical references and index.
    1. China – Economic conditions – 1976–   2. China – Economic
policy – 1976–   3. State governments – China.   4. Central – local
government relations – China.   5. Decentralisation in government –
China.   6. China – Politics and government – 1976–   I. Hendrischke,
Hans J.   II. Feng, Chongyi
HC427.92.P64 1999
338.951–dc21   98–31541
                                                                          CIP

ISBN 0–415–20776–2 (pbk)
ISBN 0–415–20775–4 (hbk)

Contents

Figures

Maps

Tables

Preface

This volume is part of a project to explore the complexities of China's provinces under reform in their geographical, economic, political and cultural diversity. The project *China's Provinces in Reform* is based on the premise that major economic, social and political developments are emanating from the provinces rather than from the centre.

In this volume, seven major Chinese provinces have been analysed with regard to their variations in terms of geography, competitive and comparative advantage, economic priority, demand from the centre, political ideology and cultural policy. These determinants of emerging provincial identities provide new insights into economic strategies of individual provinces as well as their potential for interregional interaction and inter-provincial competition. The main theme of this volume is to bring to light the links between geographical constraints, economic strategy formation under market conditions and political identities.

The research heralds a general change in the understanding of contemporary China, which for decades was based on the perception of a rather conformist China, where it was safe to regard what happened in one province as representative of the whole country. Like the previous volume *China's Provinces in Reform: class, community and political culture*, edited by David S.G. Goodman, it is the result of a workshop held in China under the auspices of the Institute for International Studies of the University of Technology, Sydney and Zhejiang University in October 1996. Over forty participants from four continents discussed the chapters included in this volume as well as the equally important papers presented by Thomas Heberer, Jiao Xingguo, Linda Li, Dali Yang, Yan Chunyou and Yao Xianguo.

Thanks are due to Cathay Pacific Airlines for agreeing to provide corporate sponsorship for the workshop. The Institute for International Studies provided the essential support which made this volume possible. Moreover, the Institute's director, Professor David S.G. Goodman, laid the foundations for the establishment of a new UNSW–UTS Centre for Research on Provincial China, jointly organised by the University of New South Wales and the University of Technology, Sydney. The Centre will continue the research on *China's Provinces in Reform* with forthcoming conferences, workshops and publications.

Hans Hendrischke
Feng Chongyi

Abbreviations

ADB	Asian Development Bank
CCP	Chinese Communist Party
CPI	Consumer Price Index
FDI	Foreign Direct Investment
FYP	Five Year Plan
GDP	Gross Domestic Product
GMP	Gross Material Product
GOV	Gross Output Value
GVAO	Gross Value Agricultural Output
GVIAO	Gross Value Industrial and Agricultural Output
IOV	Industrial Output Value
NMP	Net Material Product
NTA	National Tourism Administration
PRC	People's Republic of China
RMB	Renminbi (People's Currency)*
SOE	State-Owned Enterprise
TEDA	Tianjin Economic and Technological Development Area
TFP	Total Factor Productivity
TVE	Township and Village Enterprise
VAT	Value Added Tax
WTO	World Trade Organisation

Note:
* 8.3 *yuan* (dollar) rmb [Renminbi = People's Currency] = US$1.00

1   Provinces in competition

Region, identity and cultural construction

Hans Hendrischke

China's quiet transition into the post-Deng era has disproved the speculations of impending dramatic leadership struggles and regional instability. Some dramatic scenarios were based on the link between a divided and immobilised central leadership and regional groupings breaking away from central control. The kernel of truth in these speculations is that the central government is indeed becoming less interventionist and that provincial power and influence are increasing. One of the reasons for China's apparent stability is that the two are closely linked. Essentially, a new relationship between the central and regional power structures is emerging. As the localities increase their regulatory power and independence, the centre has reacted not in an antagonistic fashion, but rather by coopting provincial leaders and negotiating issues with provinces in a more predictable manner. This has been evident since 1992 and has been confirmed by the fifteenth National Party Congress in September 1997. The much quoted team approach of the Chinese leadership not only covers central stake holders such as party, military and government, but also includes a coordination between central and local interests.

While Chinese power structures have never been transparent, much more is known about the central perspective of leadership conflicts and central–provincial relations than the provincial perspective of internal provincial politics, inter-provincial conflicts and relations with the centre. The degree of autonomy exercised by different provinces in their negotiations with the centre is difficult to assess, because it emerges as the result of an on-going bargaining process.[1] Even what constitutes local interests and who articulates them is difficult to discern.[2] As the decision-making powers by provinces over their investments are expanding, the centre is reducing its coordination of provincial economic policies. There is now considerable overlap of investment from provincial governments struggling to gain a foothold in promising business sectors. One emerging field of study is therefore the analysis of business strategies employed by provincial governments in pursuit of competitive advantages over other provinces.

Before turning to this topic, the role of provinces and competing levels of regional government coordination in China's changing economic and social geography requires attention. In the process of reform, provincial-level units have been the dominant political actors at regional level and have had to take on more tasks as the centre reduced its direct control. However, there are indications that, with increasing inter-provincial and international integration, provinces might no longer have the size and scope to provide effective economic and regulatory coordination, thus creating a role for greater regions. On the other hand, the exercise of economic control by a provincial leadership might be undermined by the factual power of sub-provincial economic regions where economic activities are concentrated. These issues gain crucial importance when industrial planning and structural policies are at stake, and policy-making moves away from vertical coordination inherited from the planned economy to the horizontal integration that comes with decentralisation.

For the foreseeable future, however, provinces are still the most likely regional sub-divisions to hold local power, as former functions of the central state, ranging from industrial and foreign trade policies to the responsibility for social security, are transferred to provinces and municipalities. Once provinces formulate their own economic and social policies and are able to articulate their specific interests in the light of their differing circumstances, the expectation is that in the process they will also gain stronger political identities.[3] Historically, many provinces have distinct cultural identities based on local history and traditions, art forms, popular beliefs and customs, local cuisine and even personal traits, among many other characteristics. The new role of provinces brings existing notions of provincial identity out of their cultural isolation by integrating them in provincial-level political and economic agendas. Provincial leaders have discovered that they can appeal to provincial loyalty as a way to gain public support for their policies. These broad institutional developments are as yet ill-defined for the simple reason that more definite forms will only emerge as different provinces find different ways to adapt to the new and changing circumstances. To address these economic, political and cultural changes is the task of the project to examine *China's Provinces in Reform* which has produced this and a previous volume of provincial studies.[4]

This volume comes amidst a range of new publications on regional and provincial China, by both Chinese and Western authors.[5] Many of these publications still focus on central–local relations and larger regional groupings such as coastal and inland provinces rather than on the role of individual provinces and inter-provincial relations. To some degree, the old paradigm of a highly centralised state dealing with individual provinces and groups of provinces by bestowing and withholding favours still holds currency, not least because the centre can wield considerable influence over provincial matters and, more generally, because a new relationship has not yet been formalised in a new institutional framework. This and the previous volume in the project to examine *China's Provinces in Reform* follow a different approach by taking the provincial perspective and concentrating on how individual provinces have actively or reluctantly embarked on a reform course in the 1980s and adapted their provincial economies, politics and culture to the market environment that emerged after 1992. This research heralds a general change in the understanding of contemporary China which for decades was based on the perception of a rather conformist China, where it was safe to regard what happened in one province as representative of the whole country.

It is worth asking why the role of individual provinces has as yet not received more attention. One factor is certainly the propensity of the centrally controlled Chinese media to play down the autonomy of provinces, and the parallel tendency of provincial media not to boast of their degree of factual autonomy and instead emphasise their congruence with central policies. The provincial studies in *China's Provinces in Reform* have demonstrated a surprising provincial variety and degree of autonomy in implementing central policies. They show that throughout the 1980s central reform policies met a very mixed response from the provinces. Mostly for fear of losing central subsidies and investment, some provinces were unwilling to accept the gradual withdrawal of the centre and resisted reform, while others were quick in making use of the opportunities they saw in reform policies and benefited greatly. The provincial studies in this and the previous volume on *China's Provinces in Reform* confirm that the final breakthrough came only in 1992. From then on all provinces had to take on additional economic responsibilities as the centre delegated more economic and social functions.

On the basis of these results, it is tempting to project what China will look like if it is composed of provincial economies under loose central control and all with similar decision-making powers over their own economic and related political and social affairs. Such projection assumes that the centre will continue to relinquish its support for individual provinces in the form of preferential policies or subsidies and instead provide a macro-economic framework designed to allow each province to maximise its own benefit under generally applicable rules. One could argue that this is far from present realities where a myriad of central and provincial institutions regulate free economic exchange between provinces, but it is certainly not far-fetched in the light of China's application to join the World Trade Organisation. As a WTO member, China's markets would not only be opened to external but also to internal competition and provinces would have to compete on an equal footing and without protective barriers.[6] But even without such external pressure they will take on additional tasks and functions.

The studies collected in this volume bring into focus some of the general implications that will arise from this change. Although each of the provincial chapters has to be broad enough to cover the specific circumstances of each province, there are nevertheless a few major issues around which the studies can be grouped. These are the relationship between provinces and other regional divisions, the way in which increasing economic interaction and competition between provinces contributes to distinct provincial identities and, finally, the process by which provinces as essentially administrative bodies are striving to become local centres of identification linking political with economic and cultural loyalties.

GREATER REGIONS, SUB-PROVINCIAL REGIONS AND PROVINCES

China's sub-division into provinces took shape during the Yuan Dynasty and its
essential principle of basing provinces on administrative rather than economic
considerations has remained in force ever since. For centuries, therefore, there
existed a separation between economic and administrative boundaries. During
this time, the central provinces remained relatively stable and well defined, albeit
with frequent minor rearrangements and border corrections. In contrast, economic
regions were defined in different ways for different purposes. In terms of natural
geography, China falls into several large regions. For late Imperial China,
William Skinner in his seminal work combined these natural features and market
structures to define nine macro-economic regions which generally cut across
provinces' borders.[7] Skinner has since used more recent and further disaggregated
data to argue that these macro-regions are still relevant to the modern Chinese
economy.[8] However, since China's early industrialisation, attention has shifted
to the division between coastal and inland regions that occurred as a result of
industrial concentration along the coast during a century of political turmoil.
An attempt to create unified administrative and economic sub-provincial regions
was made in Manchuria under Japanese occupation in the 1930s, when the
original four provinces were split up into 19 smaller provinces in order to align
administrative borders more closely with the local economic geography.[9]

Under the People's Republic of China, the separation between administrative
and economic regions remained in force. When the People's Republic of China
was founded, the new government returned to the old provincial borders and set
up a parallel structure of Greater Administrative Regions. Although these six
Greater Administrative Regions (Huabei, Dongbei, Huadong, Zhongnan, Xinan
and Xibei) geographically largely coincide with today's larger economic regions,
they fulfilled a political role at the time in giving the Communist Party more
regional flexibility in consolidating its power. After the new Constitution came
into force in 1954, these regions were abolished and the provinces reverted to
being the major sub-central political and administrative units. By that time, the
first Five Year Plan was taking shape. It confirmed the coastal–inland division of
the country as the major principle of regional economic policies. Under the first
Five Year Plan (1953–57), regional policies were designed to shift the focus of
industrial development from the relatively developed coastal region to the
underdeveloped inland areas, especially the western provinces. These policies
underpinned regional planning for the following decades. Under central planning,
the leadership in Beijing channelled investment into the inland and the western
regions. The coastal provinces had to support this redistribution of income
with reduced economic growth. The Third Front policy during the late 1960s and
the first half of the 1970s further intensified this effect when investment was
directed to inaccessible inland areas thought safe from a potential Soviet nuclear
strike. Overall, the regional bias in favour of inland development continued until
the late 1970s. Provincial governments had little influence on these regional

economic policies and acted more as agents of the central government than as representatives of local interests.

When economic reform started in the early 1980s, the separation between economic and political sub-division was nominally left untouched. The regional impetus of the initial reform period was to reverse the direction of regional economic support and make the coastal region the beneficiary of central policies. Under the Sixth and Seventh Five Year Plan, i.e. during the decade from 1981 to 1990, a whole array of economic and political incentives including centrally funded investment, fiscal support and preferential policies were directed towards the coastal region. Coastal provinces were allowed to set up special economic zones and open cities and offer other incentives to foreign and domestic investors. Coastal provinces have since attracted the bulk of domestic and foreign investment and fuelled China's strong economic growth over nearly two decades. While the coastal region prospered in overall terms, the inland and western regions suffered a relative decline in income, living standards and economic growth. In the central government's long-term economic planning, inland provinces were to provide raw material, energy and cheap labour to the coastal provinces and in turn receive industrial products, technologies and capital. They were to benefit eventually from a 'trickle down effect' radiating from the coastal regions into the inland and gradually integrating the inland with the coastal economies. However, by the end of the 1980s it had become clear that this effect was not working and that at least in the medium term, the relative economic disadvantage of the inland and western provinces was not going to be overcome.[10] This gave rise to speculation about China breaking up into different regions. This speculation generally overlooks the crucial role of provinces.

During the 1980s, the central policy of letting the coastal region 'get rich first' was generally depicted as a regional policy, based on the fact that it targeted the whole coastal belt from Dalian in northeast China to Beihai on the Vietnamese border. In line with the official Chinese view expressed in policy statements and economic documents, it is generally assumed that the central government had simply shifted its preferences. Whereas before it had given priority to the inland regions in spreading investment over the various provinces, now it began to support the coastal region in the same way. The provincial studies show that the reform process was not imposed on the provinces as a central policy that they had to adopt, but rather that they had to be won over to accept the new central–provincial relationship. In this sense, the central government's policy was not implemented on a larger regional basis as before, but on a provincial basis. The intended result of this policy, which gave economic benefits but also more responsibility over their own affairs to the provinces, was a considerable growth in provincial autonomy. The first to benefit were those coastal provinces which had natural advantages and responded positively to the central reform initiatives. The central government benefited because these were also the provinces which supported the huge growth in the national economy and were able to contribute most to central tax revenue, as the case of Jiangsu in this volume demonstrates. The centre came to depend on the continuing fast growth and stability of these provinces not only for fiscal reasons, but equally for political and social reasons. In this sense the economic focus of the country has irreversibly shifted to the major coastal provinces and no regional policies can be made against their interests. The coastal development strategy is thus not reversible in the same way as the inland-based development strategies from the 1950s to the 1970s could be reversed in the reform period. In brief, the central government has lost its previous ability to control and influence regional development, because a structural change in the relationship between centre, regions and provinces has taken place.

As the provincial studies in this volume show, during the reform period, the traditional confinement of provinces to an administrative role has largely disappeared. Provinces have increasingly adopted economic functions and the centre has voluntarily reduced its own role in the process. Preferential policies granted to coastal provinces came as an enticement to improve provincial economic performance and to reduce reliance on central financial support. The reform strategy of developing coastal provinces has had the structural effect of turning the major coastal provinces from administrative into economic actors. This structural effect is now being widened to include inland provinces as well. Provinces such as Guangdong, Fujian and Jiangsu were the first to develop their own economic policies. For certain purposes they still fulfil an agent role for the central government, for example in tax collection, but in other respects they represent local interests. Inland provinces, such as Hubei, Shaanxi or Guizhou, which still rely heavily on the central government in their economic planning, are forced to develop in a similar fashion and gradually to expand their economic responsibilities.

This situation has worsened the plight of these and other inland provinces when they demand preferential policies from the central government similar to those given to the coastal provinces. As the central government no longer has the previous mechanism of income redistribution at its disposal, it has to turn to other forms of regional policy to redress regional disparities. Beginning with the seventh Five Year Plan in 1986, and with increased emphasis in the following Five Year Plans, the focus of central–regional policy shifted from the coastal/inland/western divide to the importance of the previous Greater Regions, most of which included coastal as well as inland provinces. These regions were expected to provide the coordination between richer and poorer provinces by facilitating horizontal links, division of labour and making use of complementarities among the provinces.[11] In policy terms this was a major readjustment from encouraging unequal development during the earlier reform period to the demand for coordination and equalisation. In practical terms, however, this policy showed little effect, because the Greater Region had no administrative power and could not enforce regional integration *vis-à-vis* provincial governments. It certainly did not reduce the differences in economic development between coast and inland.[12] The ninth Five Year Plan in 1996 recognised this failure by stipulating that the seven major economic regions should concentrate on developing their comparative advantages rather than pursuing regional equalisation. This was a return to the original coastal development strategy under which the coastal provinces continued to develop their fast growing manufacturing, information and services sectors while the inland provinces concentrated on providing agricultural products and raw materials.[13]

The inability of the centre to dictate regional economic policies and the strong economic role of provinces is reflected in a new type of regional planning which focuses on smaller trans-provincial economic regions growing out of economic interchange between sub-provincial regions with specific economic advantages. Examples of such regions are the Pearl River Delta around Guangzhou, the Yangtze River Delta around Shanghai and the Bohai Ring around Tianjin. The development of these economic regions is less a matter of central planning than a concern of the provincial governments involved. Similar regional economies are expected to develop along railway lines and transportation routes between northern Liaoning, the middle part of Jilin and the southwestern part of Heilongjiang, along the middle reaches of the Yangtze River and along the Longhai railway line through parts of Jiangsu, Henan, Shaanxi and Gansu.[14] The formation of these inter-provincial economic links is an interesting development, because economically they grow out of sub-provincial economic synergies and rely on inter-provincial coordination for their administrative purposes. The central government's role in this is only one of setting the macro-economic parameters, including large-scale infrastructure planning to facilitate such synergies. One might speculate that such smaller inter-provincial regions could eventually take on provincial functions, but that is forgetting that the existing provinces no longer owe their political and economic existence to the central government. They have taken on economic, social and other political functions that would make geographical arrangements solely on economic grounds quite unlikely, as one of the political functions of provinces is to balance political and economic power.[15] A more likely scenario is a break-up of large provinces when they become too unwieldy to fulfil their political and economic roles, as was the case with Chongqing's separation from Sichuan, but with the process of the economic empowerment of provinces still under way, this could at most happen very gradually.

The new economic role of provinces in addition to their administrative functions will change China politically and economically. Historically, the centre has been able to justify its political intervention into provincial matters on economic grounds. Provincial status and acceptance of 'policies' came with the benefits of central investment, balancing of provincial budget deficits, guaranteed flow of raw materials and state purchase of products. Provincial status at the same time also meant that provinces were institutionally not able to retain the benefits of their own economic activities. As provinces are cut off from central support and become economically self-reliant, they have no choice but to pursue their own interests by asserting their own economic identity. The dynamics of economic development have shifted from the centre to the provinces, both coastal and inland, and China is now moving towards a situation where provinces increasingly have to compete against each other. New economic developments will take shape on the basis of common interest and competitive advantage between provinces.

COMPETITIVE ADVANTAGE AND STRATEGIC IDENTITY

Up to now, provinces have competed in the political realm for central investment, central subsidies and preferential policies bestowed by the centre, while their economic competition has been suppressed or mainly confined to protectionist battles. If the centre further reduces its direct intervention and makes way for open competition, provinces will have to develop their own specific economic and business strategies and might eventually gain 'competitive identities' in addition to their political and traditional cultural identities. The implications of this are considerable, because China's economic structure will change towards a common market with a stronger division of labour. The discussion of regional policies suggests that provinces should be regarded more as competitors than as collaborators acting under central or regional coordination. The competitive dimension between provinces is still anathema to Chinese political and economic discourse, but recent research on provincial development confirms that provinces are developing their own economic identities and interests. In the process they have already emerged as competitors for preferential policies and face intensifying competition for resources and markets. They will thus have to differentiate themselves from other provinces by developing distinct competitive strategies and profiles.

Where does this competition occur? Traditionally, provinces are not perceived as economic competitors, although there are many documented instances, such as the commodity wars in the 1980s,[16] where clashes of economic interests have occurred. This type of competitive behaviour was based on protectionism, and studies of emerging markets show that rivalry develops as soon as new markets open up.[17] A more recent development is competition for commercial investment, domestic as well as foreign. While foreign investment is controlled at provincial and central level and the central government can grant and withdraw preferential policies and incentives, competition for domestic investment is much less controlled by the central government and forms of competitive behaviour include the informal granting of tax preferences and incentives, such as cheaper land rates, etc. These developments point to a trend among provinces to take an increasingly active role in promoting their economic interests. The problem for the outside observer is that these measures are often commercially sensitive and that provincial institutions may have little interest in publicising them beyond the circle of potential business partners, making it difficult to assess their strategies.

One potential source for provincial strategies are the provincial long-term strategic planning targets regularly promulgated by provincial governments and party committees in annual reports and on other occasions. But these strategic targets and planning policies should not be equated with competitive strategies. They are generally based on factor endowment and focus on comparative advantage if they contain a competitive dimension. Comparative advantage as a standard measure of the economic potential of a region can be expressed through a more or less sophisticated combination of factors.[18] Comparative advantage is regarded as the driving force behind the coastal/inland dichotomy, and is also the basis for various predictions about the economic performance of Chinese regional units into the next century.[19] This approach represented a breakthrough in regional economic analysis. It yields economic growth forecasts for coastal regions of around 9 per cent and for inland regions of around 6 per cent per annum for the next decade. From the viewpoint of strategic analysis, however, these results are too undifferentiated to elucidate what options individual provinces have for improving their situation. Comparative advantage can be seen as a remnant of the planned economy, as its focus is on objective criteria, without assigning an active role and function to the competitive differentiation and positioning of individual actors. In order to comprehend the way provinces behave as competitors, how they take account of rival strategies and develop their own distinct strategies, the reliance on factor endowment needs to be expanded to accommodate competitive strategies that are designed to overcome factor disadvantages. In general economic literature, this analytical gap emerged when the economic performance of the East Asian miracle economies had to be explained.

One answer was the concept of competitive advantage which was originally developed by Michael E. Porter for the purpose of explaining the conditions for sustained economic success of industrialised economies.[20] Porter uses the term 'competitive advantage' to indicate his broader approach and sets himself apart from the narrower notion of comparative advantage. His four determinants of competitive advantage include factor conditions, demand conditions, i.e. the existence of sophisticated buyers as a stimulus to product and factor development; the existence of related and supportive industries which stimulate technical development; and product innovation and intra-industry rivalry and domestic competitive pressure as preconditions for competitiveness in other markets. These four determinants are seen as mutually reinforcing and can be represented in a diamond shaped diagram (see Figure 1.1). Together with the role of government they define the industrial environment for sustained economic progress.

Porter specifically suggests that his framework can also be applied to subnational regional units. What matters in a national or regional context are mutually reinforcing competitive advantages across a range of industries. The more different industries in one region operate in a competitive environment and influence each other as competitors and suppliers for markets, human resources and technological innovation, the greater is the likelihood that they create 'clusters' of successful industries. The notion of clusters is at the very core of the concept of competitive advantage. Clusters spreading around specific successful industries are formed by vertical or horizontal interlinkages through buyers and suppliers or through common customers and the use of the same distribution channels.[21] As the original industries are based on favourable factor conditions, sophisticated demand, availability of skills and a generally stimulating environment, other related industries are drawn into their orbit through various synergies. Such clusters are then conducive to innovation, diversification and creation of new skills. International examples of such clusters are consumer electronics in Japan, paper-related industries in Sweden and the packaging industry in Italy. In a recent study of the competitive advantage of Hong Kong, a whole set of interrelated clusters have been identified for the Hong Kong economy.[22]

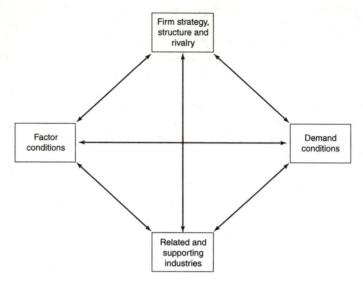

Figure 1.1 Four determinants of competitive advantage

To apply the Porter model or the further refined methodology used for the Hong Kong study to China's provinces and their industries would require large empirical research. The purpose of introducing the concept here is merely to broaden the discussion of development options of individual Chinese provinces in a competitive context. For the purpose of illustration, a first step will be to find indicators for the four determinants of competitive advantage for the provinces included in this and the previous volume. In Table 1.1, factor conditions are broadly represented by overall raw material endowment and infrastructure as well as access to domestic and foreign investment capital. A more refined approach would obviously have to include more specific physical resources, human knowledge and human resources as well as various forms of capital resources.

Demand as a determinant of competitive advantage is assumed to exist where high living standards coincide with consumer-oriented change. A striking example for the role of demand is, of course, Guangdong, with Hong Kong as a quasi domestic market. For Guangdong the Hong Kong market, quite apart from its other effects, has produced changes in factor conditions, local demand and industry structures which in turn have enabled the province to improve its position in the national market. More sophisticated buyers' markets are assumed to exist in the urban centres and provinces with higher living standards.

The existence of related and supporting industries as another determinant of competitive advantage is so far little documented in provincial studies. It will be assumed that provinces with a predominantly vertically structured state enterprise sector have fewer related and supporting industries than those with a predominantly collective economy which encourages greater horizontal links. Investment in the collective sector will therefore be used as an indicator for this

Table 1.1 Determinants of competitive advantage for Chinese provinces

Province	Factor: raw material	Factor: infra-structure	Factor: Domestic capital	Factor: FDI	Demand	Rivalry	Support industries
Guangdong		x	x	x	x	x	x
Jiangsu	x	x	x	x	x	x	x
Zhejiang	x	x	x	o	x	x	x
Shanghai		x o	x o	x	x		x
Shandong	x	x		x	x		o
Liaoning	x	x		x	x	x	x o
Tianjin		x		x o			
Guangxi	x	x			o		
Hainan	x	x	x	x			
Hubei	x	x	o				
Shaanxi	x	o					
Guizhou	x				o		
Shanxi	x	o	o				
Jiangxi	x	o					

x indicates area of strength, o indicates area of provincial development priority

determinant. Likewise, for the intensity of intra-industry rivalry and competition, the best measure for the limited purpose here seems to be the share of collective and foreign invested enterprises in provincial industrial production, as their products face full market competition. In Table 1.1, these simple indicators for the four determinants are used to produce competitive profiles for some of the provinces covered in the two volumes of provincial studies published to date.

The most distinct result is the gap between the group of leading provinces and the remaining provinces. The provinces of Guangdong and those of the Yangtze River Delta have obviously benefited from their geographical position as well as from various political and economic incentives. But the table shows that Jiangsu, Shanghai, Zhejiang and Guangdong have moved so far ahead in terms of competitive advantage that they will most likely be able to maintain a privileged position in the foreseeable future. The table also shows that the simple notion of the advantages of coastal provinces needs to be considerably refined, as not all coastal provinces and municipalities share the same advantages. Tianjin has been successful in attracting foreign investment, but has kept this burgeoning industrial sector isolated from its domestic economy which remains burdened by the legacy of state enterprises. Guangxi and Hainan, two traditionally poor coastal provinces, experienced an artificial boom in the late 1980s and the early 1990s, but were not able to translate it into long-term advantage. Shandong and Liaoning, starting from a higher level of development, were in contrast able to improve their position by encouraging local demand and the formation of supportive industries. Table 1.1 suggests that the advantage of coastal provinces does not only derive from their geographical position, but from their accumulated competitive advantages of which the geographical position is only one.

Some of the inland provinces seem to be caught in a disadvantaged position, where their original factor endowment is not supported by any of the other determinants. This leads to their demands for central support through industrial investment and infrastructure development or preferential policies similar to those enjoyed by the coastal provinces. Financial support for industrial development from the centre is an increasingly unlikely option, as most of central funding ends up in the state-owned enterprise sector. The burden of infrastructure funding is also shifting towards the provinces and central funding is concentrating on fewer major projects such as the Beijing–Kowloon railway line through the central provinces or the Nanning–Kunming railway line in the southwest. Preferential policies are often presented by provincial spokespersons as a core requirement for the economic success of inland provinces. Generally, disadvantaged provinces tend to argue that the centre is granting or withholding special policies for political reasons, but Table 1.1 indicates that there is an economic rationale in that the main recipients of preferential policies seem to be those provinces that provide a wider range of competitive advantages. The example of Jiangsu shows that the centre gained considerable additional tax revenue in absolute terms from reducing the relative tax burden for Jiangsu. In other words, preferential policies are more likely to be given to provinces which promise a return on investment for the central government in terms of higher revenues. The most likely reason why other provinces do not receive special policies is that their expected economic performance does not warrant it. The only option for inland provinces is to concentrate on their industrial infrastructure and develop competitive sectors by encouraging competition, mutual integration and the development of more competitive industrial clusters.

For China it is probably premature to look for clusters of internationally competitive industries. In international markets, China is still largely competing on price and has not made a technological impact comparable to Japan, Korea or Taiwan in their various areas of specialisation. Nevertheless, the concentration of major industries in certain provinces indicates that the formation of clusters might be well on its way. Judging from international experience, this could give those provinces a long-term advantage in certain industrial sectors and influence their long-term economic future as much as that of weaker competitors which in the longer run might have to pull out of those industries.

To illustrate the potential for the formation of industrial clusters, Table 1.2 lists the share of provinces in the production of major light industrial products for those product categories where the proportion of the province exceeds 10 per cent of national production. This simple listing, which includes all major light industrial areas except the food industry, shows that there is a distinct concentration in several sectors. Forty per cent of woollen products come from Jiangsu; three-quarters of national silk production is concentrated in Jiangsu, Zhejiang and Sichuan; half of the output in chemical and synthetic fibres is concentrated in Jiangsu, Shanghai and Zhejiang; white goods are concentrated in Jiangsu, Shanghai, Guangdong and Shandong; consumer electronics show a concentration in Jiangsu, Zhejiang and Guangdong for TV sets and a near exclusive concentration

Table 1.2 Output of major industrial products by provinces with an above 10% share – light and consumer industries, 1995 (%)

Province / Product	Jiangsu	Shanghai	Zhejiang	Guangdong	Shandong	Sichuan	Anhui	Beijing	Hebei	Henan
Knitting wool	36.1									
Woollen goods	42.5								20.6	
Yarn	15.9				12.7					
Silk	25.7		30.2			19.0				
Cloth	18.8		12.5	11.9						
Chemical fibres	29.0	10.7	10.4							
Synthetic fibres	30.6	11.2	10.6							
Bicycles	16.1	18.8	14.2					12.9		
Sewing machines	25.7	38.7		13.1						
Detergents	12.8	10.1		11.6						
Black and white TV sets	13.6	12.0	12.2	25.3		10.8				
Colour TV sets	12.2			37.1						
Electric fans	16.1		12.9	61.7						
Washing machines		15.2		19.7	10.3		13.4			
Household refrigerators		14.0		23.2	11.8		16.4			
Watches				79.9						
Radios				89.5						
Tape recorders				85.8						
Cameras				82.0						
Aluminium consumer products				56.6						
Paper, cardboard				10.2	11.3					11.7

Sources: China Statistical Yearbook 1996; Provincial China No. 3, March 1997, p. 76 ff

in Guangdong for radios, cameras and other related products. These figures point to an astonishing predominance of the Yangtze region in the more traditional areas of light industrial production and Guangdong province in the high technology products, thus indicating potential for clustering in these industries. They also give an initial indication of areas of specialisation of other provinces, such as Shandong and Anhui in white goods which might or might not lead to clustering.

Heavy industry and extracting industries are still more concentrated and, of course, also more tightly bound by factor endowment. The concentration in these areas is still very much a reflection of the structures put in place by the planned economy. Changes occurring in these sectors, for example in the car component industries supplying the major manufacturers, are not reflected in the basic figures in Tables 1.3 and 1.4. However, the concentration in a small number of provinces is obvious and points to a potential for clustering.

These preliminary tables suggest that Chinese provinces have already started a process of specialisation that will increase with the transfer of central government-owned enterprises to the provincial level, decreasing direct central interference and introducing more competitive pressure. In the process, provinces will be moving further away from their former, albeit limited, autarky to acquire different industrial profiles and specific competitive advantages. The composition of their factor endowment, the types of industries and enterprise forms, the way in which competition is controlled and encouraged, access to provincial, national and international markets and the way in which competition from other provinces is countered by government and enterprises, will all become part of the economic strategic identity of individual provinces.

As provinces are encouraged and even forced to articulate their interests in economic terms and to develop competitive economic strategies, they cannot avoid formulating their own political strategies and eventually creating their own political and cultural identities as well. This is less a question of changing general political rhetoric, than of justifying practical policies on local grounds. Once the centre devolves responsibility for social policies to the provincial level, provincial governments and party leaders have to devise their own policies and find ways to cope with specific political pressures and constraints imposed by their local situation. As policies have to be funded from local resources, they have to be justified within the different political and cultural contexts of provinces. This adds a new political dimension to the role of provincial leaders.[23]

POLITICAL AND CULTURAL IDENTITY

The most obvious examples of political constraints on provinces are internal disparities and the need for regional equalisation within a province. Locational advantages and factor endowment are seldom evenly spread through a whole province. Provinces which are considered poor in popular perception as well as in terms of aggregate statistical figures can include very wealthy areas, as is the case

Table 1.3 Output of major industrial products by provinces with an above 10% share – machinery/transport equipment, 1995 (%)

Province Product	Beijing	Jilin	Hubei	Shanghai	Jiangsu	Zhejiang	Sichuan	Tianjin
Alternators					21.6			
Metal cutting					11.3	57.7		
Motor vehicles	11.9	12.2	10.5	11.2				
Trucks	10.9	14.7	16.4				13.8	
Tractors				24.0				12.3

Sources: *China Statistical Yearbook 1996*; *Provincial China* No. 3, March 1997, p. 89 ff.

Table 1.4 Output of major industrial products by provinces with an above 10% share – heavy industries, 1995 (%)

Province Product	Shanxi	Liaoning	Heilongjiang	Shandong	Sichuan	Hebei	Shanghai	Jiangsu	Guizhou	Beijing
Coal	25.5									
Coke	39.2									
Crude oil		10.3	37.3	20.0						
Natural gas		11.8	14.4		42.7					
Pig iron	13.7					11.5	10.0			
Steel		14.0					15.2			
Rolled steel		12.0					13.2			
Plastics				11.8			11.2	12.0	19.2	12.5
Tyres				27.3						

Sources: *China Statistical Yearbook 1996*; *Provincial China* No. 3, March 1997, p. 83 ff.

in Guangxi, while the richest provinces such as Jiangsu, which lead the country on most indicators of economic success, can have deeply impoverished regions within their provincial borders. As long as the central government funded provincial budgets, poverty alleviation was one of the items for which provinces received subsidies. When these subsidies were gradually withdrawn, provincial governments with impoverished areas under their control, such as Jiangxi, Guizhou or Guangxi, continued to press the central government for a continuation of subsidies but with little success. In the late 1980s, the central government literally tried to persuade provincial governments to accept this new policy. The provincial leadership of Guangxi, for example, was even given a choice between the continuation of limited subsidies from Beijing on the one hand and a higher provincial tax retention on the other. It took several years before the provincial leadership discovered that Guangxi would have been better off with higher local tax revenue than with dwindling central subsidies. The provincial studies show that after 1992 the central government decided to reduce its role in poverty alleviation and that provincial governments had either to provide their own subsidies or develop policy alternatives. This decision was a commitment to provincial autonomy, because it forced provinces to develop their own policies and introduced an important differentiating element between provinces, as they reacted in different ways to deal with their local disparities. As the provincial studies show, the implications went far beyond the financial and administrative concerns of poverty alleviation. Provincial policies towards regional inequality and poverty are an important element in creating political and economic coherence within a province and, as they impact on overall provincial policy, form an additional dimension of provincial identity.

The question of how to deal with local disparities is primarily a political one, as it requires a choice between different policy options which affect the poorer regions of provinces as well as the more prosperous ones. The provinces faced with this problem have to find a balance between their competitive interests, which demand priority development of advantaged areas, and their social responsibility to equalise internal differentiation which primarily requires support for disadvantaged regions. The provincial studies show that different provinces opted for different policies, depending on their economic situation as well as their political outlook. In Shaanxi, the provincial leadership after some vacillation decided to opt for a coordinated development of its three major economic regions which meant that the development of the richest, central region had to be slowed down in favour of more balanced growth. A similar approach can be observed in Guizhou where the leadership tried to avoid regional polarisation at the cost of slower overall growth. In Jiangsu, on the other hand, where the local disparities between rich and poor areas are extreme, the richer part of Sunan is economically so far ahead of the impoverished counties to the north and northwest that the provincial government has the means to subsidise its impoverished counties without affecting the economic growth of the richer areas. In addition, Jiangsu seems to have struck a political balance between its economic regions with an over-representation of cadres from the poor Subei region in the provincial party and government hierarchy. Like Jiangsu, Shandong also seems to be able to provide subsidies to its poorer areas. As far as help towards self-sustaining growth is concerned, these provinces rely on a gradual trickle-down effect that is expected to work in the longer run.

As provinces assume political and economic tasks that used to be the domain of the centre, the question of their provincial political identity becomes more important. The simple categories of conservative, reformist or moderate that stem from ideological debates at the central level are not appropriate to grasp the complexities at provincial level. While provincial institutions partake in ideological debates, the provincial studies suggest that theoretical ideological considerations play only a limited role in the provincial political arena. For example, different provincial policies towards poverty alleviation pursued by Jiangsu and Shaanxi would indicate that the two provinces are in different political camps, but, as the studies show, both provinces are commonly regarded as conservative. The answer is that policy pronouncements are inadequate as indicators of provincial political attitudes. Different political affiliations are rather marked by actual provincial-level policies, more specifically, by the degree to which a province has implemented major economic reform policies and how closely it has followed central reform initiatives. Yao Xianguo has demonstrated this for Zhejiang by showing that in spite of conservative policy statements the province has been consistently quick in implementing major reform measures.[24] Such a policy orientation might therefore be called pragmatic rather than conservative. A similar case could be made for Jiangsu, whose leadership, while being reputed for its political conservatism, has been quick to embrace economic reform policies. The advantage of looking at the implementation of reform policies as an indicator of political attitude is that it gives a much more reliable link between economic and political identity than a categorisation based on ideological statements alone.

The provincial studies point to yet another dimension of provincial politics which cannot be observed at the central level, but which might eventually prepare the ground for political reforms by creating new forms of interaction between the public and political leaders. This is the emergence of a new political culture manifested in the way provincial politicians present themselves to the public in their attempts to create support for their policies by using populist means and their personal charisma. Most provincial leaders would certainly not qualify as path-breakers in this respect, but changes in political culture seem to occur in provinces where a leadership is trying to mobilise public support for economic reforms and the fight against backward-looking economic complacency. Shanxi is an example where provincial leaders made every effort to popularise themselves through media appearances, high public visibility and a general populist approach in an attempt to promote their economic reform programme. In Jiangxi, the provincial leadership has waged a campaign over years to create a new provincial identity in the obvious attempt to erase the memory of Jiangxi as a revolutionary base area entitled to compassionate support from the Communist Party for past historical merits. It would, however, be misleading to see only economic motives behind the attempts of political leaders to mobilise political support. Their aim might be to win the support of the provincial intelligentsia or to create a general political identification with the provincial leadership or provincial political culture. Provincial leaders in Shanxi and Jiangxi, for example, are exploiting a political potential that has long been dormant as particular loyalties had no place in a centrally dominated political culture. These developments at provincial level often escape general attention, because they are not reflected in immediate institutional changes, such as popular elections or formal campaigns. These provincial developments are, however, much more likely to contain the seeds of a future political culture in its concrete appearances than centrally launched initiatives for vague political reforms.

One of the most interesting findings in the provincial studies is how closely cultural identity is linked to political identity and how cultural construction works to reinforce these links. This adds to our knowledge of local cultures and identities, which is often confined to historical periods and too specific in its definition of local identities to allow comparison with the present. Authenticity of local cultural experience features strongly in cultural studies and is becoming a popular research topic.[25] In the provincial studies in these volumes, we find much less concern with local culture in provinces which are well-off economically and where the leadership is not attempting to change political attitudes than in provinces where the leadership is trying to mobilise public support. As the centre relinquishes its comprehensive ideological control, provincial leaders are defining common provincial purposes on local grounds and appeal to provincial culture and identity. Particular loyalties towards provincial culture are being fostered by a policy of cultural construction that even creates the symbols of provincial identity if they do not already exist. Jiangxi is a good example of the efforts of a provincial government which in fact is pursuing an ideological campaign against politically conservative attitudes, but has clad its argumentation in terms of a newly constructed provincial culture. One part of this construct is a link between Neo-Confucianism and the revolutionary heritage of the province in order to explain anti-commercial attitudes. The complementary construct is the proclamation of a commercial tradition predating Neo-Confucianism which serves to rally the provincial intelligentsia around the call for greater personal economic initiative and self-reliance. The artificiality of such constructs is exemplified by the 'Hubei spirit' which, in spite of the propaganda efforts by the provincial leadership, simply created no public response.

What do these observations mean for research on provincial China? They create a more flexible, multi-dimensional typology of Chinese provinces than attempts to categorise provinces by geographic position, economic features or political attitudes of the leadership. To illustrate some of these dimensions, Table 1.5 brings together a range of different provincial features and policies. This table can only in a general way point to links between economic position, political attitudes and cultural policies. As far as a pattern emerges, it is based on competitive advantage more than on other indicators. Provinces with strong competitive advantages (e.g. Jiangsu, Zhejiang, Shanghai) have been able to

Table 1.5 Economic, political and cultural features of Chinese provinces

Province	Competitive advantage	Economic priority	Demand from centre	Poverty policy	Political ideology	Cultural policy
Jiangsu	very strong	consolidation		subsidies	pragmatic	
Zhejiang	very strong	FDI			pragmatic	
Shanghai	very strong	FDI	investment			
Shandong	strong	domestic expansion		subsidies	reformist	
Liaoning	strong	domestic expansion				
Tianjin	weak	FDI	investment		conservative	preserve
Guangxi	weak	core industry		integrate	pragmatic	
Hainan	weak	FDI	preferential policies			
Hubei	moderate	FDI	preferential policies		conservative	create
Shaanxi	moderate	infrastructure	investment	integrate	conservative	
Guizhou	weak	diversification	investment	integrate	conservative	
Shanxi	moderate	infrastructure			moderate	create
Jiangxi	weak	infrastructure			moderate	create

consolidate their position, as they have economically and politically adapted to a new economic environment where the centre does not define their economic activities. Other provinces (e.g. Liaoning, Shandong) are committed to changing their previous dependence on the centre, but are still in the process of creating sufficient economic and political support. Finally, there remain some provinces which are basing their hope on being able to renegotiate their position with the centre with a view to being compensated for their contribution, usually of raw material, to the national economy. If the history of provincial reform over the last ten years is anything to go by, they will eventually also have to find their role in an environment that is controlled by market relations.

Research on these links is still in its infancy and made difficult by the lack of political transparency and the highly formalised political discourse which emphasises uniformity and consensus even where they don't exist. The provincial studies in *China's Provinces in Reform* are therefore to varying degrees able to uncover the hidden layers of intra-provincial and inter-provincial links and interactions. As much as different chapters concentrate on different aspects, they contribute to an emerging picture of provincial China that is richer in nuances and shows more potential for provincial development than previously feasible.

SEVEN PROVINCES

The seven studies presented in this volume reflect the range of provincial economic, political and cultural development. The first three chapters focus on the theme of sub-provincial variation in the three provinces of Guizhou, Shaanxi and Jiangsu, representing respectively the poor west, the central region and the developed east of China. All three provinces are affected by the withdrawal of financial support from the centre and each province has had to come to terms with this new situation in its own way. In this sense, the three studies illustrate how provincial governments are left to their own devices, even in situations where, judging by their demands, further central support seems to be the only solution to reduce poverty. The three studies also illustrate that once central support has been withdrawn, the centre does not impose any policies or solutions, but leaves it to the provinces to develop their own policies. This seems to be the case not only with poverty alleviation, but also with other policy areas, such as regional planning and industrial development.

Guizhou is most directly confronted with the problem of regional and rural poverty which, as an additional dimension, is most severe in local minority areas. Tim Oakes draws the picture of a provincial economy which has previously been able to rely on central subsidies to protect its indigenous population from commercialisation. Now, faced with the problem of dwindling subsidies, the provincial government has the dilemma that it wants its local minorities to produce marketable commodities based on their only advantage – cultural traditions – without commercialising their traditional culture. The result is predictably a quasi-colonial exploitation, as the local population controls neither production nor access to marketing channels for their products.

Andrew Watson and his co-authors, Yang Xueyi and Jiao Xingguo, illustrate how regional disparity effects economic policy-making in Shaanxi and show in detail how the provincial leadership had to decide between different options when formulating their provincial development strategy. The Shaanxi leadership in this case revised an earlier decision to stimulate growth in the richest of the three main regions of the province in favour of pulling along the poorer regions at the cost of slower overall economic development. This study also indicates that there can be a wide gap between provincial expectations of what the centre might contribute in view of the national role that a resource-rich province such as Shaanxi can play, and the actual forthcoming investment from the centre which is nowhere near the expected level.

These two studies point to an unsolved problem with central–local coordination for those provinces whose dependence on the centre has become a permanent feature of their economic set-up and whose separation from the centrally planned economy means a painful adaptation. Guizhou and Shaanxi are both important suppliers of raw materials, yet their economic decision-making seems to vacillate between efforts to maintain this role in the national economy and attempts to create province-based sources of income and advantages that will make them less reliant on the centre.

Bruce Jacobs presents a different case in analysing regional differences in Jiangsu. He argues that this rich coastal province, which has nine counties officially declared as impoverished within its borders, consists of a variety of smaller regional economies. Jiangsu's main competitive advantages derive from its position close to Shanghai. The southern part of Jiangsu is integrated into the Shanghai economy and profits from its vicinity to the large Shanghai market. The province's strategy to develop its poorer regions is based on setting up industrial zones along transportation routes. Jiangsu's policies to reduce poverty differ drastically from the approach the Shaanxi leadership has taken. Jiangsu embodies the problems of the national trickle-down effect within one province. While the region adjacent to Shanghai has reached economic standards similar to Shanghai, the poorer areas are among the poorest in China and have to rely on subsidies and development aid from the provincial government. Such disparities within a coastal province do not bode well for poorer inland provinces hoping to attract domestic and foreign investment on the basis of their lower labour costs. Jiangsu's relationship with the centre seems to be unilaterally based on Jiangsu's large contribution to the central budget. Jacobs notes that Jiangsu, in spite of its leading economic position, takes a low political profile nationally and has found a way to represent different regional interests locally. Jiangsu might exemplify a new paradigm of central–provincial relations where the province manages its own affairs in a stable political and economic environment and the centre exerts very little direct influence in matters other than macro-coordination.

Provincial strategy formation is the main theme of the following two chapters. Zhao Ling Yun describes how Hubei's leadership proposed an ambitious economic strategy which aimed at making the province the centre for the surrounding provinces in middle China. When this strategy proved to be unrealistic, the provincial leadership had to settle for a much more moderate strategy and create political support by evoking the 'Hubei spirit'. Zhao's picture of the province and its capital is one of conservative politics and holding on to economic planning with little practical business initiative emerging.

Hendrischke's chapter on Tianjin depicts another variation of provincial strategy formation. He argues that Tianjin was only partially able to make the transition from the early reform period when it played a leading role to the later reform period when it did not manage to reform its domestic economy, which remained based on state-owned enterprises. As a result, the city was pushed into economic reforms through its comparative advantage in infrastructure which attracted large-scale foreign investment but left the domestic economy lagging behind the surrounding provinces and neighbouring cities. One important reason for Tianjin's relative backwardness was the conservative outlook of the leadership which was not able to defend the city's interests against the dominating influence of neighbouring Beijing.

One theme that emerges from these studies is the formation of a provincial identity which grows out of the close linkage of political and economic strategies. As provinces pursue their political and economic interests, factors such as geographical position, relationship and competition with neighbouring provinces all play a part in defining their course of action and delineating future development options. The last two studies in this volume go one step further in specifically examining how political and cultural strategies grow out of the economic and political reform process.

David Goodman finds in Shanxi a province with an existing, historically formed provincial identity. Its cultural continuity is paralleled by a continuity in economic development policies which stretch back to the period in the 1920s when Shanxi was under the rule of an economically enlightened warlord, Yan Xishan. In the 1990s, Shanxi formulated a strategy for overtaking its neighbouring provinces, but, unlike the case of Hubei, this strategy was accompanied by a realistic assessment of its economic potential and the inherent weaknesses of the provincial economy. Unlike Shaanxi, Shanxi seems to have paid more attention to diversification and less to demanding central funding. This economic strategy was supported by a political and cultural reform programme. Shanxi's reforms were promoted by a populist leader intent on creating a political and cultural climate conducive to his economic and social reform. Shanxi in this way might be an example of how the traditional mechanism of party propaganda can be transformed and used to serve more secular efforts to create political support and goodwill.

In his chapter on Jiangxi Province, Feng Chongyi observes how a provincial leadership tried to enlist the support of the provincial elite in proselytising a liberal attitude towards economic reforms and overcoming a deeply ingrained attitude of reliance on state support. In the course of this, a new cultural identity for the province is created. Feng recognises how much this cultural construction contributed to a new provincial self-awareness among intellectuals in the province, but remains sceptical of how durable such a provincial identity can be when it is under threat from competing cultural loyalties within the province as well as from an emerging national cultural awareness related to a new lifestyle and consumerism that transcends provincial borders. This poses the larger question of how adequate provincial identity can be in such circumstances of major historical transformation.

CONCLUSION

This volume is part of a project to comprehend the complexities of China under reform by including the geographical, economic, political and cultural diversity of China's provinces while avoiding the many traps of convenient simplification. One of those has been to sub-divide China into different regions according to whatever purpose was at hand. Foreign strategy analysts and investors, for example, established their priorities by focusing on southern China. Chinese planners and politicians have their own and differing priorities in postulating regional economies, depending on whether their interests lie with attracting investment, income equalisation, regional infrastructure development or any of the other priorities that have come with economic reform. The project *China's Provinces in Reform*, now with this second volume, subscribes to none of these preconceived notions, but aims at exploring changes to China's economic, social, political and cultural set-up as they occur at provincial level, moving into yet uncharted directions.

The main, implicit hypothesis of this volume is that Chinese provinces in reform cannot be easily subsumed under larger policy frameworks such as the coastal–inland dichotomy or major economic regions. Instead, provinces have been analysed with a view to their variations in terms of geography, competitive advantage, economic priority, demand from the centre, political ideology and cultural policy as determinants of emerging provincial identities. These determinants seem to provide more subtle insights into the development of individual provinces as well as their potential for interregional interaction and inter-provincial competition. The issue of provincial identities, as it emerges from this approach, is a complex one that includes economic strategies, political ideology, social policies, cultural elements and, again to varying degrees, can be closely linked with local tradition stretching back decades or even centuries.

The drawback of this approach is that it does not lend itself to easy generalisations. The following chapters will to differing degrees focus on the broad themes of the volume. Clearly, not every province is accessible for information in the same way and research on the ground does not always yield the same insights. Overall, however, the following chapters should be able to point to directions of development and help to make sense of the often confusing variety in the political economy of Chinese provinces.

NOTES

1 See Kenneth Lieberthal and Michel Oksenberg, *Policy Making in China: Leaders, Structures, and Processes*, Princeton, New Jersey: Princeton University Press, 1988, p. 399ff.
2 See Kenneth G. Lieberthal and David M. Lampton (eds), *Bureaucracy, Politics and Decision Making in Post-Mao China*, Berkeley: University of California Press, 1992, Part IV.
3 See David S.G., Goodman, 'China in reform: the view from the provinces', in David S.G. Goodman (ed.), *China's Provinces in Reform – class, community and political culture*, London: Routledge, 1997, p. 2.
4 The first volume is David S.G. Goodman (ed.), *China's Provinces in Reform – class, community and political culture*, London: Routledge, 1997.
5 See, for example, Shaun Breslin, *Centre–Province Relations in a Reforming Socialist State*, Basingstoke: Macmillan, 1996; Yasheng Huang, *Inflation and Investment Controls in China: The Political Economy of Central–Local Relations During the Reform Era*, New York: Cambridge University Press, 1996; Wei Wei, *Zhongguo jingji fazhan zhong de quyu chayi yu quyu xietiao* [Regional Differences and Coordination in China's Economic Development], Hefei: Anhui renmin chubanshe, 1995.
6 Wei Wei, *Zhongguo jingji fazhan zhong de quyu chayi yu quyu xietiao*, p.255.
7 G. William Skinner, 'Urban development in Imperial China', in G. William Skinner, *The City in Late Imperial China*, Stanford: Stanford University Press, 1977, pp. 9–17. See also G. William Skinner, 'The structure of Chinese history', *Journal of Asian Studies*, Vol. 44, No. 2, 1985; and G. William Skinner, 'Marketing and social structure in rural China, part I', *Journal of Asian Studies*, Vol. 24, No. 1, 1964.
8 G. William Skinner, 'Differential development in Lingnan', in Thomas P. Lyons and Victor Nee (eds), *The Economic Transformation of South China – Reform and Development in the Post-Mao Era*, Ithaca, New York: Cornell University Press, 1994, pp. 17–54.
9 Joseph B.R. Whitney, *China: Area, Administration and Nation Building*, Chicago: University of Chicago Press, 1970, p. 120ff.
10 Wei Wei, *Zhongguo jingji fazhan zhong de quyu chayi yu quyu xietiao*, p. 196ff.
11 For an overview, see Terry Cannon, 'Regions: spatial inequality and regional policy', in Terry Cannon and Alan Jenkins (eds), *The Geography of Contemporary China – The Impact of Deng Xiaoping's Decade*, London and New York: Routledge, 1990, pp. 28–59; see also Liu Shidong (ed.), *Zhongguo jingji dili* [China's Economic Geography], Beijing: Gaodeng jiaoyu chubanshe, 1992, chapter 8.
12 Lu Xueyi (ed.), *21 shiji de Zhongguo shehui* [Chinese Society in the 21st Century], Kunming: Yunnan renmin chubanshe, 1996, p. 200.
13 East Asia Analytical Unit, *China Embraces the Market*, Canberra: Department of Foreign Affairs and Trade, 1997, p. 285ff.
14 Lu Xueyi (ed.), *21 shiji de Zhongguo shehui*, p. 113ff.
15 See, for example, Ma Shulin, 'Lun shengji xingzheng quhua tizhi gaige' [On the reform of the system of provincial-level administrative sub-division], *Zhanlue yu guanli*, 5 (1996), pp. 10–16.
16 See Andrew Watson, Christopher Findlay and Du Yintang, 'Who won the "wool war"?: A case study of rural product marketing in China', *The China Quarterly*, No. 118, June, 1989, pp. 213–241.
17 See Andrew Watson, 'Conflict over cabbages: the reform over wholesale marketing in China', in Ross Garnaut, Guo Shutian and Ma Guonan (eds), *The Third Revolution in the Chinese Countryside*, Cambridge: Cambridge University Press, 1996, pp. 144–163.
18 See, for example, Roger C.K. Chan *et al.* (eds), *China's Regional Economic Development*, Hong Kong: Chinese University of Hong Kong, 1996.

19 East Asia Analytical Unit, *China Embraces the Market*, p. 288ff.
20 Michael Porter, *The Comparative Advantage of Nations*, London: Macmillan, 1990.
21 Michael Porter, *The Comparative Advantage of Nations*, p. 149.
22 Michael J. Enright, Edith E. Scott and David Dodwell, *The Hong Kong Advantage*, Oxford: Oxford University Press, 1997.
23 See Kenneth Lieberthal and Michel Oksenberg, *Policy Making in China: Leaders, Structures, and Processes*, pp. 344–347.
24 Yao Xianguo and Zhou Wenqian, 'Zhejiang jingji gaige zhong de difang zhengfu xingwei pingxi' [Assessment of local government behaviour in Zhejiang's economic reforms], paper delivered at the Hangzhou Conference on Reform in Provincial China, September 1996.
25 See Tao Tao Liu and David Faure (eds), *Unity and Diversity – Local Cultures and Identities in China*, Hong Kong: Hong Kong University Press, 1996.

Guizhou Province

GENERAL

GDP (billion *yuan*)	72.00
GDP annual growth rate	8.90
as % national average	92.70
GDP per capita	2,024.80
as % national average	36.10
Gross Value Agricultural Output (billion *yuan*)	39.80
Gross Value Industrial Output (billion *yuan*)	62.90

POPULATION

Population (million)	35.55
Natural growth rate (per 1,000)	22.10

WORKFORCE

Total workforce (million)	18.90
Employment by activity (%)	
primary industry	73.00
secondary industry	9.90
tertiary industry	17.10
Employment by sector (%)	
urban	22.22
rural	77.78
Employment by ownership (%)	
state	10.58
collective	6.88
private	3.70
foreign-funded	0.11

WAGES AND INCOME

Average annual wage (*yuan*)	4,917.00
Growth rate in real wage	0.60
Urban disposable income per capita	4,221.24
as % national average	87.20
Rural per capita income	1,276.67
as % national average	66.30

PRICES

Consumer Price Index [CPI] annual rise (%)	9.10
Service price index rise	16.40
Per capita consumption (*yuan*)	1,258.00
as % national average	47.00

FOREIGN TRADE AND INVESTMENT

Total foreign trade (US$ billion)	0.50
as % provincial GDP	5.70
Exports (US$ billion)	0.40
Imports (US$ billion)	0.10
Realised foreign capital (US$ billion)	0.30
as % provincial GDP	3.90

EDUCATION

University enrolments	35,747.00
as % national average	40.70
Secondary school enrolments (million)	1.13
as % national average	68.10
Primary school enrolments (million)	4.83
as % national average	123.70

Notes: All statistics are for 1996 and all growth rates are for 1996 over 1995 and are adapted from *Zhongguo tongji nianjian 1997* [Statistical Yearbook of China 1997], Zhongguo tongji chubanshe, Beijing, 1997, as reformulated and presented in *Provincial China* no. 5, May 1998, pp. 68ff.

Guizhou Province

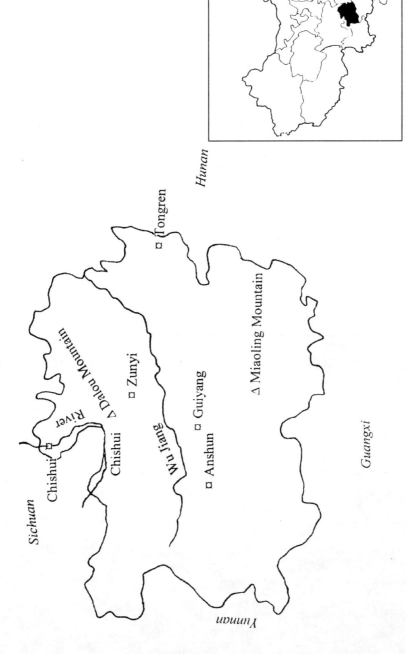

Sichuan

Chishui

Chishui River

Δ Dalou Mountain

□ Zunyi

Wu Jiang

□ Guiyang

□ Anshun

Δ Miaoling Mountain

□ Tongren

Hunan

Guangxi

Yunnan

2 Selling Guizhou

Cultural development in an era of marketisation

Tim Oakes

Guizhou Province occupies the heavily eroded limestone highlands of the eastern Yun-Gui Plateau, separating the fertile Sichuan Basin to the north from the low plains of Guangxi to the south. The mountainous setting of the province is responsible for a long history of not only relative isolation from the dominant societies and cultures of traditional China but of endemic rural poverty and a stigmatised 'frontier' cultural identity as well. Citing a long history of imperial, republican and communist efforts to tap Guizhou's resources and integrate the region politically, economically and culturally into mainstream Chinese society, Goodman has referred to the province as an example of internal colonialism.[1] Late nineteenth century British trade representative Alexander Hosie, for his part, thought it a ghostly and impecunious place, with 'sadly stunted' crops growing on 'barren and profitless' soil.[2]

Hosie's poor impressions of Guizhou as 'a huge graveyard' were in part due to several decades of disastrous rebellions which preceded his travels.[3] Such social disorder had, by that time, become common in a region whose relative inaccessibility and poverty made banditry and rebellion an attractive alternative for many locals. Chronically unstable, Guizhou's integration and assimilation to more 'civilised' Chinese ways had long been an objective of imperial governments. For the Chinese state, Guizhou not only needed economic assistance but cultural development as well. Curing Guizhou's ills of poverty and social disorder was thus partly legitimised as a cultural project aimed at the large proportion of non-Han peoples who inhabited the province. Accounting for Guizhou's poverty, and explaining its need for development, became a project in which non-Han ethnicity figured prominently. This was particularly true with respect to the region's largest ethnic group, the Miao. For the Chinese, the Miao seemed to exemplify Guizhou's poverty and need for benevolent outside help. Accounts commonly referred to Miao as so poor they worked naked in their fields.[4] But the Miao were compelling not simply for their poverty, but for their tribal 'savagery' as well. It was a common claim during the eighteenth and nineteenth century rebellions in Guizhou, that 'many of the Miao tribesmen went so far as to kill their own wives and children before embarking upon the revolt, so as to feel completely reckless of the consequences'.[5]

Guizhou's colonisation, integration and development has for centuries implied the assimilation of the region's tribal peoples and isolated subsistence farmers. China's communist leaders inherited this 'civilising project', articulating it as a campaign for 'cultural development' toward a modern socialist society.[6] This chapter ultimately seeks to explore how that campaign has changed in Guizhou during the reform era. The province's non-Han minority groups still play a pivotal role as prime subjects in the drive to modernise, but the nature of their role and their relationship to Guizhou's political economy have changed dramatically. After a summary of the historical and economic geography of the province, the chapter proceeds with two broad sections.

First, it offers an analysis of the economic situation facing Guizhou and examines modernisation efforts pursued in the first half of the 1990s. Here, two broad issues have conspired to condition the province's political economy: an impending agricultural crisis brought about by chronic rural poverty, lack of investments, limited land resources and rapidly increasing population; and a simmering fiscal crisis in which fiscal decentralisation and decline throughout China has pushed Guizhou toward increased dependence on an inadequate local revenue base. In attempting to deal with these problems, provincial leaders advocated a modernisation plan emphasising the commercial integration of Guizhou's economy with external markets. Liberalised economic policies initiated in 1992 set off a brief boom in Guizhou's urban economy. In this atmosphere of market reform, commercialising the countryside and pursuing cultural development took on a new sense of urgency among elites in minority regions.

Second, the chapter presents a case-study of how the pursuit of cultural development in an era of marketisation has caused an important shift in the relationship between non-Han ethnic groups and the project of modernisation. With ethnic tourism and traditional crafts slated to become one of the province's 'pillar' industries, minority traditions have been recognised for their potential as commodities. Cultural development has become something of a paradoxical idea, indicating the need to eradicate 'traditional thinking' while at the same time extolling ethnic tradition as a marketable commodity, that is, part of Guizhou's package of comparative advantages. Rather than indicating the blatant assimilation of earlier times, cultural development now entails the preservation and commodification of ethnic traditions which are deemed to contribute to Guizhou's overall economic development. This, however, has not necessarily altered the situation of increased vulnerability and subjugation that commercial integration has meant for many of Guizhou's rural producers. Although economic reforms clearly represent a welcome change for Guizhou's minority groups – presenting new opportunities for the promotion of ethnic identity – the pervasive metropolitan desire to preserve and commodify the exotic artefacts of ethnic tradition can be interpreted as the latest version of internal colonialism in Guizhou.

GEOGRAPHICAL AND HISTORICAL OVERVIEW

The persistence of rural poverty

Guizhou's mountainous, rocky topography has historically been unsuitable for agricultural accumulation. Local geographers classify 87 per cent of the topography as 'mountains', 10 per cent as 'hills', and the final 3 per cent as 'plains' suitable for generating an agricultural surplus. Seventy-three per cent of the landscape consists of carbonate rocks, which not only creates problems for water supply but, given the relatively wet climate (1000–1500 mm annually), leads to a deeply dissected landscape of sheer cliffs, gorges, enormous caverns and sinkholes. The eroded land not only makes agriculture difficult but continues to inhibit efficient transportation and trade. The soils are generally quite thin, often isolated amid rocky karst cones, and can be highly acid. Thirty-five per cent of cultivated land is classified in the lowest of China's three productivity categories. The province varies in elevation from around 500 metres in the east to nearly 3,000 in the west, although local vertical relief is always considerable. Only in the relatively isolated lowlands can the climate be considered subtropical, limiting rice cultivation to areas below 1,800 metres.[7]

In 1994, about 10.5 per cent of Guizhou was cultivated (1.84 million hectares). Based on the 1994 population estimate of 34.58 million, this works out to 0.053 ha per capita, or 67 per cent of China's average.[8] In 1985, the figure was 0.063 ha per capita, indicating a 16 per cent reduction in less than a decade.[9] The majority of this reduction is explained by population increase, but land loss due to erosion remains a critical problem as well. Geographers in Guizhou estimate that at least 40 per cent of the land area is experiencing moderate to severe erosion, and as land use intensifies, particularly on steep slopes, erosion rates are accelerating. (In 1975, only 11.3 per cent of Guizhou's land was suffering from erosion.)[10] They acknowledge, however, that with increasing population pressures it would be impossible to limit peasants to farming land which is less susceptible to erosion. In terms of absolute population density, the figure has tripled in less than 45 years (from 60 persons per square kilometre in 1947 to 180 in 1990). Hill estimates an agricultural density of 17 persons per hectare (equivalent to 620 persons per square kilometre of cultivated land), 'indicative of extraordinary intensity, especially considering that only 42 per cent of the cultivated land comprises irrigated rice-land (some 800,000 ha)'.[11] He further notes that in Qingzhen, in the central plateau region just west of the provincial capital where wet-rice land accounts for a mere 8 per cent of the total, the crop intensity index is an astonishing 187. Here, bare areas degraded by erosion are expanding at a rate of '200–300 ha annually'.[12]

To curb erosion and increase agricultural productivity, substantial investments are needed in irrigation expansion, afforestation, terrace engineering and grassland maintenance. Given the karst terrain, however, increasing irrigation is very expensive, since ground water is found only at a considerable depth below the surface. Nor are reservoirs always feasible given the porous quality of the

Table 2.1 Guizhou: shares of industrial and agricultural output, rural GMP and farmland, 1980–1992 (%)

Shares of GVIAO

	1980	1985	1990	1992
Agriculture	44.6	41.7	40.0	37.0
Industry	55.4	58.3	60.0	63.0
Light industry	19.5	23.2	25.4	24.9
Heavy industry	35.9	35.1	34.6	38.2

Shares of rural GMP[a]

	1980	1985	1990	1992
Agriculture	83.8	74.5	75.0	70.2
Industry	5.5	11.3	14.6	18.0
Construction	6.7	7.8	3.4	3.8
Transport	0.9	2.6	3.3	3.9
Commerce/Trade	3.1	3.8	3.7	4.1

Shares of GVAO

	1980	1985	1990	1992
Cultivation	66.5	55.4	53.5	52.1
Livestock	19.0	22.5	24.3	27.5
Sidelines	10.5	14.0	16.4	12.6
Forestry	4.0	7.8	5.5	7.4

Share of farmland, 1992

Irrigated paddy	41.8
Dry field	58.2

Note: [a] GMP, or Gross Material Product (she*hui zongchanzhi*), is the total output value of the five major material production sectors: agriculture, industry, construction, transport, and commerce. It differs from Gross National Product (GNP) in that it excludes net income from non-material services, but includes the consumption of material inputs such as raw materials and energy resources in its calculation

Source: *Guizhou tongji nianjian* [Guizhou Statistical Yearbook], *1993*, pp. 28, 188, 191, 198

bedrock. Diversification in commercial crops, livestock and timber are stressed as ways local counties can raise capital for investments. With one-quarter of the land classified as 'grassland', a considerable portion of Guizhou's agricultural output value already comes from animal husbandry (see Table 2.1). During the reform-era livestock raising has become increasingly important, accounting for 27.5 per cent of agricultural output value in 1992, up from 19 per cent in 1980.[13] Yet there are signs of severe overgrazing in certain counties. Commercial crops are encouraged, but in Guizhou nearly all cultivated land remains devoted to staple foods for local consumption: primarily rice, wheat, canola, corn and tubers.

Grain production has remained well below China's average, although it has been improving. As indicated in Table 2.2, grain productivity in Guizhou was 72 per cent of the national average in 1990. By 1994, this proportion had increased, considerably, to 85.5 per cent. Even with Guizhou's higher rate of population growth, output in per capita terms improved from 60 per cent to 73 per cent of the

Table 2.2 Guizhou: grain output and productivity

	Productivity (kg/ha)		Output (kg/per capita)	
	1990	1994	1990	1994
Guizhou	2,835	3,849	235	271
China	3,930	4,500	390	371

Source: *Zhongguo tongji nianjian* [China Statistical Yearbook] *1991*, pp. 345–348; *1995*, pp. 347, 350.

national average during the same five year period. Grain subsidies, however, remain a substantial portion of total consumption in the province, averaging between 500,000 and a million tonnes annually.[14] Imported grain costs the province an average of 700–800 million *yuan* annually, a figure roughly equal to Guizhou's annual quota subsidies from the central government.

Figures from the 1990 census indicate that 34.7 per cent of Guizhou is made up of officially recognised minority groups (see Table 2.3).[15] This is the fifth highest proportion of any province in China. With 33 different minority groups, Guizhou has the third highest number among China's provinces, after Yunnan and Xinjiang. In six counties (all in southeast Guizhou), the proportion of minorities totals over 90 per cent of the population. Nearly all (94 per cent) of the minority population is rural and agricultural; cities and towns are predominantly Han Chinese. As indicated in Table 2.3, Guizhou's population growth rate is well above China's average. Between 1970 and 1982 China's Total Fertility Rate declined by 54 per cent whereas Guizhou's declined by only 36 per cent.[16] Population growth has been highest in minority regions, where one study estimated a rate of natural increase at 23 per thousand between 1949 and 1989.[17] Local geographers estimate annual growth rates of up to 3.5 per cent in some minority regions.

There has been particular concern among government officials that rapid population growth has been outpacing food production. Between 1985 and 1988, for example, population in minority areas grew by 4 per cent whereas grain output grew by only 2.7 per cent; per capita output dropped from 372 to 366 *jin*.[18] Although this was during a period when growth rates in grain production declined throughout China due to changes in state procurement procedures in 1985, it indicates what officials see as an alarming trend in minority regions.

The autonomous prefectures of Qiandongnan, Qiannan and Qianxinan make up the southern half of Guizhou. In addition there are ten minority autonomous counties outside of these prefectures. Combined, these regions make up 55.5 per cent of Guizhou's territory and just over 40 per cent of the total population. As indicated by investment and income statistics, conditions here reflect a growing gap between minority and Han regions during the reform era.[19] Net Material Product (NMP) per capita in Guizhou's minority regions in 1985 was 43.6 per cent of China's average, and 79 per cent of the provincial average.[20] By 1990, the proportions had dropped to 30.4 per cent and 65 per cent respectively.[21] Relative

Table 2.3 Guizhou: demographic characteristics

Ethnic composition

| | (× 1,000) | | | % of total | |
	1990 census	1982 census	% change[a]	1990	1982
Total	32,391.1	28,552.9	13.4	100.0	100.0
Han	21,148.8	21,129.5	0.1	65.3	74.0
Miao	3,668.8	2,582.6	42.8	11.3	9.0
Bouyei	2,478.1	2,098.9	18.1	7.7	7.4
Dong	1,400.0	851.1	64.5	4.3	3.0
Tujia	1,045.5	1.6	63,173.2	3.2	0.0
Yi	704.7	564.6	25.3	2.2	2.0
Gelao	430.6	51.5	735.6	1.3	0.2
Shui	323.1	275.7	17.0	1.0	1.0
Hui	127.1	98.5	28.5	0.4	0.3
Bai	123.3	4.9	2,414.7	0.4	0.0

Total fertility rate	*Guizhou*	*China*
1970	7.0	5.8
1982	4.5	2.6

Rural infant mortality rate (per thousand)	*Guizhou*	*China*
UNICEF survey of 300 poor counties, 1989	108.0	68.0
Ministry of Public Health rural survey, 1994	73.2	21.5

Population growth (per thousand)

| | Guizhou | | China | |
	Birth rate	Natural increase	Birth rate	Natural increase
1981	28.0	19.4	21.0	14.5
1992	22.4	13.9	18.2	11.6
1994	22.9	14.8	17.7	11.2

Note: [a] The outstanding population growth of many minority groups in Guizhou (particularly the Tujia, Bai and Gelao) is due to the return of the nationality classification project in the 1980s and the subsequent determination of many 'pending' cases of nationality classification

Sources: Hill (1993, p. 6); *Zhongguo tongji nianjian* [China Statistical Yearbook], *1995*, p. 60; *Guizhou shengqing* [Guizhou Provincial Gazetteer], p. 430; Wong (1995)

to population distribution, state investments in minority regions have clearly been lacking. Only 10.5 per cent of Guizhou's total investment during the Sixth FYP went to minority regions. During the Seventh FYP, the proportion declined to 8.4 per cent. Minority region shares of fixed capital investments also dropped from 12 per cent during the Sixth FYP to 9.5 per cent during the Seventh.[22] Of the 49 counties comprising these regions, 39 depend on subsidies either from the province or the central government. In 1989, revenues in minority regions amounted to a mere 54 per cent of outlays, and on a per capita basis were only 16 per cent of China's average and 31 per cent of the provincial average.

Given the investment and revenue situation, it should not be surprising that the majority of what is officially defined as 'absolute poverty' in Guizhou is concentrated in minority regions.[23] In 1990, Guizhou's population accounted for about 2.8 per cent of China's total, yet it had 9.2 per cent of China's population living below the poverty line. Of the 31 counties in Guizhou (out of a total of 86) which are designated as 'impoverished counties', 21 are in minority regions, accounting for half of the total minority population in Guizhou. According to one report, the population living in absolute poverty in Guizhou was reduced from 6.14 million in 1985 to 2.22 million in 1989.[24] The same report, however, acknowledged that roughly 10–20 per cent of those whose poverty had been 'resolved' drifted back below the line each year, and criticised the 200 *yuan* per capita income line as too low to ensure that people will be able to lead productive lives.

Impoverished counties are entitled to special assistance from the province and the central government. This typically means special engineering projects (referred to as 'food and shelter projects') to help increase agricultural productivity. Special interest rates on loans for rural industries are also provided. However, aid to impoverished regions has been declining. In 1990 state assistance amounted to just over 212 million *yuan*, down from over 300 million in 1987.[25] In addition, there has been criticism of the slow development of rural industries in these regions. Many local officials refer to the 'Three Sides' problem of rural industrial development: that is, rural enterprises are only being developed next to highways, next to existing factories and next to cities. They are not, in other words, benefiting the vast majority of the rural poor who live isolated from these places. The use of the term 'Three Sides' is a deliberate reference to the legacy of 'Third Front' industrialisation in Guizhou and its 'Three Sides' principle of design, build and produce simultaneously. The enormous cost, poor performance and overall failure of many of these industries remains a significant problem for many poor regions. They contribute little to local revenues, and even though many are being converted to producing consumer goods, they are still 'stuck in a planned economy structure of production'.[26] Thus, poor counties find state investments and subsidies declining, rural industrial development uneven, and are not equipped to generate adequate revenues to expand the light industrial sector because of their economic dependence on out-dated industries left over from the height of Maoist command economics.[27]

Regional development during the Maoist era

After 1949, the central government primarily regarded Guizhou as a resource-rich province of considerable potential, especially in terms of energy, mineral and timber production. It was also a prime site for Mao's 'Third Front' defence industrial relocation policy. The three decades of Maoist rule, however, saw in

Guizhou – as with the majority of rural China – a general stagnation and decline in agricultural production and a failure to adequately address the high rates of rural poverty throughout the province. The province's inability to provide the needed inputs in the rural economy can be related to a broader political economy of unequal exchange which developed under state socialism in China. Under Maoist regional development strategies, Guizhou's links to the centre came to be dominated by industrial developments which did not fully articulate with the local agricultural economy, and the province survived on subsidies rather than developing a structurally diverse economy. While these structural features conspired to perpetuate rural poverty, official state development discourse generally blamed 'traditional thinking' and a 'low cultural level' on the part of minority and Han peasants, thereby shifting the causal focus on endemic rather than broader problems.[28] As we shall see, this remains the dominant explanation for rural Guizhou's continuing 'resistance' to modernisation.

Economic development strategies adopted by China after 1949 were drawn from the Soviet Union and its emphasis on heavy industrialisation, high rates of accumulation and investment, and rapid industrial growth at the expense of agriculture.[29] China's investment patterns have been characterised by accumulation rates averaging between 25 per cent and 35 per cent. The overwhelming bulk of this accumulation has been reinvested into heavy industry. In terms of regional development during the Maoist period, the emphasis on rapid industrialisation was combined with perceived national security needs to produce a deliberate strategy of interior industrial development. While the party's focus on interior regions at the expense of the more developed coast has been interpreted by some as a geographical expression of Maoist egalitarianism, it appears that pragmatism, more than any theories of regional social equality, was the governing principle in the PRC's regional development programme. As Kirkby and Cannon conclude, 'never in the Mao period is the theme of regional equity *per se* elevated to a matter of principle and policy'.[30] Instead, regional development policy was dictated by what was perceived as the efficient realisation of rapid industrialisation and national defence requirements.[31]

Initially, during the First FYP (1953–1957), regional development was highly planned and directed by a central government which controlled as much as 78 per cent of state expenditures (See Table 2.4). It focused on the so-called '156 key projects' which utilised Soviet aid and expertise. Seventy per cent of these projects were located in interior provinces away from the coast, and 58 per cent of First FYP industrial investments went to interior provinces.[32] Much of this

Table 2.4 China: central and local shares of state expenditure, 1955–1994 (%)

	1955	1959	1965	1971	1984	1990	1994
Central	78.1	47.6	62.2	59.5	46.6	39.8	30.1
Local	21.9	52.4	37.8	40.5	53.4	60.2	69.9

Source: *Zhongguo tongji nianjian* [China Statistical Yearbook], *1995*, p. 21

interior development was characterised by the deliberate expansion of new facilities. By the mid-1960s, for example, every provincial capital except Lhasa had its own iron and steel works. These factories were substantial symbols of socialist modernity, and as Kirkby and Cannon comment, 'no modern socialist city could hold its head up without its own steel-making facilities'.[33] Planners favoured investment in new facilities because these could be immediately translated into statistics on economic growth; new facilities could easily be planned, and they allowed the government to expand its ownership of enterprises at a time when it did not have complete control over the economy.[34]

The other important feature of regional industrial expansion was the political legacy of the revolution and the continuing perception of a hostile world beyond China. Local self-reliance was a constant theme running through Maoist politics, and was encouraged by the perception of constant danger from the outside. It was also reinforced by the vertical nature of the administrative and industrial system. After 1957, when Maoist radicalism began to dominate the Chinese political economy, the exercise of vertical authority became increasingly entrenched, particularly at the provincial level, producing a legacy of 'local encystment'.[35] The expansion of the iron and steel industry to over 2,000 state and collective enterprises by the mid-1980s reflects the fact that it was deemed important that local regions be equipped with all the necessary instruments of self-sufficient socialist modernity.[36]

While the perception of a hostile geopolitical environment helped justify the idea of local self-reliance, it also encouraged the massive relocation of China's defence industry away from the coast to the 'Third Front' provinces of the interior: namely, Guizhou, Yunnan, Sichuan, Shaanxi, Gansu, and parts of Henan, Hubei, and Hunan. Some 29,000 state enterprises were built during this period, mobilising a work force of 16 million.[37] Naughton estimates that at its peak in the late 1960s and early 1970s, two-thirds of the state's industrial budget was going to 'Third Front' investments.[38] Projects were especially costly due to their remote mountainous locations and almost non-existent infrastructure. The cost of laying railroad track in Guizhou, for example, was between four and five times higher than normal for other parts of China.

It is unlikely, however, that 'Third Front' industrialisation contributed much to regional self-sufficiency. As Naughton points out, the project was highly centralised; local governments had little say in the use of 'Third Front' funds. The command structure of the project had the authority to 'cut across functional and regional administrative boundaries, an extraordinary dispensation that was made acceptable by the urgency accorded the construction itself'.[39] 'Third Front' projects also bypassed normal material allocation procedures, sometimes skipping provincial governments entirely. Nor did the construction of these industries necessarily contribute to local economic development; few projects articulated significantly with the local economies which surrounded them. Most of the labour force for these projects, for example, was imported from other parts of the country. Indeed, 'Third Front' industrialisation, with its 'Three Sides' principle of simultaneous design, construction, and operation, reinforced the dependence of interior provinces on state subsidies, saddling them with poorly built, inefficiently managed and unprofitable industries. Even the railroads became a burden. From 1978 to 1988, 40 million *yuan* was spent repairing defects on the Chengdu–Kunming line, and over a hundred serious problem spots were still awaiting attention.[40]

Thus, even though cellularised self-sufficiency was reinforced in various ways by Maoist economic planning, the 'Third Front' experience indicates that centralisation remained a significant factor in the development of interior regions. Yet, dependence on the centre did little for the long-term economic development of Guizhou during the Maoist era. Although the central government sought to redistribute wealth in China, richer provinces seeking industrial maximisation were able to significantly determine spatial patterns of accumulation.[41] The central government's attention to development in Guizhou tended to be dominated by turning the province, with its large coal and iron ore reserves, into a centre of extraction for fuelling rapid industrial development and integration throughout southwest China.[42] During the Great Leap Forward (1958–60), nearly all state investments were diverted to mining and mineral processing, the result being a decrease in agricultural production and an increased dependence on central financial assistance.[43] Ironically, Guizhou's leaders perceived the Great Leap Forward as a turning point in provincial integration, and welcomed it as an opportunity for Guizhou to cast off its colonial status. Guizhou was even promoted as a model of the virtues of having been 'poor and blank'.[44] Ultimately, however, rapid collectivisation of agriculture and the excessive investment focus on extractive industry only led to economic and political chaos in Guizhou. Unable to implement national policies and disabled by ethnic tensions resulting from the campaign against 'local nationalism', Guizhou's entire leadership was dismissed in 1965 and replaced with functionaries from the Southwest Regional Bureau in Sichuan. It would be 15 years before a Guizhou native would once again serve among the province's leaders.[45]

This made the industrialisation of the 'Third Front' policy, which followed on the heels of the Great Leap Forward, even more likely to disregard the basic rural development needs of the province itself. Indeed, defence industrialisation only perpetuated Guizhou's economic chaos.[46] Between 1964 and 1966 a hundred major capital construction projects were carried out, and in 1966 an additional 117 projects were initiated. Yet the poor planning, design and construction of these projects, along with their enormous cost and diversion of investments, resulted in a 12 per cent decline in industrial and agricultural output from 1966 to 1969. Heavy industrial output alone declined 26 per cent, translating into a 47 per cent decline in revenues. This represented a return to 1955 levels of revenue and resulted in a 214 million *yuan* budgetary deficit for Guizhou. To compensate, 'Third Front' investments in Guizhou were stepped up, and peaked in 1971 at 1.46 billion *yuan*. This did little, however, to alter the dependency structure of the economy which defence industrialisation and resource extraction created. Guizhou simply survived on subsidies – which primarily went to urban residents for the purchase of manufactured goods from wealthier provinces and food at deflated prices.

GUIZHOU'S MODERNISATION IN THE REFORM ERA

The 'Third Front' legacy

Post-Mao Guizhou still displays many of the characteristics of a province dominated by the legacy of defence industrialisation and resource extraction. It still ranks third, behind Sichuan and Shaanxi, in the size of its defence science and technology industry.[47] In 1990, 84.9 per cent of Guizhou's industrial output value came from the state sector. China's average, at this time, was considerably lower at 54.6 per cent.[48] By 1994, the state share had dropped to about 70 per cent, yet the national average had declined even more, to 34 per cent.[49] Outside of Guiyang, the provincial capital, the state's share of industrial output was still as high as 82 per cent in 1995.[50] Besides the dominance of the state-owned enterprises, another feature of 'Third Front' regions is the continuing low productivity of their industries. A recent World Bank study found a close relationship between Total Factor Productivity (TFP) and the proportion of non-state industry; the study claimed that 'provinces with very low shares of non-state industry . . . had the lowest productivity'.[51] Guizhou's TFP index was found to be around 84, compared with Guangdong, Jiangsu, and Zhejiang, all with indices of over 125. Guizhou's low performance was shared by other 'Third Front' provinces, including Shaanxi, Gansu and Sichuan.

Table 2.5 gives an indication of the historical pattern of state investments in Guizhou, in which heavy industry has been overwhelmingly emphasised. In 1992, the state sector claimed 74.6 per cent of total fixed capital investments in Guizhou; only 2.5 per cent went to agriculture, while 65.8 per cent went to industry.[52] Throughout the 1980s and into the 1990s, the vast majority of industrial investment has gone toward mining, mineral processing, energy, and military industrial development. In 1992, 50.2 per cent of total industrial investments went to extractive industries.[53] (Guizhou ranks fifth in the country in coal reserves, second in aluminum resources, and third in manganese reserves.[54] It also ranks among the top five provinces in hydroelectric potential.) With their large investment appetite met by central allocations, these industries have been seeing considerable growth in output (for example, 12.3 per cent in 1995).[55]

As part of the Eighth FYP's 'Key Regions of the Comprehensive National Development Plan' put forth by the National Planning Commission, three key regions were selected in Guizhou for the large-scale development of energy and mineral resources. Finalised in August 1990, this plan, which covered nearly two-thirds of Guizhou's territory and 70 per cent of its population, brought the

Table 2.5 Guizhou: total state sector investments, 1950–1990 (million *yuan*)

	1950–57	*1958–78*	*1979–90*
Agriculture	25	580	647
Light industry	15	345	2,457
Heavy industry	66	8,226	11,323

Source: *Guizhou shengqing* [Guizhou Provincial Gazetteer], p. 36

intensification of resource extraction to a new level. The plan was to centrally administer 19 key regions throughout China. In Guizhou, it called for the development of 14 major hydroelectric power stations, 12 major coal-fired power stations, and intensification of coal, aluminum, iron ore, manganese, phosphorus, sulfur and gold mining.[56] The plan also called for the creation of 'processing chains', vertically integrated sets of industries taking advantage of their geographic proximity in key mining cities such as Liupanshui.[57] This represented a recognition that, 'because of low prices for the primary products', Guizhou's mining centres 'cannot build up a sufficient urban infrastructure'.[58]

At the same time, the comprehensive development plan further emphasises the centre's prescription for Guizhou as a net energy and raw materials provider in light of the increasing obsolescence of its industrial manufacturing sector left over from the 'Third Front' era. These enterprises have seen almost no growth in output in the 1990s, and are recognised as one of the weak links in Guizhou's modernisation efforts.[59] In an effort to make these industries profitable, many have been converted to consumer goods production and moved to new development zones near Guiyang, Anshun and Zunyi. Yet, this transformation of Guizhou's ordnance industry has also entailed a weaning from central investments.[60] Thus, the comprehensive development plan means an increased concentration of central investment in the energy and mining sectors, while the province is given the responsibility of reviving a derelict manufacturing industry.

The impact of fiscal decentralisation and decline

During the reform era the redistributive effectiveness of the central government has declined considerably. Since 1980, a trend toward local self-financing has generated growing regional economic disparities.[61] As previously indicated in Table 2.4, the central government's share of the budget has dropped from roughly 47 per cent in 1984 to 30 per cent in 1994. At the same time, government revenues have declined to 12.7 per cent of GNP in 1994. Mirroring a pattern which has become familiar throughout provincial China, Guizhou is faced with increasing fiscal responsibilities and increasingly inadequate revenues; it has thus taken to reaching 'beyond the budget' to generate revenues through extra-budgetary and self-raised funds.[62] At the same time, the centre's ability to address regional economic disparities through budgetary manipulation has declined. Of the centre's budgetary transfers to provinces, only quota subsidies are based on need, and by 1990 these accounted for only 15 per cent of total transfers. Over 50 per cent of transfers were earmarked grants, the overwhelming majority of which were absorbed as price subsidies in grain, oil and cotton for relatively prosperous urban populations.[63]

Between 1988 and 1994, Guizhou received annual fixed quota subsidies of 740 million *yuan*, representing a significant proportional decline in central transfers as the provincial budget expanded.[64] As indicated in a recent Asian Development Bank (ADB) report, in the early 1980s subsidies financed nearly 60 per cent of Guizhou's total budget. By 1993, this figure was down to less than 20 per cent. In

1995, 70 per cent of total fixed capital investments were financed by the province, a significant increase over the 1992 figure of 48 per cent.[65] By the 1990s, the provincial government was no longer able to transfer its diminishing subsidies to counties and instead was extracting a surplus from them to finance provincial outlays. This has resulted not only in inadequate attention to agricultural investment and rural poverty, but to a proliferation of damaging fees and surcharges on rural households and industries as counties scramble to meet their remittance quotas. The ADB report charges that, 'in Guizhou, since 1988, the entire rural sector has acquired net remitter status, so that the rural sector may be supporting the urban sector'.[66] Poor counties have thus seen very little growth in expenditures, while even relatively wealthy counties are strapped with heavy revenue sharing burdens which dampen whatever comparative advantages they've been able to muster. The consequences of this at the local level will be revisited in the final section of the chapter.

In an effort to arrest fiscal decline and increase central revenue shares, a new tax sharing arrangement was introduced by the Ministry of Finance in 1994. This shifted the bulk of turnover taxes (VAT, business tax and product tax) to the centre, and created a new consumption tax on luxury goods, including alcohol and tobacco, also to be remitted directly to the centre. This recentralisation of revenues has in fact been an on-going trend throughout the reform era; whereas in 1980 the centre collected only 19 per cent of state revenues, by 1994, it was collecting nearly 58 per cent.[67] According to the ADB, in the short run at least, these developments exacerbate Guizhou's financial difficulties. The majority of revenue expansion for counties has come from turnover taxes, and the loss of these indirect revenues in the rural sector will put significant stress on counties to find new sources of income. At the same time, many Guizhou counties have been able to capitalise on a comparative advantage in tobacco and liquor production. They now face the loss of the majority of these revenues to the centre.

During the 1980s, the central government tried to compensate for economic difficulties in the interior by introducing a number of development funds for minority regions, revolutionary base areas and impoverished counties. In terms of direct aid, however, these funds did not amount to much. In 1986, they equalled only 0.1 per cent of China's national income, and were being distributed to 60 per cent of all of China's counties.[68] The meagre amount of these funds were yet another indication 'that the centre is severely strained in its fiscal resources, and its transfers are generally insufficient or ineffective in raising the growth of capital investment in these poor regions to match the national level'.[69] In the 1990s, these development funds continue to be the primary source of central investment in most counties, but their effectiveness remains minimal. As will be discussed in the final section of this chapter, they're now typically used to cover the everyday expenditures of county budgets, such as salaries for teachers and government cadres, rather than stimulating the development projects for which they are intended.

Pursuing market socialism in Guizhou

Guizhou's pursuit of the virtues of commercialism and market-driven economic development should be seen in light of a dependent relationship to the centre defined by energy and mining development and the fiscal crisis accompanying this relationship. Throughout China, local governments have been faced with the contradictory combination of fiscal decentralisation (giving them more responsibility for managing their budgets) and fiscal decline (making it necessary for them to cover more of their expenditures). The fiscal burdens of this situation have resulted in a tremendous amount of local activity in independently promoting regional economic development, especially by expanding the light industrial sector. This has often led to irrational duplication and regional protectionism.[70] It has also led to a flurry of real estate and trade speculation aimed at attracting fast capital from domestic and foreign sources. This is perhaps most clearly manifest in rapid expansion in Guizhou of special economic development zones and glitzy trade fairs in 1992–93. Like neighbouring Guangxi to the south, 1992 marked the real beginning of economic liberalisation in Guizhou. With encouragement from the State Council, and the appointment of a new governor (Liu Shineng), the province attempted to ride the coattails of Deng's 1992 southern tour by cashing in on the southern China development boom. Despite the noticeable improvements in the urban economy which resulted, however, liberalisation has yet to alter the structural factors which contribute to Guizhou's overall economic difficulties.

While Guizhou's relationship to the centre continued to be dominated by investments in energy and mineral resource extraction, the provincial capital quickly became the site of intense land speculation. Provincial leadership managed in July 1992 to negotiate with the State Council for Guiyang's preferential status as an 'interior open city'. This set off a small real estate boom and, by May of 1993, 25 real estate development companies had been established, half of them with external funds. Indeed, with land one-third to two-thirds less expensive in Guiyang than Guangdong, 45 per cent of all private external investments in Guizhou in 1993 were in real estate.[71] The sudden flurry of construction was quite noticeable to the citizens of Guiyang, who by 1993 were comparing Guiyang to a frontier town where wealth easily comes and goes. An even more indicative example of Guizhou's pursuit of fast capital is found in the 1992 purchase of 330 hectares of land at the booming Guangxi port of Beihai, ostensibly for an export development and processing zone but more likely as a simple attempt at land speculation.[72] This turned out to be a poor investment which nevertheless created quite a stir. Entrepreneurs in Guiyang talked glowingly of Guizhou's new link to world trade, despite the fact that in 1996 the land remained undeveloped.

Much of the real estate boom took place in newly established economic development zones outside of Guiyang. These zones were initiated by the relocation of many 'Third Front' enterprises, referred to as the policy of 'coming down from the mountains and out of the valleys'. Along with their relocation, these enterprises began switching to consumer goods production. In 1979, 10 per cent of Guizhou's military industrial production was in consumer goods; by 1992 the proportion was up to 72 per cent.[73] Faced with the state's expectations of accountability, these firms hoped their new location in 'hi-tech development zones' would act as a springboard for attracting external investment. By 1993, for example, they had established linkages with over 150 'window enterprises' in the open cities along the coast in order to facilitate export-oriented production and attract investment deals. The first and largest of these zones was at Xintianzhai – the 'Guiyang Hi-Tech Industries Development Zone' – which was established, with State Council approval, by the 1992 relocation of the Zhenhua Electronics Group.[74] An additional three zones were established the same year by the provincial government; they were located in Guiyang (at Xiaohe), Zunyi and Anshun. Determined not to miss out, Guiyang's municipal government also established its own zone at Baiyun, and other municipalities and counties quickly followed suit. The entire Bijie Prefecture was granted state-level status as a 'Poverty Alleviation Experimental Zone'. Then, in 1994, Qiandongnan Miao and Dong Autonomous Prefecture was designated a state-level 'Experimental Development Zone' for minority regions by the State Nationalities Affairs Commission.[75]

Bolstered by the establishment of this experimental zone in Qiandongnan, the prefectural capital of Kaili in turn established its own 'Economic and Technological Development Zone'. The zone's policies, outlined in draft version provided by a city official in 1994, give an indication of how localities tried to attract external investment. Tax policies in Kaili include five-year income tax holidays followed by another five years of reduced taxes (tax holidays are even longer for 'hi-tech firms'), VAT reductions and waivers, subsidies for firms which face tax hardships, and tax holidays of various lengths for land, property, transportation and employment. In addition, the majority of taxes for the first six years (following the tax holiday) will be returned to the place from which the new firm's investments came. Land rents and utility fees are reduced, especially for 'hi-tech' and tourist enterprises. Kaili, which in 1965 became a centre for 'Third Front' electronics enterprises, is especially hoping to capitalise on this legacy by attracting investment in modern electronics production.

The establishment of these development zones between 1992 and 1994 was accompanied by a marketing and promotional blitz unlike anything the province had ever witnessed before. For provincial leaders, Guizhou's modernisation was to become a spectacular event, attracting tourist-investors from the wealthier regions of China and the world. Tourism, in fact, was slated to become one of the province's 'pillar industries', with plans calling for tourism revenues to contribute as much as 20 per cent to Guizhou's income by 2010 (in 1993, tourism contributed about 5 per cent).[76] If successful, such a plan would lift tourism to the same level of importance as the province's other recognised 'pillars': coal mining, hydroelectricity, mineral processing, defence industry and agriculture. Tourism was promoted as a vanguard industry, opening the way for other processes to gain a foothold in Guizhou, particularly external investment and commercial integration of the rural economy with external markets. This idea was championed by the phrase 'economic trade performing on a stage built by tourism', which was soon found in nearly all local media coverage of commercial development projects. Tourism was to be the principal vehicle by which potential investors and consumers were brought to Guizhou. It would also serve as a primary means by which the countryside could cast off its 'traditional thinking' and adopt a 'commercial conscience' in order to solve its impending subsistence crisis. Symbolically illustrating the important role of tourism, Guizhou's only high-grade highway was completed in 1991, between Guiyang and Huangguoshu Falls, the province's most popular tourist attraction. When this highway was built, 20 per cent of Guizhou's administrative village seats were still roadless.[77] With primitive transport conditions throughout the province, the construction of a high-grade highway to a site of 'non-productive' economic activity represented a significant commitment to initiating the basic infrastructure investments necessary for selling Guizhou.

Ethnic minority culture became a fundamental feature of Guizhou's promotional activities, both in terms of using exotic cultural representations as enticements for potential investments, and as a feature of market socialism's potential for rural development in minority regions. Indeed, tourism itself was thought to be ideally suited for these regions by taking advantage of the conditions which made them so poor: harsh but scenic mountainous environments and socio-cultural distance from modern Chinese economies and lifestyles. The representations of minority culture which became ubiquitous features of promoting the province would not only make Guizhou more interesting to outsiders, but were meant to establish a model for the 'cultural development' of minority groups themselves, conditioning them to articulate symbolic cultural practices with commercial projects. Tourism was thus seen not simply as a propaganda and marketing tool for Guizhou, but also as a process of development and integration encouraging minority regions to become more modern.

The most visible signs of Guizhou's modernisation-as-spectacle were found in a rash of flashy trade fairs in 1992 and 1993. While these can be interpreted, in part, as manifestations of the local initiative spurred by Deng's southern tour, they were also orchestrated as part of several centrally promoted tourism campaigns sponsored by the National Tourism Administration (NTA). In 1992, the province held a 'batik festival' in Anshun and a 'liquor culture festival' in Zunyi. The following year, there was an 'azalea blossom festival', while the former 'liquor culture festival' was combined with a 'Huangguoshu sightseeing festival'. This latter event was partly funded by the NTA and was one of five official events throughout the country marking 'China Scenery Tourism Year'. Guizhou's selection for NTA funding in 1993 was treated as a crucial opportunity for economic development; 'Huangguoshu Sightseeing and International Famous Liquor Festival' became the largest commercial event in Guizhou's history, promoted with the phrase 'let the world understand Guizhou, let Guizhou align with the world'.

These festivals were very large-scale undertakings which combined ethnic cultural performances, traditional crafts demonstrations and numerous exhibitions of local products, especially liquor. The azalea festival, for example, sought to combine tourism and trade under the principle of 'lure business through festivals, lure investment by favouring business, develop trade, expand external economic cooperation'. The festival focused on Guizhou's '100 *li* azalea belt,' a scenic attraction along the border between Dafang and Qianxi counties. Dafang is one of Guizhou's 31 impoverished counties. During the festival, *Guizhou Daily* ran an article entitled 'Economy Performing on a Stage of Flowers' which described Dafang's various natural resources awaiting investment and exploitation. Other articles followed, over the course of the week, on investment opportunities throughout the Dafang region. The paper also ran full colour pages of advertisements for Guizhou enterprises, most of which were participating in the commodities exhibition. *Guizhou Daily* also emphasised ethnic activities in its coverage, pointing out that the region's rich minority culture made it an ideal place to invest in ethnic tourism development.[78]

The Huangguoshu festival was an even bigger event. With the extra boost of NTA funds, millions of *yuan* were spent beautifying Guiyang and the nearby scenic sites for the week-long festival. The festival featured an 'International Children's Crafts Festival' (with children's performance troupes from China, the USA, Vietnam, Laos, Burma, Japan and France), a parade featuring elaborate floats sponsored by various local distilleries, ethnic song and dance performances at Huangguoshu Falls, and no less than seven different commodities and crafts exhibitions. The largest of these was held in the provincial exhibition centre, which was renamed the 'International Economic and Technological Trade Centre' to better capture the heady spirit of the fair. The festival was attended by the head of the NTA, along with numerous central party officials, and a random assortment of foreign ambassadors. It was covered by *Guizhou Daily* with four consecutive days of colour photographs and advertisements. As with the azalea festival, it also provided an opportunity to print numerous stories on development and modernisation throughout the province. The unprecedented extravagance of the festival, however, compelled the newspaper to run an editorial cautioning enterprise managers against the flagrant waste of valuable funds on lavish banquets and, ironically, the use of 'too many advertisements'.[79]

In trying to ensure their success as public relations events, the provincial government arranged to have 1.85 billion *yuan*, worth of economic cooperation projects, which had actually been negotiated throughout the preceding year, to be finalised during the festivals. *Guizhou Daily* reported that the total business volume for the 1993 festivals exceeded 3.65 billion *yuan*, that nearly 10,000 tourists and business representatives attended, and that over US$70 million in foreign direct investment was negotiated. A total of 33 joint venture/cooperation projects were negotiated, a number which, if finalised, would account for 15.5 per cent of all such contracts in Guizhou between 1980 and 1992.[80] By 1996, however, officials in the provincial government privately acknowledged that many of these business deals were never finalised. Looking back on the festivals, one official told me bluntly that the trade fairs had been 'a huge waste of money' for the province.[81] Indeed, since 1993 there have been no more large-scale trade fairs held in Guizhou. Yet, while the festivals were perhaps a failure in economic terms, reinforcing Guizhou's disadvantaged position in pursuing the newly mobile capital of post-1992 China, they were nevertheless profoundly cultural events, not simply for the tourists visiting the province, but especially for people in Guizhou itself. The festivals provided a brief tangible model of 'cultural development' and commercial integration combined with celebrations of tradition and symbolic cultural diversity.

As if to emphasise the disappointing results of the early 1990s, by 1996, tourism too was – at least temporarily – on the decline. According to a source within the tourism bureau, the first eight months of 1996 saw a dramatic decline in tourist arrivals compared to the same period in 1995. A combination of poor leadership, drastic cut-backs in the tourism bureau's budget, the consequent lack of marketing and inability of local agencies to offer competitive prices compared to those in neighbouring Yunnan was to blame.[82] Other officials recognised the growth targets for Guizhou tourism – culminating in earning 20 per cent of provincial income by 2010 – as impossible to reach; it is doubtful that tourism's contribution will increase beyond 10 per cent during this period. Thus, Guizhou's income dependence on its mining and energy sectors is likely to continue well into the next century.

The frontier-type boom-town atmosphere that characterised much of urban Guizhou during this time had its political ramifications as well. While it is difficult to assign causality to specific individuals, Guizhou's spectacular but largely wasteful pursuit of market socialism coincided with the tenure of provincial party secretary Liu Zhengwei (appointed in 1988) and governor Liu Shineng (appointed in 1992). Both were outsiders, brought in to help revitalise the local economy. Yet, as has been the tradition in Guizhou, locals regarded them as temporary functionaries 'doing time' in Guizhou while waiting for a better appointment. Liu Shineng, from Beijing, had replaced the popular yet conservative Wang Chaoren, a Miao from Guizhou's Huangping county. Wang's popularity derived from the fact that he was the first native governor since 1965. After an eight year tenure, however, his replacement in 1992 by an outsider from Beijing was an indication from the centre that the province needed some stirring up. Neither the new governor nor Secretary Liu ended up staying in Guizhou long, however. Secretary Liu was demoted to a minor post in Beijing in 1994 after his wife was arrested for fraudulent real estate speculation in Guiyang. Likewise, Liu Shineng was returned to Beijing in 1995 after three years of watching Guizhou's high-profile development schemes fall flat. Many intellectuals in Guiyang felt that such leaders came to Guizhou simply to make some money in the boom-town environment before getting a 'real' post somewhere else. By 1996, it seemed little had changed. The governor's post was being filled on an interim basis by a Liaoning native, Wu Yixia, and the new party secretary, Liu Fangren, was also an outsider. Guizhou leadership – being largely non-local – has not presented a significant challenge to the centre's prescribed role for the province; nor has it been able to develop a coherent development strategy of its own, beyond reaffirming in vague terms the need for commercialisation and 'cultural development'.

Despite the problems indicated above, the modernisation-as-spectacle approach to development did nevertheless have a notable impact on Guizhou's urban economy. Provincial exports increased 64 per cent between 1990 and 1993, while imports jumped 94 per cent. Urban consumer spending was up 34 per cent during the same period, matching similar growth in urban per capita incomes.[83] Yet, overall per capita consumption in 1994 remained the lowest in China at 735 *yuan* (42 per cent of the national average) indicating the influence of rural Guizhou's stagnant growth; rural per capital expenditures in Guizhou were the third lowest in China in 1995.[84] Urban–rural disparities have been increasing in Guizhou. Development zones have primarily benefited urban residents, whose lives are already subsidised by the state in many ways.[85] From 1990 to 1993, nominal incomes per capita in rural households increased 16 per cent, less than half the figure for urban residents.[86] Investments in Guizhou's energy production primarily benefit urban heavy industries (consuming roughly 78 per cent of all commercial electricity in the province). The other major beneficiary – urban households – consumed ten times as much electricity as rural households in 1995, despite the fact that they accounted for merely 14 per cent of the total population.[87] Furthermore, the focus on speculative development in trade and real estate resulted in the virtual ignoring of agriculture's plight. As agricultural investments stagnate, rural industrialisation is supposed to fill in the gap. But the obstacles to establishing this sector remain difficult to overcome.

As the core of rural development in Guizhou, rural industrialisation is to be based on the idea of 'leading sectors', in which limited investment resources are focused on particular commercial products. According to one report these sectors coalesce into three areas: commercialised agricultural production (for example, tobacco, timber, tung oil and livestock), traditional specialities (such as liquor, cigarettes, and ethnic textiles and handicrafts), and household appliances.[88] The expansion of commercial crop, timber, and livestock production and processing has been emphasised not only as the primary means by which households and local governments should increase incomes and revenues, but as a necessary step in reducing pressure on Guizhou's marginal upland soils. It has been acknowledged, however, that most regions have not created adequate economies of scale in commercial farm production to make the investments worthwhile. This is officially blamed on the 'small peasant economy mentality' which favours subsistence and self-sufficiency. In reality, however, local governments simply cannot put more land into commercial production because of the extreme population pressures and subsistence crisis which they already face.[89] Although one report calls for 70 per cent of all state poverty alleviation investments to go to commercial crop production, the local realities make such a plan unfeasible for local governments to implement.[90]

Thus, beyond the fringes of urban centres such as Guiyang, Zunyi and Anshun, provincial leaders have still seen very little satisfactory progress in commercialising the rural economy according to the ideals of market socialism. Indeed, the ideals of socialism in any form are increasingly questioned in the impoverished regions of rural Guizhou. On a 1996 visit to Bijie, Jiang Zemin made a point of reassuring the poor households he visited that 'China is still a socialist country'. But a group of Beijing reporters covering the secretary's visit, upon visiting impoverished villages near Guiyang, rhetorically asked if Guizhou even had a Communist Party at all. Despite all the efforts of the early 1990s, the overall picture of Guizhou's economy has changed little in structural terms. While industry and agriculture contributed nearly equal parts to the provincial GVIAO in 1994, they did so with vastly different employment figures: industry accounted for roughly 8 per cent of the workforce whereas agriculture accounted for nearly 75 per cent.[91] State-level investments continue to be dominated by mining and energy development.[92] Rural commercialism remains stubbornly undeveloped and calls for 'cultural development' as the remedy have only intensified. In this light, minority groups occupy the symbolic heart of campaigns which call for changing the 'traditional thinking' of the rural sector. Despite recent setbacks, tourism has been the major success story in these campaigns; in particular, commercial ethnic crafts production has stood out considerably as one of the more hopeful prospects for rural economic transformation and ethnic cultural development in Guizhou. In sum, Guizhou's hopes for rural development and poverty alleviation are increasingly wrapped up in the commercial potential of ethnic minorities, whose rural lives have for so long exemplified the province's 'backwardness'.

CULTURAL DEVELOPMENT IN AN ERA OF MARKETISATION

As evidenced by the trade fairs of 1992–93, 'selling Guizhou' has most succinctly meant 'selling Guizhou's traditions', its liquor and tobacco culture, its harsh yet poetic scenery and its ethnic exoticism. While the economic benefits of this approach have been questionable, the local social and cultural changes resulting from the province's attempt to establish its comparative advantage have been significant, particularly for minority groups. The promotion of commercialism has provided a new means for elites to express the ethnic and regional autonomy of their groups, but it has also brought a host of new economic and political contradictions for many sectors of minority society. These issues are addressed in this final section.

The discourse of 'cultural development' among minority elites

'Cultural development' encompasses the Chinese state's twin goals of regional political and economic integration along with the nurturing of a national civic culture based on the ideals of socialism. It is most commonly used to refer to the development of ethnic minority regions. In specific post-Mao terms, it implies the attainment of literacy (in standard Chinese), an education in science and technology, understanding of modern commerce, expertise in enterprise management, and even an entrepreneurial spirit. But in Guizhou 'cultural development' has more specifically come to mean the creative blending of traditional arts and crafts, cuisines and performances with modern commercialism, that is, the commodification of tradition. Cultural development enables a sense of local cultural autonomy and preservation, even as economic and social integration proceeds towards the state's desired goals of nation-building.

Local minority elites enthusiastically embrace 'cultural development' not only for the purposes of economic development, but more importantly as a means of maintaining a distinct sense of regional ethnic identity even as China's modernisation and integration ensues. Thus, economic development plans in minority regions are infused with a strong commitment to the preservation of those minority traditions which articulate well with the needs of commercialism and capital accumulation.[93] In Guizhou, any activity which celebrates cultural traditions and 'local colour' while at the same time promoting commercial economic development and further integration into broader markets, is upheld as an example of 'cultural development'. Newspapers are full of examples. During the 1993 azalea blossom and Huangguoshu famous liquor festivals, *Guizhou Daily* ran several such stories. One covered the opening of scenic Sajin gorge by Fuquan county, which had invested over 870,000 *yuan* in developing the site. The new tourist site opened with a three day 'Sajin Nationality Song and Dance Festival', coinciding with the Huangguoshu famous liquor festival; according to county officials, the festival would 'highlight how modern civilisation and traditional customs complement each other in cultural development'. A Huangping county crafts factory was also praised in *Guizhou Daily* for making toys to be sold all over China, which 'combined traditional skills with modern ideas'. It was with such a combination, the journalist commented, that minority groups would finally 'go to the world'.[94]

'Going to the world', in fact, has been the rallying cry among scholars and officials promoting the development of Guizhou's minority regions. What is significant about this is not simply that it represents national integration, but that it is celebrated by local elites as the means by which they may become modern while retaining the traditions and customs which mark them as distinctive and around which they seek to maintain a sense of nationality identity. State-sponsored integration is enthusiastically embraced by Guizhou's minority leaders if it leaves open a space for local cultural autonomy. As one scholar claimed, 'the question of turning traditional culture into a cultural commodity, and marketing that commodity domestically and internationally, is not simply one of economics, but of the *value* of a particular nationality group'.[95] Ethnic cultural commodification, he continued, is a bridge between nationality groups and modernity; the goal is not simply to sell nationality culture, but to develop it.

In November of 1990, the Guizhou Nationalities Cultural Studies Association held its annual meetings in Kaili, and the theme for the conference was 'Moving Guizhou's nationality cultures to the world'.[96] Papers were delivered on the subjects of preserving traditional nationality culture and on how to articulate nationality traditions with the needs of modernisation.[97] A paper by Shi Chaojiang was illustrative of the general tone of the conference. Entitled 'Traditional Miao culture and socialist modernisation', the paper first described the various features of traditional Miao culture which were positive attributes for a modernising society. Because of their history of migration and perseverance in the face of adversity and hostility, the Miao had a 'pioneer spirit' of mutual aid and assistance. They were used to being cast out into the wilderness and being forced to make it productive. This was precisely the spirit, Shi exclaimed, needed to build socialist modernisation. The Miao were also very democratic, and valued social equality. They had a spirit of industriousness and hard work, and they believed, like Deng Xiaoping, in 'seeking truth from facts'. Yet the Miao also exhibited some conflicts with the spirit of modernity. While their high moral and ethical standards were to be praised, their morality of respect for the natural environment conflicted with modernisation's need for exploitation of natural resources! The Miao had for too long been isolated subsistence farmers and harboured a 'small peasant economy mentality'. Their deep rooted religious beliefs prevented the popularisation of scientific knowledge, and their insistence on marrying locally kept the population from being invigorated by outsiders. Shi concluded that these conflicts with modernity needed to be 'put in order' and discarded. The former aspects of Miao culture which articulated positively with modernisation should be supported and promoted.

Added to this message of selective cultural engineering, which was repeated in most of the papers, were accounts of how Guizhou's nationality traditions formed the very touchstone of China's socialist modernisation. In the essay which introduced the published papers from the conference, it was argued that nationality culture was the basis for China's industrialisation and modernisation, and that it provided China with distinctiveness in the face of 'Westernisation' and prevented assimilation as China entered the global economy. In fact, nationality culture was already more modernised than most people thought. Nationality culture in Guizhou, the essay enthusiastically declared, already reflected the world's twenty-first century desires. 'People in the twenty-first century will thirst for the kind of cultural traditions we have in Guizhou.' To quench this thirst, Guizhou hospitably offered not only bowl upon bowl of rice wine proffered to tourists by jovial villagers, but beautiful batiks and embroidery patterns, reed pipe dancing, the 'oriental disco' of Miao song and dance troupes, the 'oriental choir' of Dong village girls, literature, legends and more.[98]

This approach to 'cultural development' not only allows for the selective breeding of symbolic cultural diversity as the captive antidote to modernity's cravings, but enables local leaders to actively confront the sense of loss which over four decades of socialist modernisation has engendered. The paper delivered by Wu Dehai, an active Miao scholar and former prefectural governor, openly discussed his discomfort with the 'decline' of traditional nationality culture in the face of modernisation. Wu lamented that traditional festivals and reed pipe meetings had declined in popularity since the 1950s; there was less diversity in the songs and dances performed. Many instruments which used to be around were no longer played. Fewer and fewer people knew the old myths and legends, new buildings used less traditional architecture, and traditional nationality medicine was rarely practised anymore. As a Marxist, he had to admit that this was something of an historical inevitability, and the positive result of progressing to a more advanced stage of history. But he also believed in Marx's claim that we are the makers of our own history, albeit within conditions not of our own choosing. This, he claimed, was why 'going to the world' was so important. The world was increasingly interested in preserving cultural traditions, and Guizhou's nationality groups simply needed to link their futures to this larger trend by creating more tourist sites, museums, 'cultural departments' and stronger laws preserving people's traditional customs.

Selling Guizhou: cultural development in practice

Efforts to commercialise rural production systems and transform the 'traditional subsistence mentalities' of minorities have encouraged the rapid growth of ethnic crafts commodity production in Guizhou. In the autonomous prefecture of Qiandongnan, ethnic crafts production has expanded into one of the most important sectors of an incipient rural industrialisation. Yet, beyond the promotions of elites, the process of commercialising and standardising ethnic crafts production is a project full of paradox and contradiction for local ethnic producers. In trying to combine two different cultural economies in Guizhou – those of commercialism and subsistence – ideas of development, modernisation and progress have been combined with those of cultural preservation. The idea of modernisation based on preserving nationality tradition, an idea now enthusiastically embraced by local leaders throughout Guizhou, may in fact be resulting in a new form of internal colonialism.

In brief, two dominant ideologies can be identified regarding nationality culture in Guizhou. On the one hand, preserving 'traditional nationality culture' has become important for China's projects of nationalism and modernisation, since 'tradition' forms both the ideological glue to build an imagined national community and the means by which local nationality groups can commercially participate in national integration without feeling like they are losing their local cultures. On the other hand, pursuing economic and cultural development in order to combat rural poverty, eradicate subsistence and 'small peasant mentalities', and otherwise transform the nature of rural production systems, has meant that 'nationality traditions' are only preserved if they can accommodate commercial production and exchange. Combined, these ideologies have generated an environment in rural Guizhou in which cultural development and the preservation of 'authentic nationality culture' legitimise a division of labour in which rural labour remains subordinated to urban capital. Nationality traditions of producing elaborate crafts, particularly batik and embroidery, are valued for their commercial potential in spurring the development of a rural revenue base and increasing household incomes, as well as for their 'museum value' as artefacts of national folk tradition worthy of preservation. The ideology of preservation, in this case, colludes with capital to fossilise rural modes of crafts production as a national cultural resource, and as a reservoir of skilled yet cheap exploitable labour.[99]

In rural Guizhou, particularly Qiandongnan, this process can be seen in several ways. The nationality groups of Qiandongnan, particularly the Miao, have become well known for the embroidered textiles they produce. Embroidery was a skill acquired by girls at a very early age, and was used to make elaborate clothing to wear at festivals and other important social occasions. Concern among local minority officials that with modernisation these skills would die out encouraged the promotion of economic schemes which would convince rural households that traditional skills could in fact be exploited to increase their incomes. This would enable modernisation without losing an important resource of nationality culture and identity. In Taijiang county, for example, the local nationalities commission became involved in attracting a number of coastal trading companies to set up labour-intensive, export-oriented textile factories. In 1994 there were at least three of these operating in Taijiang, as well as in at least six other county towns throughout Qiandongnan. One of the Taijiang factories was set up by a Jiangsu company to produce tie-dyed silk cloth to be exported to Japan. It employed about a hundred women, recruited from the countryside, who sat all day tying up thousands of tiny dot patterns on silk. They were paid six *yuan* for every 10,000 ties, and although the manager said they could typically produce 5,000 ties per day, workers on the shop floor told me that the most anyone earned was between 30 and 40 *yuan* per month.[100] Another Taijiang factory employed a similar number of rural women earning similar wages making embroidered cloth for export to Southeast Asia. I visited similar factories throughout the prefecture, and in all cases women lived in factory-provided dormitories, but were responsible for their own food. Employment averaged about a hundred per factory, and wages seldom exceeded 50 *yuan* per month. Because of special policies developed to attract this kind of economic activity to Qiandongnan (such as those in Kaili's special economic development zone discussed above), local governments were in fact collecting few tax revenues from these factories.

When asked in 1994, an officer at the Taijiang Nationalities Commission justified these exploitative ventures by stressing that they only represented a first step in modernisation. He likened them to a window through which more coastal companies could see the county's investment potential. He said that Taijiang's rural households still had few opportunities to earn a cash income, and that these factories would help generate a 'commercial consciousness' in the countryside. He did not believe that future development might be truncated by using Guizhou's countryside purely as a source of cheap labour and enhancing capital accumulation opportunities for coastal companies dabbling in international trade. But by 1996, the county's attitude had changed considerably. The county had refused to renew any leases for the coastal-run factories, citing insufficient pay and poor working conditions. For Taijiang, the previous goal of attracting external investment at any cost had, as with the province in general, clearly backfired. 'We lost money and the workers were treated badly,' a Nationalities Commission officer admitted. Furthermore, the county no longer had any funds available for promoting commercial crafts production. The county Nationalities Commission annual appropriation of 10,000 *yuan* had been cut, and what funds they did receive in the form of development grants were being swallowed up by day-to-day administrative expenditures and salaries.[101]

Thus, by 1996, the local state's role in promoting rural 'commercial consciousness' had diminished considerably. In Taijiang, all hopes for this were being pinned on private urban entrepreneurs. Yet the state still played a role in promoting an ideology of development in which Guizhou's peasantry is portrayed as harbouring a subsistence mentality from a pre-modern stage of production and culture. The state's campaign to commercialise the countryside has involved the mythic construction of a purely subsistence economy in 'backward mountain areas' such as Qiandongnan. Peasants are represented as locked within a 'small peasant economy mentality' until 'liberated' by the state and its urban entrepreneurial representatives as they benevolently spread the winds of reform to even the most tenacious strongholds of custom.[102] To reveal the presence of a thriving 'commercial consciousness' among the Miao, independent of state reforms, would be to open up a whole new line of argument concerning the economic backwardness of the mountain areas. More importantly, it would undermine the exoticism which – for urban entrepreneurs – is the commercial attraction of the Miao. That they come from a subsistence, tradition-bound society is what makes Miao embroidery so 'authentic' to a new class of urban Chinese consumers. Miao society must be constructed in this way if it is to remain commercially attractive to outsiders. Such is the contemporary pattern of Guizhou's internal colonialism. Ideology and expectations of ethnic remoteness have become part of a process seeking to preserve an idealised subsistence mode of production and, thus, preventing ethnic commodity production from initiating independent rural accumulation.

The desire for authenticity complements well the dominant patterns of capital accumulation in Guizhou's growing crafts industry. As ethnic tourism in the region has grown, urban entrepreneurs have set up numerous state-sponsored crafts factories, most of which are located in Kaili, with others in Taijiang, Liping and Huangping counties. With inadequate capital and a very limited market, many of these shut down after only a few months of operation, are combined with other operations or are acquired by larger state units which can afford to subsidise them, such as timber companies or the army. Those which survive do so only by establishing market links with coastal China and/or Hong Kong and Taiwan. Unlike the examples discussed above, such as the silk tie-dye factory in Taijiang, these factories seek to manufacture marketable products featuring 'authentic' ethnic crafts, such as wallets and clothing made with cloth embroidered or batiked in traditional patterns. While they tend to employ a number of rural women on-site, mainly to perform final assembly tasks, the majority of production occurs within village households on a contractual basis. The manager of Guizhou's largest crafts enterprise, the Miao Embroidery Factory in Taijiang (which is partially funded by UNICEF), estimated that 65 per cent of his factory's income came from the sale of products which have been primarily produced in rural households. The manager of a smaller factory in Huangping gave an estimate of 70 per cent for this figure. Rural women in Huangping contracting to apply the wax for batik tablecloths were earning about 10 per cent of what these tablecloths were eventually sold for.[103] At the Taijiang factory, I was told that contract producers could earn as much as 20 per cent of the final sale producing embroidered patches for wallets. With higher value items, such as clothing, however, the proportion would be much less. Nevertheless, contracts could significantly enhance a rural household's cash income.

But contract arrangements insured that control over production remained in the hands of urban factory managers who not only dictated piece-rates, but provided the 'authentic' designs and patterns in order to insure standardisation. Managers felt they were contributing to cultural development by teaching peasant households the value of money and enabling them to achieve a 'commercial consciousness'. But they also felt good about convincing peasants to respect the value of their traditions. 'If it wasn't for me,' one told me, 'peasants around here would forget their old patterns'. This attitude illustrates the colonial nature of market socialism in rural Guizhou. Contract arrangements were lauded for helping to preserve a pre-modern (that is, pre-commercial) mode of production, and for maintaining authentic nationality traditions which were important not simply for their museum value but, more significantly, for their exchange value.

The experience of the town of Shidong – in Taijiang county – illustrates the way metropolitan concerns for cultural preservation and authenticity result in increased subordination and vulnerability for Guizhou's producers of nationality culture. In addition to being a well known Miao festival site, Shidong achieved fame during the 1980s as one of Guizhou's most important ethnic crafts producing regions. Before 1990, Taijiang's Miao Embroidery Factory dealt exclusively with Shidong for its contracted embroidery. As the factory's manager, a Han, explained, 'Shidong was traditionally much more developed than Taijiang, and this legacy is still evident today. The people there are very entrepreneurial, and so it was easiest for us to get started there.' Shidong was perfect, he said, because it had developed early as an important river port; craftsmanship had become refined there. Then, after liberation, those traditional crafts were 'frozen in time', because Shidong was forgotten. Roads and railroads replaced the river as the region's most important transport network, and state investments went to developing nearby Taijiang as a government seat. By 1980, he said, Shidong had preserved a rich tradition in isolation while Taijiang had developed and become 'Hanified'. This gave Shidong new popularity in the 'cultural fever' of the reform era, and crafts production developed rapidly due to official promotion of Shidong's festivals and contracts with crafts factories.

During the 1990s, however, Shidong's position as a crafts supplier for urban commercial enterprises declined significantly. 'It is getting harder and harder to find authentic work there,' one entrepreneur in Kaili complained. 'They have become more and more influenced by Han culture, and so the patterns are not as authentic.' Another problem, he said, was that textile production in Shidong was no longer the result of a self-sufficient, enclosed economy, but an increasingly commercial one, and this had also influenced local embroidery styles. His solution to this 'contradiction' was to maintain a sort of cultural bank of authentic traditional styles, frozen in time, which would form the basis of sustained future production. 'If peasants want a job,' he said, 'they'll have to produce embroidery according to the styles we require, and these will be the authentic ones.' Other managers had come to the same conclusion about Shidong and the need to actively counter the cultural losses incurred by commercial development. The result for Shidong producers was an increased vulnerability to losing lucrative contracts unless they surrendered to the judgement of their outside employers in determining what was authentic and what was not.

A new discourse of nationalism among minority elites?

The pronouncements of 'going to the world' enthusiastically put forth in the 1990 Nationalities Cultural Studies Association meetings in Kaili, discussed above, came on the heels of the 1980s' 'cultural fever' which swept across China in the early years of the economic reforms. Since then, as a new class of urban Han entrepreneurs has emerged to commodify the exoticism of rural minorities such as the Miao, contributing to a growing spatial gap between the metropolitan coast and the rural interior, there is evidence of a growing resistance to the commercial consequences of market socialism among minority elites. Schein has argued that the hyper-commercialised culture of the West which has been introduced by Han entrepreneurs throughout the cities and towns of Guizhou – karaoke bars, night clubs, racy films, and loose sexual behaviour – have engendered a new discourse of traditional morality among minority elites in Guizhou. Faced with the commodification of so many aspects of their culture for the purposes of 'cultural development', Miao elites have taken to contrasting traditional Miao values with the wild and rootless ways of Han depravity. Schein links this attitude to a concern over the integration of Miao youth into the economy of market socialism. 'While Miao peasant regions,' she writes, 'have themselves been only minimally transformed by reform policies, what *has* happened is the partial proletarianisation of Miao young people who find wage work in urban factories and large farms, especially along the coast where local labor is already relatively expensive.'[104]

Minority elites have thus encountered an increasingly obvious contradiction in the 'going to the world' encouraged by the commercialism of cultural development efforts. While metropolitan Han are eager to consume the traditions of isolated interior mountain regions such as Guizhou, it has become clear that in the pursuit of a 'commercial conscience' the producers of ethnic minority culture – whether in contract production arrangements, urban crafts factories or coastal theme parks and hotels – have lost what elites feel to be a sense of moral autonomy. If Schein's observations are correct (and my field observations tend to concur), a new discourse of ethnic nationalism is perhaps emerging in Guizhou, a counter-discourse representing a new role for ethnic minority groups, as keepers of a non-commercialised lifestyle and traditional morality.

CONCLUSION

Given the environmental and economic problems which continue to trouble Guizhou, a semi-capitalised peasantry is perhaps a necessary step in achieving the long-term sustainability of rural production. 'Commercialising the countryside' is not, by itself, a sinister formula for the perpetuation of rural poverty. At any rate, Guizhou's rural producers appear eager for any commercial opportunity that comes along. But when commercial development remains tied to a colonial ideology of ethnic cultural authenticity, market integration simply means continued subordination and vulnerability for the rural population in minority regions. Over a period of a decade, Guizhou's ethnic groups have seen their status transformed from exemplars of impoverished rural backwardness to potential bastions of commercial modernity, the keepers of an exotic tradition metropolitan consumers are now eager to pay for. But an underlying ideology of cultural difference continues to inform these new attitudes and serves as a significant barrier separating rural ethnic regions from metropolitan Han China.

Guizhou's peripheral situation is based on a combination of factors, including a topography unsuitable for agricultural accumulation, a rapidly increasing population in many regions where resources are already marginal, and a legacy of fiscal dependence on diminishing central subsidies and unprofitable resource-extraction and defence industries. Dominated by marginal agriculture, rich in energy resources and industrial raw materials, Guizhou has long functioned as net provider in China's rapid industrial expansion, receiving little in return. While subsidies were relatively substantial, they generally went to urban consumers in the form of price subsidies and wages. Not only was rural Guizhou generally left to its own devices for inputs but, as with rural China in general, was severely squeezed to further fuel industrial growth. In the ideologically stifling atmosphere of Maoist China, there was little tolerance for ethnic differences. 'Local nationalism' was raised as a counterrevolutionary straw-man and attacked with a fervour which left rural Guizhou reeling in chaos. The 'backwardness' of ethnic groups became a convenient explanation for the countryside's failure to develop under socialism.

While such ideological rectitude for the most part died with Mao, rural Guizhou's difficulties have not abated during the reform era. The countryside has suffered the financial consequences of fiscal decline and decentralisation, providing a significant impetus for commercial development. Ethnic 'backwardness' is still trumpeted as the enemy of market socialism, but ethnic groups, ironically, now have the option of casting off their poverty by selecting a few traditions to sell in China's vigorous marketplace. Pushed by a political economy of fiscal dependency and unequal exchange, Guizhou has vigorously pursued an expanded geography of trade and investment. Indeed, it can not afford to do otherwise. But such a move has failed to produce the results which provincial leaders clearly expected, while at the same time it has brought the province's ethnic producers face to face with the ideological whims of urban consumerism. Sweeping across a landscape already prepared by decades of cultural development come the

Appendix A: Guizhou regional economic indicators, 1990 (*yuan* per capita)

	Guiyang	Liupanshui	Qianxinan	Qiandongnan	Qiannan	Tongren	Zunyi	Anshun	Bijie	Guizhou
GMP[a]	5,910	1,274	714	956	1,300	749	1,506	1,672	735	1,780
NMP[b]	2,240	544	374	517	676	425	758	704	378	654
GNP	2,907	717	454	606	802	486	889	853	449	786
Net peasant income	n/a	361	434	474	473	415	n/a	418	396	435
Government revenues	815	67	32	56	81	48	107	91	52	111
Government outlays	405	101	78	104	109	86	106	121	87	150
Grain (kg/person)	n/a	171	218	268	262	267	n/a	180	183	215

Notes: [a] GMP, or Gross Material Product, is the total output value of the five major material production sectors: agriculture, industry, construction, transport, and commerce. It differs from Gross National Product (GNP) in that it excludes net income from non-material services, but includes the consumption of material inputs such as raw materials and energy resources in its calculation
[b] NMP, or Net Material Product is the sum of net output value of agriculture, industry, construction, transport, and commerce, obtained by deducting the value of the material consumption of those sectors from the Gross Material Product
Source: Guizhou shengqing [Guizhou Provincial Gazetteer], pp. 660, 671, 682, 694, 705, 717, 728, 739, 749

contemporary ideals of tradition, authenticity and difference, their paths forged open by the accumulating logic of capital as it discovers fiscally strapped counties desperate to exploit their cheap labour for any kind of investment. Rural Guizhou may not be quite the 'barren and profitless' place which met Hosie's gaze a century ago, but a spectre of colonialism still haunts the province as it seeks to overcome this historical legacy. Minority nationality groups face the most daunting situation in this regard, for they bear the dual and contradictory symbolism of impoverished backwardness and potentially marketable modernity.

ACKNOWLEDGEMENTS

Fieldwork for this chapter was carried out in Guizhou in 1993–94 thanks to generous grants provided by the National Science Foundation and the Committee on Scholarly Communication with China. In addition, I would like to thank Kam-Wing Chan and the participants of the 1996 'China's Provinces in Reform' Workshop for their assistance, suggestions and critical comments.

NOTES

1 D. Goodman, 'Guizhou and the PRC: the development of an internal colony', in D. Drakakis-Smith (ed.), *Internal Colonialism: Essays Around a Theme*, pp. 107–124, Institute of British Geographers, Developing Areas Research Group Monograph No. 3, 1983.

2 A. Hosie, *Three Years in Western China*, London: George Philip, 1890, p. 25.

3 Ibid., p. 32. On the nineteenth century rebellions in Guizhou, see R. Jenks, *Insurgency and Social Disorder in Guizhou: The 'Miao' Rebellion, 1854–1873*, Honolulu: University of Hawaii Press, 1994.

4 The nakedness of Miao farmers, especially girls, has long been a common Chinese image to mark both the poverty and tribal primevalness of the Miao. In *The Long March* (1985), Harrison Salisbury recounts his informants' impressions of Guizhou when the Red Army passed through in 1934; the Miao were so poor, they said, that girls had to 'work naked in the fields' (p. 106).

5 H. Wiens, *Han Chinese Expansion in South China*, Hampden, CT: Shoe String Press, 1967, p. 190.

6 See S. Harrell, (ed.), *Cultural Encounters on China's Ethnic Frontiers*, Seattle: University of Washington Press, 1995, for numerous essays on the history and contemporary legacy of China's 'civilising project' along China's periphery.

7 R.D. Hill, 'People, land, and an equilibrium trap: Guizhou province, China', *Pacific Viewpoint* Vol. 34, No. 1, 1993, p. 3.

8 *China Statistical Yearbook, 1995*. Reprinted in *Provincial China* 1996, No. 1, pp. 38, 52.

9 *Guizhou tongji nianjian* [Guizhou Statistical Yearbook], *1993*, pp. 5, 7.

10 R.L. Edmonds, *Patterns of China's Lost Harmony*, London: Routledge, 1994, p. 67.

11 Hill, 1993, op. cit., p. 7.

12 Ibid., p. 15.

13 *Guizhou tongji nianjian* [Guizhou Statistical Yearbook], *1993*, p. 191.

14 *Guizhou shengqing* [Guizhou Provincial Gazetteer], p. 279. Grain subsidies in 1985, for example, amounted to 17 per cent of total grain consumed in the province.

15 The Chinese term '*minzu*' may be translated as either 'nationality' or 'ethnic group', but has no exact equivalent in English; see also note 97 below.

16 Hill, 1993, op. cit., p. 6.

17 M.W. Ran, 1991, p. 221.

18 Ibid., p. 230.

19 It should be noted that much of this gap is explained in terms of a disparity between urban and rural Guizhou in general, but is magnified when isolating for regions in which minority populations predominate.

20 Net Material Product (*guomin shouru*) is the sum of net output value of agriculture, industry, construction, transport, and commerce, obtained by deducting the value of the material consumption of those sectors from the Gross Material Product (*shehui zongchanzhi*). The disadvantage of using this indicator is that it excludes non-material production sectors such as services, education, public health, military and government administration.

21 R.S. Li, 'Guizhou shaoshu minzu zizhi difang jingji shehui fazhan qingkuan cunzai wenti ji jinhou fazhan de jianyi' [Problems concerning socio-economic development in Guizhou's minority nationality autonomous regions and suggestions for future development], in *Guizhou sheng shaoshu minzu jingji yanjiu* [Research on Guizhou's Minority Nationality Economy], Guiyang: Guizhou minzu chubanshe, 1991, p. 3.

22 Ibid., p. 5.

23 The poverty line was initially based on an administrative village (*xiang*) average per capita income of less than 120 *yuan*. In 1986, in order to cast a wider net of government assistance, the poverty line was revised to a county (*xian*) average of less than 150 *yuan* (200 *yuan* in minority regions). Authorities in Guizhou indicate that since 1993 the official poverty line in minority regions has increased to the equivalent of 300 *yuan* per capita annual income.

24 M.W. Ran, *et al.* (eds), 'Guizhou sheng shaoshu minzu pinkun diqu jingji kaifa de xianzhuang, zhiyue yinsu, yu duice' [Economic development in Guizhou's impoverished minority nationality regions: present situation, causal factors, and countermeasures], in *Kaifa Da Xinan; Guizhou, Guangxi, Xizang juan* [Develop the Great Southwest; Guizhou, Guangxi, Tibet Edition], Beijing: Xuefan chubanshe, 1991, p. 220.

25 Ibid., p. 222, and *Guizhou shengqing* [Guizhou Provincial Gazetteer], pp. 115–119. There is also less redistribution of grain from surplus regions to grain-poor regions within Guizhou. This is because of reforms meant to encourage 'agricultural growth poles' in regions suitable for agricultural accumulation. These regions have less of their grain expropriated to poor regions, so that surplus can be invested in economic crops and rural industries.

26 H. Wen, 'Guizhou shaoshu minzu diqu de qinggongye xianzhuang wenti ji jinhou de fazhan' [Light industry in Guizhou's minority nationality regions: current problems and future prospects], in *Guizhou sheng shaoshu minzu jingji yanjiu* [Guizhou Minority Nationality Research], Guiyang: Guizhou minzu chubanshe, 1991, p. 159.

27 T.H. Yan, 'Wo sheng minzu zizhi difang "ba wu" shiqi jingji shehui fazhan chutan' [Preliminary inquiry into socio-economic development in our province's nationality autonomous regions during the Eighth FYP], in *Guizhou sheng shaoshu minzu jingji yanjiu* [Guizhou Minority Nationality Research], Guiyang: Guizhou minzu chubanshe, 1991, pp. 10–22.

28 See, for example, Ran, 1991, op cit., p. 221, and Li, 1991, op cit., p. 2.

29 See K.W. Chan, *Cities with Invisible Walls; Reinterpreting Urbanisation in Post-1949 China*, Hong Kong: Oxford University Press, 1994, pp. 59–63, for a summary of China's Soviet-style development strategy during the Maoist era.

30 R. Kirkby and T. Cannon, 'Introduction', in D.S.G. Goodman (ed.), *China' Regional Development*, London: Routledge, 1989, p. 5.

31 H. Leung and K.W. Chan, 'Chinese regional development policies: a comparative

reassessment', paper presented at the Annual Meeting of the Canadian Asian Studies Association, Winnepeg, Canada, 1986.

32   Kirkby and Cannon, 1989, op. cit., p. 5.

33   Ibid., p. 6.

34   W.S. Tang, *Regional Uneven Development in China, with Special Reference to the Period Between 1978 and 1988*, Hong Kong: Chinese University of Hong Kong Department of Geography Occasional Paper No. 110, 1991, p. 33.

35   C. Wong, 'Central–local relations in an era of fiscal decline: the paradox of fiscal decentralisation in post-Mao China', *China Quarterly* No. 128, 1991, p. 712.

36   Kirkby and Cannon, 1989, op. cit., p. 11.

37   Ibid., p. 6.

38   B. Naughton, 'The Third Front: defense industrial*i*sation in the Chinese interior', *China Quarterly*, No. 115, 1988, p. 366.

39   Ibid., p. 367.

40   Ibid., p. 376.

41   Leung and Chan, 1986, op. cit.

42   Goodman, 1983, op. cit., p. 119.

43   Y.X. Chen, *et al.* (eds), (1993) *Guizhou sheng jingji dili* [Economic Geography of Guizhou Province], Beijing: Xinhua chubanshe, 1993, pp. 60–63. According to data in N. Lardy, *Economic Growth and Distribution in China*, Cambridge: Cambridge University Press, 1978, pp. 130–32, Guizhou's revenue sharing relationship with the central government became one of net recipient beginning in 1958. Up to this date it had been a net provider.

44   D.S.G. Goodman, *Centre and Province in the PRC: Sichuan and Guizhou, 1955–1965*, Cambridge: Cambridge University Press, 1986, p. 111.

45   Ibid., p. 131.

46   See Y.X. Chen *et al.* (eds), 1993, op. cit., pp. 64–67, for a summary of the impact of defence industrialisation on Guizhou's economy.

47   F. Liang, 'Guizhou's ordinance industry turns civil', *Beijing Review* (October 11–17), 1993, p. 13.

48   *Guizhou shengqing* [Guizhou Provincial Gazetteer], p. 142 and *Zhongguo Tongji Nianjian* [China Statistical Yearbook], *1995*, p. 375.

49   *Zhongguo tongji nianjian* [China Statistical Yearbook], *1995*, pp. 375, 378–79.

50   Calculated from local figures in *Guizhou nianjian* [Guizhou Yearbook], *1996*, pp. 640–710.

51   World Bank, *China; Reform and the Role of the Plan in the 1990s*, Washington, DC: The World Bank, 1992, pp. 55–56.

52   *Guizhou tongji nianjian* [Guizhou Statistical Yearbook], *1993*, pp. 99–100. In 1995 agriculture's share of fixed capital investments in Guizhou had risen to 6 per cent (*Guizhou nianjian* [Guizhou Yearbook], *1996*, p. 60).

53   Ibid.

54   *Guizhou nianjian* [Guizhou Yearbook], *1996*, p. 379.

55   Ibid., p. 59.

56   *Guizhou sheng guotu zongti guihua* [Guizhou Comprehensive Development Plan], Beijing: Zhongguo jihua weiyuanhui, 1992.

57   Deng, 1993, op. cit.

58   S.Z. Ye, 'Urban systems and the exploitation of natural resources in southwestern China', in C.T. Kok *et al.* (eds), *Arbeiten zur Chinaforschung*, Bremen: Zentraldruckerei der Universität Bremen, 1993, p. 129.

59   *Guizhou nianjian* [Guizhou Yearbook], *1996*, p. 61.

60   Liang, 1993, op. cit., p. 14.

61   C. Wong, C. Heady and W.T. Woo, *Fiscal Management and Economic Reform in the People's Republic of China*, Hong Kong: Oxford University Press, 1995.

62   In 1995, for example, provincial revenues only amounted to 45 per cent of expenditures (*Guizhou nianjian* [Guizhou Yearbook], *1996*, p. 60).

63 Ibid., p. 96.
64 Ibid., p. 92.
65 *Guizhou nianjian* [Guizhou Yearbook], *1996*, p. 60; *Guizhou tongji nianjian* [Guizhou Statistical Yearbook], *1993*, p. 102.
66 C. Wong (ed.), *Financing Local Government in the People's Republic of China* [Draft version], Manila: Asian Development Bank, 1995, p. 11.
67 *Zhongguo tongji nianjian* [China Statistical Yearbook], *1995*, p. 21.
68 P. Ferdinand, 'The economic and financial dimension', in D.S.G. Goodman (ed.), *China's Regional Development*, London: Routledge, 1989, p. 46.
69 Leung and Chan, 1986, op. cit., p. 44.
70 Wong, 1991, op. cit.
71 *Xingdao Ribao* [Xingdao Daily], 16 May, 1993.
72 See H. Hendrischke, 'Guangxi Zhuang Autonomous Region: towards Southwest China and Southeast Asia', in D.S.G. Goodman (ed.), *China's Provinces in Reform: Class, Community, and Political Culture*, London: Routledge, 1997, on the real estate speculation boom in Beihai.
73 Liang, 1993, op. cit., p. 15.
74 *Guizhou Huabao* [Guizhou Pictorial], No. 5, 1993, pp. 18–23.
75 *Qiandongnan Bao* [Qiandongnan Paper] 15 April, 1994 and N.H. Zhang, 'Minzu zizhi difang gaige kaifang shiyanqu de zhengce yanjiu [Policy research on open reform experimental zones in nationality autonomous regions], *Guizhou Minzu Yanjiu* [Guizhou Nationalities Research] No. 1, 1995, pp. 31–33.
76 Interview with Sun Jinghua, Guizhou Tourism Bureau Director of Promotion and Marketing, 1 August 1994.
77 Li, 1991, op. cit.
78 *Guizhou Ribao* [Guizhou Daily] 14–18 April, 1993
79 *Guizhou Ribao* [Guizhou Daily] 8–12 August, 1993.
80 *Guizhou Ribao* [Guizhou Daily] 17 August, 1993. See also the summary in *Guizhou Huabao* [Guizhou Pictorial] 1993, No. 6, pp. 6–15.
81 Interview with Tourism Bureau official, Guiyang, 28 October 1996.
82 Interview with Tourism Bureau official, Guiyang, 28 October 1996.
83 *Guizhou tongji nianjian* [Guizhou Statistical Yearbook], *1993*, pp. 159, 161, 338–39.
84 *China Statistical Yearbook, 1995*. Reprinted in *Provincial China* 1996, No. 1, pp. 48–49.
85 See Chan, 1994, op. cit., pp. 97–114, for a summary of the many ways urban residents have been subsidised by the Chinese state.
86 *Guizhou tongji nianjian* [Guizhou Statistical Yearbook], *1993*, p. 168.
87 *Guizhou nianjian* [Guizhou Yearbook], *1996*, pp. 357 and 598.
88 Y.X. Chen and J.R. Wang, 'Guizhou jingji diyu fazhan zhanlue chutan [Preliminary inquiry into development strategies for Guizhou's economic regions], *Guizhou Shifan Daxue Xuebao* [Journal of Guizhou Normal University] Vol. 63, No. 2, 1990, pp. 1–6.
89 Hill, 1993, op. cit.
90 Ran, 1991, op. cit., p. 229.
91 *Zhongguo tongji nianjian* [China Statistical Yearbook], *1995*, pp. 86, 332, and 381.
92 *Guizhou nianjian* [Guizhou Yearbook], *1996*, p. 231.
93 G. Z. Lei, 'Shuizu wenhua yu xiandaihua [Shui culture and modernisation], *Guizhou Minzu Yanjiu* [Guizhou Nationalities Research] 1, 1992, pp. 33–36.
94 *Guizhou Ribao* [Guizhou Daily] 25 August, 1993.
95 Lei, 1992, op. cit., p. 33, my emphasis.
96 See *Guizhou sheng minzu wenhua xiehui* [Guizhou Nationalities Cultural Studies Association], *Zouxiang shijie daqiao* [Crossing the Great Bridge to the World], Guiyang: Guizhou minzu chubanshe, 1991.
97 Although the noun *minzu*, that is, 'ethnic nationality,' includes the Han, it appears that when used as an adjective the term rarely, if ever, refers to the Han. Just as 'ethnic' is rarely thought of as applying to dominant racial groups (such as white Caucasians in

the United States), '*minzu*' is often assumed to simply refer to minority groups. That, at least, appeared to be the case at this conference. '*Minzu*' is a less exclusive term than 'minority *minzu*,' but the issues being discussed dealt quite exclusively with those concerning minority groups.

98 By 1993 promoting Guizhou as an authentic breath of fresh air for modern tourists had become quite popular among tourism planners in general. The following piece of promotional literature is illustrative:

> Guizhou is both new and ancient. Development has started late here. Guizhou has been little affected by the pollution of modern industry, nor has it been assaulted by modern civilisation. Nature is still pristine here, and people still preserve their traditional cultures. There has been very little change here, little cultural corruption from the outside. The mountains are green, the water clear. And because they're spread out all over, one can see *minzu* customs just about anywhere.
>
> Guizhou's environment gives people a sense of returning to nature. This is something the people of the developed countries crave for. And Guizhou's minorities inspire people to value the preservation of living culture. In some parts of the world, all people have is staged culture. But in Guizhou, tourists can enter the villages and houses of the minorities, share their lives, understand them
>
> (Deng, 1993, pp. 8–9)

99 This pattern has been described in other developing world situations in terms of 'articulation of modes of production'. Citing research by Wolpe, Hall provides the following statement which resonates strikingly with the situation in Guizhou:

> In South Africa, the tendency of capital accumulation to dissolve other modes is cross-cut and blocked by the counter-acting tendencies to conserve the non-capitalist economies – on the basis that the latter are articulated in a subordinate position to the former. Where capitalism develops by means, in part, of its articulation with non-capitalist modes, 'the mode of political domination and the content of legitimating ideologies assume racial, ethnic and cultural forms and for the same reasons as in the case of imperialism . . . political domination takes on a colonial form. [Wolpe] adds: 'The conservation of non-capitalist modes of production necessarily requires the development of ideologies and political policies which revolve around the segregation and preservation and control of African "tribal" societies' – that is, the relation assumes the forms of ideologies constructed around ethnic, racial, national, and cultural ideological elements.
>
> (Hall 1979, 322)

My intent here, however, is not so much to present a theoretical argument about the nature of capitalist expansion than simply to point out the similarities between modernisation in Guizhou and neo-colonial patterns of development in other parts of the world.

100 For comparison, average monthly income in 1992 for wage earners in Taijiang was 165 *yuan* (*Guizhou tongji nianjian* [Guizhou Statistical Yearbook, *1993*, p. 95).

101 Interview with Taijiang Minorities Affairs Commission officer, 4 November 1996.

102 This ideology is illustrated in a chapter, about one of Taijiang's most successful ethnic crafts producers, in a book entitled *Zhongguo qiye yinghao* [The Heroes of Chinese Enterprise]. The chapter chronicles the history of a Miao villager named Pan Yuzhen in a way which stresses how she was coaxed out of her 'pre-modern' thinking to blossom as a successful entrepreneur and culturally developed citizen of 'new China'. The chapter begins with the following paragraph:

> It used to be that the Miao women living amid the mountains believed in the tradition of making embroidered clothing only for their own use. They would

never think of giving it to outsiders, and certainly would never think of selling it. This was the law of tradition. Embroidery was never to be used for anything but making oneself beautiful, especially for marriage. But in 1979, the reforms swept through China like a flood, and in the mountains the pool in which commerce was thought to be shameless started to ripple. The winds of reform were felt by one woman there, who turned against traditional rules, broke the customs, and sold her first piece of embroidery. Since then, she has travelled China from south to north, and has brought the Miao out of the mountains and into the world of commerce. From the point of a needle, they have filled the earth with embroidery, and leapt to earning over 800,000 *yuan*. This is not dream; this is a very true story.

(S.H. Zhang, 1993)

Passages like this reflect an ideology which explains problems of rural poverty and lack of local capital accumulation not in terms of broader structural mechanisms that perpetuate peripheral status, but as a result of centuries of backward traditions awaiting the arrival of the state's enlightened modernisation policies to finally break them down. That this ideology perpetuates a fiction about the Miao was clear to Pan Yuzhen herself. Interviewing her in Taijiang, I asked about this passage and she claimed that it misrepresented the Miao. In fact she insisted on taking me to a remote periodic market near Taijiang to prove it. At the market, she pointed out the lively trade going on in silver ornaments, embroidery and batik, items whose commercial value are thought only to be realised once tourists stumble upon the scene. 'These markets have always been busy selling these things,' she said. There was no 'law of tradition' preventing their sale. Silver ornaments, she said, had always been a specialist's trade, and most embroidery designs were actually purchased from skilled artists who specialised in drawing them.

103 Contract producers earned 3.5 *yuan* per piece, with each piece selling for 35 *yuan*. Working 12 hours non-stop, a woman could produce two pieces.
104 Schein, L., 'The other goes to market: the state, the nation, and unruliness in contemporary China', *Identities* Vol. 2, No. 3, 1995, p. 18.

REFERENCES

Chen, K. (ed.), *Guizhou sheng nongcun jingji quhua* [Regional Economic Plan for Rural Guizhou], Guiyang: Renmin chubanshe, 1989.
Chen, Y.X. and Wang, J.R., 'Guizhou jingji diyu fazhan zhanlüe chutan' [Preliminary inquiry into development strategies for Guizhou's economic regions], *Guizhou Shifan Daxue Xuebao*, Vol. 63, No. 2, 1990, pp. 1–6.
Chen, Y.X. *et al.* (eds), *Guizhou sheng jingji dili* [Economic Geography of Guizhou [Province], Beijing: Xinhua chubanshe, 1993.
Clarke, S. R., 'The province of Kweichow', in M. Broomhall (ed.), *The Chinese Empire; a General and Missionary Survey*, London: Morgan and Scott, 1907, pp. 251–270.
— —, *Among the Tribes in South-West China*, London: Morgan and Scott, 1911.
Deng, Z.B., 'Shanguo 'tiantang' de shuguang: guanyu Guizhou fazhan lüyouye yu kaifa ziyuan zhi yantao' [Dawn of a mountain kingdom paradise: a study of exploiting resources and developing Guizhou's tourism industry], paper presented at the Mainland–Taiwan Tourism Conference, Taibei, 1993.
Diamond, N., 'The Miao and poison: interactions along China's southwestern frontier', *Ethnology*, Vol. 27, No. 1, 1988, pp. 1–25.
Goodman, D., 'Guizhou and the PRC: the development of an internal colony', in

D. Drakakis-Smith (ed.), *Internal Colonialism: Essays Around a Theme*, Institute of British Geographers, Developing Areas Research Group Monograph No. 3, 1983, pp. 107–124.

——, *Centre and Province in the PRC: Sichuan and Guizhou, 1955–1965*, Cambridge: Cambridge University Press, 1986.

Guizhou gaige kaifang bianji xiaozu [Guizhou Open Reform Editorial Small Group] (ed.), *Guizhou gaige kaifang de shinian, 1978–1988* [Ten Years of Open Reform in Guizhou, 1978–1988], Guiyang: Guizhou renmin chubanshe, 1988.

Guizhou minzu diqu sishinian, 1949–1989 [Forty Years in Guizhou's Minority Regions], Guiyang: Guizhou minzu chubanshe, 1991.

Guizhou nianjian [Guizhou Yearbook], Guiyang: Guizhou nianjian chubanshe, various years.

Guizhou shaoshu minzu [Guizhou Minority Nationalities], Guiyang: Guizhou minzu chubanshe, 1991.

Guizhou sheng guotu zongti guihua [Guizhou Provincial Comprehensive Development Plan], Beijing: Zhongguo jihua weiyuanhui, 1992.

Guizhou sheng minzu wenhua xuehui [Guizhou Provincial Nationality Cultural Studies Association], *Zouxiang shijie daqiao* [Crossing the Great Bridge to the World], Guiyang: Guizhou minzu chubanshe, 1991.

Guizhou shengqing (xiuding ben) [Guizhou Provincial Gazetteer, Revised Edition], Guiyang: Guizhou renmin chubanshe, 1993.

Guizhou sheng renkou dituji [Population Atlas of Guizhou Province], Beijing: Zhongguo ditu chubanshe, 1994.

Guizhou tongji nianjian [Guizhou Statistical Yearbook], Beijing: Zhongguo tongji chubanshe, various years.

Guizhou xianqing [Guizhou County Gazetteer], Beijing: Zhongguo tongji chubanshe, 1992.

Hill, R.D., 'People, land, and an equilibrium trap: Guizhou province, China', *Pacific Viewpoint*, Vol. 34, No. 1, 1993, pp. 1–24.

Hosie, A., *Three Years in Western China*, London: George Philip, 1890.

——, *On the Trail of the Opium Poppy; a narrative of travel in the chief opium-producing provinces of China*, London: George Philip, 1914.

Jenks, R., *Insurgency and Social Disorder in Guizhou: The 'Miao' Rebellion, 1854–1873*, Honolulu: University of Hawaii Press, 1994.

Lee, J., 'Food supply and population growth in southwest China', *Journal of Asian Studies*, Vol. 41, No. 4, 1982, pp. 711–746.

Lei, G.Z., 'Shuizu wenhua yu xiandaihua' [Shui culture and modernisation], *Guizhou minzu yanjiu* [Guizhou Nationality Research], 1,1992, pp. 33–36.

Li, R.S., 'Guizhou shaoshu minzu zizhi difang jingji shehui fazhan qingkuang cunzai wenti ji jinhou fazhan de jianyi' [Problems concerning socio-economic development in Guizhou's minority nationality autonomous regions and suggestions for future development], in *Guizhou sheng shaoshu minzu jingji yanjiu* [Research on Guizhou's Minority Nationality Economy], Guiyang: Guizhou minzu chubanshe, 1991, pp. 1–9.

Liang. F., 'Guizhou's ordinance industry turns civil', *Beijing Review* (October 11–17), 1993, pp. 12–15.

Lin, Y.H., 'The Miao-Man peoples of Kweichow', *Harvard Journal of Asiatic Studies*, Vol. 5, No. 3, 1941, pp. 261–344.

Ran, M.W. *et al.* (eds), 'Guizhou sheng shaoshu minzu pinkun diqu jingji kaifa de xianzhuang, zhiyue yinsu yu duice' [Economic development in Guizhou's impoverished minority nationality regions: present situation, constraints and countermeasures], in *Kaifa da Xinan; Guizhou, Guangxi, Xizang juan* [Develop the Great Southwest; Guizhou, Guangxi, Tibet Edition], Beijing: Xuefan chubanshe, 1991, pp. 218–232.

Spencer, J. R., 'Kueichou: an internal Chinese colony', *Pacific Affairs*, 13, 1940, pp. 162–172.

Wen, H., 'Guizhou shaoshu minzu diqu de qinggongye xianzhuang wenti ji jinhou de fazhan' [Light industry in Guizhou's minority nationality regions: current problems and future prospects], in *Guizhou sheng shaoshu minzu jingji yanjiu* [Guizhou Minority Nationality Research], Guiyang: Guizhou minzu chubanshe, 1991, pp. 150–161.

Wiens, H., *Han Chinese Expansion in South China*, Hampden, CT: Shoe String Press, 1967.

Wong, C. (ed.) *Financing Local Government in the People's Republic of China* [Draft version], Manila: Asian Development Bank, 1995.

Yan, T.H., 'Wo sheng minzu zizhi difang "ba wu" shiqi jingji shehui fazhan chutan' [Preliminary inquiry into socio-economic development in our province's nationality autonomous regions during the Eighth FYP], in *Guizhou sheng shaoshu minzu jingji yanjiu* [Guizhou Minority Nationality Research], Guiyang: Guizhou minzu chubanshe, 1991, pp. 10–22.

Zhang, N.H., 'Minzu zizhi difang gaige kaifang shiyanqu de zhengce yanjiu' [Policy research on open reform experimental zones in nationality autonomous regions], *Guizhou minzu yanjiu* [Guizhou Nationality Research], 1, 1995, pp. 31–33.

Zhou, C. *et al.* (eds), *Guizhou jindaishi* [A Brief History of Guizhou], Guiyang: Guizhou renmin chubanshe, 1987.

Shaanxi Province

GENERAL

GDP (billion *yuan*)	117.50
GDP annual growth rate	10.20
as % national average	106.30
GDP per capita	3,317.50
as % national average	59.20
Gross Value Agricultural Output (billion *yuan*)	45.90
Gross Value Industrial Output (billion *yuan*)	123.90

POPULATION

Population (million)	35.43
Natural growth rate (per 1,000)	15.00

WORKFORCE

Total workforce (million)	18.00
Employment by activity (%)	
primary industry	58.50
secondary industry	19.00
tertiary industry	22.50
Employment by sector (%)	
urban	26.11
rural	73.89
Employment by ownership (%)	
state	19.44
collective	23.89
private	8.33
foreign-funded	0.11

WAGES AND INCOME

Average annual wage (*yuan*)	4,882.00
Growth rate in real wage	0.70
Urban disposable income per capita	3,809.64
as % national average	78.70
Rural per capita income	1,165.10
as % national average	60.50

PRICES

CPI annual rise (%)	9.70
Service price index rise	17.10
Per capita consumption (*yuan*)	1,431.00
as % national average	53.50

FOREIGN TRADE AND INVESTMENT

Total foreign trade (US$ billion)	1.80
as % provincial GDP	12.40
Exports (US$ billion)	1.10
Imports (US$ billion)	0.70
Realised foreign capital (US$ billion)	0.40
as % provincial GDP	2.60

EDUCATION

University enrolments	134,868.00
as % national average	154.20
Secondary school enrolments (million)	1.57
as % national average	94.20
Primary school enrolments (million)	4.74
as % national average	120.30

Notes: All statistics are for 1996 and all growth rates are for 1996 over 1995 and are adapted from *Zhongguo tongji nianjian 1997* [Statistical Yearbook of China 1997], Zhongguo tongji chubanshe, Beijing, 1997, as reformulated and presented in *Provincial China* no. 5, May 1998, pp. 68ff.

Shaanxi Province

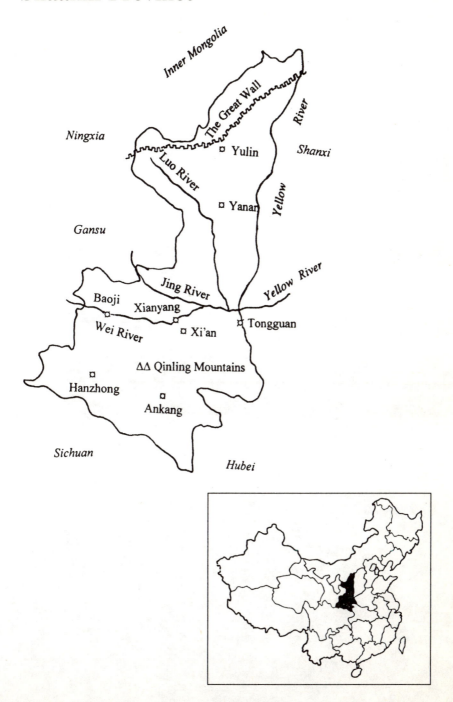

3 Shaanxi

The search for comparative advantage

Andrew Watson, Yang Xueyi and Jiao Xingguo

Like deeply etched skin, the loess dominates the face of Shaanxi.[1] From the deserts and sandy hills of the north, through the ravines, gullies and plateaus of the central layer, down to the rich valley of the Wei, it moulds the life of its people. The air they breathe is flavoured by its fine dust. It is only in the south, protected by the Qinling Mountains, that the loess has no presence, and the environment is part of a different natural world.[2] The contrast between the two regions north of the Qinling, Shaanbei and Guanzhong, and Shaannan to the south is thus profound. The north is part of the Yellow River system. The climate ranges from warm temperate to semi-arid, with long cold winters. Its grains are wheat, maize and the coarse grains of north China. The south is a mountainous zone which stands at the headwaters of the Han River and links naturally to the Yangtze River basin. Its climate is mild and wet, and its products of rice, tea and silk are characteristic of the south.

All three regions are distinct. Shaanbei borders on the deserts of Inner Mongolia. Its climate is very dry, and its rainfall is unreliable. Its population is sparse, and it is the poorest region. Guanzhong centres on the Wei River valley. The major cities of Xi'an, Xianyang and Baoji are located within it. It has always had the most productive agricultural land, and it is the heart of Shaanxi. The south, though continuously under Shaanxi administration, shares more in common with the mountainous areas of Sichuan.[3] Its shortage of farming land has long made it a poor region, and its population grew historically as a result of immigration by people who, for various reasons, were forced into a more isolated and marginal area.

The economic differences between the three regions are summarised in Table 3.1. The table shows clearly that Shaanxi is dominated by Guanzhong. The region has around 60 per cent of the population and produces even higher proportions of its output. The city of Xi'an alone has around 60 per cent of provincial industry and produces over 30 per cent of provincial GDP.[4] Guanzhong is thus the core social and political region of the province, balanced to the north and south by two much poorer areas. Indeed one image of the province is that of Guanzhong carrying two burdens, like a peasant with a loaded shoulder pole.

History dominates the province's image of itself. Deep in the loess at Huang Ling lies the tomb of the Yellow Emperor. At times it is still decorated by wreaths

Table 3.1 The regions of Shaanxi Province, 1994

	Shaanxi	Guanzhong	%	Shaannan	%	Shaanbei	%	Sum of Regions*
Population (m)	34.02	20.24	59.5	8.85	26	4.93	14.5	34.02
GNP (bn yuan)	84.983	62.320	72.1	15.692	18.1	8.459	9.8	86.471
Fixed Assets (bn yuan)	28.329	18.055	74.7	3.883	16.1	2.218	9.2	24.156
GVAO (bn yuan)	30.238	21.104	60.0	8.966	25.5	5.112	14.5	35.182
GVIO (bn yuan)	100.976	85.701	81.6	12.983	12.4	6.3	6.0	105.004
Grain output (millions of metric tonnes)	9.446	6.0158	59.0	2.3726	23.3	1.8068	17.7	10.1952

Note: * The Yearbook notes that the sum of the regions is not always the same as the provincial figure but does not explain why. Presumably statistical categories differ. The percentages are based on the sum of regions

presented by local officials in respect for the mythical founder of the Chinese nation.[5] At Wugong, a county town to the northwest of Xi'an, lies a cluster of key agricultural colleges. They mark the site where Hou Ji, Prince Millet, the agricultural deity credited with the early development of agriculture, was said to have served under the legendary Emperor Shun. All of the great dynasties of the early empire emerged in the Wei River valley. The tombs of the Zhou, Qin, Han and Tang dominate the landscape along the river's banks. The soil is rich with their relics, and their triumphs are commemorated in Xi'an by the Bei Lin (the Forest of Steles) and by the rich collection of the Provincial Museum. The walls and towers of Xi'an embody a tradition that places Shaanxi at the heart of China's cultural roots, and much of the modern architecture has a particular archaic style, pointing towards the Han and the Tang. The people of Shaanxi are thus sharply conscious of their heritage.

In late imperial times, however, the province became a relative backwater. The economic forces of China moved east and south.[6] It was not until the Long March that Shaanxi was brought back into the heart of revolutionary change when a new tradition of survival against adversity was symbolised by the 'Yan'an Way'.[7] Yet once the Base Area was abandoned after 1946, the focus again shifted elsewhere. The economic, political and social centres of the nation are still the key economic areas of later times.

Nevertheless, as the old headquarters of the revolution and the gateway to the northwest, Shaanxi retained a pivotal role in regional issues under the planned economy. It was home to the party's Northwest Bureau until the mid-1960s and a major focus for planned development in the early planning period. Some 24 of the 156 key projects of the First Five Year Plan were located in Shaanxi, and the province became the centre of large military, textile, electrical machinery and machine-building industries. This trend was reinforced by the policies of the 1960s and early 1970s which emphasised building up the 'rear areas' and developing the 'Third Front' as a strategic goal of dispersing industrial development. Whatever the cost in market economy terms,[8] the plan system delivered substantial industrial development to the province, primarily concentrated in the Guanzhong region along the Long–Hai railway. By the late 1970s, therefore, Shaanxi's industrial output ranked high in the national economy, and its scientific and technical level was among the best that the planned economy could deliver, even though much of this growth and investment was characterised by low levels of productivity and poor returns.[9] In contrast to the industrial growth, however, the harsh and arid climate meant that Shaanxi's agriculture remained relatively poor. A dual economy was created, as a number of inherent economic disparities remained unresolved under the planned development.

Economic reform after 1978 gradually undermined Shaanxi's status in the planning system and turned the advantage of a large state investment into a burden of inefficiency. The national focus shifted rapidly towards the coast, as did the bulk of the investment. Furthermore, the booming growth of the coast was based on the import of new technology, which rapidly made the province's stock of equipment and skills obsolete. The surge of coastal development almost invisibly eroded the industrial base of the province and challenged it to redefine its role and its strategy. Shaanxi's contemporary development can be characterised by the contrasts between its profound cultural heritage, its legacies of the planning period and its new role as a poor relative of the dominant east. The reform process requires the province to identify a strategy for growth by searching for new comparative advantage in an evolving market system.

This study explores the way Shaanxi responded to the changed economic environment during the reform period. It begins with a discussion of how to define Shaanxi as a region and draws some comparisons with other provinces. The aim is to locate Shaanxi within a typology of regional models. The following section examines the evolution of Shaanxi's development strategy during the years 1978 to 1995. This leads into an analysis of the actual growth performance over the period. The provincial-level analysis is then broken down into a discussion of contrasting development at a sub-provincial level, focusing on the disparities between Guanzhong, Shaannan and Shaanbei and on the implications of those differences for understanding the nature of provinces as a coherent entity. The conclusion brings these various themes together by summarising the issues now confronting Shaanxi.

DEFINING SHAANXI AS A REGION

The issue of centre–local relations is always crucial in large countries, and it has been fundamental throughout China's history. The establishment of the People's Republic tilted the balance sharply in favour of the centre, though friction between central control and local initiative persisted and was expressed in terms of the balance between 'branches and areas'.[10] Centralised control through the branches of the ministries created problems for local coordination and innovation in the areas. Decentralisation, especially the administrative form favoured by Mao, created problems of control and macro management. The reform period has introduced both economic and administrative decentralisation. Administrative decentralisation has given greater authority to local levels of government, but it does not change the basic nature of the planned economy. Economic decentralisation gives autonomy to independent units of production and, by its nature, demands interaction through the market. Both kinds of decentralisation have extended the operational powers of the provinces and given the issue of centre–local relations a sharp contemporary relevance, dominated by its economic content.

Jae Ho Chung argues that there are three general perspectives on this issue.[11] These are cultural, structural, and procedural. The cultural perspective is based on local history and provincialist values. The structural emphasises the distribution of power between the centre and the localities. The procedural focuses on the processes for bargaining and interaction between the different levels of government. Chung argues against a narrow focus on budgetary and resource allocation issues in favour of a broader approach which accepts that the relationship between the centre and the provinces is not a zero-sum game, that there are variations in the balance between central control and local autonomy across a spectrum of issues for each province, and that the level of analysis should extend beyond the province–centre framework to embrace both sub-provincial and supra-national linkages. His comments provide a useful correction to the dominant focus on economic issues that have characterised much of the discussion outside China of centre–local relations during the reform period. The level of analysis, in particular, is a point which is explored at some length below. Nevertheless, at certain periods of time, one or other of the variables involved has played the major role, and there can be no doubt that the economic relationship between province and centre has been at the core of the key changes of the reform period. The position taken here, therefore, is that understanding the economic basis for central–provincial relations is crucial to understanding policy choices at the provincial level.

During the 1980s, the introduction of budget contracting and its impact on centre–provincial relations led to a growing emphasis on the emergence of local economic identities.[12] This culminated in the 'commodity wars' of the late 1980s[13] and in the increasing difficulty faced by the central government in exercising macro-economic controls. Much of the growth in the economy was monopolised at provincial levels, central revenue came under pressure, and the ratio of central investment in total investment declined.

These changes not only affected central–local interaction but also the relationship between different provinces. The operation of the state grain marketing system during the 1980s, for example, meant that grain producing provinces transferring grain supplies out at low state prices were, in effect, subsidising those provinces which received large allocations of cheap state grain.[14] The net effect was to put pressure on the budgetary position of the grain surplus provinces and to ease the budgetary position of the deficit provinces. Since the former were often poorer agricultural provinces and the latter richer industrialised ones, the transfer effect was regressive. In this case, therefore, the conflict of interest was not between the centre and the province but between the provinces.

Issues of this kind have led some to argue that regionalism poses a challenge to the integrity of the Chinese economic and political system. That potential was recognised and addressed by the central leadership in the fiscal and financial reforms begun in 1994, and it continues to receive attention in economic and political discussion in China.[15] In addition, the regional inequalities of income and economic development generated during the 1980s and early 1990s have led to a renewed emphasis on regional policy in the Ninth Five Year Plan adopted in March 1996.[16]

In retrospect, many aspects of the economic competition between the centre and the provinces can be seen as transitional, reflecting the friction between the remnants of the plan system and the emerging market forces. Local government systems still have considerable ability to intervene in the economy, despite the ultimate reform goal of separating administrative and economic responsibility. Nevertheless, even though such friction continues to exist, there are still many countervailing forces for integration between centre and locality. Among these are the political authority of the party and administrative systems, the increasing sophistication of central macro-economic management through tax and banking reform, and the emergence of more integrated marketing networks across provincial boundaries which serve to promote provincial interdependence.[17]

The responses of provinces to these forces generated by the reforms is largely defined by the level and nature of their economic and social development. Coastal provinces with high rates of growth, large non-state sectors and substantial budget revenues are more able to finance their own development. For them, a lower level of dependence on central economic intervention is realistic, and greater economic autonomy is often desirable. For less-developed provinces with slow growth, large numbers of state enterprises and poor finances, greater independence is neither feasible nor desirable. In the latter case, reliance on central support is important, and there is considerable sensitivity to central decisions over the distribution of funds and projects. While their local economic interests are clear and they can be expected to work towards them, such provinces are not able to and would not want to adopt a strongly independent economic position in conflict with the centre.

Defining the nature of Shaanxi as an economic region and the location of the province in the range of provincial types thus requires consideration of a number of factors. The key ones are those of location and endowment, economic structure and fiscal relationships with the centre.

Location and endowment

In terms of location and endowment, Shaanxi is usually seen as part of the northwest, on the edges of the old heartland of Chinese culture and transitional to outlying provinces stretching into central Asia. In the view of some, this is an advantage since it offers an intermediary role between the eastern and western parts of China.[18] The fact that Guanzhong sits astride the key rail link between the coast and Xinjiang and that Xi'an is the dominant industrial centre between the two ends adds to this perception. Nevertheless, in terms of the three broad zones of east, west and centre now commonly used in regional analysis in China, Shaanxi lies on the western edge of the central zone. What is more, the coastal bias in development policies after the mid-1980s served to highlight the province's remoteness from the areas of fastest growth. As He Jinming, the former first secretary of the provincial government, noted, in 1987 at a regional development conference in Lanzhou the Beijing participants argued that the coast should be the focus for immediate rapid development and the northwest would have to manage as it could until the benefits of coastal growth began to trickle down.[19] The interior location that had been a benefit during the plan period, especially when the strategic emphasis was on the development of dispersed 'Third Front' industrial centres, suddenly became an obstacle; and the lack of direct interaction with the world economy and the shift of the investment focus towards the coast heralded a sharp relative decline in Shaanxi's economic position.

The evolution of reform policies and the preferential policies towards the coast after the mid-1980s thus worked to the disadvantage of Shaanxi, and it is no surprise to find Zhao Bingzhang and Zhang Baotong arguing that: 'The current division of the distribution of China's productive forces into east, centre and west, and the strategy of gradual development moving from east to west does not correspond to the actual distribution of productive forces and, therefore, does not benefit the development of the Chinese economy.'[20] This disadvantage is one that Shaanxi shares with many of the interior and western provinces, especially those that benefited from the plan system such as Sichuan and Hubei. As Dorothy Solinger has shown, however, the key issue here is the impact of preferential policies from the centre.[21] In Wuhan, another example of an inland centre of planned economic development, advantages in terms of transport infrastructure, an industrial structure not that dissimilar to coastal cities and a reform oriented leadership were unable to compensate for the bias of central policies. Location and the concentration of plan industries are therefore only part of the equation.

The northwest location also defines the basic parameters for Shaanxi's agriculture. Bordering on the more arid zones of the interior, the province faces problems of cold, dry winters and variable summer rainfall. Yields and per capita supplies of most crops are generally well below average. In 1994, for example, the output of grain per hectare was only 56.5 per cent (2,544 kg compared with 4,500 kg) and peasant per capita income was some 65.9 per cent (805 *yuan* compared with 1,221 *yuan*) of the national average.[22] The differences between the harsh, dry north and the moist south of the province also creates substantial variations in sub-provincial agricultural systems. The constraints of the loess in the north and the mountains in the south mean that the most productive region is Guanzhong. Shaanbei and Shaannan are both much poorer.

Of the remaining location and endowment factors, three key issues stand out: water, transport, and energy and minerals. Water is a basic constraint on Shaanxi's development. Per capita water resources are only slightly over half the national average.[23] It was estimated that in 1990 guaranteed water supplies were 29 per cent less than demand and that the deficit would still be of the order of 20 per cent in the year 2000.[24] The issue affects both industry and agriculture, and is particularly severe in Guanzhong and Shaanbei. Since the late 1980s, Xi'an has only been able to obtain around half of its potential water demand, and controls on supply have been common. The recent opening of a major supply canal cannot fill the gap,[25] and the city will continue to be short of water until a large project in the Qinling Mountains is completed some years hence. Shaannan, by contrast, has ample rainfall and river flows. However, the exploitation of its water resources, especially for hydroelectricity, requires substantial capital inputs, something which both the prefectures and the province lack. The Han River in Shaannan is said to be able to support eight major dams but only two have been constructed. Further development will require major investment by the central government.

Transport suffers from a similar lack of investment. The location of the province, protected by the Yellow River to the east and the mountains to the south, has historically given it a relative isolation from the eastern provinces.

The pass where the Wei River flows into the Yellow River has always been the strategic entry point, and it is the route through which the main transport link to the province and to the northwest, the Long–Hai railway, runs. This line, which crosses Guanzhong, is a vital route, but its capacity is stretched. This is an important constraint on the outward links from the province.

Within the province, north–south links are limited. The rail line from Xi'an to Ankang follows a circuitous route through the Qinling Mountains, and the journey takes almost 20 hours.[26] The line northwards to Yan'an was not completed until the early 1990s, and Yulin is linked to Inner Mongolia by a line from Shenmu to Baotou. Plans are under way for a link from Shenmu to Yulin and thence to Yan'an and for a coal transport line from Shenmu to the coast, but the completion times are many years away. While road transport is improving and there has been much development in the 1990s, reliability is often poor, especially in the loess region and in the southern mountains. In 1988, all-weather routes only accounted for 44.6 per cent of roads.[27] Overall, therefore, the lack of transport infrastructure is a major problem, particularly in terms of limiting development at the local level and providing links out of the province. In 1995, it was seen as an important obstacle to the new policies aiming to encourage investment to shift from the coast towards the west.[28]

Energy development in Shaanxi has been substantial during the reform period. In particular the discovery and exploitation of coal in the northern part of the province has accelerated through a combination of both large enterprise investment and rural enterprises. Shaanxi forms part of the Shanxi–Shaanxi–Inner Mongolia coal field, which holds over 50 per cent of China's total coal reserves. The emphasis on the energy sector adopted as part of the revision of national industrial strategy in 1994 was seen as a significant gain for the province,[29] and especially as an avenue of development for the poor north. Guaranteed reserves (*baoyou chuliang*) of coal in the province rose from 99.886 billion tonnes in 1985 to 161.84 billion tonnes in 1994.[30] The 1985 reserves made Shaanxi the third largest coal centre in the country, but its output was only fourteenth.[31] The subsequent discoveries have begun to push the province up the table of energy producers, and it now receives considerable emphasis in national plans for energy development.

Coal-mining development has taken place in Yulin and Yan'an Prefectures and in western Guanzhong. Together these areas account for over 90 per cent of the reserves. The most spectacular growth has been in the Shenmu–Fugu area, bordering on Inner Mongolia and northern Shanxi. In 1985, it accounted for 78.4 per cent of provincial reserves, and new discoveries have since increased its share. The coal is of high quality, with low sulphur content and easily mined. It is being developed by the national Shenhua Corporation, a new semi-independent corporation under the management of the State Planning Commission. By 1996, the verified reserves (*tanming chuliang*) of this area were reported to be around 223.6 billion tonnes, with even more in prospect.[32] According to local officials, the early phase of Shen–Fu coal exploitation in the mid-1980s was based on a model of local small-scale mines proposed by Zhao Ziyang. Later, this approach was seen as wasteful of the resource, and a large-scale modern mining company was established. Major central initiatives are thus beginning to exploit these reserves, and the development of the energy sector in the north is becoming one of the growth poles of the province. The current plan is for an annual output of 30 million metric tonnes, making it second only to Datong in Shanxi at 32 million metric tonnes.

Nevertheless the full utilisation of the coal reserves is constrained by a shortage of capital and infrastructure.[33] Large-scale mine development requires large amounts of capital, but the transport constraints at present mean that current capacity cannot be fully utilised and the return on the investment is slow to materialise. The Daliuta Mine was operating at half capacity when visited in mid-1996 and the major limitation was the lack of railway capacity to move the coal. A direct line to the coast is under construction, and the first stage to Shuozhou across the Yellow River in Shanxi was opened on 1 July 1996.[34] The coast will not be reached until the year 2002, however, when greater exports will become possible. Meanwhile, coal must move out via Baotou in Inner Mongolia, and wagons are limited. What is more, there is a back-haul problem, since the wagons have to return empty. As a result, the local market price for coal is 42 *yuan* a tonne compared with the plan price of 66 *yuan*. While the potential for long-term development would appear good, the immediate returns are limited. The area is also surrounded by major coal producing areas in Shanxi and Inner Mongolia, which are already well developed. Successful competition is difficult at this stage.

Associated with the coal, oil and natural gas have also been developed. The gas reserves are substantial and one of the largest in the country.[35] A local chemical industry is developing in Yulin as a result. As discussed below, there are also plans to export gas to other provinces. Oil reserves are more limited, but exploitation, which in 1985 was estimated to be only one thousandth of the geological reserve, has begun to accelerate.[36]

Finally, electricity supply is also constrained by lack of investment. The major coal deposits in the north cannot be fully exploited for electricity because of lack of water. The coal-fired electricity stations being built along the Wulanmulun River at Daliuta in Shenmu, for example, cannot produce reliably because of the uncertainties of water supply, and a plan to divert Yellow River water is under consideration. What is more, the differences in the grid system between 500 kV for the north China grid, in which Shanxi is located, and 330 kV for the northwest, in which Shaanxi is located, adds a technical obstacle to the flow of electricity across boundaries.

Hydroelectricity capacity is only substantial in Shaannan, where high rainfall, mountainous topography and the Han River offer opportunities to build dams. The costs of such dams are, however, enormous, and they require central government approval and investment. As a result only a small proportion of the Han River potential has been developed.[37] Overall, therefore, Shaanxi is more dependent on coal as a primary source of energy than the country as a whole (86.9 per cent in 1994 compared to 78 per cent),[38] and it needs much investment to bring its electricity supply up to potential demand. In the mid-1980s, electricity had to be supplied from outside,[39] and in early 1996 the provincial governor, Cheng Andong, still saw it as a bottleneck which could not be overcome for some time.[40]

The net effect of these locational and endowment factors underline the problems facing Shaanxi. The development of transport and energy infrastructure requires large amounts of capital. That, in turn, is dependent on either central government grants and loans or on the capacity of the province to raise capital on its own. Since the province is a deficit province, the latter course is not easy. Even in central government-aided projects, where the centre provides 70 per cent of the funds, the province and its prefectures often find it difficult to raise the remaining 30 per cent through bank loans because, in view of their poor revenue base, banks are unwilling to lend. This contrasts with coastal provinces, where local revenue surpluses are always available as counterpart funds for project development. Under these circumstances, Shaanxi continues to depend on central policy initiatives and project approval processes and its potential for independent provincial policy remains constrained.

Economic structure

The economic structure of provinces in China can be analysed both in terms of the relative proportions of different sectors in their total GDP and in terms of the role of different types of ownership. The former gives an indication of relative levels of development. A higher ratio for agriculture, for example, is typically associated with a lower level of GDP. The latter is particularly important in respect of industry, since it reflects the extent of the reform process and the diversification of economic operation. A higher ratio of state-owned enterprises, for example, suggests that the reforms have had less impact on the structural transformation of the local economy.

In terms of GDP, Shaanxi ranked twenty-first among all provinces in 1994 and in per capita terms it ranked twenty-seventh.[41] Its per capita GNP and urban incomes are generally 150 to 230 per cent below those of the coastal provinces.[42] Furthermore, its position in a number of these indicators has tended to decline. Peasant per capita net income fell from being equal to the national average in 1978 to being only 61 per cent of the national average in 1995.[43] Figure 3.1 compares the structure of Shaanxi and national GDP for 1978 and 1994. Shaanxi began with a larger role for the primary and secondary sectors and a smaller role for the tertiary sector. This reflected the relatively high level of state industrial investment under the plan system and the continued emphasis given to agricultural self-sufficiency. As is typical under a planned economy, the tertiary sector was less developed, and this feature was even more marked in Shaanxi. By the end of the period, the primary sector had experienced a relative decline but was still above the national average, and the secondary sector had declined to below the national average. In effect the acceleration in the growth of manufacturing and light industry in other parts of China compared with the slower growth in Shaanxi meant that there had been a relative decline in the significance

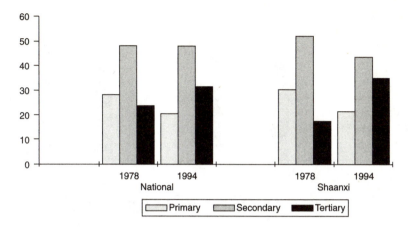

Figure 3.1 GDP structure (%)
Source: National and Provincial Yearbooks, various years

of its industrial sector. Meanwhile Shaanxi's tertiary sector had grown substantially in line with the national trend. Its relative importance in the province was boosted because of the poorer performance of the secondary sector.

The factors behind this picture become clearer when seen in terms of the gross value of output (GVO) measure in Figure 3.2. At the beginning of the period, the structure of the Shaanxi economy was very similar to that of the national economy. By 1994 agriculture had declined but much less than the national average, so that it still played an important role in the Shaanxi economy. Light industry had declined at a time while the national average had grown substantially, and heavy industry had risen to well above the national figure. In other words, the structure of the Shaanxi economy had gone against the national trend by reinforcing the role of heavy industry and by experiencing a relative decline in the role of light industry. This change underlines the fact that the province remains predominantly focused on the role of heavy industry. It has yet to develop the same level of light industrial and labour-intensive manufactures as other parts of the country. In other words, the underlying industrial structure has been slow to change.

This latter point is further illustrated in Figure 3.3 which gives the ratio of industrial output value by ownership. At the national level, there has been a dramatic transformation of the role of state-owned enterprises whose share in industrial output value has shrunk from around 78 per cent to less than 31 per cent. In 1978, Shaanxi state-owned industry was slightly above the national average. By 1994, the state sector had declined but still remained above 57 per cent. Meanwhile the non-state sector had grown to 42 per cent but lagged some 23 points behind the national average, which was over 65 per cent. The Shaanxi economy had therefore not developed the collective, rural enterprise, private and foreign sectors at the same rate as the developed coastal provinces, and the industrial structure was thereby more heavily burdened by the problems of

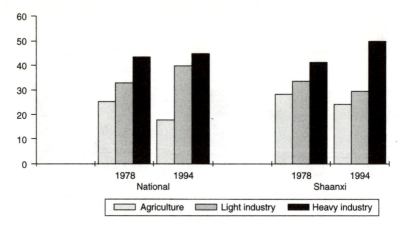

Figure 3.2 Gross value of output by sector (%)
Source: National and Provincial Yearbooks, various years

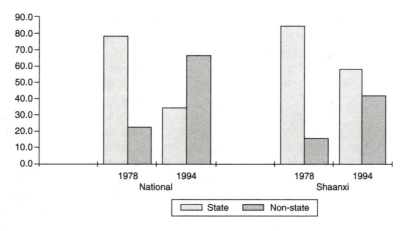

Figure 3.3 Industrial output value by ownership (%)
Source: National and Provincial Yearbooks, various years

transition that state enterprises have experienced during the reform process. Moreover, the higher the ratio of state enterprises, the greater the likelihood of economic inefficiencies in the provincial economy.

As noted above, the foundations of this industrial structure were laid during the plan period, when Shaanxi received special emphasis in the development of large and medium state enterprises and military industries. By 1985, some 68 per cent of manufacturing industrial output value was concentrated in military, electronic, machinery and textile enterprises.[44] This structure not only meant that there was a large state sector *per se*, but it also resulted in a large ratio of industries owned by the central authorities and the military system compared to those owned by the local state. In 1985, some 72 per cent of the province's 291 large and medium enterprises were centrally owned, and there were nearly one hundred military enterprises, making Shaanxi the second largest military industry province.[45] In 1993, the gross value of output of industries under central departments still accounted for 39.7 per cent of the total state enterprise output in the province. They were controlled by more than 10 central ministries and dispersed across 10 provincial cities and prefectures. The same concentration applied to scientific, technical and educational personnel, with very high proportions of them under the management of central departments. In 1995, for example, military industries had 20 per cent of the province's state enterprise fixed assets, employed 42 per cent of scientific and technical personnel, but only had a 40 per cent equipment utilisation rate.[46] The familiar problems of friction between branches and areas and among branches have thus always been present in the province. There is also a perception that the province has been too dependent on central investment for its growth, and the large ratio of centrally owned enterprises demonstrates that the locally resourced economy is relatively underdeveloped.

Ultimately, therefore, Shaanxi shares a number of constraints and problems with other provinces which were developed during the plan period. These include Heilongjiang, Liaoning and Jilin in the northeast, and Hubei, Sichuan and Gansu in the centre and west. Although, as Solinger has shown, there are important particular characteristics in each of these areas which must be taken into account when analysing their individual reform paths,[47] the features that gave them advantages in the plan period have, in the course of the reforms, become constraints on their growth. As such, they can be expected to prefer policies designed to ease the pressures on state enterprises and to look for central support in handling their difficulties in the transition to a market economy. They can also be expected to be less enthusiastic about policies which promote a regional bias in development towards the coast and to prefer policies which are sectorally based. Furthermore, the relative lack of diversification into dynamic new sectors makes their economies more reliant on centrally funded projects as a way of stimulating local growth. The power of the centre to affect such regions thus remains very strong. As Solinger puts it, 'decentralization has heightened influence at the subnational level only where other conditions – conferred from the Centre itself – were also present.'[48] These conditions include such things as preferential policies, high local profit retention ratios and incentives for foreign investment.

Fiscal position

Shaanxi's reliance on the centre is even more clear when the structure of the provincial budget is analysed. Table 3.2 and Figure 3.4 give an overview of Shaanxi's revenue and expenditure within the budget. It clearly shows that Shaanxi has been a deficit province since the reforms began, and that the deficit has tended to worsen over time. What is more, the reforms in tax procedures introduced in 1994, which aimed at increasing the central share of revenue, mean that the deficit should now be calculated at a much higher level (4292.7 million *yuan* for 1994 compared to 220.5 million under the old system). Overall,

Table 3.2 Budget income and expenditure, 1978–1994 (million *yuan*)

Year	Revenue	Expenditure	Balance
1978	1975.87	1830.26	145.61
1979	1680.10	1956.17	−276.07
1980	1581.05	1828.37	−247.32
1981	1345.38	1638.87	−293.49
1982	1356.22	1729.93	−373.71
1983	1450.07	1880.76	−430.69
1984	1531.24	2274.71	−743.47
1985	2029.67	2750.07	−720.40
1986	2409.07	3559.31	−1150.24
1987	2818.05	3780.51	−962.46
1988	3387.88	4458.35	−1070.47
1989	3896.03	5078.70	−1182.67
1990	4119.01	5390.62	−1271.61
1991	4513.91	5827.81	−1313.90
1992	5095.39	6526.54	−1431.15
1993	6289.82	7539.85	−1250.03
1994	8331.11	8551.58	−220.47

Source: *Shaanxi tongji nianjian 1995* [Shaanxi Statistical Yearbook], p. 148. The figures for 1994 are calculated according to the pre-tax reform method to make them consistent

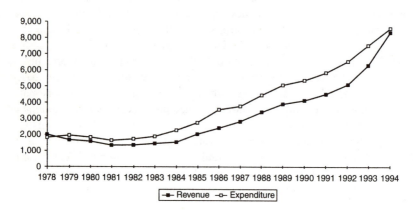

Figure 3.4 Shaanxi budget revenue and expenditure (m¥)
Source: Table 3.2

therefore, the province is dependent on central allocations to sustain its budget expenditure. A similar picture is evident at county level, with a majority of the 105 or so counties running substantial deficits.[49] This situation not only makes the province dependent on central fiscal allocations but also limits its flexibility in developing projects on its own initiative. What is more, the higher returns to be found in the coastal region have led to a flow of capital out of Shaanxi.[50]

Implications

The above analysis demonstrates that the scope for initiative in developmental policies in Shaanxi is subject to strong locational, structural and fiscal constraints. These constraints have acted as a brake on the ability of the province to respond to the economic and administrative decentralisation of the reform period. They have also magnified the effects of the regional bias of the coastal development strategy and of a lower level of interaction with the world economy. Shaanxi thus falls into the category of provinces which benefited from the plan system and which have undergone a relative decline as the reforms evolved. Its level of economic dependency on the central government is much higher than that of coastal provinces which have experienced rapid growth and have much lower ratios of state-owned industry. However, while these structural features are fundamental constraints, policy also matters. The way in which a province bargains with the centre and shapes its local development strategy has crucial implications for its economic development and its ability to respond to the changing economic environment. These issues are explored in the following section.

THE EVOLUTION OF DEVELOPMENT STRATEGY, 1978–1995[51]

Shaanxi is said to be a conservative province in which 'official thinking and status' are always given priority. It has tended to be slower in experimenting with reforms and has waited for official sanction before adopting new policies. This view is one that is commonly held across the province, and it has been noted by many outside observers both within and outside China. Indeed, as Kevin Lane has shown, at the outset of the reform period Shaanxi was still enthusiastically implementing the priorities of the plan system and of the Cultural Revolution, and it was slow to abandon its commitment to the set of policies which had shaped its economic structure before 1978.[52] The perception is that the province lags at least six months to a year behind other areas. Furthermore, in the cycles of reform policy, Shaanxi has been more cautious. For example, during the austerity period of 1989–91 some in Shaanxi were quick to put the brake on township and village enterprises (TVEs) at a time when the coastal provinces gave less emphasis to central calls for restrictions on their development.[53] This was seen by many as an example of the way coastal provinces have accelerated their development in contrast to the more conservative policy approach of Shaanxi. The image of the province, for both locals and outsiders, is thus orthodox and passive rather than progressive and innovative. Whatever the reality of the natural constraints, this policy character is seen as part of the explanation for the relative decline of the province and for its lack of dynamic innovation.

Most observers of Shaanxi's development strategy during the reform period argue that the province has passed through three main phases. The first phase from 1978 to around 1984 is primarily seen as one of overcoming old ideological restrictions and correcting the errors of the past. It focused on the political tasks of removing the orthodoxy of the Cultural Revolution and the plan system. At the same time it saw the introduction of the rural reforms. As elsewhere in China, this process was accompanied by debate over the orientation of the production responsibility system. Certainly some cadres at the basic level in Shaanxi saw it as a retreat from socialist ideals of collective farming.[54] This caution was given as one explanation for the relatively slow development of TVEs in the province. Nevertheless, evidence from the mid-1980s suggests that, even if slower, the process followed much the same course as it did in other provinces.[55]

The second phase from 1985 to 1991 saw the first efforts to develop a distinctive provincial strategic plan.[56] That strategy aimed to build on the existing industrial foundation and called for reform of the economic system, greater opening to the outside world and more efficient growth. In particular it set a series of production targets for the year 2000 and raised a number of strategic issues. These included: (1) giving emphasis to science and education based on the concentration in these sectors built up during the plan period; (2) the stable development of agricultural production and a new focus on TVE growth; (3) continued emphasis on the machinery and textile industries; (4) the development of infrastructure and basic industries such as energy and transport; and (5) the development of tourism. The latter was based on the province's historical roots, and during the early 1980s it had been a subject of debate, with more cautious officials concerned at the impact of foreign influences.

One particular issue was the strategy for sub-provincial development. The initial formulation was to 'develop Guanzhong as the key point and to support the development of Shaannan and Shaanbei'. In some ways, this regional emphasis can be seen as the local equivalent of the national model of focusing on coastal development first. At the same time it reflected the reality of the economic importance of the Guanzhong area. Such formulations, however, were seen to neglect the needs of the poorer regions. Subsequent reformulations thus shifted towards 'develop Guanzhong as the key point and actively develop Shaannan and Shaanbei' or 'develop Guanzhong as the key point and accelerate the development of Shaannan and Shaanbei'. The successive changes reflected the debate over the strategic emphasis within the province and made concessions to the concerns of basic level officials. The most recent policies therefore stress the need to 'reduce gradually the economic differentials between Guanzhong and Shaannan and Shaanbei'.[57]

The most significant factors during this period, however, were external. The adoption of the coastal development strategy by the central government reduced the amount of resources flowing to Shaanxi through the plan system. The effects of the 'commodity wars' of the period also weakened state enterprises in their efforts to compete with the emerging non-state sectors, especially those in the textile industries which were so important to the Shaanxi economy. In addition, the impact of the austerity programme of 1989–91 tended to bite harder in areas with a larger proportion of state enterprises. Overall, therefore, the province did not succeed in making any major breakthroughs in its development programmes during this time. The explanation lies in both the endowment constraints discussed above and in the slowness of the province to adopt active policies to promote change in the industrial structure and to diversify the economic system.

The third phase began in 1992 and saw a search for strategies to overcome some of the constraints Shaanxi faces. In particular, the province was now sharply aware of the extent to which it had fallen behind the coastal zone. Reflecting the renewed central emphasis on reform symbolised by the publicity given to Deng Xiaoping's southern tour, the province set out to accelerate the processes of structural reform and opening. The realignment of central policy away from a regional bias towards a sectoral bias was also seen as an opportunity for Shaanxi to make up lost ground. The beginning of this shift came with the national outline for long-term development put forward in 1991. This stressed the need to develop basic industries and infrastructure.[58] It was not, however, fully articulated until the State Industrial Policy was proclaimed in 1994. This stated unequivocally that: 'The state will gradually shift preferential economic policies in investments, loans, project distribution and foreign capital use from regions to industries, and will give necessary assistance to major projects for development and construction of the central and western regions.'[59] This combination in the national strategy of a reaffirmation of open policies, an emphasis on energy and infrastructure and a downgrading of the coastal bias offered a new opening to Shaanxi. Nevertheless, the economic and locational advantages of the coast remain entrenched, and it is recognised that development will still mean finding ways of interacting with the coastal provinces and complementing their growth as they shift towards higher levels of capital intensity and require more energy and raw materials.[60]

The challenge now facing the province is whether local enterprises can learn to compete effectively with their coastal rivals on the domestic and international markets, despite the differential impact of preferential policies from the centre and of the limitations imposed by the absence of truly competitive markets. The obstacles are many, and it is not surprising to find the governor, Cheng Andong, adopted a cautious tone in a recent speech on provincial development.[61] He listed a number of problems. He noted that per capita GDP is among the lowest in the country and that, since incomes are also well below the national average, 'even small fluctuations in prices can influence social stability'. He pointed out that some 40 per cent of state enterprises in the province were in difficulty and that 'over 100,000' state enterprise workers and 'over 200,000' rural enterprise workers were not getting their wages. He listed water supply, transport and electricity as major bottlenecks, the latter being an especially severe constraint on all forms of production. He also stressed that there was low efficiency and few new products and that Shaanxi had not yet developed any prominent sectors, brands or regional specialities. Nevertheless, Cheng argued that the greater macro-economic stability after the high inflation of 1993 and 1994 and the shift in central government policies towards the interior regions were positive factors. He was also encouraged by the acceleration in TVE growth after 1992 and by the fact that Shaanxi met its target for foreign investment of US$410 million in 1995 at a time when the country as a whole was experiencing a slow-down.[62] His priorities for investment remained focused on basic infrastructure such as water, roads and electricity and on the need to increase agricultural output.

Against this background, the most recent statement of provincial strategy is embodied in the Ninth Five Year Plan and the goals of development by the year 2010.[63] This summarises the developments of the previous plan period and sets out the various targets for the next 15 years. The general strategies remain those of achieving greater efficiency, more diversification of the economic system through the growth of the non-state sector (to grow from 50 per cent to 70 per cent of industrial output by 2000), greater openness to the world economy, reliance on the established educational and scientific base in the province, more investment in agriculture, further diversification of the industrial structure and better use of resources.[64] While the thrust of the plan underlines the increasing sense of urgency in the province of the need to break away from its more conservative past, the basic themes of development and of the relationship between the sub-provincial regions remain focused on the familiar themes. The need for investment in water, transport, energy and basic raw materials again receive stress. Provincial development strategy thus continues to look for some fundamental breakthroughs in the face of severe constraints.

Overall, therefore, Shaanxi's development policies since 1978 have been characterised by a great slowness to respond to the opportunities offered by the reforms and an unwillingness at many levels in the hierarchy to abandon either the priorities of the plan system which formed the basis of Shaanxi's earlier development or the left bias of the Cultural Revolution. While location and endowment constraints have presented major difficulties in the context of reform goals, conservative policies have delayed the search for a new path.

ECONOMIC PERFORMANCE, 1978–95

The above periodisation characterises Shaanxi's development in terms of the key policy changes adopted by the central government. The first phase was dominated by the rural reforms. The second phase marked the shift to urban reform issues. And the third phase reflected the decisive adoption of the goal of building a socialist market economy that followed on from Deng Xiaoping's Southern Tour. Overall, therefore, it tends to support the view that the province has not been a reform innovator but has tended to react to changes in central orientation.

A different perspective on this periodisation is to examine the actual economic effects of the changes taking place. Some indicators of Shaanxi's economic performance during the reform period relative to the nation as a whole are given in Figure 3.5. These indicators show that in important areas such as per capita income, GDP and per capita gross value of industrial output, Shaanxi has passed through a period of consistent relative decline, regardless of the various policy phases. Furthermore, the gaps between the provincial and national figures are widening.

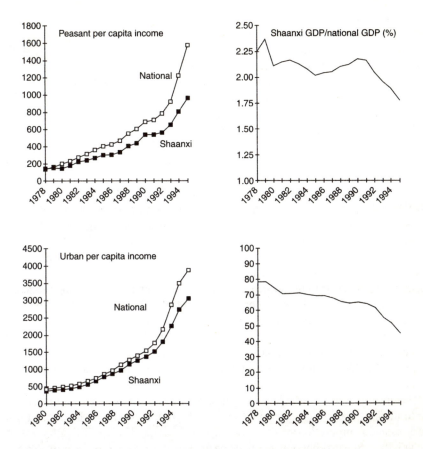

Figure 3.5 Shaanxi and national economic indicators, 1978–1994/5
Source: National and Provincial Yearbooks, various years

In the first phase the main changes were in the countryside. They resulted in substantial improvements in output and growth in peasant incomes. Nevertheless, as shown in Figure 3.5, the rate of growth was slower than the national average, with the result that peasant income in Shaanxi declined compared with that of peasants elsewhere.[65] The slow relative growth of the TVE sector was a major contributor to this growing disparity.[66] At the same time, the continued momentum of the plan system in the Sixth Five Year Plan during the first half of the 1980s saw further state industrial investment in the province. This meant that the industrial structure was slow to change. In the view of Zhang Baotong, this represented a lost opportunity since the province did not come to terms with the underlying implications of the reforms and was encouraged to stick with its established framework.[67] Indeed, Kevin Lane cites evidence to show that Shaanxi continued to emphasise heavy industrial development throughout the 1980s and was slow to shift to consumer products, with the result that it lagged well behind its competitors.[68]

During the second phase, the emphasis in central policy shifted to the coast. In effect the growth of coastal industries based on new technology meant that the older established industries of Shaanxi rapidly became obsolete, and the skills of the large scientific and technical workforce also became out-dated. As experienced elsewhere in the inland provinces, the coastal developments began to draw human talent and capital away. Efforts to develop a strategy for Shaanxi to respond to the coastal emphasis thus stressed that if a way were not found, 'the economic gap with the coastal provinces would widen'.[69] The goal of the development plans announced in 1988 was that Shaanxi should transform its economic structure, open up to foreign technology, shake off its self-reliant inward focus, attract coastal investment in its raw materials and become more commercialised. As shown by the indicators in Figure 3.5, however, the gap between the province and the coast did not close. Instead, it was intensified by the strict austerity policies carried out in Shaanxi during the period 1989 to 1991, when the curves began to turn sharply as Shaanxi's position deteriorated.

The third phase of growth with its strong emphasis on more open reform policies has yet to lead to an upswing in Shaanxi's development. As Cheng Andong made clear in his speech given at the beginning of 1996,[70] the problems remain entrenched, and Shaanxi has yet to identify and develop those sectors and industries in which it can compete effectively with other provinces. While energy and raw materials would seem sectors in which the province has a natural comparative advantage, the realisation of that potential requires infrastructure and capital, and that, in turn, needs central approval and funding for large projects. In addition, the role of the existing state industrial system as a basis for future development remains problematic. The adjustment costs of transforming them into market-focused, efficient producers are high in a province where they form a substantial proportion of the economy as a whole. The issue is also one of relativities. Shaanxi not only has to catch up with the coastal provinces, it also has to grow at a much faster rate if it hopes to overcome the widening gaps in development. Without central government assistance such a task would seem to be very difficult.

SUB-PROVINCIAL ISSUES: GUANZHONG, SHAANNAN AND SHAANBEI

The previous discussion has examined the performance of Shaanxi as a whole and its relationship to the centre. At various points, however, the extent of sub-provincial variation has been underlined. In the following discussion, we return to the issue of the 'level of analysis' raised by Jae Ho Chung and examine the relationship between provincial and sub-provincial development.

As noted above, since the late 1980s, an issue of debate within the province has been the formulation of the development strategy in terms of the relationship between Guanzhong and the poorer regions to the north and south. Whatever the formulation, the reality of the dominance of Guanzhong is inevitable. As shown in Table 3.1, it has 60 per cent of the population and accounts for between 60 and 80 per cent of various types of economic output. It also has the bulk of accumulated investment. Although the regional bias of the late 1980s means that Guanzhong has lost its momentum and its role as the economic dynamo of the province has weakened a little,[71] the future of the province will continue to rely on the performance of this sub-region. In contrast, around half of all Shaanxi's counties are officially designated poor counties and these are concentrated in the north and south.[72] Given their constraints of climate and terrain, the two poles of the province thus face major problems of development. Even if the energy resources of Shaanbei were to result in substantial development there, it is unlikely that its economy could develop the complexity and diversity of Guanzhong.

In many ways, the relationship between the provincial government and the officials in the regions and prefectures mirrors that between the central authorities and the province. As part of the provincial administrative system, regional administrators are appointed by the provincial personnel departments and form part of an integrated public service. During their career, they may well be moved between counties or from county to prefecture and from prefecture to province. Their perspective is thus not a narrowly local one. Nevertheless, their administrative work is dependent on a flow of policies and resources from provincial level to sustain local development. It is therefore inevitable that at various times and over various issues, they will disagree with the provincial priorities or argue that their locality is not getting the resource allocations that it needs. The debate over the formulation of the provincial development slogan reported above reflected these concerns.

Table 3.3 presents comparative data for the ten prefectures in Shaanxi in 1995. The data demonstrate clearly the extent of regional variations within Shaanxi, with Guanzhong being above average for many of the key indicators. The variations also illustrate some important nuances within that general picture. In terms of GNP per capita, Xi'an dominates the province. The other major industrial centres of Baoji, Xianyang, Tongchuan and Hanzhong are substantially below it, though this may reflect a larger ratio of agricultural population within them. The fact that Hanzhong ranks fifth shows the way the 'Third Front' strategy led to a dispersal of industrial investment to local centres. Xi'an also dominates in terms of urban incomes and revenue per capita. Apart from Xi'an, however, urban incomes across the province are relatively even, suggesting that variations in wage rates are relatively low. Revenue per capita also tends to follow the pattern of industrialisation, with the agricultural prefectures well below the average.

Turning to agriculture, the pattern is more mixed. Since 1995 was a year of severe drought in the province, the picture presented by the data may be atypical. In terms of peasant per capita income, the more urbanised and industrialised prefectures dominate, underlining the extent to which peasant income growth has been related to the expansion of off-farm income. The grain and edible oil figures may well reflect both the drought and local cropping practices. Overall, therefore, the province has some marked variations in economic performance, and the

Table 3.3 Shaanxi prefectural economic development levels, 1994–1995

	GNP per capita 1994 (yuan)	Revenue[1] (yuan per capita) 1995	Peasant income (yuan per capita) 1995	Net urban income (yuan per capita) 1995	Grain per capita (jin) 1995	Edible oil per capita (jin) 1995
Provincial average	2,355	107	923	2,708	538	22
Xi'an	4,590	281	1353	4,139	542	7
Xianyang	2,552	103	999	2,565	625	19
Tongchuan	2,529	107	844	2,184	372	14
Baoji	3,229	114	945	2,857	598	25
Weinan	1,936	101	991	2,570	622	29
Guanzhong average	2,967	141	1,026	2,863	552	19
Yan'an	2,287	135	912	na	692	24
Yulin	1,382	54	837	2,212	420	27
Shaanbei average	1,835	95	875	2,212	556	26
Shangluo	1,129	44	615	na	340	6
Ankang	1,504	50	862	2,636	574	28
Hanzhong	2,407	82	870	2,502	590	41
Shaannan average	1,680	59	782	2,569	501	25

Notes: [1] Revenue is government income left in the prefecture for own use, including extra-budgetary income and excluding central deductions
[2] Grain excludes miscellaneous grains
[3] Edible oils are expressed as raw materials and not pressed oils

Sources: Col 1: Shaanxi tongji nianjian 1995 [Shaanxi Statistical Yearbook], pp. 37–38
Cols 2–6: Interview with Mr Huang Jianjun, Deputy Head, Hanzhong Prefecture Statistical Bureau, 20 June 1996

realities of these local variations are explored in more detail in the following discussion of Hanzhong and Ankang Prefectures in the south and Yulin Prefecture in the north.

Hanzhong and Ankang

Hanzhong and Ankang are two of the three prefectures that make up the Shaannan region, the other being the poorest of all, Shangluo.[73] The area lies in the precipitous Qin-Ba ranges and is characterised by a lack of flat arable land. The landscape has also hindered the development of transport. The lack of farmland has meant that, despite the relatively favourable climate, the region has always been poor.[74] The one exception is the small basin of Hanzhong, where the combination of good land and plentiful water in the Han River has established a reputation for prosperous farming in the southern style, especially in Hanzhong County. Given its locational constraints, agriculture remains a major sector in the Hanzhong economy. It still accounted for 42 per cent of agricultural and industrial GVO in 1990 and industrial per capita output value was only one-third of the provincial average.[75]

Hanzhong Prefecture has always been the most prosperous in Shaannan, and its economy is based on its agriculture and on a number of industries developed there during the plan period. By 1984, the output of the 73 national and provincial state enterprises in Hanzhong accounted for nearly 39 per cent of prefectural industrial GVO, and the aircraft and machine building industries were important local sectors.[76] Prefectural state enterprises were mainly concentrated in construction materials, medicines, food processing, machinery and textiles. As is the case for the province as a whole, however, many of these state-operated industries are now inefficient and obsolete.

Hanzhong is currently focusing on identifying new areas of comparative advantage in the mineral, biological and water resources it shares with the neighbouring prefectures. These resources are, in fact, seen as the basis for the development of Shaannan as a whole.[77] Nevertheless, there is some uncertainty in the prefecture over their relative merits. The minerals require considerable capital to exploit and their development is constrained by the lack of transport. Local officials estimate that there is an annual shortage in outbound rail capacity of around 1.2 million tonnes. What is more, some of the minerals, like limestone, are plentiful elsewhere and cheap. The biological resources include such things as mushrooms, tea and Chinese medicines. These are already developing but, even with improvements in quality, could not be seen as a key sector. Water resources for hydroelectricity are large but, as noted above, require capital resources beyond the means of the prefecture for development. There is also a concern that too much industrialisation might threaten the environment in the basin area. Overall, therefore, the concept of development based on the three major resources is proving difficult to realise.

Ankang shares many of the features of Hanzhong but it is constrained by poorer agricultural conditions and an absence of any major industrial development. The lack of arable land is particularly severe, and the landscape is a maze of steep mountains and narrow valleys. This has forced the population to clear and farm precipitous slopes, much steeper than the 25° limit imposed by the land law. Local officials concede that there is nothing to be done about this since there is no alternative land to which people could be moved. Transport and infrastructure constraints also hindered industrial development in Ankang until the 1970s. In 1991, industrial output value was still only 34 per cent of total GVIAO.[78] The development of Ankang has to rely on the same set of resources as Hanzhong, but the problems of lack of capital and infrastructure are even more severe.

Officials in both prefectures say that Shaannan does not attract enough investment from the central and provincial levels. The proposals that are put forward in the various development strategies therefore tend to languish for lack of the resources to implement them. An example of this was the 10 billion *yuan* promised by the central government in the Eighth Five Year Plan for the development of TVEs in the northwest. Only 4 billion was realised, less than the amount provided in the previous plan period.[79]

One of the problems of Shaannan is the lack of a strong focus for its development strategy. Guanzhong is the key point for provincial development, and Shaanbei now has an overall emphasis on energy. The problem was discussed at a Shaannan Economic Work Conference in 1992, where the role of hydro-electricity, minerals and biological resources was again affirmed.[80] More recently proposals have centred on the concept of the Han River Industrial Corridor.[81] The idea was modelled on the proposal for a Yangtze Development Corridor and surfaced in a regional development conference during 1994. It was then approved by the Provincial People's Congress. It is now a feature of all provincial statements on regional development.[82] Its central idea is to integrate the main cities along the Han River by rail and road into a united industrial system and open an outlet to the Yangze.[83]

As yet, however, the proposal remains unrealised. The 1994 conference suggested that the Provincial Planning Commission should establish a 'corridor development company' but this has not been done.[84] In the absence of an organising unit to lobby for funds and develop projects, little practical work has ensued. What is more, such an organisation has to be established at provincial level. Local officials argue that if they set up their own body, it would lack both funds and authority. For the moment, therefore, the proposal has little specific content.

At present, local integration is mainly in the form of consultation among the six prefectures in the Qin-Ba area (the three in Shaanxi, Daxian in Sichuan, Yunyang in Hubei and Luoyang in Henan). These hold annual economic cooperation meetings to deal with matters of trade and economic cooperation, but there is no over-arching organisation. This form of consultation is an example of how sub-provincial levels can maintain practical links directly across provincial boundaries. Other local examples include the exchange links between Lan'gao County in Ankang and Kunshan City in Jiangsu. These links were set up as part of the central strategy of requiring developed areas in the east to support the backward areas of the interior. Ankang Prefecture also maintains offices in Wuhan,

Shanghai, Shenzhen, Hangzhou and Xi'an in order to promote its economy and to keep an eye on its markets. These various activities involve direct contacts and do not have to be managed through the provincial level of government. They centre entirely on the practical processes of economic interaction. They do not create institutional mechanisms which replace provincial authority, but they underline the way in which market integration is encouraging the growth of linkages outside the channels of the administrative hierarchy.

Yulin

Yulin lies at the opposite end of the province.[85] Its dry climate, its constant battle to keep the sand dunes of the Maowusi Desert at bay, and its eroded loess hills form a sharp contrast with the moist mountains of Shaannan. Nevertheless, it shares a common experience of poverty. All 12 of its counties are designated poor areas. Lying along the line of the Great Wall, the prefecture has always had a strategic role. Its lack of water and its mix of sandy desert and poor quality loess has, however, meant that much of its agriculture is marginal. It has the highest per capita land ratio in the province but a low level of per capita grain output. Much of its grains are coarse grains, and it also has an extensive pastoral industry of sheep and goats. Since the 1950s, much effort has been made to control the advance of sand dunes from the north and to develop irrigated agriculture in the valleys. This has enabled some improvement in output, but the average level of peasant income is still very low.

Until the mid-1980s, the economic structure remained firmly based in agriculture. In 1984, only 26 per cent of GVIAO came from industry. During the late 1980s, however, the emphasis on the development of energy resources created a new dynamic of growth. Energy is now seen as the key to the prefecture's future growth and as the basis for a coal, electricity and gas development zone along the line of the Great Wall.[86] The prefecture is attracting considerable outside investment in coal and gas projects and is optimistic about its long-term prospects. The growth rate of GNP during the Eighth Five Year Plan was around 17.2 per cent a year, above the national average, and it is anticipated that Yulin will eventually emerge as a key economic centre in the province. While there is a clear focus on the sources of future growth in Yulin, however, the immediate problems remain the familiar ones of a lack of capital and infrastructure, and the difficulties of overcoming parochial perspectives based on relative isolation and a lack of understanding of the way the emerging market economy operates. The constraints of capital, water shortages and lack of infrastructure remain a brake on development. Like the local officials in the south officials in Yulin also feel that their needs do not get sufficient priority in central and provincial allocations of resources.

Within the vision of 'energy-led' development, however, a number of organisational and practical problems have emerged. The shortage of capital means that prefectural and county projects find it hard to get support. This contrasts with the major national projects like the Shenhua Corporation mines in Shenmu. There is thus the potential for conflict between the various administrative levels involved in regional energy development. Yang Qiubao discusses contradictions over such items as resource utilisation, land use, labour allocation, water allocation, environmental degradation and the distribution of benefits.[87] Such contradictions also involve the interaction between central and local authorities and between the enterprises and local government. The Daliuta Mine, for example, no longer provides employment for peasants displaced by its mines since they do not have the necessary skills. It only pays compensation for the land. Since it uses modern imported technology, most of its workforce is skilled labour brought from other mining areas.[88] As a more market-focused organisation, it does not seek to run all of the social services it needs, like the old state enterprise system. It pays taxes and expects the local government to provide them. The mine operators also complain that unlike Inner Mongolia, where coal development is given priority and the province doesn't charge for the land, Shaanxi offers less favourable consideration.

In this respect, the operation of energy taxes also varies across the country. Under the policy of relieving the burden on poor areas, the tax levels in Shaanxi are lower than elsewhere. Table 3.4 sets out some comparisons. In the view of local officials, the policy works to local disadvantage. It means that the major source of local wealth is taxed at a low level, and this makes it difficult to generate increased revenues to fund further development.

The resources of Yulin do, however, offer some useful advantages for the prefecture in dealing with outside units. Beijing wants to build a gas pipeline to obtain its supplies of natural gas direct from Yulin. According to the local officials, the issue is being negotiated directly between Beijing and Yulin. Yulin is willing to sell the gas to Beijing, but as part of the deal it is asking Beijing to build a road from Yulin to Beijing alongside the pipeline, to lay down a gas pipe system in Yulin City for local gas distribution and to provide large investments in industrial enterprises in Yulin. Whatever the eventual outcome of such negotiations, it is another example of how emerging market relationships are providing a basis for direct economic interaction between different parts of China, without the need to work through the hierarchy of administrative levels.

This brief analysis of the disparities among Shaanxi's prefectures has illustrated a number of important issues. First, research into the nature of

Table 3.4 Energy taxes in selected regions

Item	Shaanxi	Elsewhere	
Coal (*yuan* per tonne)	0.50	Shanxi	2.50
Gas (*yuan* per '000 cubic metres)	2.00	Sichuan	15.00
		Daqing	12.00
Oil (*yuan* per tonne)	2.40	Daqing	24.00
		Evergreen	12.00

Source: Interview 30 June 1996

provincial development needs to take account of the substantial variations which can exist at sub-provincial levels. Few provinces are homogenous, and their strategies have to take account of the considerable differences in local endowments and circumstances. Second, regional development within a province can generate strategic debates in much the same way as provincial development can generate debates with the centre over national policy. Third, regional competition for scarce resources works in much the same way within provinces as it does between them. Finally, the evolution of market interaction is offering new avenues for interaction between sub-provincial levels across provincial boundaries in ways that were not possible under the strict territorial-administrative boundaries of the plan system.

CONCLUSION: SEARCHING FOR COMPARATIVE ADVANTAGE

The evolution of Shaanxi's development strategy during the reform period demonstrates the way in which aspects of the province's endowment and its legacy of the plan period have constrained its strategic choices. It also underlines how the introduction of the emerging market system has transformed the underlying balances of the provincial economy. The planned economy delivered substantial benefits to Shaanxi. The province established a large industrial base and developed a strong cadre of scientific and technical personnel. The combination of the shift towards economic efficiency based on market relationships and the regional bias towards the coast which resulted from the reform process undermined that foundation and left the province seeking a new focus. The province has had to look for new areas of comparative advantage while, at the same time, bearing the costs of the transition and competing in the face of central preferential policies directed towards other areas. Against the background of these constraints, administrative decentralisation, which gave more authority to local levels of government, and economic decentralisation, which gave more independence to economic units, have not automatically led to greater dynamism within the province. The freedom for manoeuvre remained within the limits established by central policies. The result was a relative decline.

Alongside the problems of endowment, legacy and central bias, the nature of administrative leadership in Shaanxi was also a key issue in its response to the reforms. Shaanxi has been noteworthy for its conservative and cautious provincial establishment. Cadres at all levels were slow to shift from the priorities of the pre-reform period. They attempted to maintain the focus on planned heavy industry at a time when the central government was shifting to other priorities and dramatically reducing the flow of resources on which Shaanxi had relied. There was thus a delay in revitalising the province and a slowness in developing new sources of growth.

The problems faced by Shaanxi fall into two categories. The first set is shared with those provinces which also have a large proportion of state enterprises. The market environment has revealed their inefficiencies, and the transitional costs of restructuring are high. The second is shared with the other provinces in the interior who have seen the coastal areas leap ahead as a result of central decisions. The absence of properly integrated markets and the relative lack of capital, infrastructure, human resources and access to world markets makes the challenge of defining a new economic role forbidding. The inclination towards caution and conservatism in policy change in Shaanxi not only tended to delay adjustments to the reform process but also slowed down the search for a decisive shift in provincial strategy.

Against that background, Shaanxi's search for a new development formula has, as yet, not been able to identify novel sources of comparative advantage. The regional variations within the province have also shown how the same problems have been at work at sub-provincial level. Potential answers put forward in provincial strategies and debated over the past ten years have included such suggestions as:

- revitalising the electronics, machine-building and textile industries established during the plan period;
- promoting the raw material and energy sectors in order to meet the needs of rapid growth along the coast;
- promoting labour-intensive industries to take over from those along the coast as the latter move up the capital-intensive ladder;
- accelerating openness to foreign trade and investment; and
- acting as an intermediary between eastern China and the northwest.

Many of these proposals could well contribute to a solution to Shaanxi's dilemma. The lower level of provincial GDP implies that it has a lower standard of living but that its labour will remain cheaper than that along the coast, giving it the opportunity to compete on labour costs. Its lack of quality consumer products means that it makes sense to try to compete in raw material supply and intermediate products. The problem, however, is that realisation of such strategies relies on investment in transport, energy and infrastructure within the province.

Overall, Shaanxi's experience underlines the extent to which provincial development is shaped by central policies. Shaanxi's original strengths were the creation of the planned system. Its reforms began as a response to central initiatives. The erosion of its established industrial base and its relative decline were largely the consequence of central policies which favoured other regions. The revival of its hopes in the mid-1990s were again the consequence of the central government's acknowledgement of a need to shift from a regional bias to a sectoral bias and of a need to direct resources towards the provinces that had been left behind. The formulation of the provincial development strategy during the reforms and the outcome of various initiatives were thus profoundly influenced by the impact of national-level policies. Ultimately the solution to the constraints on provincial development will also require support from the central government in the form of capital and infrastructure. While the evolution of market forces can be expected to encourage the development of regional specialisation, the adjustment costs for Shaanxi are thus likely to remain high. Shaanxi's search for comparative advantage still has some distance to go.

ACKNOWLEDGEMENTS

Research for this chapter was supported by a University of Adelaide small ARC grant and by the Shaanxi Academy of Social Sciences. Mr Li Sanhuai of the Academy also provided much help during fieldwork in the province. Watson is very grateful for their support and assistance and for the help given by the many officials in the regions of Shaanxi visited. The authors also thank the participants in the workshop, 'China Provinces in Reform', Zhejiang University, 20–24 October 1996 and Dr Christopher Findlay for their helpful comments.

NOTES

1 For an excellent photographic survey of the loess region see, Wang Yongyan (ed.), *Zhongguo huangtu* [Loess in China], Xi'an: Shaanxi renmin chubanshe, 1980.
2 For further information on the agricultural regions of Shaanxi see, Shaanxi Normal University Geography Department, *Shaanxi Sheng Ankang Diqu Dilizhi* [The Geography of Ankang Prefecture, Shaanxi Province], Xi'an: Shaanxi renmin chubanshe, 1986; *Shaanxi sheng Yulin diqu dilizhi* [The Geography of Yulin Prefecture, Shaanxi Province], Xi'an: Shaanxi renmin chubanshe, 1987; and *Shaanxi Sheng Weinan diqu dilizhi* [The Geography of Weinan Prefecture, Shaanxi Province], Xi'an: Shaanxi renmin chubanshe, 1990; Northwest University Geography Department, *Shaanxi nongye dili* [The Agricultural Geography of Shaanxi], Xi'an: Shaanxi renmin chubanshe, 1977; and Chen Mingrong, *Qinling de qihou yu nongye* [The Climate and Agriculture of the Qinling Mountains], Xi'an: Shaanxi renmin chubanshe, 1988.
3 The Qin-Ba Mountains area embracing parts of Shaanxi, Sichuan and Hubei forms a coherent natural economic zone. See also Jiao Xingguo (ed.), *Baituo Pinkun de Tansuo: Shaan-nan Qin-Ba shanqu tuopin kaifa yanjiu* [An Exploration of Breaking Free from Poverty: Research into Poverty Alleviation and Development in the Qin-Ba Mountain Area of Southern Shaanxi], Xi'an: Shaanxi renmin jiaoyu chubanshe, 1991.
4 Interview, Mr Shi Zhuya, Director, Xi'an Planning Commission, 19 June, 1996.
5 In 1994 a large international ceremony in memory of the Yellow Emperor was held, attended by the Chairman of the CPPCC, Li Ruihuan, the Provincial Party Secretary Zhang Boxing, and the Provincial Governor, Bai Qingcai, *Shaanxi nianjian 1995*, p. 11.
6 See Chi Ch'aoting's concept of 'key economic areas' in *Key Economic Areas in Chinese History*, first published 1936, reprinted New York: Paragon, 1963.
7 Mark Selden, *The Yenan Way in Revolutionary China*, Cambridge, Mass.: Harvard University Press, 1971.
8 Cyril Lin, 'China's economic reforms 2: western perspectives', *Asian-Pacific Economic Literature*, Vol. 2, No. 1, March 1988, pp. 1–25 argues that the inefficiencies and losses in terms of economies of agglomeration have amounted to a substantial burden on the economy as a whole.
9 Kevin P. Lane, 'One step behind: Shaanxi in reform', in Peter Cheung, Jae-ho Chung

and Lin Zhimin (eds), *Provincial Strategies of Economic Reform in China*, Armonk, NY: M. E. Sharpe, 1998.

10 See Jonathan Unger, 'The struggle to dictate China's administration: the conflict of branches vs areas vs reform', in *The Australian Journal of Chinese Affairs*, No. 18, July 1987, pp. 15–45 .

11 Jae Ho Chung, 'Studies of central–provincial relations in the People's Republic of China: a mid-term appraisal', *The China Quarterly*, No. 142, June 1995, pp. 487–508.

12 Christine P. W. Wong, 'Central–local relations in an era of fiscal decline: the paradox of fiscal decentralization in post-Mao China', in *The China Quarterly*, No. 128, March 1991, pp. 691–715 and Jean Oi, 'Fiscal reform and the economic foundations of local state corporatism in China', in *World Politics*, Vol. 45, No. 1, 1992, pp. 99–126. For contrasting Chinese views on the economic significance of economic regionalism in the reform period, see Sheng Liren and Dai Yuanchen, 'Woguo "zhuhou jingji" de xingcheng ji qi biduan he genyuan' [The formation of the 'warlord economy' in China: defects and origin], *Jingji Yanjiu* [Journal of Economic Research] No. 3, 1990, pp. 12–19 and Wu Minyi, 'Guanyu difang zhengfu xingwei de ruogan sikao' [Some thoughts on local governments' behaviour], *Jingji Yanjiu* [Journal of Economic Research], No. 7, 1990, pp. 56–59.

13 See, for example, Andrew Watson, Christopher Findlay and Du Yintang, 'Who won the "wool war"?: A case study of rural product marketing in China', *The China Quarterly*, No. 118, June 1989, pp. 213–241.

14 For a more detailed discussion of this issue see Andrew Watson and Christopher Findlay, 'Food and profit: the political economy of grain market reform in China', paper presented to the conference on *Grain market reform in China and its implications*, East West Centre, Hawaii, September 1995. The issue is also explored by Nicholas Lardy, *China's Interprovincial Grain Marketing and Import Demand*, United States Department of Agriculture, Economic Research Service, Agriculture and Trade Analysis Division, September 1990 and Chu Yijie, 'Liangshi diaochushi de ku zhong' [The difficulties of grain transfers are heavy] *Jingji Cankao* [Economic Information], 8 June 1989, p.1.

15 See Huang Xiaoguang, 'Caizheng tizhi gaige yu difang baohuzhuyi' [Reform of the fiscal system and regional protectionism], *Jingji Yanjiu* [Economic Research], No. 2, 1996, pp. 37–40 and Wang Maolin, 'Revealing new connotation on correctly handling relations between central and local authorities', *Renmin Ribao* [People's Daily], 2 May 1996, p. 9, English version in *Summary of World Broadcasts, Asia-Pacific*, FE/2619/G/9, 23 May 1996.

16 'Outlines of the Ninth Five Year Plan for National Economic and Social Development and the Long-Term Target for the Year 2010 of the People's Republic of China', Xinhua News Agency, 18 March 1996.

17 One of the clearest examples of this at work is the growing strength of the national free market network for fruits and vegetables. See Andrew Watson, 'Conflict over cabbages: the reform of wholesale marketing in China', in Ross Garnaut, Guo Shutian and Ma Guonan (eds), *The Third Revolution in the Chinese Countryside*, Cambridge: Cambridge University Press, 1996, pp. 144–163.

18 See the discussion in Zhao Bingzhang and Zhang Baotong, *Shaanxi jingji fazhan zhanlüe zonglun*, [A Comprehensive Strategy for Shaanxi's Economic Development], Xi'an: Sanqin chubanshe, 1988, pp. 1–15.

19 Interview, 18 June 1996.

20 Zhao Bingzhang and Zhang Baotong, *Shaanxi jingji fazhan zhanlüe zonglun*, p. 4.

21 Dorothy J. Solinger, 'Despite decentralization: disadvantages, dependence an ongoing central power in the inland – the case of Wuhan', *The China Quarterly*, No. 145, March 1996, pp. 1–34.

22 State Statistical Bureau, *Zhongguo tongji nianjian 1995* [China Statistical Yearbook, 1995], Beijing: Zhongguo tongji chubanshe, 1995, p. 280 and p. 350.

23 Research Team for the Social and Economic Development Strategy for Shaanxi 1996–2010, 'Shaanxi zouxiang 21 shiji de zhanlüe sikao' [Strategic thinking for Shaanxi for the 21st century], Part 1, *Renwen Zazhi* [The Journal of Humanities], No. 4, 1995, p. 6.

24 Zhao Bingzhang and Zhang Baotong, *Shaanxi jingji fazhan zhanlüe zonglun*, pp. 367–368.

25 *Renmin Ribao* [People's Daily], overseas edition, 1 July 1996, p. 1.

26 A direct route that is under construction will reduce that to four hours.

27 Zhao Bingzhang and Zhang Baotong, *Shaanxi jingji fazhan zhanlüe zonglun*, p. 8.

28 Research Team for the Shaanxi 1996–2010 Social and Economic Development Strategy, 'Shaanxi zouxiang 21 shiji de zhanlüe sikao', Part 1, p. 5.

29 The policy was articulated in the State Council's 'Outline for State Industrial Policy in the 1990s', 25 March 1994, made public in June 1994. See *Summary of World Broadcasts, Asia-Pacific*, FE/2033/S1/1, 28 June 1994.

30 Zhao Bingzhang and Zhang Baotong, *Shaanxi jingji fazhan zhanlüe zonglun*, p. 116 and Shaanxi Statistical Bureau, *Shaanxi tongji nianjian* [Statistical Yearbook of Shaanxi], Beijing: Zhongguo tongji chubanshe, 1995, p. 10.

31 Zhao Bingzhang and Zhang Baotong, *Shaanxi jingji fazhan zhanlüe zonglun*, p. 116.

32 Interview at Daliuta Mine, 29 June 1996. Around the same time, prefectural officials reported 159.54 billion tonnes of verified reserves for the whole prefecture. The inconsistencies in the figures for the reserves indicate the rapidity of growth and the rising expectations in the area.

33 See the discussion in Yang Qiubao, 'Xibei ziyuan fuji qu de jingji kaifa zhanlüe' [The strategy for the economic development of the resource-rich areas in the northwest], *Shaanxi Shifan Daxue Xuebao (Zhexue Shehui Kexue Ban)* [Journal of Shaanxi Normal University (Social Science)], Vol. 25, No. 2, June 1996, pp. 19–26.

34 *Renmin Ribao* [People's Daily], overseas edition, 1 July 1996, p. 1.

35 Research Team for the Social and Economic Development Strategy for Shaanxi 1996–2010, 'Shaanxi zouxiang 21 shiji de zhanlüe sikao', Part 2, Vol. 5 1995, p. 42.

36 Zhao Bingzhang and Zhang Baotong, *Shaanxi jingji fazhan zhanlüe zonglun*, p. 117.

37 Kang Suirun, *Quyu jingji yanjiu wenji* [Essays on Regional Economy], Xi'an: Shaanxi renmin chubanshe, 1994, p. 21.

38 Shaanxi Statistical Bureau, *Shaanxi tongji nianjian 1995*, p. 132 and State Statistical Bureau, *Zhongguo tongji nianjian 1995* [China Statistical Yearbook, 1995], Beijing: Zhongguo tongji chubanshe, 1995, p. 199.

39 Zhao Bingzhang and Zhang Baotong, *Shaanxi jingji fazhan zhanlüe zonglun*, p. 118.

40 Cheng Andong, 'Cheng Andong shengzhang tan Shaanxi jingji fazhan wenti' [Governor Cheng Andong discusses issues in Shaanxi's economic development], *Shaanxi Xinxibao* [The Shaanxi Reporter], 18 January 1996, p. 1 and p. 5.

41 State Statistical Bureau , *Zhongguo tongji nianjian 1995*, p. 33.

42 Research Team for the Social and Economic Development Strategy for Shaanxi 1996–2010, 'Shaanxi zouxiang 21 shiji de zhanlüe sikao', Part 1, p. 5.

43 Shaanxi Statistical Bureau, *Tongji Yu Shehui*, No. 1, 1996, p. 47.

44 Wang Ziyi, 'Shaanxi quanmin qiye gaige mubiao moshi tantao' [A discussion of the target model for the reform of enterprises owned by the whole people in Shaanxi], *Shaanxi Shifan Daxue Xuebao (Zhexue Shehui Kexue Ban)* [Journal of Shaanxi Normal University (Social Science)], No. 3, 1989, p. 40.

45 Ibid. The central enterprises also had over half of enterprise fixed assets, He Jinming (ed.), *Shaanxi xian qing* [The Counties of Shaanxi], Xi'an: Shaanxi renmin chubanshe, 1985, p. 1051.

46 Research Team for the Social and Economic Development Strategy for Shaanxi 1996–2010, 'Shaanxi zouxiang 21 shiji de zhanlüe sikao', Part 1, p. 2.

47 Dorothy J. Solinger, 'Despite decentralization: disadvantages, dependence an ongoing central power in the inland – the case of Wuhan'.

48 Ibid., p. 33.
49 Zhao Bingzhang and Zhang Baotong, *Shaanxi jingji fazhan zhanlüe zonglun*, p. 320 point out that in 1980 some 67 counties were in deficit and by 1983 this had grown to 72. The number of counties has varied over time with administrative reorganisation but is generally around 105–108, including county-level cities.
50 Kevin P. Lane, 'One step behind: Shaanxi in reform'.
51 The following discussion is based on interviews with a number of officials and economists in the province in June–July 1996, on Zhao Bingzhang and Zhang Baotong, *Shaanxi jingji fazhan zhanlüe zonglun*, and on sources such as the *Shaanxi nianjian* for various years.
52 Kevin P. Lane, 'One step behind: Shaanxi in reform', cites considerable evidence to show the slowness with which officials throughout Shaanxi moved from the left policies and perspectives of the Cultural Revolution. He also provides a detailed discussion of the conservative character of the Shaanxi leadership at most levels during the reform period.
53 The *Shaanxi nianjian* 1990, p. 130 reports that in 1989 a trend to negate township and village enterprises arose but that this was overcome by a series of reports and speeches by provincial leaders.
54 This was the case at the model Fenghuo Brigade in Liquan County which was visited in October 1981 and was then opposing household contracting. See the discussion in Andrew Watson, 'Agriculture looks for "shoes that fit": the production responsibility system and its implication', *World Development*, Vol. 11, No. 8, August 1983. Kevin P. Lane, 'One step behind: Shaanxi in reform', also cites evidence to indicate that Shaanxi did not move positively towards household contracting until after 1982.
55 CCP Central Secretariat, *Zhongguo nongcun shehui jingji dianxing diaocha*, [Typical Surveys of Rural Social and Economic Development in China], Beijing: Zhongguo shehui kexue chubanshe, 1988, pp. 418–437. A fuller version of this report and its supplementary materials can be found in Shaanxi Rural Policy Research Office, *Shaanxisheng nongcun shehui jingji diaocha* [Shaanxi Rural Economic and Social Surveys], Xi'an: Shaanxi renmin chubanshe, 1986.
56 The strategy was proclaimed in a series of speeches by the provincial party secretary, Zhang Boxing, (see, for example, 'Jin yi bu jiefang sixiang, da dan gaige kaifang, nuli jiakuai wo sheng shehuizhuyi xiandaihua jianshe de bufa' [Further emancipate thinking, be bold in reform and opening up, strive to accelerate our steps in socialist modern construction], 29 April 1988, printed in *Shaanxi Ribao*, 7 May 1988 and reprinted in *Shaanxi nianjian 1989*, Xi'an: Shaanxi renmin chubanshe, 1989 pp. 1–14), and by the provincial governor, Hou Zongbing (see, for example, 'Zhengfu gongzuo baogao' [Government work report], 18 May 1988, in *Shaanxi nianjian 1988*, Xi'an: Shaanxi renmin chubanshe, 1988, pp. 1–13). It is outlined as 'Shaanxisheng jingji he shehui fazhan zhanlüe gangyao 1988 – 2000' [Outline of Shaanxi Economic and Social Development Strategy, 1988 – 2000], *Shaanxi nianjian 1989*, pp. 24–28, and elaborated in Zhao Bingzhang and Zhang Baotong, *Shaanxi jingji fazhan zhanlüe zonglun*.
57 Shaanxi Planning Commission, *Kua shiji de hongwei lantu: 1996–2010* [The Great Blueprint for the Next Century: 1996–2010], Xi'an: Shaanxi renmin chubanshe, 1996, p. 7.
58 'Outline of the ten-year programme and the Eighth Five Year Plan', *Renmin Ribao* [People's Daily], 16 April 1991. See *Summary of World Broadcasts, Part 3, Asia-Pacific*, FE/1058/C1/1–29, 29 April 1991.
59 State Council's 'Outline for State Industrial Policy in the 1990s', 25 March 1994, English version made public in June 1994. See *Summary of World Broadcasts, Asia-Pacific*, FE/2033/S1/1, 28 June 1994.
60 Research Team for the Social and Economic Development Strategy for Shaanxi 1996–2010, 'Shaanxi zouxiang 21 shiji de zhanlüe sikao', Part 1, pp. 1–2.
61 Cheng Andong, 'Cheng Andong shengzhang tan Shaanxi jingji fazhan wenti'.

62 According to the *Zhongguo tongji nianjian 1995*, p. 600, Shaanxi's realised foreign investment in 1995 was US$392.44, a rise of 59 per cent over 1994. National growth in the same period was only just over 11 per cent.

63 Shaanxi Planning Commission, *Kua shiji de hongwei lantu: 1996–2010* [The Great Blueprint for the Next Century: 1996–2010], Xi'an: Shaanxi renmin chubanshe, 1996.

64 Ibid., pp. 70–73.

65 For an analysis of regional disparities in rural incomes see Scott Rozelle, 'Stagnation without equity: patterns of growth and inequality in rural China's rural economy', *The China Journal*, No. 35, January 1996, pp. 63–92. Though not the worst performer, Shaanxi's peasant income growth was among the slow growth group of provinces.

66 For an analysis of the differences between coastal and interior TVE development, see Andrew Watson and Harry X. Wu , 'Regional disparities in rural enterprise growth', in Christopher Findlay, Andrew Watson and Harry Wu (eds), *Rural Enterprises in China*, London: Macmillan, 1994, pp. 69–92.

67 Interview, 19 June 1996.

68 Kevin P. Lane, 'One step behind: Shaanxi in reform'.

69 Chen Jiazhen, Pu Zhijin and Li Shousheng , 'Shaanxi jingji zai yanhai fazhan zhanlüe zhong de xuanze' [The choices for the Shaanxi economy under the coastal development strategy], *Shaanxi Ribao* [Shaanxi Daily], 3 June 1988, p. 2.

70 Cheng Andong, 'Cheng Andong shengzhang tan Shaanxi jingji fazhan wenti'.

71 Research Team for the Social and Economic Development Strategy for Shaanxi 1996–2010, 'Shaanxi zouxiang 21 shiji de zhanlüe sikao', Part 2, *Renwen Zazhi* [The Journal of Humanities], No. 5, 1995, pp. 40–41.

72 Ibid., pp. 42–43 reports that 18 counties out of the total of 23 in Yan'an and Yulin Prefectures in Shaanbei are poor counties and that the three prefectures of Hanzhong, Ankang and Shangluo in Shaannan have over half of the province's five million poor.

73 The following discussion is based on interviews with local officials carried out in June 1996. The developmental problems of the region are explored in Jiao Xingguo (ed.), *Baituo pinkun de tansuo: Shaan-nan Qin-Ba shanqu tuopin kaifa yanjiu* [An Exploration of Breaking Free from Poverty: Research into Poverty Alleviation and Development in the Qin-Ba Mountain Area of Southern Shaanxi], Xi'an: Shaanxi renmin jiaoyu chubanshe, 1991. Extensive additional information on Ankang can be found in Kang Suinian, *Quyu jingji yanjiu wenji* [Essays on Regional Economy], Xi'an: Shaanxi renmin chubanshe, 1994.

74 In the late 1970s the central government designated it as one of the ten poorest regions in the country. Zhao Bingzhang and Zhang Baotong , *Shaanxi jingji fazhan zhanlüe zonglun*, p. 252.

75 Research Team for the Social and Economic Development Strategy for Shaanxi 1996–2010, 'Shaanxi zouxiang 21 shiji de zhanlüe sikao', Part 2, p. 43.

76 He Jinming (ed.), *Shaanxi xian qing* [The Counties of Shaanxi], Xi'an: Shaanxi renmin chubanshe, 1986, pp. 531–532.

77 Research Team for the Social and Economic Development Strategy for Shaanxi 1996–2010, 'Shaanxi zouxiang 21 shiji de zhanlüe sikao', Part 2, p. 43, Zhao Bingzhang and Zhang Baotong, *Shaanxi jingji fazhan zhanlüe zonglun*, pp. 254–56, and Xu Shanlin, 'Zhuazhu lishi jiyu, jiakuai Shaannan jingji kaifa [Grasp the historical opportunity, accelerate the development of Shaannan], *Shaanxi Ribao*, 14 June 1992, p. 2.

78 Kang Suinian, *Quyu jingji yanjiu wenji*, p. 20.

79 Interview, Ankang, 24 June 1996.

80 Xu Shanlin, 'Zhuazhu lishi jiyu, jiakuai Shaannan jingji kaifa', p. 2.

81 For a general discussion of this idea see Kang Suinian, *Quyu jingji yanjiu wenji*, pp. 12–19.

82 See, for example, Cheng Andong, 'Guanyu zhiding Shaanxi sheng guomin jingji he shehui fazhan "jiu-wu" jihua he 2010 nian yuanjing mubiao jianyi de shuoming' [On

the drawing up of the Ninth Five Year Plan for the economic and social development of Shaanxi Province and the long-term targets for the year 2010], *Shaanxi Ribao*, 14 November 1995, pp. 1–2 and Shaanxi Planning Commission, *Kua shiji de hongwei lantu: 1996–2010* [The Great Blueprint for the Next Century: 1996–2010], Xi'an: Shaanxi renmin chubanshe, 1996, p. 97.

83 Research Team for the Shaanxi 1996–2010 Social and Economic Development Strategy, 'Shaanxi zouxiang 21 shiji de zhanlüe sikao', Part 2, pp. 43–44.

84 Interview, Ankang, 24 June 1996.

85 The following discussion is based on interviews carried out in Yulin from 28 June to 1 July 1996. A major source of historical detail can be found in Yulin Prefecture Gazetteer Editorial Group, *Yulin diqu zhi* [Yulin Prefecture Gazetteer], Xi'an: Xibei daxue chubanshe, 1994.

86 Shaanxi Planning Commission, *Kua shiji de hongwei lantu: 1996–2010* [The Great Blueprint for the Next Century: 1996–2010], Xi'an: Shaanxi renmin chubanshe, 1996. pp. 96–97.

87 Yang Qiubao, 'Xibei ziyuan fuji qu de jingji kaifa zhanlüe' [The strategy for the economic development of the resource-rich areas in the northwest], *Shaanxi Shifan Daxue Xuebao (Zhexue Shehui Kexue Ban)* [Journal of Shaanxi Normal University (Social Science)], Vol. 25, No. 2, June 1996, p. 25.

88 Interview, Daliuta, 29 June 1996.

REFERENCES

Ankang City Local Gazetteer Editorial Committee, *Ankang xian zhi* [Ankang County Gazetteer], Xi'an: Shaanxi renmin chubanshe, 1989.

CCP Shaanxi Provincial Committee Research Office, Shaanxi Academy of Social Sciences and the Shaanxi Social Sciences Association, *Shaan qing yaolan* [An Outline of Shaanxi], Xi'an: Shaanxi renmin chubanshe, 1986.

Chen Mingrong, *Qinling de qihou yu nongye* [The Climate and Agriculture of the Qinling Mountains], Xi'an: Shaanxi renmin chubanshe, 1988.

Editorial Group, *Shaanxi nongye jiegou 1949–1986* [The Agricultural Structure of Shaanxi, 1949–1986], Beijing: Zhongguo tongji chubanshe, 1987.

He Jinming (ed.), *Shaanxi xian qing* [The Counties of Shaanxi], Xi'an: Shaanxi renmin chubanshe, 1986.

Jiao Xingguo (ed.), *Baituo pinkun de tansuo: Shaan-nan Qin-Ba shanqu tuopin kaifa yanjiu* [An Exploration of Breaking Free from Poverty: Research into Poverty Alleviation and Development in the Qin-Ba Mountain Area of Southern Shaanxi], Xi'an: Shaanxi renmin jiaoyu chubanshe, 1991.

Kang Suinian, *Quyu jingji yanjiu wenji* [Essays on Regional Economy], Xi'an: Shaanxi renmin chubanshe, 1994.

Lane, Kevin P, 'One step behind: Shaanxi in reform', in Peter T.Y. Cheung, Jae-ho Chung and Zhimin Lin (eds), *Provincial Strategies of Economic Reform in Post-Mao China: Leadership, Politics and Implementation*, Armonk, NY: M.E. Sharpe, 1998.

Northwest University Geography Department, *Shaanxi nongye dili* [The Agricultural Geography of Shaanxi], Xi'an: Shaanxi renmin chubanshe, 1977.

Research Team for the Social and Economic Development Strategy for Shaanxi 1996–2010, 'Shaanxi zouxiang 21 shiji de zhanlüe sikao' [Strategic thinking for Shaanxi for the 21st century], Part 1, *Renwen Zazhi* [The Journal of Humanities], No. 4, 1995, pp. 1–8 and Part 2, No. 5, 1995, pp. 40–46 and 69.

Shaanxi nianjian, Xi'an: Shaanxi renmin chubanshe, various years.

Shaanxi Normal University Geography Department, *Shaanxi sheng Ankang diqu dilizhi* [The Geography of Ankang Prefecture, Shaanxi Province], Xi'an: Shaanxi renmin chubanshe, 1986.

—— , *Shaanxi sheng Yulin diqu dilizhi* [The Geography of Yulin Prefecture, Shaanxi Province], Xi'an: Shaanxi renmin chubanshe, 1987.

—— , *Shaanxi sheng weinan diqu dilizhi* [The Geography of Weinan Prefecture, Shaanxi Province], Xi'an: Shaanxi renmin chubanshe, 1990.

Shaanxi Planning Commission, *Kua shiji de hongwei lantu: 1996–2010* [The Great Blueprint for the Next Century: 1996–2010], Xi'an: Shaanxi renmin chubanshe, 1996.

Shaanxi Province Gazetteer Editorial Committee, *Shaanxi shengzhi* [Shaanxi Province Gazetteer], Xi'an: Shaanxi renmin chubanshe, many volumes in progress.

Shaanxi Rural Policy Research Office, *Shaanxisheng nongcun shehui jingji diaocha* [Shaanxi Rural Economic and Social Surveys], Xi'an: Shaanxi renmin chubanshe, 1986.

Shaanxi Statistical Bureau, *Shaanxi tongji nianjian* [Shaanxi Statistical Yearbook], Beijing: Zhongguo tongji chubanshe, various years.

Wang Yongyan (ed.), *Zhongguo huangtu* [Loess in China], Xi'an: Shaanxi renmin chubanshe, 1980.

Yan'an Prefecture Statistical Gazetteer Editorial group, *Yan'an diqu tongji zhi* [Yan'an Prefecture Statistical Gazetteer], Beijing: Zhongguo tongji chubanshe, 1995.

Yulin Prefecture Gazetteer Editorial Group, *Yulin diqu zhi* [Yulin Prefecture Gazetteer], Xi'an: Xibei daxue chubanshe, 1994.

Zhao Bingzhang and Zhang Baotong, *Shaanxi jingji fazhan zhanlüe zonglun*, [A Comprehensive Strategy for Shaanxi's Economic Development], Xi'an: Sanqin chubanshe, 1988.

Zhu Chuzhu (ed.), *Zhongguo renkou: Shaanxi fence* [The Chinese Population: Shaanxi Volume], Beijing: Zhongguo caizheng jingji chubanshe, 1988.

Jiangsu Province

GENERAL

GDP (billion *yuan*)	600.40
GDP annual growth rate	12.20
as % national average	127.10
GDP per capita	8,444.70
as % national average	150.70
Gross Value Agricultural Output (billion *yuan*)	182.40
Gross Value Industrial Output (billion *yuan*)	1,155.60

POPULATION

Population (million)	71.10
Natural growth rate (per 1,000)	12.10

WORKFORCE

Total workforce (million)	37.50
Employment by activity (%)	
primary industry	41.60
secondary industry	33.30
tertiary industry	25.20
Employment by sector (%)	
urban	26.40
rural	73.60
Employment by ownership (%)	
state	15.47
collective	31.20
private	7.20
foreign-funded	1.10

WAGES AND INCOME

Average annual wage (*yuan*)	6,603.00
Growth rate in real wage	0.30
Urban disposable income per capita	5,185.79
as % national average	107.20
Rural per capita income	3,029.32
as % national average	157.30

PRICES

CPI annual rise (%)	9.30
Service price index rise	12.30
Per capita consumption (*yuan*)	1,557.00
as % national average	95.50

FOREIGN TRADE AND INVESTMENT

Total foreign trade (US$ billion)	20.70
as % provincial GDP	28.70
Exports (US$ billion)	11.60
Imports (US$ billion)	9.10
Realised foreign capital (US$ billion)	5.50
as % provincial GDP	7.60

EDUCATION

University enrolments	220,575.00
as % national average	125.70
Secondary school enrolments (million)	3.24
as % national average	97.00
Primary school enrolments (million)	6.88
as % national average	87.00

Notes: All statistics are for 1996 and all growth rates are for 1996 over 1995 and are adapted from *Zhongguo tongji nianjian 1997* [Statistical Yearbook of China 1997], Zhongguo tongji chubanshe, Beijing, 1997, as reformulated and presented in *Provincial China* no. 5, May 1998, pp. 68ff.

Jiangsu Province

Shandong

□ Xuzhou

□ Lianyungang

Hongze Lake
□ Huaiyin

Yellow Sea

□ Yancheng

Anhui

Nanjing □ Yangzhou

□ Zhenjiang

Yangtze River

Changzhou □

□ Nantong

□ Wuxi

Shanghai

□ Suzhou

Lake Tai

Zhejiang

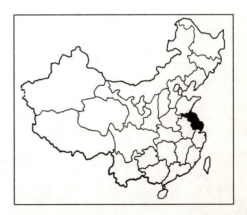

4 Uneven development:

prosperity and poverty in Jiangsu

J. Bruce Jacobs

Jiangsu is unquestionably one of China's most important provinces. With the fourth largest provincial population, Jiangsu is China's leading province in both agriculture and industry[1] as well as a key provider of human resources for the nation. Yet summary descriptions mask significant regional variegation within the province. Wealthy southern Jiangsu, the home of the famous 'Sunan [Southern Jiangsu] model' of Township and Village Enterprises (TVEs), is one of China's richest regions – an area where reform has taken root. Leaders in northern Jiangsu, an area of considerable poverty, have found it difficult to implement reform. This regional disparity within Jiangsu, which concerns Jiangsu's provincial leadership, forms an underlying theme of this chapter.

The chapter begins with an examination of Jiangsu's economic history and administrative evolution as a province. A section on the province's geography is followed by an analysis of the province's regions. The chapter then examines the origins of the 'Sunan Model', a key element leading to Sunan's development as one of China's wealthiest regions. After analysing the reasons for the disparities between North and South Jiangsu, the chapter explores Jiangsu's economic modernisation and the province's economic development strategies. This section concludes with a detailed look at the province's poverty alleviation strategies as outlined in a recent provincial party document. The final section considers political dimensions, including the province's status as a 'cash cow' for the centre, Jiangsu's weakness at the provincial level, and the conservatism of the provincial leadership.

ECONOMIC HISTORY AND ADMINISTRATIVE EVOLUTION

The development of the Lower Yangtze Valley – the heartland of modern Jiangsu Province – into a 'Key Economic Area' of China took several centuries. The great Former Han historian, Sima Qian (145–90? BC), wrote that the Lower Yangtze Valley was a

> large territory sparsely populated, where people eat rice and drink fish soup, where land is tilled with fire and hoed with water [i.e. slash and burn

cultivation]; where people collect fruits and shellfish for food; where people enjoy self-sufficiency without commerce. The place is fertile and suffers no famine and hunger. Hence the people are lazy and poor and do not bother to accumulate wealth. Hence, in the south of the Yangtse and the Hwai [Huai], there are neither hungry nor frozen people, nor a family which owns a thousand gold.[2]

The development of the Lower Yangtze Valley only began following the collapse of the Latter Han in AD 220. In the intervening 360 years of political division between the fall of the Han and the establishment of the Sui Dynasty (581–617), many northerners fled war and chaos in their homelands and settled in the comparatively peaceful Lower Yangtze Valley.[3] These emigrés looked condescendingly on the native southerners but, as non-Han 'barbarians' continued to control the North for centuries, the northern emigrés gradually assimilated.[4] In 609, southern Chinese provinces accounted for only 12.4 per cent of the registered Chinese population.[5] Yet, the vast quantity of resources devoted during the Sui Dynasty to building the Grand Canal – an infrastructure project still important in contemporary Jiangsu – shows the growing importance of Lower Yangtze wealth to the political centre in North China.

The civil wars following the collapse of the Sui Dynasty and the founding of the Tang Dynasty (618–906) led to further migration south. By 742 – after just 133 years – the proportion of the registered population living in southern China had more than doubled to 27.7 per cent.[6] The great mid-Tang Dynasty rebellion of An Lushan (755–763) created another massive migration from North to South.[7] By about 800 the Lower Yangtze Valley paid 90 per cent of the total land tax[8] and by the eleventh century southern China had 'well over half the entire Chinese population'.[9] The collapse of the Northern Song (960–1127) and establishment of the Southern Song (1127–1279), with its capital in Hangzhou, led to another important migration from north to south.[10] Without doubt, the Lower Yangtze Valley was the 'Key Economic Area' of China during the Yuan (1280–1368), Ming (1368–1644) and Qing (1644–1911) dynasties.[11]

Jiangsu only became a province in 1667. Before then, the current territory of Jiangsu Province was usually divided into different administrative units.[12] In the Tang, Song and Yuan dynasties, northern Jiangsu belonged to northern administrative units while southern Jiangsu belonged to southern administrative units.[13] During the Ming, the whole of Jiangsu belonged to Nan Zhili.[14] In 1645, the newly ascendant Qing established Jiangnan Province which included both Jiangsu and Anhui. A series of administrative changes culminated with the establishment of Jiangsu Province in 1667 with the provincial capital in Suzhou, where it remained until the end of the dynasty, while the Governor-General over Jiangsu and Anhui provinces was located in Nanjing.[15]

In April 1927, the Nationalists established their national capital in Nanjing. The following year they made Nanjing and Shanghai special municipalities, thus detaching them from Jiangsu Province. Zhenjiang became the provincial capital[16] because it was easier to control, being close to Nanjing, and because it was accessible to areas north of the Yangtze River. Suzhou was too far south, though the puppet government of Wang Jingwei established its provincial government there.[17]

After the Communists liberated Nanjing on 23 April 1949, Nanjing remained a centrally administered (i.e. provincial-level) municipality. Except for Xuzhou and Lianyungang, which temporarily became part of Shandong, the rest of Jiangsu was divided into two administrative offices.[18] The Northern Jiangsu (Subei) Administrative Office, established on 21 April 1949, had its headquarters in Taizhou. The Southern Jiangsu (Sunan) Administrative Office, established on 26 April 1949, was located in Wuxi, an industrial city located near the geographic centre of the administrative area. This two-fold division occurred because northern Jiangsu was liberated considerably earlier than southern Jiangsu and the leaders of the two areas faced different problems.[19]

The Communists re-established Jiangsu Province in 1953. In 1954 and 1955 two Anhui counties were restored to Jiangsu while two Jiangsu counties were returned to Anhui. In 1958 ten Jiangsu counties were shifted to Shanghai Municipality. In 1983 Jiangsu abolished prefectures and fully implemented a system of prefectural 'municipalities managing counties'. Following the 1983 reform, Jiangsu had 11 prefectural municipalities and 64 counties and county-level municipalities,[20] a situation which persisted until mid-1996.

The system of municipalities managing counties received its major impetus in Liaoning during the late 1950s. This owed to Liaoning's strong industrial base and the relative development of its urban economy.[21] In 1959 and 1963, Liaoning was the only mainland province without prefectures,[22] though by 1977 Liaoning had three prefectures and still had two prefectures in 1983 when Jiangsu abolished the unit.[23] The Liaoning case had, however, proved 'this structure could be feasibly implemented in economically developed prefectures'.[24]

In his report on the Sixth Five-Year Plan (1981–1985), Premier Zhao Ziyang noted:

> We must take cities which are comparatively well-developed economically as centres to pull along the surrounding countryside, to organise production and circulation in a unified way, and to gradually form economic districts of various sizes and various types which rely on cities.[25]

In 1982 the Party Central Committee and the State Council issued a notice on reforming prefectures and at the end of the year Jiangsu became the first 'experimental point'.[26]

Jiangsu provincial leaders responded quickly. In early 1983 First Party Secretary Xu Jiatun went to Liaoning and another Party Secretary visited Zhejiang to examine the situations in those provinces. The provincial party committee and government prepared a document for the Party Central Committee and the State Council and in March 1983, with State Council approval, Jiangsu abolished its prefectures and completely implemented a system of prefectural-level municipalities. The province, which had had seven prefectures and seven prefectural-level municipalities from 1971,[27] thus reduced its prefectural-level units from 14 to 11.

This system was supposed to enable wealthier urban areas to assist poorer rural areas. Politically, it provided an additional level of people's congresses which prefectural municipalities, unlike prefectures, have. However, the changes were not without negative consequences. First, because prefectures did not own enterprises, counties controlled industries. With the change, prefectural municipalities often established enterprises in urban districts, so counties often felt they did less well under the new system. Second, municipalities without counties did not have expertise in handling agriculture. After becoming prefectural municipalities, they often did not manage the new rural areas under their jurisdiction well. Over time, this problem has been resolved.

Third, some new prefectural municipalities lacked the economic power to 'pull along the surrounding countryside'. Prior to the 1983 change, Yangzhou and Taizhou had equal administrative status under Yangzhou Prefecture as well as similar economic strength. After the change, Yangzhou gained prefectural status while Taizhou became a subordinate county-level municipality under Yangzhou. In the words of Fei Xiaotong, this created a problem of 'non-adaptability between administrative and economic divisions'. Yangzhou, despite its administrative superiority, could not 'pull' Taizhou economically, thus creating a situation in which a 'small horse pulls a big cart'.[28]

From 1983 to mid-1996, Jiangsu had 11 prefectural municipalities which, in addition to urban districts and suburban districts, contained 64 counties and county-level municipalities. As can be seen from Table 4.1[29], the span of the prefectural municipalities varied considerably. The larger cities, with more urban and suburban districts, are either south of the river or in the far north.

Until 1996, with two exceptions, all of the prefectural municipalities managed three to seven county-level units. The two exceptions, Huaiyin and Yangzhou, controlled 11 and ten county-level units respectively. According to a Huaiyin Municipal Government source, these numbers were too difficult for the prefectural municipality to manage, especially in terms of economic development. Accordingly, in mid-1996, Huaiyin and Yangzhou were divided. Huaiyin retained six of the county units while the new prefectural municipality, Suqian, gained four. (Guannan County was transferred to Lianyungang, which now has four county-level units.) Taizhou also gained prefectural status and controls four of the county units originally in Yangzhou. This should help solve the problem of 'non-adaptability between administrative and economic divisions', discussed above, which Fei Xiaotong raised in 1984, the year following the implementation of the prefectural municipality system.[30]

According to a Jiangsu authority, Premier Li Peng approved the division of Huaiyin and Yangzhou because the new total of 13 prefectural units was still less than the 14 units which had existed before 1983. Proposals to split Yancheng and Xuzhou were therefore not approved. Many localities wish to increase their status and the centre wanted to forestall applications from other provinces.

Table 4.1 Administrative structure of Jiangsu prefectural municipalities, 1983–1996, 1996–

Prefectural municipality	Urban district	Suburban district	Total districts	County-level municipalities	Counties	Total county-level units
1983–1996						
Nanjing	10		10		5	5
Wuxi	5		5	2	1	3
Xuzhou	5		5	2	4	6
Changzhou	3	1	4	2	1	3
Suzhou	3	1	4	5	1	6
Nantong	2		2	4	2	6
Lianyungang	4		4		3	3
Huaiyin	2		2	2	9	11
Yancheng	1	1	2	1	6	7
Yangzhou	1	1	2	8	2	10
Zhenjiang	2		2	2	2	4
TOTAL	38	4	42	28	36	64
1996–						
Nanjing	10		10		5	5
Wuxi	5		5	2	1	3
Xuzhou	5		5	2	4	6
Changzhou	3	1	4	2	1	3
Suzhou	3	1	4	5	1	6
Nantong	2		2	4	2	6
Lianyungang	4		4		4	4
Huaiyin	2		2	1	5	6
Suqian	1		1		4	4
Yancheng	1		1	1	7	8
Yangzhou	1	1	2	3	2	5
Taizhou	1		1	4		4
Zhenjiang	2		2	2	2	4
TOTAL	40	3	43	26	38	64

Sources: Calculated from *Jiangsu tongji nianjian 1996*, p. 9; *Xinhua ribao*, 12 August 1996, p. 1

Two other changes occurred in the mid-1996 revisions. First, the former Suqian county-level municipality was divided into an urban district and a new county, Suyu. Second, taking account of long-requested appeals, the Yancheng Suburban District was restored to its former status as Yancheng County.[31] Because most of the fieldwork was conducted prior to the official announcement of the 1996 divisions, and statistical sources at the time of writing still had not divided Huaiyin and Yangzhou prefectural municipalities, statistical data in this chapter do not reflect the mid-1996 adjustments.[32]

Four of the 13 prefectural municipalities are south of the Yangtze River (from east to west): Suzhou, Wuxi, Changzhou and Zhenjiang. The city of Nanjing, to the west of Zhenjiang, is on the south bank of the Yangtze River, but the prefectural municipality of Nanjing has counties on both banks. Eight of the prefectural municipalities are north of the Yangtze. Nantong is across the Yangtze from Shanghai and Suzhou. Taizhou is to the west of Nantong and Yangzhou is further west. Yancheng is on the coast north of Nantong while

Huaiyin is west of Yancheng. Suqian is northwest of Huaiyin. The northernmost prefectural municipalities are Lianyungang on the coast and Xuzhou in the north-westernmost portion of Jiangsu.

A majority of the county-level units in the southeastern prefectural munici-palities and in Yangzhou, Taizhou and Nantong have been granted municipal status, indicating a greater degree of urbanisation (Table 4.1). Counties must meet three conditions to be eligible for upgrading to county municipality status: (1) a permanent population of 100,000; (2) a GDP of 100 million *yuan* in the county seat; and (3) a total county GDP of 3,000 million *yuan*. Counties wish to receive municipal status for four very concrete reasons. First, higher levels give county-level municipalities favourable tax treatment. A county only retains 3 per cent of its fiscal revenues for local construction while a county-level municipality retains 8 per cent. This is because a 'city' requires more facilities, such as better roads and parks. Second, county-level municipalities, with 'vice-prefectural status', are half a grade higher than counties in the administrative system. This gives all cadres in a county-level municipality higher status and higher pay. Third, Chinese trademarks require the place name as part of the brand name. Consumers believe a product originating from a city is better than one from a rural area, so municipal status helps sell local products.[33] Finally, county-level municipalities, unlike counties, become a line-item in the provincial budget and gain direct access to provincial authorities.[34] For these reasons, many counties apply for municipal status. The centre has a quota for each province. Many counties in central and western China, which barely meet the criteria, receive municipal status, but elevation in Jiangsu is more difficult owing to the quota.[35]

GEOGRAPHY

Located on the Yellow Sea in the middle of China's Pacific coastline, north of Shanghai and Zhejiang, east of Anhui and south of Shandong, Jiangsu with an area of 102,600 square kilometres accounts for about 1 per cent of China's total area. Ranked twenty-fourth in size, Jiangsu is one of the PRC's smallest provinces – larger only than Zhejiang, Ningxia and Hainan. In 1995, Jiangsu had a population of 70,660,200 million – 5.8 per cent of China's population – ranking fourth behind only Sichuan, Henan and Shandong. With 689 persons per square kilometre – more than five times the national average – Jiangsu has China's highest provincial population density. The population is overwhelmingly Han, with non-Han accounting for only 0.2 per cent.[36]

Among China's provinces, Jiangsu ranks first in the proportion of its area in plains and in water. Hills account for only 14.3 per cent of area, the lowest proportion in China. Most of the hills are located in the northeastern and south-western parts of the province. Plains account for 68.8 per cent of area. Jiangsu has four major plains: the Huang-Huai or Huaibei between the Yellow and Huai rivers, the Jiang-Huai between the Yangtze and Huai rivers, the coastal plain and the Yangtze Delta.[37]

Fresh water covers 16.9 per cent of Jiangsu's area and the province contains 10.43 per cent of China's fresh-water surface area[38] The province has 290 lakes, which include Hongze Lake and Lake Tai, China's third and fourth largest, as well as 2,100 rivers and canals.[39] Water transport is important to Jiangsu's economic development. The Yangtze River, one of the world's largest and economically most important rivers, flows west to east through southern Jiangsu. The Grand Canal, which totals 690 kilometres in Jiangsu, provides an important north–south transport route within the province. Smaller rivers and canals provide a network of water routes in many parts of the province.[40] In his classic 1930s study of Kaixiangong, a village in southeastern Jiangsu near Lake Tai, Fei Xiaotong describes the importance of 'agent boats which offer [villagers] a free daily service to purchase necessities from the town and [who] derive their income from acting as selling agents'.[41] Unlike many parts of China, south-eastern Jiangsu lacked periodic markets because the water-transport networks obviated the need.[42]

Jiangsu has considerable arable land, about 69 million mu. This accounts for 4.7 per cent of China's total arable land and covers 45.1 per cent of Jiangsu's total area. Irrigated fields account for 63 per cent of the arable land with the remainder consisting of dry fields. Forests account for only 5 per cent of Jiangsu's area, while the scattered pastoral lands account for even less.[43] These resources in arable land and water have enabled Jiangsu to have China's highest provincial agricultural product and second highest provincial product of agriculture, forestry, animal husbandry and fishing after Shandong.[44] (In recent years Jiangsu has surpassed Sichuan and Guangdong.)

Jiangsu also has an important, expanding land resource in its tidal flats. The Pacific Warm Current picks up silt from the Yangtze River which it deposits on the Nantong and Yancheng coasts. A written source says this land already totals 5,250,000 mu on the mainland with a total 7,200,000 mu including offshore sand shoals. In Yancheng prefectural municipality, where this process creates 50,000 mu of new land annually, the tidal lands total 6,800,000 mu. The land is dyked and used initially to grow sea grass, to graze goats and to build fish ponds. After two or three years it is suitable for growing cotton or rice.[45] One of China's first modern entrepreneurs, Zhang Jian (1853–1926), became involved in such land reclamation in 1900.[46]

Although Jiangsu has some important mineral deposits, it clearly lacks sufficient resources for its industry. Coal, located primarily around Xuzhou in the northwest is the chief energy source, though petroleum and natural gas have also been discovered. Metals include iron reserves of 600 million tonnes as well as some lead, zinc, silver, copper and manganese. Non-metals produced include limestone, quartzite, marble, granite, diamonds, salt, kaolin and clays.[47] Having its sources of energy and raw materials as well as its markets external to the province, Jiangsu has specialised in industrial processing and 'learned comparatively early how to use the methods of market adjustment to solve the contradictions between production, supply and marketing'.[48] Even with its lack of resources, Jiangsu ranks first among China's provincial-level units in industrial production with industrial value almost 24 per cent greater than Guangdong, the second-ranking province.[49]

THE REGIONS OF JIANGSU

The uneven development of Jiangsu becomes clear with a few statistics presented in a recent analysis of Jiangsu development. The most prosperous southeastern section (Suzhou, Wuxi, Changzhou) only has 19 per cent of the province's population and 17 per cent of the province's area, yet produces 41 per cent of the provincial GDP. On the other hand, the poorer northern region (Huaiyin, Suqian, Yancheng, Xuzhou and Lianyungang) has 44 per cent of the province's population, 51 per cent of its area, and yet produces only 19 per cent of its GDP. Furthermore, the annual growth rate of the southeastern region was 43.2 per cent, while the northern region grew only at the rate of 16.8 per cent.[50]

Any analysis of Jiangsu development clearly requires attention to regions within Jiangsu, but considerable debate exists concerning what in fact constitutes coherent regions within the province. Most simply, Jiangsu has been divided into two regions, north and south of the Yangtze River. This division has historical origins and the terms Jiangbei and Jiangnan have been used for centuries.

The ecological origins of poverty in Jiangbei, to be discussed below, forced many Jiangbei people to migrate to Jiangnan and to Shanghai, where they often undertook menial jobs. In Shanghai, the term 'Jiangbei person' or 'Jiangbei swine' became an epithet. 'Subei', meaning northern Jiangsu, replaced 'Jiangbei', but people of Subei origin continued to face discrimination despite the use of a more politically correct term. From the outside, i.e. in Shanghai, people from Jiangsu north of the Yangtze River could be lumped together, but in fact the circumstances and backgrounds of people from Huaiyin were very different from those of Yangzhou or Nantong.[51] Thus, the term 'Subei' to describe all of Jiangsu north of the Yangtze River is not very useful. Similarly, there is tremendous variation among those areas in Jiangsu south of the Yangtze River.

Another approach to regional analysis in Jiangsu uses the concept of development along transportation lines. Thus, the slogan 'three alongs' (*san yan*) argues development should occur along the Yangtze River, along the coast and along the eastern Longhai railway between Xuzhou and Lianyungang. This last is the eastern portion of the proposed Asia–Europe Continental Land Bridge which has its eastern terminus in the port of Lianyungang.[52] Unfortunately, this scheme omitted Huaiyin, the poorest, most populous and largest in area of Jiangsu's pre-1996 prefectural municipalities.

This 'three alongs' approach has led to an important recent attempt to classify Jiangsu into four 'economic belts' (*jingji dai*), the 'three alongs' plus 'along the Grand Canal'. This scheme ultimately fails because six of Jiangsu's 13 prefectural municipalities belong to two belts and because each belt has huge internal variegation, but we present the scheme both for its heuristic and descriptive value and because 'three alongs' and 'four alongs' gained some official imprimatur as part of provincial economic development strategies in the late 1980s–early 1990s and mid-1990s respectively.[53]

1   *The Yangtze River economic belt* The eight prefectural municipalities (Nanjing, Zhenjiang, Changzhou, Wuxi, Suzhou, Yangzhou, Taizhou and Nantong) in this belt account for 54.8 per cent of the province's population, 47 per cent of its area, and 81 per cent of its GDP. The Yangtze River links the region to Shanghai and the world and to the interior provinces of Anhui, Jiangxi, Hubei, Hunan and Sichuan, and the belt has several ports which together can handle over 100 million tonnes of cargo annually. The economic belt dominates Jiangsu's economy, producing 87 per cent of the provincial industrial product. Yet, with 48 per cent of the province's arable land and with 70 per cent of the labour force in non-agricultural occupations, the belt produces more than half of the province's grain, tea, vegetable oil, aquatic products and silkworm cocoons. The belt has 93 per cent of the province's foreign-invested enterprises. Furthermore, the belt is rich in human resources with 61 institutions of higher learning – 84 per cent of the provincial total, and 131 scientists and technicians for every 10,000 persons.[54]

2   *The Coastal economic belt* This economic belt, consisting of three prefectural municipalities (Nantong, Yancheng and Lianyungang), has 27.5 per cent of the province's population, 29.6 per cent of its area, but only 18 per cent of its GDP. The belt produces 32 per cent of the provincial agricultural product, but only 12 per cent of its industrial product. The region has abundant marine resources and its ports have good potential, but overall the belt's 'economic strength is comparatively weak'.[55]

3   *The Rail Land Bridge economic belt* This belt in the northernmost part of Jiangsu consists of two prefectural municipalities (Xuzhou and Lianyungang) which account for 17 per cent of the province's population and area, but only 10 per cent of its GDP. In addition to having abundant mineral resources, this belt has transportation assets. Xuzhou is known as the 'Thoroughfare of Five Provinces', connecting Jiangsu by rail with southern and southwestern Shandong, eastern Henan and northern Anhui. Lianyungang connects the sea with the continent and Shandong with central Jiangsu. The Asia–Europe Continental Bridge from Lianyungang to Rotterdam will connect to 11 Chinese provinces. With Lianyungang as the 'bridgehead' for the Land Bridge, the economic belt – and Jiangsu as a whole – should benefit.[56]

4   *The Grand Canal economic belt* This economic belt includes six prefectural municipalities (Xuzhou, Huaiyin, Suqian, Yangzhou, Taizhou and Zhenjiang), but excludes Suzhou, Wuxi and Changzhou, which are also along the canal. This belt has 44 per cent of Jiangsu's population and 49 per cent of its area, but only 30.6 per cent of its GDP, 42 per cent of its agricultural product and 23 per cent of its industrial product. Ironically, most

of the advantages mentioned for this belt apply primarily to Xuzhou, Yangzhou, Taizhou and Zhenjiang, which also belong to other economic belts.[57] Poor Huaiyin and Suqian have few of these assets.

Until recently, the Jiangsu leadership divided Jiangsu into two areas, Subei being all areas north of the Yangtze and Sunan all areas to the south. In 1983 the Jiangsu Provincial Party Committee and Provincial Government proclaimed the 'regional economic development strategy' of 'Vigorously improve Sunan, accelerate the development of Subei'.[58] This geographical division along the Yangtze has concerned Chinese scholars. An important contemporary analysis argues that Nantong should be included in Sunan.[59] Fei Xiaotong placed Nantong in Sunan together with Suzhou, Wuxi and Changzhou, but excluded Nanjing and Zhenjiang. However, even though southern Nantong belonged to the Shanghai Economic Region, he felt some concern with this classification because northern Nantong is well beyond Shanghai's influence. Fei proposed a Central Jiangsu (Suzhong) region,[60] and a modification of this has now become policy. The current categorisation overcomes many of these defects. Sunan includes Suzhou, Wuxi, and Changzhou. Subei includes Huaiyin, Suqian, Yancheng, Lianyungang and Xuzhou. Suzhong contains Nanjing, Zhenjiang, Yangzhou, Taizhou and Nantong. This chapter adopts this three-fold regional classification.[61]

Sunan

The Sunan region has several characteristics. Its wealth is based on collectively owned Township and Village Enterprises (TVEs), which provide the basis of the 'Sunan model', discussed below. The region has seven of China's ten most prosperous counties. All three prefectural municipalities unquestionably belong to the 'inner core' of the Shanghai economic region and all three speak languages belonging to the Shanghai (*Wu*) family of languages.

Nanjing and Zhenjiang clearly do not belong to this region. They have not relied on TVEs. Economically, they have lagged far behind the Sunan region and Nanjing has only leapt ahead economically since about 1993–1994. They speak languages belonging to the Mandarin family of languages rather than the Shanghai family. (The linguistic border is at Danyang, in the eastern part of Zhenjiang prefectural municipality.)

The case of Nantong, as mentioned earlier, is more complex. Southern Nantong is in the Shanghai sphere of influence. Furthermore, according to interviews, Nantong has used the TVE model, being second only to Suzhou in the number of TVEs in 1983. Yet, an earlier analysis of Shanghai's economic integration places only Suzhou, Wuxi and Changzhou in the 'inner core'. Nantong as well as Nanjing and Zhenjiang belong to the 'outer core'.[62] Linguistically, the languages of Nantong are very complex and even those areas which speak Shanghai-related languages vary considerably from standard Shanghainese.[63] Substantial parts of Nantong speak Mandarin-based languages. At present transport between Shanghai and Nantong remains inconvenient, normally requiring three and a half hours by car (and ferry), though the hydrofoil has reduced this time to two hours. Nantong is also the main port on the north bank of the Yangtze River. For all these reasons, Nantong is best placed in the Suzhong region.

Suzhong

In some ways the Suzhong region may seem a bit of a residual region, but it does have some coherence. The entire area lies on the Yangtze River. Most parts speak Mandarin-based languages. Large state-owned enterprises have played an important part in the region's economy. While less prosperous than Sunan, the Suzhong region is considerably more urbanised and prosperous than Subei.

Subei

Unlike the Sunan and Suzhong regions which have the valuable Yangtze River, the Subei region is afflicted by the Huai River. Historically, the Subei region was prosperous and more developed than the Suzhong and Sunan regions and even after the Northern Song Dynasty (960–1127) the Huai was an important transportation artery. All this changed in 1194 when the Yellow River shifted south and usurped the bed of the Huai River. The Yellow River, owing to its passage through the loess soil of northern China, has the world's highest silt content. As it deposits silt, its river bed has risen higher than the surrounding plain, thus creating horrendous floods when the dykes have broken. The Yellow River created this problem in Subei by depositing vast amounts of silt in the region.

As a result the Huai River no longer had an exit to the sea. Many lakes were flooded and dykes broken to form the great Hongze (literally 'flooded marshes') Lake. But the Hongze Lake could not contain all of the Huai River's water and more flowed to the Gaoyou region where 36 small lakes became the Lake Gaoyou. From 1400 to 1905, the Huai had 350 major floods.[64] Not surprisingly, these floods created many refugees. The name of a new prefectural municipality reflects this situation – Suqian literally means to 'move house'. In the words of an important economic history of Jiangsu:

> From this we can see that in the history of Subei economic development, 1194 is an unforgettable year. It was Subei's turning point from honour to disgrace and from prosperity to decline. The structure of a progressive Subei and a backward Sunan began to be smashed.[65]

One Subei informant, who called the Yangtze a good, positive river, referred to the Huai as 'destructive'.

The unremittingly flat ecology of the Subei plain strikes a visitor.[66] Hongze Lake, which covers 2069 square kilometres, is only a few metres deep and the lake bed is much higher than the surrounding plain to the east, thus giving rise to the name 'Suspended Lake'. If the dyke burst, Hongze County and much of

Huaiyin prefectural municipality would be flooded. Water flows from Hongze Lake in three rather unsatisfactory ways. First, it can flow north to the New Yi River (along a channel widened in the 1960s) and then east to Lianyungang. Ironically, when there is too much water from Shandong, the water in this channel can flow south as well! Second, it can flow east to the sea through the Subei Irrigation Main Channel, which was constructed in the 1950s across the northern part of Yancheng prefectural municipality. Finally, it can flow south through man-made channels to Lake Gaoyou and the Grand Canal to the Yangtze River. A CCTV programme referred to Huaiyin as 'The Land Floating on Water'. These water resources provide Huaiyin (including Suqian) with potential, but they also present unremitting danger.

Yancheng prefectural municipality to the east of Huaiyin, where the Yellow River also deposited huge amounts of silt, is similarly flat and low. The vast majority of Yancheng has an elevation of less than 5 metres above sea level.[67] Chinese in imperial times referred to the Yancheng area as the bottom of a cauldron – it was difficult to get the water out. Fresh water flooded in from the west while sea water sometimes flooded in from the east. The marshes provided some cover for the Communists during the Anti-Japanese War, and Yancheng became the headquarters of the New Fourth Army on 25 January 1941.

Clearly, these ecological factors have contributed to Subei's poverty. Compared to Sunan and Suzhong, the Subei region has relatively little urbanisation and industrialisation. In Shuyu, a poor county south of Hongze Lake in Huaiyin prefectural municipality, the first industry arrived only in the 1960s when, under Mao Zedong's policy of dispersing industry to the interior, the county obtained six military factories. In contrast to Sunan with its collective ownership, Subei has very little collective ownership; private ownership predominates.[68]

Table 4.2,[69] which gives per capita national income for each prefectural municipality, clearly demonstrates the tripartite regional classification has validity. The three Sunan prefectural municipalities have the highest per capita income while the four Subei prefectural municipalities have the lowest. The four Suzhong prefectural municipalities fall in between.

Table 4.3[70] shows the proportion of non-agricultural population in each prefectural municipality in 1995. Generally, Sunan has the highest proportion of non-agricultural population while Subei has the lowest. Nanjing, the provincial capital and by far Jiangsu's largest urban centre, is the main exception, while Xuzhou and Lianyungang have marginally larger non-agricultural populations than Yangzhou. Overall, however, Sunan has the greatest degree of urbanisation while Subei has the least.

Table 4.4[71] shows GDP by sector. With the exception of Nanjing, the Subei prefectural municipalities have the highest proportion of GDP in the primary sector and the lowest in the secondary industry, while Sunan has the highest proportion in the secondary sector and the lowest in the primary sector. Nanjing's secondary sector fits the regional analysis, but its role as a capital and its high urbanisation mean it has an especially large tertiary sector and a very small primary sector.

Table 4.2 Per capita national income

Region	Prefectural municipality	yuan
Sunan		
	Suzhou	5,677
	Wuxi	6,005
	Changzhou	3,868
Suzhong		
	Nanjing	3,481
	Zhenjiang	3,405
	Yangzhou	2,163
	Nantong	2,044
Subei		
	Huaiyin	1,105
	Yancheng	1,435
	Lianyungang	1,477
	Xuzhou	1,508

Source: *Jiangsu shixian jingji 1993*, pp. 10–12

Table 4.3 Non-agricultural population, 1995

Region	Pref. mun.	Population	Non-ag. pop	% Non-Ag
Sunan		13,357,500	4,675,600	35.00
	Suzhou	5,729,100	1,688,500	29.47
	Wuxi	4,291,900	1,807,700	42.12
	Changzhou	3,336,500	1,179,400	35.35
Suzhong		25,080,400	7,331,500	29.23
	Nanjing	5,217,200	2,590,400	49.65
	Zhenjiang	2,632,700	837,600	31.82
	Yangzhou	9,388,100	1,787,400	19.04
	Nantong	7,842,400	2,116,100	26.98
Subei		30,244,900	5,076,600	16.78
	Huaiyin	10,301,800	1,300,800	12.63
	Yancheng	7,835,300	1,384,200	17.67
	Lianyungang	3,596,300	705,400	19.61
	Xuzhou	8,511,500	1,686,200	19.81
All Jiangsu		68,682,800	17,083,700	24.87

Source: *Jiangsu Statistical Yearbook 1996*, pp. 324–326

Table 4.5[72] shows industrial output by ownership. The collective sector is clearly predominant in Sunan, accounting for over 60 per cent of industrial output. Interestingly, the collective sector also accounts for more than half of industrial output in Zhenjiang, Nantong and Yancheng. Overall, the collective sector is weakest in Subei. The relatively high proportion of state industry in Subei is due to the region's very low industrialisation. Nanjing and Xuzhou, on

Table 4.4 GDP by sector, 1995 (%)

Region	Pref. Mun.	Primary (%)	Secondary (%)	Tertiary (%)
Sunan		7.89	59.88	32.23
	Suzhou	8.90	60.17	30.93
	Wuxi	5.30	59.62	35.08
	Changzhou	10.77	59.68	29.55
Suzhong		14.88	53.50	31.62
	Nanjing	7.61	52.13	40.25
	Zhenjiang	11.76	56.54	31.70
	Yangzhou	16.84	55.92	27.24
	Nantong	23.25	50.19	26.57
Subei		34.28	39.04	26.69
	Huaiyin	43.31	33.39	23.30
	Yancheng	36.91	38.10	24.99
	Lianyungang	38.49	34.53	26.98
	Xuzhou	24.51	45.29	30.20
All Jiangsu		16.52	52.74	30.74

Source: Calculated from *Jiangsu Statistical Yearbook 1996*, pp. 321–323

Table 4.5 Industrial output by ownership, 1995 (%)

Region	Pref. mun.	State	Collective	Private	Jt. stock	Foreign	HK–Taiwan
Sunan		18.52	61.14	0.02	2.54	8.09	7.08
	Suzhou	17.76	60.62	0.02	0.90	10.95	8.09
	Wuxi	16.28	65.04	0.02	3.03	6.83	6.81
	Changzhou	24.62	54.64	0.02	5.24	4.19	5.34
Suzhong		35.71	42.44	0.05	5.47	7.82	6.86
	Nanjing	58.95	24.29	0.08	2.26	8.29	4.35
	Zhenjiang	29.76	56.65	0.01	1.66	6.44	5.12
	Yangzhou	24.78	48.70	0.07	11.36	3.28	9.35
	Nantong	20.16	52.32	0.00	3.66	14.87	7.95
Subei		47.55	43.85	0.12	1.59	3.40	3.16
	Huaiyin	51.16	41.79	0.04	3.06	1.29	2.42
	Yancheng	36.35	55.13	0.30	1.08	3.11	3.72
	Lianyungang	44.47	39.50	0.00	1.49	7.95	5.96
	Xuzhou	56.99	36.22	0.06	1.07	3.37	2.04
All Jiangsu		30.03	50.98	0.05	3.53	7.21	6.35

Source: Calculated from *Jiangsu Statistical Yearbook, 1996*, pp. 345–347

the other hand, have strong state sectors because they are the locations of heavy industry. Yangzhou has relatively large proportions of its industrial output produced by joint stock enterprises and Hong Kong–Taiwan invested enterprises. Some believe the Hong Kong and Taiwan investors have located in Yangzhou because it is President Jiang Zemin's native place. Nantong, the site of a substantial textile industry, has an important foreign invested sector. Explicit private ownership is negligible in the industrial sector.

These tables show the wide variations in wealth and development among the three regions of Jiangsu. These regional differentiations hold over a wide variety of political, social and economic variables, such as per capita fiscal income and expenditure, educational levels, educational facilities, medical facilities, and economic growth rates.

THE 'SUNAN MODEL'

In the context of post-Mao economic reform, many people attribute the wealth of Sunan to the 'Sunan Model' of industrialisation through collectively owned Township and Village Enterprises (TVEs).[73] Despite the promulgation of the 'Sunan model' as a phenomenon of the post-Mao reforms, the development of TVEs has strong roots in the Maoist and even the pre-Communist periods. In his classic 1930s study of a Sunan village, Fei Xiaotong discusses collective silk industry and other enterprises at some length.[74] When Fei revisited the village in 1957, he discovered people were actually poorer than in the 1930s because Communist policies had shifted these industrial activities from villages to towns and cities, thus removing an important source of village income.[75] For his troubles on behalf of the people, Fei was condemned as a 'Rightist'.

Fei maintains that the importance of rural industry arose from Sunan's unfavourable population to land ratio:

> Due to its large population and insufficient arable land, southern Jiangsu is an area where agriculture and industry have long been closely linked together, each supplementing the other. . . . As early as the 1930s, when I first investigated a village in this region, I found that quite a few peasant households derived half of their income from agriculture and half from handicraft industry. Indeed, in a place with such high population density and limited farm land as southern Jiangsu, it is impossible to get rich by farming alone. To really prosper, one must in addition develop the processing of farm and sideline products as well as the household handicraft industry.[76]

According to Fei and others,[77] the problems of population pressure and surplus labour became so severe in the 1960s and 1970s that some measures had to be taken.

Fei argues the surplus labour and tradition of village industry facilitated the establishment of rural industry, but that external factors were essential to its development in the mid-1970s. As he explains, during the Cultural Revolution

normal production in big and medium-sized urban enterprises was inter-
rupted when their workers began making 'revolution'. However, people
cannot live without commodities. As the situation in the countryside was
then relatively stable, the production of some commodities which could not
be carried out in the cities was shifted to the countryside.[78]

In establishing such rural production, Fei emphasises the importance as
'go-betweens' of urban-educated youths and cadres who had been sent down to
the countryside and retired workers who originally hailed from rural areas.[79]
Such 'connections were a catalytic agent for the development of rural industries,
which then gradually established closer and closer relations with large and
medium-sized cities after 1978'.[80]

In considering the success of TVEs, a number of points need to be made. First,
the establishment of TVEs in Sunan predated the reform period. Sunan had a
tradition of rural industry which cadres revived in the mid-1970s owing, at least
partly, to population pressures. Many TVEs began their existence as 'commune
and brigade industries'. Second, both under Mao and during the post-Mao
reforms, the collective sector has always produced a relatively large proportion
of Jiangsu's industrial output. In 1978, even before the reforms began, over
one-third of Jiangsu's industrial output came from collective enterprises. During
1962–1985, the collective sector usually accounted for a larger proportion of
industrial output in Jiangsu than in the whole of China or in Liaoning and
Guangdong.[81] Third, the importance of Shanghai as a provider of capital,
technology, materials, trained personnel and markets cannot be exaggerated.
Sunan TVEs have greatly benefited from the position of Sunan as part of the
'inner core' of the Shanghai economic region.[82]

Finally, the categorisation of TVEs as 'collective' deserves further scrutiny.
In an important study of TVEs, Wan Jieqiu argues that the 'collective ownership'
of Sunan TVEs 'is in fact a type of local government ownership'.[83] The term
'collective' has become a bit of a fetish. The establishment of rural industries
prior to the commencement of the reform period forced local cadres to use the
strategy of the 'collective'. (State ownership was reserved for county and higher
levels.) Sunan and places like Nantong which established 'collectives' at this time
have retained this form as it has proven successful and familiar. Later developing
areas, like Subei, lack a collective base and in fact the government now urges
the establishment of private enterprises.[84] Thus, Subei has considerably less
collective ownership.

EXPLAINING THE NORTH–SOUTH DIFFERENCES

How should we explain the vast differences between the development of Sunan
and Subei? Significantly, interviews conducted in all three regions of Jiangsu
with a wide variety of people, including government and party officials, scholars,
business people, workers and peasants from all parts of the province, provided a

remarkable congruence of reasons to explain the divergence between Subei and Sunan. These interviews raise six inter-related factors which have led to Subei's poverty.

1   *Environment* In addition to the ecological causes of Subei's impoverishment discussed earlier, Subei's environment contributes to its poverty in other ways. The sandy and salty soil is poor. Irrigation is also poor. Except for coal in Xuzhou, the area lacks substantial mineral resources. Geographically, Subei lacks a Shanghai or a major urban centre to stimulate its economy. The poor environment has prevented development and consequent urbanisation. Rather than have urban centres stimulating and supporting the countryside, rural Subei supports the somewhat parasitic Subei urban centres. Subei lacks the advantages bestowed by the Yangtze River on Sunan. Rather, it must deal with the tribulations which the Huai delivers.

2   *Weak economic base* As Tables 4.3 and 4.4 show, more than 80 per cent of the Subei population who work in agriculture produce less than 35 per cent of the GDP. The industrial base is very weak and most areas had no industry prior to 1949 – and often for many years afterwards. Factories are few and usually small. Furthermore – and not surprisingly considering the weak economic base – there is a great shortage of investment capital. The government no longer provides funds for enterprises and Subei finds it difficult to raise funds from banks or attract overseas investment.

3   *Low levels of education and training* Unlike Sunan, which has a long tradition of education dating back to the imperial periods, Subei has very low levels of education and training. Jiangsu is renowned for its higher educational institutions, but almost all are in Nanjing and Sunan. Subei lacks trained cadres. It has few people trained in science and technology. The province sends in a 'Science and Technology Deputy County Executive' into each county-level unit for two- or three-year stints, but one or two such cadres in each county cannot solve the comparative absence of scientific and technological skills and training in Subei.[85] In addition, Subei cadres lack the concepts of the 'commodity economy'.

   Thus, Subei lacks many types of human resources. It lacks scientists and technicians. It lacks managers. It lacks enlightened cadres. And it lacks a skilled workforce. The region is caught in a vicious cycle. The workforce, lacking opportunities, does not obtain training. But, because the workforce is unskilled, Subei does not attract investment which would help train the labour force.

4   *Poor transportation infrastructure* Unlike Sunan which has the Yangtze River, canals, railways and now major roads, Subei has lacked good transportation. The only railway until recently was the Longhai across the northernmost part of the province. A new local railway is being built from Xuzhou to Zhejiang, but local funds have had to be used. The few airports are small and have only sporadic services. The Huaiyin airport has closed. One can fly from Yancheng to Beijing and Foshan, but not to

Nanjing, the provincial capital. The Grand Canal has not provided adequate transportation. Until recently roads too have been poor. Even today the roads between Huaiyin and Yancheng are very poor. This lack of transportation infrastructure has inhibited Subei's economic development.

In recent years, Subei has adopted the Shandong slogan of 'To become wealthy, first build roads'. Three major national roads – Beijing–Fuzhou, Beijing–Shanghai and Heilongjiang–Hainan – will pass through Huaiyin, while a lower level national road is being constructed from Lianyungang to Shanghai. Three first-grade provincial roads – Nanjing–Lianyungang, Nanjing–Xuzhou and Huaiyin–Jiandu – are basically finished and a Yancheng to Nanjing road through Yangzhou is under construction. Subei leaders feel these new transportation links will help improve the Subei economy.[86]

5 *Poor government strategies* Some people criticise government economic strategies in Subei. Rather than attempt to industrialise or to use the Sunan strategies in Subei, the government should have used comparative advantage. In this view, Subei economic strategy should have emphasised developing its agriculture, then moving to agricultural processing and light industry before heavy industry. Agricultural sidelines should also have been stressed rather than such heavy industry as cars and tractors.

6 *Culture* Virtually every interviewee contrasted Sunan and Subei cultures. Sunan people are astute and sagacious. They are open to new ideas. They are entrepreneurial. They are happy dealing with the market economy and the world economy. Subei people, on the other hand, are described as conservative. They have the concepts of small-scale peasants. If they have enough to eat, wear and live, they are satisfied. They lack a sense of the 'commodity economy'.

Subei people have the northern Central Plains culture of places like Henan. They are simple and honest and very hard-working. They are frank and outspoken. But they lack drive and are happy with the status quo. Owing to their geographical location and the lack of transportation links, they have fewer contacts with the outside. In the cold Subei winter, people sit in the sun with their arms inside their padded jackets trying to stay warm, while their Sunan compatriots are out trying to make money. These conservative attitudes hinder Subei cadres who are concerned with their own power and position. Subei cadres often lack solidarity and factional divisions often occur between families, lineages and clans.

These cultural generalisations may seem gross and even libellous. Yet, they were repeated many times by Subei people as well as by Sunan people. Such Chinese stereotypes as northerners being 'straight and honest, simple and enduring' while southerners from the Yangtze Valley are 'clever and sharp, cunning businessmen', and northerners being 'tall, strong, honest and brave' while southerners are 'small, delicate, smart and gentle' have been traced back at least 800 years to the Song Dynasty.[87] The inability of Sunan cadres working in Subei to improve the Subei economy suggests these cultural factors together with the other constraints do inhibit Subei's development.

The differing economic situations in Subei and Sunan have greatly affected the career choices of potential leaders in each region. In Sunan, people want to go into business where they can earn much more than those who work in government. In Subei, owing to the limited business opportunities, people prefer to work in government where they have an 'iron rice bowl' and earn more than small business people. A Chinese businessman starkly confirmed this contrast when he said he would prefer to invest in Sunan where he would deal with an enterprise rather than in Subei where he would have to work with government.

ECONOMIC MODERNISATION

Jiangsu ranks fourth among China's mainland provinces in per capita GDP (excluding the provincial-level municipalities) after Guangdong, Zhejiang and Liaoning (see Table 4.6).[88] As noted earlier, this overall wealth conceals considerable intra-provincial variation. The richest counties exceed Shanghai in per capita GDP, while Jiangsu's poorest counties have levels comparable to China's poorest provinces. (See Table 4.6 for selected provincial data and Table 4.9 for selected Jiangsu county data).

Under Mao Zedong, Jiangsu did relatively poorly in terms of economic development. During 1952–1978, China's GDP grew at an annual rate of 6.1 per cent, but Jiangsu's growth rate was only 5.2 per cent. In the 1950s and 1960s, Jiangsu was a major agricultural province, but industry remained under-developed. The secondary sector did not exceed the primary sector in GDP value until 1972 and even the tertiary sector was larger than the secondary sector for many years during the 1950s and 1960s. Jiangsu did not receive even one of the 156 major projects of the First Five-Year Plan (1953–1957) and 'got even less of a turn' during the 'Third Front' period. Only in the latter part of the 1970s did Jiangsu receive a chemical fertiliser plant in accord with the development idea that 'industry should aid agriculture'.[89]

In the 1970s the structure of the Jiangsu economy underwent a fundamental change, 'using the opportunities from the development of Shanghai's processing industry'. Sunan's TVEs rose quickly. The secondary sector, which exceeded the primary sector only in 1972, accounted for more than half of provincial GDP by 1977.[90] During this period Jiangsu's economy worked under the difficulty of having 'two key elements external to the province': natural resources and markets. The industrial economy had four key characteristics: (1) industrial processing predominated, (2) small and medium enterprises accounted for 98.6 per cent of enterprises with only 1.4 per cent considered large scale, (3) collective ownership predominated, and (4) local enterprises dominated with over 90 per cent of enterprises belonging to municipalities and counties and less than 10 per cent under the province.[91] (This may be one reason that the province in Jiangsu is perceived as weak, a topic discussed further below.)

Table 4.6 Per capita GDP (RMB¥) in selected provincial-level units, 1994

Province	Per cap. GDP
Shanghai	15,204
Beijing	10,265
Tianjin	8,164
Guangdong	6,380
Zhejiang	6,149
Liaoning	6,103
Jiangsu	5,785
Fujian	5,386
Hainan	4,820
Shandong	4,473
Heilongjiang	4,427
Anhui	2,521
Sichuan	2,516
Yunnan	2,490
Henan	2,475
Jiangxi	2,376
Shaanxi	2,344
Tibet	1,984
Gansu	1,925
Guizhou	1,553

Source: China Statistical Yearbook 1996, p. 45

As Table 4.7[92] shows, Jiangsu has had two major periods of rapid growth from July 1984 until December 1988 (when macro-economic controls slowed the entire Chinese economy) and since February 1992.[93] This post-Mao growth has relied on small and medium-sized TVEs using their adaptive capacities to take advantage of opportunities for development. But Jiangsu economists now see the small size of TVEs and the poor quality of their products as a weakness. In the period until 2010, Jiangsu hopes to continue to use its comparative advantage, but to accelerate the development of economies of scale including the building of large-scale backbone enterprises and large-scale enterprise groups. The province also hopes to attract some large and competitive transnational corporations, which are competitive in international markets, to increase economies of scale and improve products.[94]

Meeting in December 1994, the Ninth Jiangsu Provincial Party Congress agreed on three key strategies for the development of Jiangsu in two stages to 2000 and to 2010: 'Use Science and Education to Make the Province Prosperous', 'Internationalisation of the Economy' and 'Joint Development of Regions'. These strategies are meant to sustain an annual GDP growth rate of 12 per cent until 2000 (with a primary sector growth rate of 4 per cent, a secondary sector growth rate of 11.5 per cent and a tertiary sector growth rate of 16 per cent). Such growth would lead to a sectoral distribution of 9.5 : 52.5 : 38.0[95] compared to the 1995 ratios of 16.4 : 52.7 : 30.9.[96] The growth of the

Table 4.7 Growth rates of Jiangsu GDP, 1972–1995

Year	% increase
1972	6.3
1973	8.7
1974	0.6
1975	7.1
1976	2.1
1977	7.7
1978	23.1
1979	19.8
1980	7.1
1981	9.4
1982	11.5
1983	12.2
1984	18.6
1985	25.6
1986	14.3
1987	23.8
1988	31.1
1989	9.3
1990	7.2
1991	13.1
1992	33.4
1993	40.4
1994	35.3
1995	27.1

Source: Calculated from *Jiangsu Statistical Yearbook 1996*, p. 31

tertiary sector has been slower than planned and the 1994 plan goal was lowered from the 40 per cent approved in 1993. In 1995, the planned goal for the tertiary sector in 2000 was again dropped by two per cent to 36 per cent.[97]

The strategy of 'use science and education to make the province prosperous'

In January 1989, responding to Deng Xiaoping's statement that 'Science and Technology is the first productive force', Jiangsu became the first province to announce the strategy of 'using science and technology to make the province prosperous'. In August 1994 this slogan was changed to 'Use Science and Education to Make the Province Prosperous' with the understanding that the meaning was to encompass the whole content of the former slogan as well as to recognise that 'education is the mother of science and technology'. At the end of the year, this slogan became the first of three strategies for Jiangsu's economic and social development.[98] This strategy used an important comparative advantage. While Jiangsu had gained little industry under Mao, it had developed many large, high-standard science and technology research organisations. At the end of 1988 Jiangsu had over one million science and technology personnel in over 600 research organs. The province had 70 institutions of higher education and led the country in number of students.[99]

Jiangsu's agriculture and industry had not used these science and technology resources. At the beginning of the twentieth century, science and technology contributed less than 20 per cent to the growth of agricultural production. Now, with the use of chemical fertilisers, modern irrigation and mechanisation, science and technology contribute to 60–80 per cent of agricultural growth rates in developed countries. During 1981, the contribution of science and technology to agricultural growth was only 35 per cent in China and 40 per cent in Jiangsu.[100] Similarly, the contribution of science and technology to industrial growth in developing countries can reach 60 per cent. In Jiangsu during the period 1981–1985 it was only 29 per cent and during 1986–1990 it was even lower. In original value, only 7 per cent of Jiangsu industrial equipment reached international standards and only 23 per cent reached advanced domestic standards. The quality of products was also low.[101]

This strategy appears to have been successful. From 1987 to 1993 the role of technology in agricultural growth increased from 4.2 per cent to 46.34 per cent and the figures in industry increased from 13.2 per cent to 37.4 per cent. In addition the numbers of science and technology personnel reached 1,721,100 people in 1993, an increase of 67.90 per cent over 1987. Those actually involved in research and development increased by 20,000. For every 10,000 persons, Jiangsu has 247 science and technology personnel with 58 persons actually involved in research and development, proportions four times the national average. From 1987 to 1993, the funds invested in research and development increased 3.18 times, an average annual increase of 21.31 per cent.[102]

The strategy of 'internationalisation of the economy'

The strategy of internationalisation of the economy is also making progress. From 1978 to 1993 total trade (imports and exports) increased at an annual rate of 22.2 per cent.[103] Table 4.8[104] provides several indicators of internationalisation. Both imports and exports have increased at very high rates since 1992. The proportion of primary products exported has declined while that of manufactured products has increased. Actual foreign investment has also increased and foreign-invested firms now account for close to 40 per cent of exports. By September 1994 actual foreign investment had reached US$7,603 million in 24,064 enterprises.[105] At present, Sunan and areas along the Yangtze River have reached the goal of the three 'one-thirds': the export of one-third of industrial sales, foreign investment in one-third of enterprises and foreign investment reaching one-third of fixed capital investment.[106]

The strategy of 'joint development of regions'

The strategy of 'joint development of regions' argues all regions of Jiangsu must be developed at the same time. According to a source with close links to the

Table 4.8 Indicators of internationalisation of Jiangsu economy (in US$ million)

	1985	1990	1991	1992	1993	1994	1995
Imports	294.92	744.57	1,043.77	1,581.50	2,740.90	3,885.72	5,002.24
% increase	n/a	n/a	40.18	51.52	73.31	41.77	28.73
Exports	1,558.51	2,949.95	3,460.53	4,670.95	5,958.61	9,024.26	11,792.18
% increase	n/a	n/a	17.31	34.98	27.57	51.45	30.67
% for. invest. firms	n/a	n/a	n/a	27.98	38.07	40.83	36.72
% primary products	n/a	20.43	18.27	12.98	10.23	9.85	8.33
% manufact. prod.	n/a	79.57	81.73	87.02	89.77	90.15	91.67
Actual foreign invest.	93.26	438.61	n/a	n/a	3,287.35	4,468.22	5,287.01
% increase	n/a	n/a	n/a	n/a	n/a	35.92	18.32

Note: n/a: not available in cited sources or not applicable
Sources: Chu Dongtao, *Jiangsu jingji fazhan zhanlüe*, pp. 92–93 and *Jiangsu Statistical Yearbook 1996*, pp. 257, 259–260, 265

Jiangsu Provincial Party Committee, it has taken some time for the Jiangsu leadership to recognise that since the beginning of the post-Mao reforms in late 1978, 'In overall terms, Jiangsu's economic development has been good, but the contradiction of the imbalance between north and south has been notably conspicuous'.[107] According to this source, Jiangsu's approach to regional development can be divided into four stages.

In the first stage, during the late 1970s and early 1980s, development strategy emphasised the whole rather than parts, but in fact each locality basically 'struggled for itself' and the economic disparities between Sunan and Subei actually increased. In the second stage, during the mid-1980s, the 1983 slogan 'Vigorously Improve Sunan, Accelerate the Development of Subei' was promulgated and the leadership began to look at the potential of impoverished Subei. However, the role of Subei was still to 'assist' the richer areas.[108]

In the late 1980s and early 1990s, more and more people began to discuss the importance of a regional development strategy for Jiangsu. During this period the 'three along' strategy was developed, which 'emphasised the importance of transportation arteries to bring about economic development. This model was, of course, better than the model [of the second period], but it also revealed many shortcomings' for, as noted above, this strategy did not include the poor areas along the Grand Canal nor did it include hilly areas. 'This left a "hole" in the major framework for the economic development of the whole province'.[109]

The fourth period began in the mid-1990s with the incorporation of the fourth 'along'.[110] The strategy now emphasises dividing tasks according to complementarity and comparative advantage to help all areas. The strategy also calls for increased horizontal economic links and technical cooperation between governments and enterprises.[111] Such links, which resemble sister cities, include Zhangjiagang Municipality in Suzhou with Feng County in Xuzhou, and Xishan Municipality in Wuxi with Shuyu County in Huaiyin. According to the provincial party newspaper, reporting on a group of 30 Xishan enterprise and township leaders visiting Shuyu, such links are 'to select capable cadres to help the poor counties attract projects, technology and capital as well as to train people and organise the export of labour' in order to enable the impoverished counties to escape poverty and gain prosperity.[112]

The data in Table 4.2, based on entire prefectural municipalities, fail to reflect the true range of wealth and poverty in Jiangsu. Table 4.9[113], based on county-level (and urban district) data, shows the extreme gap between the wealthiest parts of Sunan and the impoverished areas of Subei. As noted above, comparison with Table 4.6 shows the wealthiest parts of Sunan are among China's most prosperous, while the poor areas of Subei have standards of living similar to China's poorest provinces. Sunan has seven of China's ten 'strongest' county-level units[114] and Jiangsu has fully one-quarter of China's hundred 'strongest' county-level units,[115] but Jiangsu also has nine counties which are officially impoverished. Thus, over one-half of Jiangsu's 64 county-level units belong to China's economic extremes – among its richest hundred county-level units or its most poverty-stricken.

Counties vary greatly in their ranking on different parameters. No one county is the poorest on every scale. In order to pick a sample of the wealthiest and poorest, the top six and the bottom five counties (and urban districts) were picked on the basis of per capita national income in 1992. As a Jiangsu Provincial Party document[116] calls Huaiyin, Lianshui, Xiangshui, and Guannan counties 'the most difficult' in terms of poverty alleviation, the last three were added to the sample.

Table 4.9 suggests ratios between richest and poorest often exceed 10:1. Such ratios affect per capita GDP, per capita use of electricity and distribution of telephones. Even though the poor counties are subsidised (spending much more than their fiscal income), the rich units can spend many times more per capita. (The urban districts are able to spend much more per capita than the county-level municipalities.) Hospital beds and doctors are also far more readily available in the rich areas of Sunan than in the poor areas of Subei.

The Jiangsu Provincial Party Committee has recently demonstrated its commitment to poverty alleviation. Following the 1994 Provincial Party Congress, which approved the three strategies for economic development, the party issued three documents on poverty alleviation: Document No. 1 (1995), Document No. 5 (1996) and Document No. 26 (1996). The last contains concrete proposals to assist impoverished counties and suggests some of the difficulties which have arisen in this work. Document 26 begins:

> In recent years, economic and social matters in the various poverty relief counties and the 68 impoverished townships of Huaibei [Subei] have developed relatively well, and most will be able to alleviate poverty and reach a decent standard of living according to schedule. But there are still some counties and townships in which development remains very difficult. The stabilisation of poverty alleviation and acceleration of development in

Table 4.9 Wealth and poverty in Jiangsu Province, 1995

County-level unit	Per cap. inc. (RMB¥) (1992)	Per cap. GDP (RMB¥)	Per Cap. kWh per year	Phones per 100 persons	Per Cap. fiscal income (RMB¥)	Per Cap. fiscal expend. (RMB¥)	Hospital beds per 10,000	Doctors per 10,000
Wealthy units								
Wuxi Urban District, Wuxi Pref. Mun.	8,228	20,065	3,099	34.7	2,212	912	61.0	43.0
Taicang Mun., Suzhou Pref. Mun	7,664	18,947	1,720	19.0	797	302	29.0	19.3
Xishan Mun., Wuxi Pref. Mun.	7,430	21,444	2,605	n/a	1,039	368	26.1	14.4
Zhangjiagang Mun., Suzhou Pref. Mun.	7,036	22,459	2,269	13.1	867	414	26.8	15.1
Suzhou Urban District, Suzhou Pref. Mun.	6,737	14,035	1,994	33.0	1,563	733	53.5	46.7
Kunshan Mun., Suzhou Pref. Mun.	6,539	17,254	1,592	14.9	881	464	26.5	18.2
Poor units								
Huaiyin Co., Huaiyin Pref. Mun	839	2,338	264	1.3	89	133	6.8	6.8
Feng Co., Xuzhou Pref. Mun.	799	2,643	203	1.2	119	160	10.1	7.6
Suining Co., Xuzhou Pref. Mun.	785	2,436	196	1.3	93	132	9.2	6.0
Shuyang Co., Huaiyin Pref. Mun.	763	1,816	167	1.2	64	104	8.7	6.6
Binhai Co., Yancheng Pref. Mun.	740	1,900	194	1.5	86	138	9.6	9.3
Lianshui Co., Huaiyin Pref. Mun.	916	1,817	218	1.1	77	133	11.5	7.4
Guannan Co., Huaiyin Pref. Mun.	920	1,941	216	1.4	102	132	10.7	6.9
Xiangshui, Yancheng Pref. Mun.	1,110	2,622	331	2.4	103	148	17.9	10.8

Note: in 1992 Taicang was a county and Xishan Municipality was Wuxi County. In 1996 Guannan County was shifted from Huaiyin to Lianyungang Prefectural Municipality and Shuyang County became part of the new Suqian Prefectural Municipality
Sources: for per capita national income in 1992, see *Jiangsu shixian jingji 1993*, pp. 10–12, 309; 1995 data calculated from *Jiangsu Statistical Yearbook 1996*, pp. 321–326, 363–365, 375–377, 384–386

these places is the keystone in implementing the province's objective of an assault on poverty.[117]

The document outlines a number of organisational measures which suggest difficulties in implementing poverty alleviation work. The document increases the membership of the Poverty Alleviation Work Teams sent to four counties and maintains the strength of teams in other counties. Furthermore, it strengthens the leadership of the work teams. The work team leader must be a 'responsible comrade' of a leading organ who actually goes and works on the 'first front'. The leaders must leave their work in their original units and actually undertake the poverty alleviation work. Furthermore, each work team must have two deputy leaders, possessing provincial department or bureau status, including one with financial expertise. If the original organs find 'sending a Work Team Leader difficult because they truly have insufficient numbers of leaders, they can appoint an additional leader after reporting to and receiving permission from the Provincial Party Committee'.[118]

The document differentiates programmes according to area. In the four 'most difficult counties' (Lianshui, Xiangshui, Guannan and Huaiyin) work will continue at both county and township levels. In Binhai and Shuyu counties the work will concentrate on the township level. In other counties the work will focus on particular townships and villages. The document increased provincial financial commitments to poverty alleviation in 1997. The working cash fund is increased by 120 million *yuan*. The four provincial commercial banks are to increase their loans by 80 million *yuan*. The provincial Planning and Economic Commission, the provincial Agricultural Development Bank, and the Nanjing branches of several banks are also to increase their poverty alleviation funds. Non-refundable aid funds are also to be increased to improve agricultural land of low and medium productivity, to build local roads and village electricity networks, to extend electricity to all natural villages, to improve sanitation, water, broadcast, postal and telecommunications facilities in villages and to repair dangerous school buildings and medical facilities.

According to the document, the relevant prefectural municipalities and counties must be involved. The poverty alleviation counties must specially allocate poverty alleviation funds to townships, villages and households. Provincial funds must be allocated to counties and townships in order to actually achieve results. 'Poverty alleviation funds must be concentrated to support projects which directly help improve peasant incomes. Sixty per cent of loans must be used for agriculture, diversification and processing industry for agricultural subsidiary products'.[119] The document makes clear that these funds are not to be used for 'ordinary industrial projects'. Furthermore, 'for new industrial projects, emphasis must be placed on supporting projects which involve north–south links'.[120] To achieve these aims the document tries to establish controls over allocation and spending of funds.

In accordance with Document 5 (1996), Document 26 reiterates the importance of north–south links between municipalities and counties. The top party and government leader must personally lead this link work and establish a specialised work group. The Sunan cadres sent to Subei must be responsible county-level leaders who must actually go to Subei to work. The leadership group of such Sunan counties and municipalities can be increased by one person.

The document calls for combining north–south links with the process of industrial transfer, a process in which the provincial Planning and Economic Commission should assist. 'In order to guarantee the efficiency of poverty alleviation projects, in poverty alleviation counties more than 50 per cent of industrial projects funded from the poverty alleviation monies must be spent on north–south link projects'.[121] The Sunan counties and municipalities must also send some enterprise and technical cadres to form expert teams to provide guidance in matters of management, technology and markets to projects in linked counties.

The document emphasises:

> Solving the livelihood problems of the masses must be given first priority. . . . This is the heart of economic work in the economically weak Huaibei region. . . . Beginning now, until each poverty alleviation county reaches key poverty alleviation targets in peasant income, rate of straw houses and safe drinking water, counties and poverty alleviation townships are not permitted to build new office buildings, are not permitted to buy prestige cars, are not permitted to build high-class hotels and are not permitted additional mobile phones.[122]

In conclusion, the document provides some additional concrete measures. It promises to assist fiscal debt in the impoverished areas. For 1997 it allocates 23 million *yuan* for roads in impoverished areas, including 13 million *yuan* in the four most difficult counties. It continues the extension of electricity policy for another two years. It increases the allocation of 25 million *yuan* for improvement of village water supplies by an additional 5 million *yuan*. And it allocates a special fund of 4 million *yuan* to repair houses of especially poor families in the four poorest counties.[123]

Political dimensions

Although Jiangsu clearly ranks as an important province, paradoxically the province itself appears weak. Furthermore, the provincial leadership is perceived as 'conservative'. Although the problems facing a large province are considerably more complex than in a provincial-level municipality, in Jiangsu – unlike Shanghai – a field researcher does not sense an efficient, powerful and relatively unified leadership successfully implementing a substantial reform programme.[124] In Jiangsu, leadership at sub-provincial levels seems more relevant.[125]

One major reason for Jiangsu's weakness at provincial level is that the province makes a disproportionate contribution to central government revenues. Since 1983 Jiangsu has ranked second (to Shanghai) among provincial-level units in contributions to central revenues. Jiangsu contributes about 60 per cent of its fiscal revenues to the centre and these account for about one-quarter of the centre's fiscal income.[126] Thus, while Jiangsu serves as a 'cash cow' for the central government, the province has comparatively few financial resources.

China's arcane fiscal system, to quote senior Chinese economists in Beijing and the provinces, remains 'secret', 'unfair', 'defective' and 'unable to satisfy requirements'. Basically, each provincial-level unit negotiates a minimum or base amount to be paid to the central government annually. Two systems prevail. Guangdong arranged to keep the full surplus over and above its base amount. Shanghai and Jiangsu had to pay a fixed proportion of their fiscal revenues above the base amount to the centre. While historical circumstances played a role in determining the base amount each province must pay, the system is extraordinarily arbitrary and secret. Thus the base amount as well as any percentages above the base amount paid to the centre depend upon historical background, the negotiating skills of the provincial representatives and any 'particularistic ties' which the provincial officials may have with the centre. To the best of the writer's knowledge, no source provides details of contracts between the centre and each of the provincial-level units.[127] According to Jiangsu provincial leaders, the 1993 fiscal reforms including the use of VAT and specific allocations of tax revenues to the centre and to localities helped Jiangsu somewhat, but the former inequities in the system remain. Unlike Shanghai, which persuaded the centre to allow it to retain a larger share of revenues locally,[128] Jiangsu is still forced to send a large proportion of its fiscal revenues to the centre. A reputable source confirms that Jiangsu contributed about 60 per cent of its fiscal revenues to the centre during 1949–1985 (see Table 4.10),[129] lending credence to claims that Jiangsu now contributes 11,000–15,000 million *yuan* annually to central coffers. According to a senior provincial leader, the provincial budget is only 4,000 million *yuan* and this budget must pay for all salaries and construction as well as support Subei.

Table 4.10 Jiangsu contributions to central fiscal revenues, 1949–1985

Period	RMB¥ (million)	Jiangsu Revenue (%)
1949–52	1,222	76.00
1953–57	2,754	61.64
1958–62	4,204	42.16
1963–65	2,825	56.07
1966–70	6,349	59.00
1971–75	11,772	59.73
1976–80	16,661	59.83
1981–85	23,479	64.21
Total	69,266	59.79

Source: Dangdai Zhongguo de Jiangsu, I, p. 596 (Table 14)

A second reason for provincial weakness is that wealthy areas apparently retain fiscal revenues locally. County enterprises and TVEs pay very few taxes and their profits go to local governments rather than the province. While concrete statistics are virtually impossible to obtain,[130] observers argue that in Sunan the best roads are local, unlike most places where the national roads, followed by provincial roads, are the best. Similarly, locally-funded public buildings in Sunan are excellent. Yet, on a comparative basis, Sunan suffers in the proportion of fiscal income it retains and the per capita fiscal expenditure it makes when compared to several Chinese municipalities (see Table 4.11).[131] Wuxi Municipality alone pays as much tax to the centre as Shandong province.[132] A third reason for provincial weakness is the shortage of provincial enterprises discussed above.[133] In view of the difficulties facing central and western provinces with large numbers of state-owned enterprises, discussed in other chapters of this volume, this may be a blessing in disguise.

An important source verifies this analysis of provincial weakness: 'Fiscally, in addition to sending revenues to the centre, a large proportion is left in localities. Provincial-level finances are threadbare. Money and credit . . . is basically stripped off to the municipalities. The ability of the province to shift and control [funds] is weak and it is very difficult to concentrate strength to do anything substantial'.[134]

As a province Jiangsu is also weak in that it lacks a sense of cultural identity. As noted earlier, Sunan and Subei have very different cultures. Jiangsu people are more likely to identify with localities, though when in other provinces or overseas they may say they are from Jiangsu. Yet, even then, no one can identify a Jiangsu culture and any efforts to define such a culture usually draw on Sunan characteristics to represent the province as a whole. Unlike the provincial leaderships in Shanxi and Jiangxi, as discussed elsewhere in this volume, Jiangsu's leadership has not attempted to create a 'new' provincial culture.

Table 4.11 A comparison of Sunan's fiscal situation with that of some Chinese cities

Place	Fiscal Exp./ Fiscal Inc. (%)	Per cap. Fiscal Exp. (RMB¥)
Sunan	37.59	171.07
Beijing	89.30	686.20
Tianjin	73.78	529.26
Shanghai	51.19	736.72
Guangzhou	63.85	551.94
Dalian	75.00	470.45
Shenyang	69.64	414.31
Qingdao	56.70	231.76
Shenzhen	97.77	1,609.81
Hangzhou	46.37	228.02
Nanjing	49.24	229.97
Xiamen	79.24	966.54

Source: Zhou Haile, *Suxichang fazhan baogao*, p. 68 (Table 7)

Within Jiangsu, the provincial leadership is widely perceived as 'conservative' for two inter-related reasons: its origins and its desire to curry favour with the centre. Under Mao Zedong, most provinces were ruled by outsiders. Sichuan had its 'Shanxi Gang' (also known as the 'Potato Clique'),[135] while Zhejiang had its Shandong Gang. Guangdong was dominated by Shandong, Hebei and Shanxi cadres, Fujian by Shandong and Shanxi cadres, Hunan by Hebei and Shanxi cadres and Anhui by Chahar cadres. Manchurians dominated Jiangxi, but Yanan people dominated Manchuria.[136] In this context, Jiangsu was unusual in being controlled by a group from within the province, the 'Subei Gang'. To some extent, the patterns of outsider dominance relate to which armies 'liberated' areas and established control. The New Fourth Army, based in Yancheng from 25 January 1941, formed a significant group within the Chinese Communist military during the Anti-Japanese War and Civil War. Not surprisingly, many of these cadres helped liberate areas of Jiangsu south of the Yangtze River.

An examination of Jiangsu Party leaders during 1949–1986 suggests that claims of a 'Subei Gang' do have validity. Biographical data obtained for 36 leaders[137] reveal that 23 of the leaders came from outside Jiangsu, but that 12 had served in the New Fourth Army and another had served the Communists in senior Subei government positions. The ten outsiders who did not serve in the New Fourth Army included some particularly prominent Chinese leaders – Ke Qingshi, Liu Bocheng, Song Renqiong, and Xu Shiyou. The outsiders with New Fourth Army background also included some nationally prominent leaders – Chen Peixian, Jiang Weiqing, Peng Chong and Su Yu. Of the 13 leaders from Jiangsu, eight came from Subei, while two of the five from Sunan had served in the New Fourth Army. (For the purposes of this analysis, Subei includes all areas north of the Yangtze River, since discussions of the 'Subei Gang' include people from Nantong and Yangzhou. This is appropriate because this was the area of the Subei Administrative Office from 1949 until Jiangsu province was re-established in 1953 and because Nantong was an important revolutionary area.) Four key Jiangsu provincial leaders in the post-Mao period leaders all hailed from Subei: Xu Jiatun (from Rugao in Nantong), Hui Yuyu (Guannan in Huaiyin), Han Peixin (Xiangshui in Yancheng) and Gu Xiulian (Nantong).

The 'Subei Gang' also appears to have had prominence at lower levels. A sample of eight Subei county gazetteers suggests local Subei people dominated leadership posts in Subei. In Wuxian, a Sunan county now in Suzhou prefectural municipality, Subei (and Shandong) cadres held the position of County Executive from 1949 until 1981 (except in 1954–1957 when a local held the position). In 1981 a local was appointed. People from the Huaiyin and Yancheng areas also served as leaders of the Wuxian People's Congress from 1949 to 1987 when a local was elected.[138] Observers suggest many current provincial department heads are also from Subei.

The current top Jiangsu leadership also has strong Subei representation. At least seven of ten top leaders – Party Secretary Chen Huanyou (Nantong) and six of eight Vice-Governors – come from Subei. The Governor, Zheng Silin, comes from Suzhou, though he worked in other provinces for some time. Of the two remaining governors (native place unknown), one worked in Subei and the other in Sunan.

The 'Subei Gang' continues in power because people place their followers in good positions. Overall, because they have been less exposed to the outside world than Sunan people, Subei people are perceived to be more conservative. Furthermore, as noted earlier, the differing economic situations in Subei and Sunan have meant Subei people prefer to work in government while Sunan people have many other opportunities. All of these factors explain the predominance of the 'Subei Gang' in politics and its conservatism.

Jiangsu observers feel the leadership is also too timid and too obedient. Provincial leaders wanting to curry favour with higher levels are unwilling to risk upsetting the centre. Thus, for example, provincial leaders are unwilling to bargain for a change to make Jiangsu's fiscal arrangements more equitable. This timidity and obedience to higher authority means the provincial leadership lacks daring and vision – in other words, is conservative.

Conclusion

Although generally perceived to be a wealthy, well-endowed province, within its relatively small area Jiangsu encompasses many of the regional problems facing China as a whole. Sunan is among China's wealthiest areas, but Subei is among the poorest. Furthermore, Jiangsu's provincial government, like the central government, complains that it lacks adequate financial resources to solve these regional disparities.

In retrospect, Jiangsu is fortunate in lacking substantial state-owned enterprises. But the provincial strategy of seeking economies of scale has yet to be realised and the loss of flexibility to adapt to rapidly changing markets – a key strength of the TVEs – may be lost to the Jiangsu economy if this strategy is pursued. On the other hand, Jiangsu is well-endowed with talented and trained science and technology personnel as well as entrepreneurial business people. Sunan also benefits from being part of the Shanghai economic region's 'inner core'.

Ultimately, however, Jiangsu's success as a province requires solving the Subei problem. Poverty alleviation is difficult in the best of circumstances, and Jiangsu suffers from a weak provincial government. Furthermore, it suffers from a poorly developed sense of provincial identity, which in part derives from its relatively short history as a province and from the wide divergence of cultures within its borders. Conceivably, as the 'plan' decreases and the 'market' increases in importance, the role of the provincial level in Jiangsu could decline even further. If that should eventuate, the prospects for rapid development in Subei will be bleak.

ACKNOWLEDGEMENTS

This chapter is part of a larger project on central–local relations partially funded by an Australian Research Council (ARC) Large Grant. The author expresses gratitude to the ARC, to Nanjing University, and to numerous scholars, party and government officials in Jiangsu for their guidance, support, encouragement and hospitality. He also especially thanks Dr Lijian Hong, a Departmental and project colleague, for his insights and suggestions and Dr Antonia Finnane, a noted Australian specialist on the history of Jiangsu, for her advice and wisdom.

NOTES

1 *Zhongguo tongji nianjian 1996* [China Statistical Yearbook 1996], pp. 70, 356, 404.
2 Quoted from Chi, p. 98. Although Chi cites the quoted passage from *Shiji*, ch. 102, it actually appears in ch. 129.
3 Chu, *Jingji shi gao*, p. 568.
4 Wright, p. 49.
5 Twitchett, pp. 22–23.
6 Ibid., p. 23.
7 Chu, *Jingji shi gao*, pp. 568–569; Twitchett, pp. 23–26.
8 Chi, p. 125.
9 Twitchett, p. 23.
10 Chu, *Jingji shi gao*, p. 569.
11 Chi, pp. 146–148; Chu, *Jingji shi gao*, p. 569.
12 Ibid., p. 13.
13 For details of the administrative arrangements for contemporary Jiangsu from the Qin to the Yuan dynasties, see ibid., pp. 15–18.
14 Ibid., p. 18.
15 Details in ibid., pp. 18–19. For subprovincial administrative arrangements during the Qing see ibid., pp. 20–21.
16 Ibid., p. 21.
17 Interview.
18 Chu, *Jingji shi gao*, pp. 21–22.
19 *Jiangsu sheng dashiji*, pp. 1–2; interview.
20 *Zhonghua . . . shouce*, pp. 206–207; Chu, *Jingji shi gao*, p. 22.
21 *Zhonghua . . . shouce*, p. 125.
22 Ibid., pp. 29–40.
23 Ibid., pp. 42, 49.
24 Ibid., p. 125.
25 Ibid.
26 Ibid.
27 *Dangdai Zhongguo de Jiangsu*, I, p. 153.
28 Fei, 'Small Towns in Central Jiangsu', in Fei *et al.*, *Small Towns*, pp. 167–168.
29 Calculated from *Jiangsu tongji nianjian 1996*, p. 9; *Xinhua ribao*, 12 August 1996, p. 1.
30 Fei, 'Small Towns in Central Jiangsu', pp. 167–168.
31 *Xinhua ribao*, 12 August 1996, p. 1 and interviews.
32 In using Chinese statistics, it is best to bear in mind the cautionary maxim, 'Officials make statistics, statistics make officials' *(guan chu shuzi, shuzi chu guan)!* See *Liaowang xinwen zhoukan* [Outlook Weekly], No. 8 (20 February 1995), pp. 20–21.

33 Interviews.
34 David Zweig makes this point in 'Institutional Constraints' and personal communication.
35 Interviews.
36 This paragraph is drawn from Zhang, pp. 23, 27; Chu, *Jingji shi gao*, p. 31; *Zhongguo tongji nianjian 1996*, p. 70; *Jiangsu tongji nianjian 1996*, p. 49.
37 Zhang, pp. 23–24; Chu, *Jingji shi gao*, pp. 25–26.
38 Zhang, pp. 23–24.
39 Chu, *Jingji shi gao*, p. 27.
40 Chu, *Jingji shi gao*, pp. 27–28. For more details on Jiangsu's water resources, see ibid., pp. 28–29.
41 Fei, *Peasant*. p. 249.
42 I am indebted to Professor G. William Skinner for this point.
43 Zhang, p. 25; Chu, *Jingji shi gao*, p. 26.
44 *Zhongguo tongji nianjian 1996*, p. 356.
45 Chu, *Jingji shi gao*, p. 26; interviews in Yancheng Municipality. The figures for the area of tidal flats vary even in the official Jiangsu Party newspaper. *Xinhua ribao*, 12 July 1996, p. 4 states Yancheng has a total of six million mu of tidal flats, accounting for 70 per cent of the provincial total. This would give a provincial total of 8.57 million mu, but *Xinhua ribao*, 17 July 1996, p. 3 says the provincial total is 9.8 million mu.
46 Chu, *Reformer*, pp. 114–127.
47 Zhang, p. 25; Chu, *Jingji shi gao*, pp. 24–25.
48 Ibid., p. 51.
49 *Zhongguo tongji nianjian 1996*, p. 404.
50 Zhang, p. 8. These statistics are based on 1992 data.
51 For an historical consideration, see Finnane, 'Origins', pp. 211–238. From a Shanghai perspective see Honig, *Creating* and Jacobs, p. 166.
52 Zhang, p. 12 and interviews.
53 Chu, *Jingji fazhan zhanlüe*, pp. 114–115.
54 Zhang, pp. 28–30. See also Chu, *Jingji fazhan zhanlüe*, pp. 115–119.
55 Zhang, pp. 30–31. See also Chu, *Jingji fazhan zhanlüe*, pp. 119–122.
56 Zhang, pp. 31–33. See also Chu, *Jingji fazhan zhanlüe*, pp. 122–125.
57 Zhang, p. 33; area figures calculated from *Jiangsu jiaotong lüyou tuce*, pp. 3–19. See also Chu, *Jingji fazhan zhanlüe*, pp. 125–127.
58 Chu, *Jingji shi gao*, pp. 566–567, 570.
59 Ibid., p. 569.
60 Fei Xiaotong, 'Xiao chengzhen, Subei pian' [Small Towns, Subei chapter], in *Xiao chengzhen, xin kaituo*, pp. 7–8. For a translated version, see Fei, 'Small Towns in Northern Jiangsu', in Fei *et al.*, *Small Towns*, pp. 88–89. The Shanghai Economic Region, established in 1982, originally covered 57 counties in the Yangtze River Delta. In December 1984, after Fei wrote his article, the Shanghai Economic Region was expanded to encompass Jiangsu, Zhejiang, Jiangxi and Anhui. On the Shanghai Economic Region see Jacobs and Hong, pp. 239–240.
61 This tripartite division is used in an important economic analysis of Jiangsu: Chu, *Jingji shi gao*, pp. 574–576. However, this division into three regions only occurs after an extensive analysis using two regions: Sunan with six municipalities (the five south of the Yangtze plus Nantong) and a Subei with five pre-1996 municipalities (the four northern municipalities and Yangzhou), ibid., pp. 569–574.
62 Jacobs and Hong, pp. 241–242. Some unpublished materials from Professor G. William Skinner contributed to this analysis.
63 Interviews and discussions with Ms Zhang Xin, a specialist in Nantong languages from the Shanghai International Studies University, have assisted understanding of this point.

64   On the Huai River, the following sources have been especially useful: Chu, *Reformer*, pp. 145–161; Chu, *Jingji shi gao*, pp. 567–568; Finnane, 'Water, Love, and Labor', pp. 662–65; and Finnane, 'The Administration of Water Control'.

65   Chu, *Jingji shi gao*, p. 568.

66   The Subei field research was conducted in – and hence these remarks apply primarily to – Huaiyin (including Suqian) and Yancheng, which account for two-thirds of the area and three-fifths of the population of Subei.

67   *Yancheng shixian gailan*, p. 10.

68   This point is made in numerous interviews and Ho.

69   *Jiangsu shixian jingji* 1993, pp. 10–12.

70   Calculated from *Jiangsu tongji nianjian* 1996, pp. 324–326.

71   Calculated from ibid., pp. 321–323.

72   Calculated from ibid., pp. 345–347.

73   There is a huge literature on TVEs. For a good introduction in English, see Zweig, 'Rural Industry'; for a key Chinese study see Zhou.

74   Fei, *Peasant*.

75   For his 1957 report, see Fei, *Chinese Village Close-Up*, pp. 158–196.

76   Fei, 'Small Towns, Great Significance – A Study of Small Towns in Wujiang County', in Fei *et al.*, *Small Towns*, pp. 36–37. The original Chinese text is considerably more acerbic: Fei, 'Xiao chengzhen, da wenti [Small Towns, Great Issues]' in *Xiao chengzhen, da wenti*, p. 21.

77   Fei, 'Small Towns, Great Significance', p. 38; Fei, 'Xiao chengzhen, da wenti', p. 22; Zhao, pp. 260, 266.

78   Fei, 'Small Towns, Great Significance', p. 39. The original also makes reference to the importance of completing the plan for export products: Fei, 'Xiao chengzhen, da wenti, p. 23.

79   Fei, 'Small Towns, Great Significance', p. 39; Fei, 'Xiao chengzhen, da wenti, p. 23.

80   Fei, 'Probing Deeper into Small Towns – A Study of the Small Towns in the Four Municipalities of Southern Jiangsu', in Fei *et al.*, *Small Towns*, p. 72. The Chinese text adds a sentence on the importance of the Third Plenum in promoting and strengthening this process: Fei, 'Xiao chengzhen, zai tansuo [Small Towns, Further Explorations]' in *Xiao chengzhen, da wenti*, p. 48.

81   Prime, pp. 200–202.

82   Jacobs and Hong, pp. 241–243.

83   Wan, pp. 4–5 et passim.

84   Interviews. Fei Xiaotong also makes this point: Fei, 'Xiao chengzhen, Subei pian', p. 24. For a translated version, see Fei, 'Small Towns in Northern Jiangsu', p. 113.

85   In addition, these cadres have difficulty penetrating local society. However, counties welcome them as a source of *guanxi* with research institutes. In Nantong, the prefectural municipality sends a 'Science and Technology Deputy Township Head' to all township-level units.

86   The importance of roads is indicated by the number of reports in the official Jiangsu Provincial Party daily during August–October 1996: *Xinhua ribao*, 14 August, p. 1 (3 articles); 29 August, p. 1; 3 September, p. 1; 13 September, p. 1; 14 September, p. 1; 15 September, pp. 1, 4; 16 September, p. 1; 17 September, p. 4; 19 October, p. 12; 26 October, p. 1 (2 articles including XHRB commentator). (The run of newspapers available to the writer during these months was not complete.)

87   Eberhard, pp. 598, 601–606. A variety of scholars clearly place Subei in North China and Sunan in South China: see, for example, Cressey, p. 120; Buck, p. 26; Eberhard, pp. 598–599; G. William Skinner, 'Regional Urbanization in Nineteenth-Century China', in Skinner (ed.), pp. 215, 218–219; Skinner, 'Cities and the Hierarchy of Local Systems', in ibid., pp. 342–343.

88   *Zhongguo tongji nianjian 1996*, p 45, which provides 1994 data. Per capita GDP in

Jiangsu increased from 5,785 *yuan* in 1994 to 7,299 *yuan* in 1995, see *Jiangsu tongji nianjian* 1996, p. 31.

89 Chu, *Jingji fazhan zhanlüe*, p. 2. For the proportions of Jiangsu's economy in each sector (1952–1995), see *Jiangsu tongji nianjian 1996*, p. 33.
90 Chu, *Jingji fazhan zhanlüe*, p. 2; *Jiangsu tongji nianjian* 1996, p. 33.
91 Chu, *Jingji fazhan zhanlüe*, p. 3.
92 Calculated from *Jiangsu tongji nianjian 1996*, p. 31.
93 Chu, *Jingji fazhan zhanlüe*, p. 3.
94 Ibid., pp. 15–16.
95 Ibid., pp. 42–44.
96 *Jiangsu tongji nianjian 1996*, p. 33.
97 Interview.
98 Chu, *Jingji fazhan zhanlüe*, p. 62.
99 Ibid., pp. 63–64.
100 Ibid., pp. 64–65.
101 Ibid., p. 63.
102 Ibid., pp. 70–71.
103 Ibid., p. 92.
104 Ibid., pp. 92–93 and *Jiangsu tongji nianjian 1996*, pp. 257, 259–260, 265.
105 Chu, *Jingji fazhan zhanlüe*, p. 93.
106 Ibid., pp. 94–95.
107 Ibid., p. 111.
108 Ibid., p. 114.
109 Ibid., pp. 114–115.
110 Ibid., p. 115.
111 Ibid., pp. 128, 131–132.
112 *Xinhua ribao*, 4 July 1996, p. 4.
113 Per capita national income for 1992 from *Jiangsu shixian jingji 1993*, pp. 10–12, 309; data for 1995 calculated from *Jiangsu tongji nianjian 1996*, pp. 321–326, 363–365, 375–377, 384–386.
114 Interviews.
115 *Jiangsu tongji nianjian 1996*, p. 500.
116 Zhonggong Jiangsu, p. 2.
117 Ibid., p. 1. The four pre-1996 prefectural municipalities in Subei had a total of 782 townships (274 urban townships and 508 rural townships); calculated from *Jiangsu tongji nianjian 1996*, p. 9.
118 Zhonggong Jiangsu, p. 2.
119 Ibid., p. 3.
120 Ibid., pp. 3–4.
121 Ibid., p. 4.
122 Ibid., p. 5.
123 Ibid., pp. 6–7.
124 For Shanghai, see Jacobs, p. 186 et passim.
125 For an important study of Zhangjiagang Municipality in Suzhou Prefectural Municipality, see Zweig, 'Developmental Communities' For an excellent comparison of leadership in Zhangjiagang and Nantong Municipality, see Zweig, 'Institutional Constraints'
126 *Dangdai Zhongguo de Jiangsu*, I, p. 592 and interviews.
127 This draws on Jacobs and Hong, p. 227.
128 Ibid., pp. 232–234; Jacobs, pp. 169–172.
129 *Dangdai Zhongguo de Jiangsu*, I, p. 596 (Table 14).
130 One scholar joked that if Premier Li Peng asked for the statistics he *might* obtain correct figures. For others, the task is 'hopeless'.
131 Zhou, p. 68 (Table 7).

132 Interview.
133 Chu, *Jingji fazhan zhanlüe*, p. 3.
134 Zhang, pp. 8–9.
135 Hong, p. 204.
136 Interviews including Professor Hu Hua.
137 During the period, Jiangsu had 39 Party leaders: *Dangdai Zhongguo de Jiangsu*, II, pp. 825–830. Biographical data for 36 of these were obtained primarily from *Zhongguo renming* supplemented by Ma.
138 Wuxian County Gazetteer (publication data unavailable), pp. 774, 776.

REFERENCES

Buck, John Lossing, *Land Utilization in China*, Nanking: University of Nanking, 1937; reprinted New York: Paragon Book Reprint Corp., 1968.

Chi, Ch'ao-ting, *Key Economic Areas in Chinese History as Revealed in the Development of Public Works for Water Control*, 2nd edition, London: George Allen & Unwin, 1936; reprinted New York: Paragon Book Reprint Corp., 1963.

Chu Dongtao (chief editor), *Jiangsu jingji fazhan zhanlüe* [Jiangsu Economic Development Strategies], Nanjing: Hehai daxue chubanshe, 1995.

——, *Jiangsu jingji shi gao* [Draft Economic History of Jiangsu], Nanjing: Nanjing daxue chubanshe, 1992.

Chu, Samuel C., *Reformer in Modern China: Chang Chien, 1953–1926*, New York: Columbia University Press, 1965.

Cressey, George B., *Asia's Lands and Peoples: A Geography of One-Third the Earth and Two-Thirds Its People*, New York and London: McGraw-Hill, 1944.

Dangdai Zhongguo de Jiangsu [Contemporary China's Jiangsu], 2 vols., Beijing: Zhongguo shehui kexue chubanshe, 1989.

Eberhard, Wolfram, 'Chinese Regional Stereotypes', *Asian Survey*, Vol. 5 No. 12 (December 1965), pp. 596–608.

Fei Hsiao Tung (Fei Xiaotong), *Chinese Village Close-Up*, Beijing: New World Press, 1983.

——, *Peasant Life in China: A Field Study of Country Life in the Yangtze Valley*, London: Routledge & Kegan Paul, 1939.

——, *Small Towns in China - Functions, Problems & Prospects*, Beijing: New World Press, 1986.

——, *Xiao chengzhen, da wenti* [Small Towns, Great Issues], First Collection, Nanjing: Jiangsu renmin chubanshe, 1984.

——, *Xiao chengzhen, xin kaituo* [Small Towns, New Development], Second Collection, Nanjing: Jiangsu renmin chubanshe, 1986.

Finnane, Antonia, 'The Administration of Water Control under the Qing: The Case of Xiahe, 1684–1796', unpublished paper presented at the Asian Studies Association of Australia Conference, Adelaide, 1988.

——, 'The Origins of Prejudice: The Malintegration of Subei in Late Imperial China', *Comparative Studies in Society and History*, Vol. 35 (1993), pp. 211–238.

——, 'Water, Love, and Labor: Aspects of a Gendered Environment', in Mark Elvin and Liu Ts'ui-jung (eds), *Sediments of Time: Environment and Society in Chinese History*, Cambridge and New York: Cambridge University Press, 1998, pp. 657–690.

Ho, Samuel P.S., *Rural China in Transition: Non-agricultural Development in Rural Jiangsu, 1978–1990*, Oxford: Clarendon Press, 1994.

Hong, Lijian, 'Sichuan: Disadvantage and Mismanagement in the Heavenly Kingdom', in David S.G. Goodman (ed.), *China's Provinces in Reform: Class, Community and Political Culture*, London: Routledge, 1997, pp. 199–231.

Honig, Emily, *Creating Chinese Ethnicity: Subei People in Shanghai, 1950–1980*, New Haven and London: Yale University Press, 1992.

Jacobs, J. Bruce, 'Shanghai: An Alternative Centre', in David S.G. Goodman (ed.), *China's Provinces in Reform: Class, Community and Political Culture*, London and New York: Routledge, 1997, pp. 163–193.

Jacobs, J. Bruce and Lijian Hong, 'Shanghai and the Lower Yangzi Valley', in David S.G. Goodman and Gerald Segal (eds), *China Deconstructs: Politics, Trade and Regionalism*, London and New York: Routledge, 1994, pp. 224–252.

Jiangsu jiaotong lüyou tuce [Atlas of Jiangsu Transportation and Tourism], Shanghai: Zhonghua ditu chubanshe, 1995.

Jiangsu sheng dashiji (1949–1985) [Record of Major Events in Jiangsu Province (1949–1985)], Nanjing: Jiangsu renmin chubanshe, 1988.

Jiangsu shixian jingji 1993 [The Economy of Jiangsu Municipalities and Counties 1993], Nanjing: Jiangsu sheng tongji ju, 1993.

Jiangsu tongji nianjian 1996, [Statistical Yearbook of Jiangsu 1996], Beijing: Zhongguo tongji chubanshe, 1996.

Ma Hongcai (ed.), *Xinsijun renwu zhi* [Biographies of New Fourth Army Personages], Nanjing: Jiangsu renmin chubanshe, 1985 (Vol. I), 1986 (Vol. II).

Prime, Penelope B., 'Central-Provincial Investment and Finance: The Cultural Revolution and Its Legacy in Jiangsu Province', in William A. Joseph, Christine P.W. Wong and David Zweig (eds), *New Perspectives on the Cultural Revolution*, Cambridge and London: Council on East Asian Studies/Harvard University, 1991, pp. 197–215.

Skinner, G. William (ed.), *The City in Late Imperial China*, Stanford: Stanford University Press, 1977.

Twitchett, Denis, 'Introduction', in Denis Twitchett (ed.), *The Cambridge History of China, Volume 3, Sui and T'ang China, 589–906*, Part I, Cambridge: Cambridge University Press, 1979, pp. 1–47.

Wan Jieqiu, *Zhengfu tuidong yu jingji fazhan – Sunan moshi de lilun sikao* [Government Promotion and Economic Development – Thoughts on the Theory of the Sunan Model], Shanghai: Fudan daxue chubanshe, 1993.

Wright, Arthur F, 'The Sui Dynasty (518–617)', in Denis Twitchett (ed.), *The Cambridge History of China, Volume 3, Sui and T'ang China, 589–906*, Part I, Cambridge: Cambridge University Press, 1979, pp. 48–149.

Xinhua ribao [New China Daily], Nanjing.

Yancheng shixian gailan [An Overview of Yancheng's Municipalities and Counties], Yancheng: Yancheng shi difang zhi bangongshi, 1988.

Zhao Dexin, *Zhonghua renmin gongheguo jingji shi, 1967–1984* [Economic History of the People's Republic of China 1967–1984], Zhengzhou: Henan renmin chubanshe, 1989.

Zhang Feng (ed.), *Zou xiang 21 shiji de Jiangsu* [Jiangsu Heading Towards the 21st Century], Nanjing: Jiangsu renmin chubanshe, 1995.

Zhonggong Jiangsu shengwei bangongting wenjian, Su ban fa (1996) 26 hao [Document No. 26 (1996), Jiangsu Provincial Party Committee Office], 6 December 1996.

Zhongguo renming da cidian: dangdai renwu juan [Biographical Dictionary of Famous Chinese: Volume of Contemporary Persons], Shanghai: Shanghai Cidian chubanshe, 1992.

Zhongguo tongji nianjian 1996 [China Statistical Yearbook 1996], Beijing: Zhongguo tongji chubanshe, 1996.

Zhonghua renmin gongheguo xingzheng quhua shouce [Handbook of Administrative Divisions in the People's Republic of China]; edited by Minzheng bu xingzheng quhua chu [Department of Administrative Divisions, Ministry of Civil Affairs], Beijing: Guangming ribao chubanshe.

Zhou Haile (chief editor), *Suxichang fazhan baogao* [A Report on the Development of the Suzhou-Wuxi-Changzhou Region], Beijing: Renmin ribao chubanshe, 1994.

Zweig, David, '"Developmental Communities" on China's Coast: The Impact of Trade, Investment and Transnational Alliances', *Comparative Politics*, Vol. 27, No. 3 (April 1995), pp. 253–274.

— —, 'Institutional Constraints, Path Dependence, and Entrepreneurship: Comparing Nantong and Zhangjiagang, 1984–1994', in Jae Ho Chung (ed.), *Agents of Development: Sub-Provincial Cities in Post-Mao China*, London: Routledge, in press.

— —, 'Rural Industry: Constraining the Leading Growth Sector in China's Economy', in *China's Economic Dilemmas in the 1990s: The Problems of Reforms, Modernization, and Interdependence*; edited by the Joint Economic Committee, Congress of the United States, Armonk, N.Y. and London: M.E. Sharpe, 1993, pp. 418–436.

Hubei Province

GENERAL

GDP (billion *yuan*)	297.00
GDP annual growth rate	13.20
as % national average	137.50
GDP per capita	5,099.10
as % national average	91.00
Gross Value Agricultural Output (billion *yuan*)	114.10
Gross Value Industrial Output (billion *yuan*)	483.60

POPULATION

Population (million)	58.25
Natural growth rate (per 1,000)	16.10

WORKFORCE

Total workforce (million)	26.90
Employment by activity (%)	
primary industry	50.10
secondary industry	21.90
tertiary industry	28.00
Employment by sector (%)	
urban	36.43
rural	63.57
Employment by ownership (%)	
state	21.56
collective	33.83
private	15.24
foreign-funded	0.37

WAGES AND INCOME

Average annual wage (*yuan*)	5,099.00
Growth rate in real wage	−1.30
Urban disposable income per capita	4,364.00
as % national average	90.20
Rural per capita income	863.62
as % national average	96.80

PRICES

CPI [Consumer Price Index] annual rise (%)	9.40
Service price index rise	18.80
Per capita consumption (*yuan*)	1,954.00
as % national average	73.00

FOREIGN TRADE AND INVESTMENT

Total foreign trade (US$ billion)	2.90
as % provincial GDP	8.00
Exports (US$ billion)	1.50
Imports (US$ billion)	1.30
Realised foreign capital (US$ billion)	1.10
as % provincial GDP	3.10

EDUCATION

University enrolments	189,909.00
as % national average	132.10
Secondary school enrolments (million)	2.63
as % national average	96.20
Primary school enrolments (million)	7.00
as % national average	108.00

Notes: All statistics are for 1996 and all growth rates are for 1996 over 1995 and are adapted from *Zhongguo tongji nianjian 1997* [Statistical Yearbook of China 1997], Zhongguo tongji chubanshe, Beijing, 1997, as reformulated and presented in *Provincial China* no. 5, May 1998, pp. 68ff.

Hubei Province

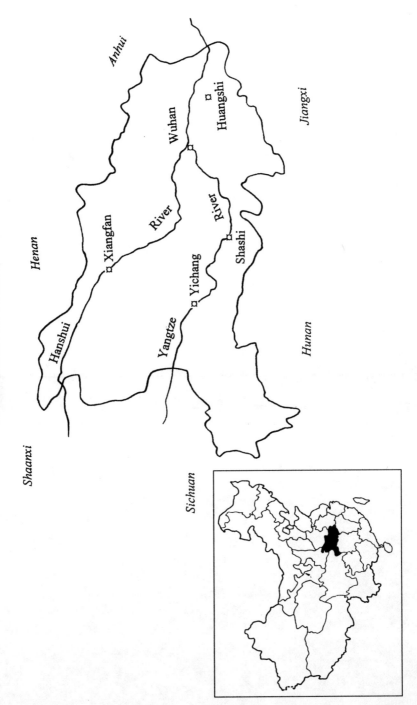

Anhui

Henan

Shaanxi

Hanshui

Xiangfan

Wuhan

River

Yichang

Yangtze

Sichuan

River

Shashi

Huangshi

Jiangxi

Hunan

5 Hubei

Rising abruptly over central China?

Zhao Ling Yun

The general pattern of China's social economic development since the 1980s has been characterised by the widening gap between coastal and central-western provinces and by the efforts of the latter in catching up with the former. Located at the centre of central China, Hubei epitomises the basic characteristics of the central provinces, such as a solid Chinese Communist Party (CCP) basis, large population, rich natural resources and a relatively high level of heavy industrialisation. Hubei was favoured by the central government in the pre-reform era, but fell out of favour in the 1980s. As with all of the central-western provinces, Hubei began to lag behind the coastal provinces in the reform era and has been trying to catch up since the late 1980s.

In the pre-reform era, Hubei had been favoured by the planned economic system and its strategy of heavy industrialisation. As one of the key areas to receive centrally allocated investment, Hubei had developed into one of the major industrial and agricultural bases in China and economically was the most powerful province in central China before 1985. However, since the mid-1980s, Hubei began to lag behind not only the coastal provinces but also the other central provinces in social and economic development. In response, and in an attempt to restore its historical position by overtaking the other central provinces and catching up with the coastal provinces, the provincial leadership in 1987 raised the slogan of 'Rising Abruptly over Central China'.

The process of economic reform and development has since resulted not only in changes to Hubei's economic structure, but also in social and political changes. Social integration on the one hand was accompanied by social disintegration, social stratification and social conflicts on the other. The politics of Hubei have also undergone some changes. Pressure groups have emerged and are starting to play an increasing role in political life; there are more players in the provincial political arena and political governance has been moving towards more transparency and rule by law.

THE POSITION OF HUBEI IN CHINESE HISTORY

Hubei,[1] the cradle of Chu Culture over 2,000 years ago, was one of the birthplaces of Chinese civilisation. Hubei's central geographical location has facilitated the interchange between and integration of regional cultures in northern and southern China. Hubei was also one of China's earliest centres of industrialisation. Modern industrial enterprises in China were established by the influx of technical equipment and Western management after the Opium War. The Chinese did not join foreign investors in establishing modern enterprises in the Hubei area until 1890, when Zhang Zidong, the governor-general of Hubei, Hunan, Guangdong and Guangxi, officially founded four enterprises for military equipment.[2] These were among the first modern enterprises in China. By the end of the nineteenth century, Wuhan, then known as Hankou, developed a fairly large industrial sector and earned the reputation of being 'China's Pittsburgh' or 'China's Manchester'.[3]

Owing to Hankou's opening as a trading port in 1858, Hubei was integrated into the world economy long before other inland provinces. By the end of the Qing Dynasty, the United Kingdom, the United States, Russia, France, Japan, Germany, Italy, Belgium, Denmark, the Netherlands, Sweden and Mexico had established consulates in Hankou. Foreign banks had established more than ten branches in Hubei and developed a well-functioning short-term capital market which financed import and export trade. By 1905, 114 foreign-owned trading firms were engaged in exporting Hubei's agricultural produce and local specialties. Although Wuhan's opening to the outside world occurred about 20 years later than the opening of the coastal ports of Shanghai, Guangzhou, Xiamen, Fuzhou and Ningbo, in foreign trade volume it was second only to Shanghai and compared favourably with Tianjin and Guangzhou by the end of the 1890s. Hence it was also known as the 'Chicago of the East'. With its relatively high level of modern industrial and commercial development, it was not surprising that Hubei became a centre of China's bourgeois revolution led by Dr Sun Yat-sen in the early twentieth century. It was in Wuchang, another part of Wuhan, that the 1911 Revolution, which brought the Qing Dynasty as well as dynastic rule in China to an end, started.

Hubei also occupies an important place in the history of the CCP before 1949. Hubei was among the provinces where Communist groups had emerged before the CCP was founded nationally. Among the 13 representatives of the first National Congress of the CCP, five were from Hubei. Some key figures of the CCP, such as Lin Biao and Li Xiannian, were born in Hubei. Among 254 marshals, generals and lieutenant-generals of the People's Republic of China before 1965, 49 were born in Hubei, ranking next only to Hunan in numbers.

Hubei was entirely brought under the rule of the CCP on 18 November 1949 when Hefeng County was taken over from the Guomindang. The provincial party, government and military bodies were established on 20 May 1949. Li Xiannian was appointed the party secretary of Hubei Province, chairman of Hubei People's Council and commander of Hubei Military Region. In June 1956, the first Provincial Party Congress established a provincial secretariat with Wang Renzhong as its first secretary. The Second Congress was held four years later, in April 1960. Wang Renzhong continued to hold the position of first secretary. The Third Congress was held in March 1971 and the position of the first secretary was taken by Zeng Shuyu, the former commander of Wuhan Military Region, who remained in the position until it was taken by Cheng Pixian in December 1977 after the Cultural Revolution had concluded. In response to Deng Xiaoping's call to rejuvenate and professionalise provincial party officials, the provincial party leadership witnessed a big change in 1983, when Guan Guangfu was appointed as party secretary and the average age of the members of the party secretariat was brought down by eight years to 56.5 years. Three of the four provincial party secretaries, including Guan, were university graduates. Guan's term of office lasted until 1994, when Jia Zhijie took over the position.

The first provincial People's Congress in Hubei was held in August 1954. Liu Zihou was elected as the provincial governor and Zhang Tixue the vice-governor. On 15 January 1956, Zhang Tixue was elected as the governor in the third session of the First Congress and re-elected in the Second and the Third Congress. During the Cultural Revolution, the Hubei Provincial Revolutionary Committee was set up in February 1968, chaired by Zeng Shiyu, who was succeeded by Zhao Xinchu on 30 December 1977. In January 1980, the Provincial Revolutionary Committee was replaced by the Provincial Council, with Han Ningfu as the governor. Since then, the position of governor was successively held by Huang Zhizhen, Guo Zhenqian, Guo Shuyan, Jia Zhijie and Jiang Zhuping.[4]

Generally speaking, the political situation of Hubei during the period from 1949 to 1956 was stable, even though the collectivisation of agriculture and the handicraft industry and the socialist transformation of 'capitalist industry and commerce' did great harm to peasants, handicraftspeople and 'capitalists'. Hubei carried out quite radical policies during the period of the Great Leap from 1958–1960, due largely to the influence of its party secretary, Wang Renzhong, who was widely regarded as one of the most radical provincial secretaries at that time. The slogan 'to make a great leap forward in agricultural production', with the call for doubling or even tripling the output of grain, cotton and oil-seed within ten years, was first raised in Hubei, as early as November 1957. The exaggeration of agricultural production, known as 'launching satellites', was widespread in Hubei. One such 'satellite' that caused a national sensation was the news that rice paddy output per *mu* had reached 18,478.35 kilograms. Hubei declared the completion of the establishment of communes in its countryside on 1 October 1958. Some of these communes even proclaimed the 'realisation of Communism'. Wang Renzhong was one of the provincial secretaries who had deeply influenced Mao's impression of the potential of China's agricultural production at the time.[5]

Hubei was thrown into chaos during the Cultural Revolution. Intellectuals were the first to be affected. Li Da, one of the founding members of the CCP and the interpreter of Mao's philosophical works, then president of Wuhan University, together with the party secretary and the vice-president of the university, were labelled 'The Village of Three in Wuhan' on 13 June 1966 and dismissed. This was the start of the Cultural Revolution in Hubei. In July, some of the major provincial party and government leaders, including vice-governors Cheng Yixin and Liu Jisun, and a large number of cultural officials were dismissed from their posts. The first Red Guard organisation was formed in August 1966 among high school students, and more than ten organisations of this kind sprang up among university students. They closed the *Hubei Daily* and took over the *Wuhan Evening Paper* on 16 November 1966, marking the beginning of their activities to seize power. Then Party Secretary Wang Renzhong, Governor Zhang Tixue and a large number of party and government leaders were repudiated. More than 4,500 cadres of the Wuhan city government and 8,000 cadres of the Hubei provincial government were sent to 'Cadre Schools' or transferred to factories and the countryside to do manual labour. During the Cultural Revolution Hubei was the first place where the military system came under wide assault. One faction of Wuhan rebel organisations attacked the headquarters of Wuhan Military Region led by Commander Cheng Zaidao and Political Commissar Zhong Hanhua in April 1967. Jiang Qing met the leaders of the rebel organisations and called for further attacks on 16 April. This resulted in the nation-wide assault on the military system and the increase of 'Armed Battles'.

Hubei started to redress the injustices of the Cultural Revolution soon after it concluded. The provincial court re-examined 7,303 'counter-revolutionary' cases and concluded 69.4 per cent of them in June 1978. All of those previously accused of having been 'Rightists' were rehabilitated in November 1978. All of the cadres sent to the countryside, factories and 'Cadre Schools' were allowed to resume their positions. The major leaders of rebel organisations were arrested and sentenced to prison in July 1982.

ECONOMIC DEVELOPMENT AND MODERNISATION

Located at the geographical centre of China and along the middle reaches of the Yangtze River, Hubei is adjacent to Anhui, Jiangxi, Hunan, Sichuan, Shaanxi and Henan. The province has an area of 185,900 square kilometres, accounting for 1.94 per cent of China's total and making Hubei the sixteenth largest province in terms of land area. According to the administrative system at the end of 1995, the province had jurisdiction over one prefecture (Xianning), one autonomous prefecture (Enshi Tujia and Miao Autonomous Prefecture) and ten prefectural-level cities (Wuhan, Huangshi, Xiangfan, Shiyan, Jinsha, Yicang, Jinmen, Erzhou, Xiaogan and Huanggang). These prefectures and cities in turn govern 41 counties, 24 county-level cities, two autonomous counties and a forest district. The province had a population of 57.72 million at the end of 1995 which was composed predominantly of Han as well as Tujia, Hui, Miao and Mongol nationalities.

Hubei enjoys favourable natural conditions for agriculture. The subtropical monsoon climate brings plenty of sunlight and warmth. The annual frost-free period lasts for 230 to 300 days and the annual rainfall is between 800 and 1,600 mm. The annual mean temperature is between 13 and 18° centigrade. Mountainous areas account for 56 per cent of Hubei, plains for 20 per cent and hilly land for 24 per cent. Apart from 1,295 hectares of cultivated land, mainly paddy fields, there are more than 1,000 lakes and 1,193 rivers with a total length of 37,000 kilometres within Hubei Province. Jianghan Plain, the well-known 'land of rice and fish', is one of China's ten main bases for the production of grain, cotton, jute, ramie, sesame and fresh water fish. Hubei is the leading province in the production of grain, cotton, fibre crops and fresh water fish. However, the province is affected by high population growth. The average area of cultivated land per capita has decreased sharply from 0.145 hectares in 1949 to 0.068 hectares in 1988, as the population grew rapidly. In 1988, the population density of Hubei was 276.7 persons per square kilometre, 2.4 times the national average. Moreover, because of numerous lakes, rivers and serious soil erosion in its mountainous areas, Hubei is very vulnerable to flooding. An evaluation made by the Research Centre for Ecology, Chinese Academy of Science, graded the quality of the comprehensive ecology of Hubei as 'worsening'.

Hubei is rich in mineral resources and hydroelectric resources. Of the 131 minerals found in China, 110 are found in Hubei, eight of them with the largest and fourteen with the second largest deposits in China. The hydroelectric resources of Hubei total 331 million kWh, ranking fourth among all provinces. The hydroelectric power generated in Hubei ranks first in China, accounting for one-fifth of the national total.

Hubei used to be known as 'China's thoroughfare', as distances from Wuhan to Beijing to the north, Guangzhou to the south, Shanghai to the east and Chengdu to the west are almost the same. Hubei is linked to all these centres by key national communication lines. Currently, two of China's major railways, namely the Beijing–Guangzhou line and the Zhicheng–Liuzhou line, run through Wuhan, and the Yangtze River, the busiest inland navigation line in China, cuts across the province. Hubei is therefore geographically well positioned to expand its links to the outside world. However, the disadvantages of Hubei with regard to natural resources are no less remarkable. Hubei lacks ordinary mineral energy resources, such as coal, gas and oil, and most of its existing mines are of low grade. While the hydroelectric resources are rich, only one-seventh of them is worth developing.

During the period from 1949 to 1979, Hubei experienced quite remarkable economic development. Hubei was favoured by the heavy industrialisation strategy and benefited from central government investment. Hubei was one of the provinces which received a major share of centrally allocated investment before 1980. During the period from 1949 to 1957, Hubei's economic development surpassed the national average. Hubei was able to made a quick post-war economic recovery and by 1951 its economy had already attained a higher level than in the pre-war period. During the First Five Year Plan, seven out of the 156 key projects supported by the Soviet Union were allocated to Hubei.[6] Total investment from 1949 to 1957 amounted to 2.5 billion *yuan*, ranking eleventh among all provinces. During the Second Five Year Plan from 1958 to 1962, Hubei's rank in total investment improved from eleventh to eighth position, and the province emerged as an important industrial base of China. During the Third and Fourth Five Year Plans, when the 'Third Front' strategy dominated planning, Hubei, together with Sichuan and Shaanxi were the main beneficiaries and

Table 5.1 Hubei's position in China's economy, 1980

Indicators	Hubei's ranking among all provincial-level units
National income	8
Gross output of agriculture	7
Gross output of industry	7
Gross value of industrial fixed assets	6
Gross value of capital and funds	3
Total investment of SOEs	3
Total grain output	4
Total cotton output	4

Source: Hao and Shen, 1992, p. 63

became strategic development areas. During this period, Hubei finalised three huge projects[7] which further reinforced its industrial capacity and consolidated its position as an industrial centre. Even at the beginning of the 1980s, when China started to shift its focus of investment away from its central inland regions to the coast, Hubei still attracted considerable funding from the central government. During the period from 1976 to 1980, centrally allocated investment in Hubei totalled 9.6 billion *yuan*, ranking third among all provinces.[8]

Largely as a result of investment by the central government, Hubei experienced rapid economic development and played an important role in the national economy. As Table 5.1 shows, Hubei was one of the most powerful provincial economies in China in 1980.

Hubei began to implement the Agricultural Household Responsibility System in the countryside in 1979 and completed the process by the end of 1983. The separation of collectives from the state and the replacement of the People's Communes by township-level government organs was completed by the end of 1984. At the same time, there were reforms at enterprise level in urban industry. In 1979, 153 enterprises were involved in an experimental increase of enterprise autonomy which included a profit-sharing arrangement between the government and the enterprises, as well as the transformation of these SOEs into independent accounting units with responsibility for their profits and losses. In 1979, Laohekou City was the first locality to introduce 'replacement of profit by taxation and coexistence of profit and taxation'. By June 1983, this reform had spread to all SOEs within Hubei Province and by the end of 1985, the taxation system had replaced the previous system of turning over profits to the state. In 1984, Hubei even appointed a German businessman as the director of a SOE for two years, the first case of its kind in China. In addition, during the period from 1986 to 1996, experiments were conducted in contracting out, leasing and share-holding of enterprises.

Macro-economic reforms concentrated on the planning and finance system. The provincial government reduced the scope of its command planning and correspondingly enlarged the scope of markets. By the end of 1985, industrial goods under the plan had been reduced from 177 to 43 categories. Others were regulated by a guiding plan and market forces. With respect to agricultural products, the provincial government maintained indicative planning over 13 products, including grain, cotton and oil seed. The number of agricultural goods under procurement planning was reduced form 23 to 14. Industrial goods under plan allocation decreased from 30 to 11, and production materials under plan allocation decreased from 254 to 53. By the end of 1985, a bank system that consisted of branches of the major banks, the China Foreign Exchange Bureau and the China Insurance Company had taken shape. It has since been playing an increasingly important role in financial regulation and control within the province.

A comprehensive reform of the economic system of urban areas with the aim of establishing key cities as regional economic centres began after 1983. From 1983 to 1985, 95 per cent of the 128 enterprises formally owned by the province were gradually handed over to regional key cities. Parallel to this, the economic authority of these cities was increased. The provincial capital of Wuhan was given the authority to effect independent planning, equivalent to a provincial-level unit directly under the central State Planning Commission. Ownership structures also experienced a remarkable change, along with the rapid development of the non-state sector. As shown in Table 5.2, the proportion of the output of the non-state sectors has grown continuously.

Table 5.2 Hubei's industrial output value by ownership, 1980–1995 (%)

	1980	*1985*	*1990*	*1995*
State sector	77.7	68.8	62.3	38.1
Collective sector*	21.8	28.7	32.6	37.0
Self-employed labourers	0.1	2.2	4.4	15.0
Private and foreign funded sectors	0.4	0.3	0.7	9.9

Note: * including urban and township and village collectives
Source: *Hubei tongji nianjian (1996)* [Hubei Statistical Yearbook (1996)], Zhongguo tongji chubanshe, 1996, p. 33

Economic reform undoubtedly promoted the development of the provincial economy. As shown in Table 5.3, Hubei's economy has been developing faster in the reform era than it did in pre-reform era. In the period from the 1980s, Hubei experienced its most remarkable economic growth since 1949. However, compared with other provinces, Hubei gradually started to lag behind and its importance within the national economy slowly declined after the mid-1980s, as shown by Table 5.4.

In terms of major indicators of economic growth, the gap between Hubei and coastal provinces widened in the 1980s. In terms of gross industrial output, Hubei was lagging behind some leading coastal provinces, including Shanghai, Jiangsu, Liaoning and Shandong before the reform, and the gap was further widened in the reform era as the latter provinces started to speed up their development. This is

Table 5.3 Economic growth of Hubei, 1953–1995: average annual growth rates (%)

	1953–91	1979–91	1991–95
Gross output of industry and agriculture	8.6	10.7	18.8
Gross output of industry	12.2	13.0	22.2
Gross output of agriculture	3.7	4.7	7.3
National income	6.2	8.5	na
GNP	6.5	8.7	12.9
Net incremental fixed capital	12.2	14.6	29.8
Total retail of social commodities	9.5	13.8	23.3
Total import and export	na	17.3	25.5
Fiscal revenue	na	8.9	na

Source: *Hubei tongji nianjian (1992)* [Hubei Statistical Yearbook (1992)], Zhongguo tongji chubanshe, 1992, pp. 64–67; *Hubei tongji nianjian (1996)* [Hubei Statistical Yearbook (1996)], Zhongguo tongji chubanshe, 1996, pp. 29–31

Table 5.4 Hubei's ranking position among all provinces: selected indicators

	1980	1985	1991
National income	8	9	9
Gross output of industry and agriculture	7	10	11
Gross output of industry	7	8	8
Gross agriculture output	8	9	7
Original value of the fixed capital of SOEs	4	na	7
Total investment in capital construction of SOEs	3	12	11
Total grain output	4	6	7
Total cotton output	4	4	5
Total retail of social commodities	6	7	9
Total export	na	10	13
Total foreign investment	na	9	10
Actual income of urban citizens	na	17	17
Per capita net income of peasants	na	8	19
Per capita net income of workers in SOEs	24	na	25
Per capita net income of workers in collective enterprises	16	na	22

Source: *Hubei tongji nianjian (1992)* [Hubei Statistical Yearbook (1992)], Zhongguo tongji chubanshe, 1992, p. 68

clearly visible from total social output, as shown in Table 5.5. The annual growth rate of total social output of Hubei actually lagged behind the national average rate, let alone the rates of the coastal provinces. More embarrassing was the fact that some other provinces, such as Guangdong, Zhejiang and Hebei, had only taken a relatively short time to overtake Hubei in terms of gross industrial output.

More importantly, Hubei's original leading position among provinces in China's central belt and among the provinces in the central Yangtze region[9] were challenged after the mid-1980s. Up to 1986, Hubei, in terms of gross industrial and agricultural output, had been leading among the nine provinces of the central belt which, apart from Hubei, includes Heilongjiang, Jilin, Inner Mongolia,

Table 5.5 Annual growth rate of total social output of Hubei, selected coastal provinces and national average, 1979–1990 (%)

	Annual growth rate
Hubei	14.97
Zhejiang	19.98
Guangdong	19.91
Shandong	18.02
Jiangsu	18.00
National average	15.35

Source: Hao and Shen 1993, p. 8

Shaanxi, Henan, Anhui, Hunan and Jiangxi. However, it was overtaken by Henan in 1987.

There is no simple explanation for the relative economic slow-down of Hubei since the mid-1980s. One factor was the decline of total investment in Hubei during the 1980s. Total investment from the central government started to decline as the focus of central investment gradually shifted from central China to the coastal areas. Central government investment in Hubei was reduced from 9,634 million *yuan* during the Fifth Five Year Plan to 9,300 million *yuan* during the Sixth Five-Year Plan (1981–1985). This was a negative influence on Hubei's economy, which had become quite dependent on investment from the central government. During the second half of the 1980s, Hubei was not able to increase investment from other sources: for example, local government investment, foreign investment and private investment. Thus, during the period from 1980 to 1985, when average national growth in investment amounted to 41.6 per cent, total investment in Hubei grew only by 25.6 per cent, ranking last among all provincial-level units. During these years, seventeen provincial-level units doubled their total investment and Guangdong and Shanghai increased their total investment by 300 per cent. Hubei, starting off with the second largest amount of total annual investment among all provinces at the beginning of the decade, dropped to eleventh position by the end of it. Hubei's economic growth was fundamentally affected by this decrease in investment. The province gradually lost its advantage in fixed industrial assets and its rank declined from fifth position before 1983 to sixth in 1984, seventh in 1987 and eighth in 1989.

In addition, Hubei was burdened with an out-dated industrial basis. Hubei had undertaken a renewal of equipment and a transformation of large-scale industrial enterprises in the early 1950s and during the period of the 'Third Front' construction in particular. As shown in Table 5.6, most of the Hubei's industrial factories were built before the 1970s. Moreover, the depreciation rate of Hubei was only 4.15 per cent, lower than the national average level of 4.45 per cent. This restricted Hubei's ability to provide the necessary funds for replacement of equipment and transformation of enterprises. The transformation of the numerous enterprises originally built for military purposes and located in inaccessible areas such as mountain valleys was extremely costly.

Table 5.6 Obsolescence of Hubei's factories
by the end of the 1980s

Building time	Percentage
Before 1949	11.6
1950s	34.7
1960s	19.1
1970s	29.6
1980s	5.0

Source: Hao Shen p. 91

To make things worse, the financial responsibility system in which revenue and expenditure were fixed for five years and the governments at different levels were made responsible for their own finances worked to weaken rather than strengthen the accumulative and financial ability of Hubei. Wuhan, the largest city in Hubei, carried an even heavier financial burden, as some large enterprises, such as Wuhan Iron and Steel Company, one of the largest of its kind in China, were handed over to Wuhan by the central government. At the same time, Wuhan had to transfer a considerable proportion of its financial revenue to the central budget. During the Sixth and Seventh Five Year Plans, investment by the central government in Wuhan was sharply cut down. With only 11,726 million *yuan*, Wuhan only ranked ninth among China's twelve major cities. At the same time, Wuhan's revenue retention rate was only 17 per cent after the city achieved provincial-level planning status in 1985.[10] Wuhan had the highest ratio of revenue transfer and the lowest retention rate among all cities with independent planning status after 1985. In 1989, Wuhan made the second largest revenue contribution to the central budget after Shanghai.

During the 1980s, Hubei's conservative provincial leadership was overcautious in implementing economic reforms. In retrospect, a group of scholars and government consultants analysed that during the 1980s, 'the major leaders of Hubei failed to try their best in economic reforms and development' and that 'there were too many remnants of small production and subsistence economy mentality and a strong inertia from the planned economic system in Hubei. As a result, the provincial leadership lacked a sense for openness, competition, science and technology, quality and marketisation.' They went on to criticise: 'The provincial leadership seemed to be cowardly and overcautious rather than enterprising and pioneering, dogmatic and imitative rather than creative and flexible, indulging in idle talk rather than effective action' and that 'officials at all levels paid too much attention to increasing "output value", neglecting quality and efficiency in economic growth, as their achievements were evaluated according to "output value" by corresponding higher government bodies.'[11]

As a result of conservatism and overcautiousness, Hubei missed many favourable opportunities for economic reform and development. Hubei lagged behind coastal provinces in introducing foreign capital and opening to the outside world. Foreign capital introduced to Hubei constituted only 1.63 per cent of the national total in 1988 and further declined to 0.7 per cent of the national total in 1989. In 1987, Hubei ranked ninth among all provinces in attracting foreign capital and declined to tenth position in 1988 and the eleventh in 1989. When there was a widespread increase in utilising foreign capital across the country in the first part of 1990, Hubei was one of the three provinces that experienced a decrease. Moreover, there existed some structural problems in utilising foreign capital in Hubei. During the 1980s, direct investment accounted for only 16 per cent of foreign capital in Hubei, much lower than the national average of 30 per cent. The average amount of foreign investment in Sino–foreign joint venture enterprises in Hubei was US$410,000, much lower than the national average of US$690,000.

Hubei lagged behind the coastal provinces in bringing the economy out of the 1989–1990 recession, since it implemented especially severe policies during the post-1989 austerity period. The province terminated a total of 801 construction projects with an overall investment value of 1,287 million *yuan*. Qinghai and Hubei had already been the two provinces that implemented the harshest investment restrictions as part of their austerity policies in 1988. In addition, Hubei also restricted the development of township and village enterprises and the private sector. The number of the township and village enterprises declined from 1,093,000 in 1988 to 1,043,000 by the end of 1991. Finally, Hubei was reluctant to develop market structures. As a result, in the wake of Deng Xiaoping's southern trip in 1992, the industrial and economic recovery of Hubei lagged behind the achievements of other provinces.

THE STRATEGY OF RISING ABRUPTLY OVER CENTRAL CHINA

Aware of the need to address the province's relative backwardness, Party Secretary Guan Guangfu at the Eighth Session of the Fourth Provincial Congress of the CCP in Hubei in December 1987 officially proposed a 'Strategy of Rising Abruptly over Central China'. This proposal was a reflection of the sense of crisis and an initial response to the challenges from the surrounding provinces. The Fifth Provincial Congress of the CCP in Hubei in December 1988 and a session of this Congress in January 1991 confirmed this strategy and demanded further improvement. Over 200 scholars and government consultants from more than 40 units were organised to do research and expand on this strategy. Their final report was presented to the provincial leadership in November 1991. In this report, central China was defined as comprising the seven provinces of Hubei, Henan, Anhui, Jiangxi, Hunan, Sichuan and Shaanxi. These provinces are more or less at the same level of socio-economic development and share some historical and cultural features. Historically, Hubei had a close relationship in supplying resources and trading with the other six provinces.

The strategy of 'Rising Abruptly' defined a number of broad policies for the province, such as coordinating economic with scientific, technological and social development rather than pursuing one-sided economic development, aiming for a long-term, sustained and coordinated development of the economy rather than a short-term 'Great Leap Forward', surpassing the national average in economic growth and efficiency and gradually gaining a position among the more advanced provinces, serving overall national development by creating a link between the eastern and western areas and becoming the strongest province and a pole of growth for central China.

In more detailed terms, 'Rising Abruptly' also included quantitative targets to ensure that the province's GNP, national income, gross industrial and agricultural output, financial income, volume of imports and exports, and output of major industrial and agricultural products would reach the highest level among the central Chinese provinces. In terms of economic efficiency, including the proportion of comprehensive material resources consumption in national income, the tax contribution per 100 *yuan* industrial fund and the productivity of SOEs, Hubei was to maintain the highest level among all provinces in central China. It was to lead all central provinces in its speed of technological progress and its technological level of major industries as well as in the contribution of technological progress to economic growth. Finally, Hubei's income per capita (including income per capita of peasants) and living standards were to be the highest among all central provinces.

'Rising Abruptly' was to be realised by 2020, with Hubei's GNP, output of major industrial and agricultural products and economic efficiency among the leading provinces in China. The target for per capita GNP was an increase of 300 per cent during the period from 1996 to 2020 to reach US$2,500 by 2020. These objectives were to be achieved in three stages. During the preparatory stage from 1991–1995, Hubei was to convert its growth-oriented economic development to efficiency-oriented development. The annual growth rate of total industrial and agricultural output was targeted at a moderate 6.4 per cent and that of GNP at 5.5 per cent. The period of initial take-off from 1996–2000 was to bring industrial restructuring and major technological progress with a growth rate of total industrial and agricultural output of 8.5 per cent and GNP growth of 6.6 per cent. The goal of 'Rising Abruptly' was to be achieved during the period from 2001–2020. The realisation of these objectives would be to give Hubei a leading position over other provinces in central China, over Chinese coastal provinces and a place internationally among medium-developed countries.

This quite ambitious strategy was not implemented according to the original blueprint. This is at least partly due to the faults of the strategy itself. First of all, Hubei people, especially grass-root officials, had little interest in this strategy and lost their confidence in the provincial leadership. Second, there was no consensus among the provincial leadership regarding this strategy. Two provincial governors, Guo Zhengqian and Guo Shuyan, could not agree with Party Secretary Guan on the strategy and ended their terms of office in Hubei prematurely. Third, the strategy was not clearly formulated and appeared unrealistic to many officials. Finally, the neighbouring provinces did not lend their support to the strategy. Shaanxi, Gansu, Ningxia to the northwest and Sichuan, Guizhou and Yunnan to the southwest organised themselves in alternative forums, such as the Forum for Coordinated Development of Northwestern Provinces and the Cooperative Conference for Economic Development of Southwestern Provinces, to collectively bargain with the central government for preferential policies and funding. To the other provinces in central China, the implementation of Hubei's strategy implied economic domination by Hubei which was not acceptable. As a result, there was no meaningful arrangement for economic cooperation among the provinces of central China and their relationship remained much more competitive than cooperative. They were described as 'a sheet of loose sand'.

Modification of the strategy

Deng Xiaoping's southern tour in early 1992 was a watershed for Hubei Province, as it resulted in the reappraisal of the 'Rising Abruptly' strategy. Deng talked to the top provincial leaders of Hubei on his way to south China and the provincial leadership responded to Deng's talks by loosening the restrictive policies formulated in the period from 1989–1991. Since then, Hubei has been speeding up its pace in developing township and village enterprises, the private and foreign-funded sectors and the market economy as a whole.

Another factor in the re-appraisal of the strategy was the 'Three Gorges' project, which was approved by the National People's Congress in April 1992. The total investment for this project is estimated to reach about 200 billion *yuan*. This project offers golden opportunities for Hubei, which serves as a major base for material supply and logistics. The huge demand for steel and other building materials, machinery, transportation and financial services will be a major boost for Hubei's relevant industries and sectors. The provincial government has been bargaining with the central government to deepen its involvement in the project and encouraged provincial enterprises to participate in the bidding process for supply of materials, equipment and services.

Third, the new provincial leadership formed in 1994, with Jia Zhijie as party secretary and Jiang Zhuping as governor, took a more practical and enterprising position. Jia had formerly served as governor of Gansu and Jiang had served as vice-minister of the Ministry of Aviation. Their professional background enabled them to take a more realistic attitude towards the problems of the province and of its development strategy. Party Secretary Jia reportedly was concerned that conservatism still occupied people's minds and that in such a situation 'Rising Abruptly' was only an idle dream. The new leadership decided to modify the strategy of 'Rising Abruptly over Central China' and renamed it 'Rejuvenating and Rising Abruptly'. In December 1994, as a part of their reform, Jia advocated the 'Hubei Spirit' which emphasised solidarity, creativity, flexibility and courage as essential qualities.[12]

The modified strategy was incorporated in Hubei's 'Ninth Five Year Plan and Long-Term Objectives by 2010'. According to the new strategy, Hubei was to achieve rejuvenation and an abrupt rise of Hubei's economy by 2010, ten years earlier than the previous strategy. Hubei as a 'large industrial and agricultural province in central China' was still to be developed into the 'economically most powerful province in central China' and through a 'fundamental transformation' become fully integrated with the national and international economic systems. The revised objectives for social and economic development by 2010 include a GDP increase of 400 per cent over that of 1980 and a per capita GDP of 10,000 *yuan*.

The new strategy differed slightly from the previous one. First of all, omitting to mention Hubei's dominant position 'over central China', it was more modest and more acceptable to the neighbouring provinces. Second, providing concrete indexes for the growth rates of major items which were based on a comprehensive evaluation of the national and Hubei's economic potential made the revised strategy more feasible and realistic. Third, the new strategy contained a series of supporting sub-strategies regarding the development of agriculture, science and technology, infrastructure and other sectors. Finally, the propagation of the so-called 'Hubei Spirit', as part of this strategy, provided the necessary propagandistic support.

THE SOCIAL IMPACT OF ECONOMIC REFORM

Economic reforms and development since the 1980s became stimuli to social and political change in Hubei, including social stratification, a faster pace of migration, accelerated urbanisation and value changes. The class structure of Hubei has markedly changed since the 1980s. As Table 5.7 shows, there has been a phenomenal increase of those employed in the self-employed, private and foreign-funded sectors. This means that a new social stratum of private business people is emerging.

Table 5.7 Change of the structure of employment (000s)

	SOEs	Urban collectives*	Private and foreign funded	Self-employed workers	Rural
1980	4,042.1	1,001.1	na	28.8	14,797.4
1985	4,573.2	1,578.3	3.5	221.0	16,005.2
1990	5,241.2	1,729.1	15.2	270.9	17,531.9
1995	5,691.2	1,378.8	353.8	1391.5	16,971.7

Note: * excluding employment in township and village enterprises
Source: *Hubei tongji nianjian 1996* [Hubei Statistical Yearbook (1996)] Zhongguo tongji chubanshe 1996, p. 61

The internal structure of traditional classes in China has also changed. The number of workers in collectives has increased more rapidly than that of workers in SOEs. Peasants, according to a survey, can be stratified into eight groups according to their income levels and social status. These groups are: agricultural labourers, peasant workers, hired labourers, peasant intellectuals, self-employed labourers, entrepreneurs, managers of town and township enterprises and rural administrators.

The income gap between different groups has been widening. As shown in Table 5.8 and Table 5.9, the index of consumption of the non-agricultural population has been increasing more rapidly than that of agricultural population, and the wage level of workers in SOEs and urban collectives has lagged behind that of employees in private and foreign-funded enterprises.

Table 5.8 Indexes of consumption of non-agricultural and agricultural populations (1978 = 100)

Year	Total	Non-agricultural	Agricultural
1980	117.7	121.0	116.1
1985	219.1	233.2	212.2
1990	291.8	312.9	281.5
1995	434.7	615.1	340.1

Source: *Hubei tongji nianjian 1996* [Hubei Statistical Yearbook (1996)] Zhongguo tongji chubanshe, 1996, p. 170

Table 5.9 Wage levels of workers in different sectors (*yuan* per capita)

Year	SOEs	Collectives	Private and foreign-funded enterprises
1980	744	619	n.a
1985	1082	867	988
1990	2045	1467	2259
1995	4991	3308	5093

Source: *Hubei tongji nianjian 1996* [Hubei Statistical Yearbook (1996)] Zhongguo tongji chubanshe, 1996, p. 66

Migration has been an evident phenomenon in Hubei since the 1980s. During the five years from July 1985 to July 1990, cross-counties and cities migration totalled 1,866,410; immigration to Hubei from other provinces was 431,745 and emigration from Hubei to other provinces 346,274, accounting for 58.31 per cent, 23.13 per cent and 18.55 per cent respectively of the total. As shown in Table 5.10, moving from the countryside to cities and towns constituted the main flow, accounting for 48.03 per cent of the total, followed by movement from cities and towns to other cities and towns.

Further analysis reveals that newly emerging medium-sized industrial cities, such as Shashi and Yichang, had the highest emigration rates. The emigration rate of Shashi during this period was 13.264 per cent, and that of Yichang 11.736 per cent. The migratory preference of the population was influenced by topographic characteristics. The migratory preference in plains was higher than that in mountainous areas: both immigration rates and emigration rates were higher in

Table 5.10 Directions of migration in Hubei, July 1985–July 1990 (%)

	To villages	To towns	To cities	Total
From villages	9.10	10.11	37.92	57.13
From towns	1.73	4.52	16.91	23.16
From cities	1.69	3.42	14.60	19.71
total	12.52	18.05	69.43	100.00

Source: Gu and Jian, *Dangdai Zhongguo renkou liudong yu chengzhenhua* [Migration and Urbanisation in Contemporary China], p. 81

plains than in mountainous areas. More importantly, the migratory preference was highly positively related to the level of economic development. The higher the level of economic development and the higher the income level, the higher the emigration rate and immigration rate, and vice versa. As shown in Table 5.11, the basic reasons for migration included marriage, business and seeking refuge with relatives.

Table 5.11 Reasons for migration in Hubei (%)

	Hubei as a whole	Cities as a whole	Countryside as a whole	Urban area of Wuhan	Suburban areas of Wuhan
Job transfer	9.57	8.78	10.55	6.57	12.74
Job assignment on graduation	5.35	5.07	5.71	2.87	2.72
Business engagement	25.90	32.60	17.64	34.84	27.40
Studies and further training	14.83	19.33	9.27	27.29	3.88
Refuge with relatives	6.10	5.75	6.52	5.26	5.45
Retirement	0.65	0.49	0.86	0.43	1.81
Family reunion	10.65	9.87	11.62	7.47	13.63
Marriage	12.76	7.16	19.68	5.58	20.06

Source: Gu and Jian, *Dangdai Zhongguo renkou liudong yu chengzhenhua* [Migration and Urbanisation in Modern China], p. 87

The speed of urbanisation of Hubei has been impressive. Since 1982, the increase of urban population in Hubei has been faster than the national average. But this does not necessarily mean that all of this population has been 'urbanised'. The administrative arrangement allowing 'counties to be governed by cities' and 'counties to be transformed into cities' had much to do with the rapid increase of 'urban' population. By the end of 1995, all prefectures in Hubei except for Xianning were transformed into prefecture-level cities, and 24 counties were reclassified as county-level cities. As shown in Table 5.12, during the period from 1982 to 1990, the growth rates of the urban population of newly established county-level cities exceeded that of the provincial average.

Table 5.12 Level and speed of urbanisation in the newly established county-level cities of Hubei Province, 1982–1990 (%)

	Urbanisation level in 1982	Urbanisation level in 1990	Average growth rate of urban population from 1982 to 1990
Hubei as a whole	17.32	29.64	8.24
Zhaoyang	5.15	21.54	21.49
Macheng	4.62	13.81	15.94
Wuxue	7.33	32.23	22.76
Xiaogan	7.57	18.16	13.23
Yingcheng	10.27	18.50	21.61
Anlu	8.53	13.70	7.56
Guangshui	7.31	19.47	15.06
Xianning	16.56	36.37	12.99
Puji	16.30	43.51	15.47
Xiantao	5.83	22.34	19.93
Shisou	6.70	23.39	18.10
Honghu	9.03	35.50	20.28
Tianmen	6.24	18.50	15.92
Qianjiang	4.86	39.78	31.42
Danjiangkou	27.45	24.22	0.01
Zhicheng	13.83	36.61	13.11
Dangyang	8.76	27.92	16.78
Lichuan City	3.06	9.36	16.71

Source: Gu and Jian, *Dangdai Zhongguo renkou liudong yu chengzhenhua* [Migration and Urbanisation in Modern China], p. 304

Economic reform and development have also resulted in ideological and value change. People in Hubei today tend to be sceptical towards the traditional ideas of socialism and adopt more flexible attitudes towards political issues. The older generation, especially those working in large SOEs, still maintain their confidence in socialism and the leadership of the CCP. The younger generation, however, tends to search for new ideas from the West, although their political enthusiasm has diminished after their dream of Western-style democracy broke in 1989. The majority of youth today seem to concentrate more on economic issues, particularly after Deng's Southern Tour in 1992.

Individualism has taken root in people's minds and maximisation of self-interest has been widely accepted. This is evident in people's choices of occupations. Income has become the most important factor for people when choosing their occupations. Many people change their jobs frequently and hold two or more posts concurrently in order to maximise their personal income. A survey in Hubei showed that 30 per cent of young people think that collectivism is out of date, and 47.9 per cent of young people argue that personal advantage has top priority in the hierarchy of national, collective and personal interests.

Materialism seems to be more and more influential in social life. Being rich has become one of the most remarkable symbols of achievement in life. There are frequent reports about beautiful girls accompanying the new rich for money and about party and government officials developing close personal relationships with the new rich for various purposes. People, especially young people, feel elated when they are able to consume foreign products and prestigious goods. Many shop signs were adorned with the words 'King', 'Queen', 'Prince' and 'Princess'. This phenomenon was widely publicised by mass media as 'aristocratisation', leading to a ban of this kind of shop sign by the Wuhan city government.

Personal life has become more liberalised. Cohabitation without marriage, adultery, pre-marital sexual activity and even polygamy are especially ascribed to the new rich and seem to have become acceptable to a certain degree to young people. An investigation showed that pre-marital pregnancies have increased sharply. In Wuhan city, 39,000 pre-marital abortions were registered in 1982 and 65,000 in 1984. An investigation into the sexual behaviour of university students in the Wuhan area shows that 11 per cent of male and 12 per cent of female students had had pre-marital sexual experiences.

INTEREST AND PRESSURE GROUPS

Economic reform, development and opening have resulted in a gradual process of democratisation in Hubei. One visible sign of this has been the presence of various pressure groups. The process of social stratification forms a foundation for the presence of pressure groups with different sectoral interests.

Some groups had existed before the reform era, such as the Trade Unions, the Women's Association, the Youth League and the Association of Industry and Commerce. They were established and controlled by the CCP and usually played a supportive role in implementing policy decisions made by the party. However, in the reform era this has changed. Trade unions, for example, have been playing a more important and active role in the policy setting of relevant areas. First of all, as the workers in SOEs have become more vulnerable to the negative consequences of economic reform, especially hyperinflation, poor social security and restructuring and liquidation of enterprises, trade unions have become more active in protecting the interests of workers. In accordance with instructions from the national Federation of Trade Unions, the provincial Federation of Trade Unions demanded that the trade union leaders of SOEs with a share-holding structure should be brought into the governing bodies of these corporations. At the same time, trade unions in individual enterprises have bargained on behalf of workers with the managers and even with the responsible government organs regarding welfare and other issues. On some occasions, trade union representatives in poorly run SOEs successfully rejected restructuring proposals.

Some new pressure groups have emerged in the reform era. The Association of Individual Labourers, for example, represents the interests of self-employed workers *vis-à-vis* the government bodies concerned. It is interesting that self-employed workers have started to organise their own trade unions. It is reported that 234 individual labourers in Qingshan District of Wuhan City organised a trade union, which is the first of its kind in China. The members of this union regard themselves as labourers and part of the working class. The union is endorsed by the district's official trade union leaders who support the individual labourers' endeavours to protect themselves and settle conflicts between the self-employed and responsible government bodies. The government bodies concerned, however, hold a negative attitude, arguing that the major function of trade unions is to coordinate labour–capital relations and that the trade union of individual labourers will not be able to do so. The City Federation of Trade Unions has held a cautious attitude toward the presence of this new trade union and expressed 'concern' in a diplomatic manner.[13]

The Association of Entrepreneurs was formed in 1993 and membership included over 300 owners of private enterprises. The aims of this association are to protect the interests of entrepreneurs in Hubei and coordinate the relationship between entrepreneurs and the government. The founder of the association was a government official, the director of the 'Provincial Centre for Economic Research'. In this sense, the association cannot claim to be the formal organisation of an interest group. However, the association has been warmly welcomed by entrepreneurs who have taken it as their own organisation and hope to present their ideas and protect their interests through it. The fact that it is semi-governmental in nature might be advantageous for entrepreneurs trying to get access to political power.

The peasants have also made attempts to protect their interests by forming informal and formal organisations. The peasants had been favoured by the implementation of the Household Responsibility System and the increases in prices for agricultural products before 1985. However, this benefit has to a large extent been eroded by the price increases for industrial goods, such as fertiliser, chemicals and pesticide and by numerous government charges. As a response, peasants in Hubei made use of traditional forms of organisation such as lineage organisations, as well as government-sponsored institutions such as Autonomous Committees of Villagers to protect their interests. Major responsibilities of the Autonomous Committee include collecting ideas and complaints from the villagers, making decisions regarding important issues within the village, supervising governmental affairs within the village, developing public welfare and protecting the interests of the villagers. It is reported that one villagers' meeting was successful in rejecting demands to pay 1 million *yuan* in excessive charges to higher authorities.[14]

Some organisations cater for special needs. Realising that the process of social and economic changes created various disadvantaged social groups which needed special protection and assistance, a group of young jurists at Wuhan University in 1993 organised the Centre for the Protection of the Interests and Rights of Disadvantaged Social Groups, offering free legal service and advice. Since its inception, numerous individuals from disadvantaged social groups have appealed to the Centre for legal support. There are other private social initiatives. China Green Village for Children, which was praised as the 'Number One Village on the

Earth', was established by a middle school English teacher in Wuhan in 1988. It aims to adopt orphans and protect their rights. The Marriage Post for Women was organised by a divorced woman in 1994, helping divorced or abused women.

POLITICAL CHANGE

Generally speaking, with economic reform and development, the pattern of governance in Hubei has been changing in the direction of democracy, openness and rule of law. The provincial leadership has been trying to open up and broaden decision-making processes by introducing some democratic mechanisms, such as consultation with the democratic parties, advisory bodies and academic organisations, as well as solicitation of ideas and opinions from the public through the mass media. Some academic organisations and advisory bodies act as 'think tanks'. The Hubei Provincial Centre for Economic Research, established on 10 September 1983, was formed as an advisory body to the provincial leadership regarding strategic issues of economic development. Other examples are the Advisory Committee of Wuhan City Government and a large number of academic organisations at universities in Wuhan. These organisations are usually financed by either government or business and are increasingly able to provide specific expertise.

As a new development, the mass media have become more influential in policy-making and implementation. A number of policies made by the government have been widely discussed and debated in the mass media, ranging from whether or not Wuhan should build an underground railway to how the city government should manage its rubbish disposal. It was to a large extent due to the lengthy reports on rural difficulties and complaints by the media that the provincial government decided to reduce various excessive charges on peasants.

As to the tendency towards rule of law, the provincial government has issued a great number of laws and regulations, trying to regulate political, economic and social life. For example, an examination system has been implemented for the nomination and promotion of officials up to the level of department of provincial government, making at least some posts open for public competition on the basis of merit. The provincial leadership also seems to be more determined to strengthen law enforcement. Some high ranking leaders, such as Chen Shuiwen, a former vice-governor, were dismissed or sentenced to prison because of corruption.

The provincial leadership before 1994 was criticised as conservative not only in economic matters, as analysed above, but also in political affairs. The party secretary, Guan Guangfu, was accused of having an ossified and rigid ideological outlook and of implementing central government policies harmful to Hubei, while failing to make use of policies that could have had a positive impact on the province. Examples cited are that Hubei carried out a campaign against 'bourgeois liberalisation' among intellectuals as early as summer 1981 with the result that intellectuals were thrown into fear again with the experience of the Cultural

Revolution still fresh in their memory. In June 1989, Hubei was one of the provinces where students strongly responded to the 'Tiananmen Square Incidents', and where they were severely punished later.

Due largely to the conservatism in political and ideological affairs, the provincial leadership was overcautious in pushing economic reform. No significant steps were taken towards the reform of large SOEs, as the leadership was too concerned with social stability and the situation of workers. Actually, Hubei, especially Wuhan, produced a number of successful ideas regarding the reform of SOEs, such as bankruptcy, mergers, restructuring by introducing foreign capital, privatisation and leasing. All of these served to inspire and enlighten other provinces and were put into practice in many other places, but not in Hubei. A popular saying claims that Hubei produces more talk and less action, whereas Guangdong provides more action and less talk. Upholding the dogma that the SOEs should always be the mainstay and dominant part of a socialist economy, the provincial leadership did little to develop township and village enterprises and private enterprises. As mentioned earlier, Hubei carried out an over-austere policy during the period from 1989–1991, whereas the coastal provinces, such as Guangdong and Shandong, implemented Beijing's policy in a quite flexible and experimental manner.

Political conservatism and the overcautious manner in economic reform resulted in a relatively backward situation for the province which in turn frustrated its people, especially grassroots officials who were disaffected with the provincial leadership. In the election of the People's Representatives in 1993, more than half of voters cast negative votes for Secretary Guan Guangfu. Officials also took a sceptical or satirical attitude towards Guan's strategy of 'Rising Abruptly over Central China'. When joking about someone's big belly, they would use the term 'rising abruptly'.

The new leadership which succeeded Guan Guangfu has begun a struggle against conservative attitudes. Secretary Jia concluded that the most serious problem for Hubei was that 'the thoughts and minds of Hubei people have not been liberated enough'. He launched a campaign to advocate the 'Hubei Spirit' in mid-1995 with the hope of overcoming conservative attitudes in Hubei and gaining moral support for his reforms from the people.

CONCLUDING REMARKS

Before the 1980s, Hubei's pace and pattern of social and economic development was to a large extent determined by the policies of the central government. Central government investment in heavy industry and 'Third Front' projects had helped to develop Hubei into a relatively highly industrialised province as well as a major agriultural production base. Hubei was favoured by investment from the central government on the one hand, and had to provide a large portion of agricultural resources on the other. These were the legacies inherited from the pre-reform era. In the reform era, as a result of the decline of investment and absence of preferential policies from the central government, Hubei faced serious difficulties and came to lag behind other provinces in social and economic development.

The realisation that a rejuvenation of Hubei's economy and an overall improvement of the provincial situation had to be based on local efforts took a long while. The 'Rising Abruptly' strategy was a response to the unsatisfactory situation as well as a reflection of the desire to restore the historical position of the 'heavenly favoured province'. To what extent Hubei will be able to rise depends on whether it is able to deal with its difficulties. First of all, it depends on whether Hubei can improve its relationship with neighbouring provinces, in particular in linking up with them to bargain collectively for more investment and equal treatment with the coastal provinces by the central government. Second, it depends on whether or not the provincial leadership can successfully overcome conservatism in the province. It is hard to make an optimistic prediction, as only the top leaders have been replaced. Most officials at various levels in the provincial hierarchy are former members of Guan's leadership who hold deeply entrenched conservative attitudes. Third, it depends on whether or not the province can find a new relationship with its major city of Wuhan. The relationship between the province and Wuhan City has not been friendly and is unlikely to improve fundamentally in the short run. This uneasy relationship dates back to the early 1950s, when Wuhan as the seat of the Central-Southern Bureau of the CCP was directly governed by the central government and administratively ranked higher than the surrounding province. Then there were economic conflicts between Hubei and Wuhan. Very few officials from the city government of Wuhan were promoted to the provincial leadership of Hubei, which used to exploit Wuhan to develop other parts of the province before the city was granted the status of 'independent planning unit'. Since the independent planning status of Wuhan was abolished in 1994, the provincial leadership has been trying to do the same again. The municipal government of Wuhan has responded by concentrating on the development of Hankou, which is the part of Wuhan where the city government is seated, and by ignoring Wuchang, the seat of the provincial government. Finally, it depends on whether or not Hubei can adequately respond to the challenges from the neighbouring provinces and maintain its superior position among them. Henan, Jiangxi and Anhui have overtaken Hubei in the development of trade, agriculture and collective enterprises respectively. As a result, the geographical and historical advantage enjoyed by Hubei have vanished. In a word, it is hard to predict whether Hubei will successfully rise and again become the economically most powerful province in central China.

NOTES

1 The name of the province Hubei [north of the lake] refers to its location to the north of Dongting Lake in the middle reaches of the Yangtze River.
2 These were Hubei Gun Factory, Hanyang Steel Factory, Daye Iron Mine and Jiangxia Maanshan Coal Mine.

3 For details see Xu Penghang, *Hubei gongye jingji fazhan shi* [A History of Industrial Development in Hubei], Beijing: Zhongguo tongji chubanshe, pp. 14–21.
4 Before taking their positions in the provincial leadership, Guan Guangfu was the president of the Hubei Branch of the People's Bank of China, Jia Zhijie and Jiang Zhuping were engineers, Guo Shuyan was the vice-minister in charge of the State Science and Technology Commission.
5 Wang was thought of highly by Mao at that time. For details see Bo Yibo, *Ruogan zhongda juece yu shijian de huigu* [A Review of Some Important Events and Decisions], Beijing: Zhonggong zhongyang dangxiao chubanshe, 1991, p. 346.
6 These projects were Wuhan Iron Company, Wuhan Heavy Machinery Factory, Qingshan Thermal Power Station, Wuhan Changjiang Bridge, Wuhan Boilers Factory, Wuchang Ship-building Factory and Wuhan Combined Meat Processing Factory.
7 These projects were the Second Motor Factory, the 1.5 Metre Rolling Mill and Gezhouba Dam.
8 See Hao Fuyi and Shen Zuliang, *Shiji zhi jiao de zhanlue juece* [The Strategic Choice at the Turn of the Century], Wuhan: Hubei renmin chubanshe, 1993, pp. 55–6.
9 'Central region' and 'central belt' are differently defined, with the former consisting of Hubei, Hunan, Henan, Sichuan, Shaanxi, Anhui and Jiangxi, and the latter consisting of these seven provinces as well as Heilongjiang, Jilin, Inner Mongolia and Shanxi.
10 This ratio was originally 19 per cent according to the arrangement between the central government and Wuhan. The Hubei provincial government held back 2 per cent.
11 For details see Hao Fuyi and Shen Zhuliang, 1993, pp. 97–8.
12 Jia actually imitated Jiang Zemin, who earlier in 1994 had summarised the 'Zhangjiagang Spirit' by four almost identical terms.
13 *Wuhan Wanbao* [Wuhan Evening Post], 21 September, 1996.
14 *Wuhan Wanbao* [Wuhan Evening Post], 24 September, 1996.

REFERENCES

Gu Shengzu and Jian Xinhua, *Dangdai Zhongguo renkou liudong yu chengzhenhua* [Migration and Urbanisation in Contemporary China], Wuhan: Wuhan daxue chubanshe, 1994.
Hao Fuyi and Shen Zuliang, *Shiji zhi jiao de zhanlue juece* [The Strategic Choice at the Turn of the Century], Wuhan: Hubei renmin chubanshe, 1993.
Hu Changyi, *Hubeisheng guotu guihua* [The Programme for Land Utilisation in Hubei], Wuhan: Hubei renmin chubanshe, 1991.
Pi Minxiu, *Wuhan jin bai nian shi* [A History of Wuhan in the Last Hundred Years], Wuhan: Huazhong gongxueyuan chubanshe, 1985.
Solinger, Dorothy J., 'Despite Decentralisation: Disadvantages, Dependence and Ongoing Central Power in the Inland: the Case of Wuhan', *The China Quarterly*, No. 145, March 1996, pp. 1–34.
Wang Wenlian and Wu Mianjian, *Zhongguo Hubei* [China's Hubei], Beijing: Renmin chubanshe, 1995.
Xu Penghang, *Hubei gongye jingji fazhan shi* [A History of Industrial Development in Hubei], Beijing: Zhongguo tongji chubanshe, 1993.
Yang Jiazhi and Jiang Jianmin, *Wuhan: Zhongguo disan jia zhengquan jiaoyisuo lixiang zhi di* [Wuhan: The Ideal Site for the Third Stock Exchange of China], Beijing: Xinhua chubanshe, 1993.

Ying Zhengtao, *Wuhan gongye jiegou yanjiu* [A Study of the Industrial Structure of Wuhan], Beijing: Kexue chubanshe, 1990.

Zhao Baojian, *Ba Wuhan jiancheng guojixing chengshi* [Develop Wuhan into an International City], Wuhan: Wuhan chubanshe, 1992.

Zhou Zaorui, *Hubeisheng jingji dili* [The Economic Geography of Hubei Province] Beijing: Xinhua chubanshe, 1988.

Tianjin City

GENERAL

GDP (billion *yuan*)	110.20
GDP annual growth rate	14.30
as % national average	149.00
GDP per capita	11,628.70
as % national average	207.50
Gross Value Agricultural Output (billion *yuan*)	14.20
Gross Value Industrial Output (billion *yuan*)	238.60

POPULATION

Population (million)	9.48
Natural growth rate (per 1,000)	10.10

WORKFORCE

Total workforce (million)	4.90
Employment by activity (%)	
primary industry	16.90
secondary industry	47.70
tertiary industry	35.40
Employment by sector (%)	
urban	65.31
rural	34.69
Employment by ownership (%)	
state	40.82
collective	38.78
private	10.20
foreign-funded	4.29

WAGES AND INCOME

Average annual wage (*yuan*)	7,643.00
Growth rate in real wage	7.90
Urban disposable income per capita	5,967.71
as % national average	123.30
Rural per capita income	2,999.68
as % national average	155.70

PRICES

CPI annual rise (%)	9.00
Service price index rise	17.40
Per capita consumption (*yuan*)	3,380.00
as % national average	126.30

FOREIGN TRADE AND INVESTMENT

Total foreign trade (US$ billion)	9.60
as % provincial GDP	72.00
Exports (US$ billion)	4.70
Imports (US$ billion)	4.90
Realised foreign capital (US$ billion)	2.20
as % provincial GDP	16.90

EDUCATION

University enrolments	71.354.00
as % national average	304.90
Secondary school enrolments (million)	0.49
as % national average	111.00
Primary school enrolments (million)	0.88
as % national average	83.40

Notes: All statistics are for 1996 and all growth rates are for 1996 over 1995 and are adapted from *Zhongguo tongji nianjian 1997* [Statistical Yearbook of China 1997], Zhongguo Tongji Chubanshe, Beijing, 1997, as reformulated and presented in *Provincial China* no. 5, May 1998, pp. 68ff.

Tianjin City

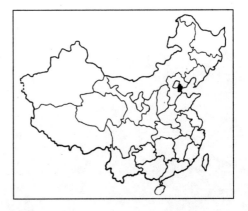

6 Tianjin – quiet achiever?

Hans Hendrischke

Tianjin presents a paradox. It is the one province-level unit in China whose *raison d'être* is clear in historical terms, but is becoming increasingly less evident under present economic conditions. Tianjin (or 'Tientsin' in the old transcription) was the economic and commercial capital of northern China for nearly a hundred years until the middle of the twentieth century, most of the time next to an economically weak national capital in Beijing. Until war erupted in China, Tianjin was China's second largest modern cosmopolitan city behind Shanghai, divided into foreign concessions and home to a Chinese industrial bourgeoisie and a worker's movement. While the memories of its former glory remain strong, Tianjin's history during the People's Republic of China is mostly one of relative decline. Its population is the smallest of the three municipalities with provincial status and its role among them is diminishing. Tianjin has the lowest living standards and per capita consumption of the three big municipalities and has been overtaken by other smaller cities. Compared to Beijing or Shanghai, Tianjin seems to lack a specific identity and purpose. Its role in the Bohai Rim Region is shared with other port cities and, above all, with Beijing. Competition for its traditional markets is growing and large cities of sub-provincial status such as Dalian, Tangshan and Qingdao are increasingly catching up with Tianjin in terms of overall economic indicators. Surprisingly, it was foreign investors who realised the advantages and economic potential of the city and who have contributed most to its recent economic growth. Since the early 1990s, Tianjin has attracted huge foreign investment projects from multinational companies such as Motorola, Heinz and Toyota which have made it their production base in northern China and expanded its economic reach far beyond the borders of the city. Yet, notwithstanding the huge economic impact of foreign-funded enterprises in its satellite towns, a near-nostalgic, conservative atmosphere prevails in Tianjin. Compared with the affluence and conspicuous consumption one finds in many of China's booming cities, the prevalence of state enterprises and Tianjin's laid-back, peaceful urban streetscape and its old-fashioned shops in the city centre are more reminiscent of the late 1970s and the pre-reform period.

How can Tianjin's relative decline in domestic economic position be explained and what is Tianjin's likely future? The study of regional and provincial economies and societies in China has moved to a level where it makes sense to study the differences between provinces in greater detail as the picture of a unified country is becoming much more differentiated. Only the study of differences seems to provide clues to what mechanisms are holding China together. Geographical location and factor endowments are obvious factors structuring Tianjin's social and economic development, but they alone cannot explain Tianjin's recent past or future. Current research is drawing our attention to the role of special policies granted by the central government,[1] as well as to the role of local leadership and the ability of localities to attract foreign investment.[2] These factors apply to Tianjin in their own specific ways. Tianjin's situation cannot be explained without taking into account the economic and political competition between Beijing and Tianjin and the specific political culture of the city. Tianjin has a comprehensive local identity, manifested in economic and social policies and the political outlook of its leadership, which sets it apart from other provincial-level municipalities and provinces. Tianjin's identity is so specific that one could even argue that previous studies on social policies which regard Tianjin as representative of China might in effect say more about the specific characteristics of the city than about China in general.[3] The following chapter addresses the linkages between factor endowment, politics and socio-economic development in Tianjin during the last decades.

It will be argued that in the case of Tianjin, there is an overall development strategy at work which operates more subtly than the city government's official planning with its general statements on the one hand and quantitative targets on the other. This overall, implicit development strategy manifests itself in a predictable attitude towards major political, social and economic issues: for example, in the continuing preference given to infrastructure investment, in maintaining state enterprises and social standards and in the segregation of foreign-funded and domestic industries. To understand this development strategy, one has to look beyond the narrow perspective of factor endowment, sectoral policies and the like and include political issues, such as the outlook of the leadership and especially the relationship of the city of Tianjin with the neighbouring national capital of Beijing, in the analysis. While the general political process surrounding the development of special economic zones, including Tianjin, has been well researched,[4] the reluctance to address the specific local political problems is hampering the usefulness of existing analyses, both in English and Chinese language publications.[5] The reluctance of Chinese authors to give public account of these political matters is understandable, but the way they are discussed internally is not much different from discussing party affiliations of state governments in the West. Tianjin's present economic and social situation has to be understood in its historical and political context. The main parts of this chapter address Tianjin's historical background, Tianjin under central planning, its entry into the reform period and its new dilemma in the 1990s.

TIANJIN'S FACTOR ENDOWMENT AND HISTORICAL BACKGROUND

Tianjin is situated approximately one hundred kilometres southeast of Beijing on the estuary of the Haihe River which flows into the Bohai Sea. The six urban districts of the city of Tianjin proper cover an area of 330 square kilometres, the municipality of Tianjin which also includes four suburban and three coastal districts as well as five rural counties is spread over an area of 11,305 square kilometres. Forty per cent of the total area is under cultivation, while approximately 20 per cent is used for residential purposes and industry. The city has ample land resources along the coast which can be used for port expansion and industrial development. By the mid-1990s, the municipality of Tianjin had a population of 9.5 million with an industrial labour force of approximately three million and a total labour force of five million. The city's transport infrastructure is well developed. The new 142-kilometre Beijing–Tianjin–Tanggu highway links the city to neighbouring Beijing. Rail links extend to Beijing to the west, Qinhuangdao, Shenyang and Harbin to the east and further up north and to Shanghai in the south. Tianjin's Xingang ('New Harbour') is China's largest man-made port and Tianjin's international airport has north China's largest cargo handling facilities. Tianjin has rich maritime resources and a long history as a salt producer. Tianjin has the Dagang Oilfield under its jurisdiction and offshore oil is produced in the Bohai Sea. The city also has its own coal reserves, as well as reserves of marble and pottery clay. Tianjin has geothermal resources of an estimated 20 billion cubic metres of hot water. The downside of this is that Tianjin is situated in an earthquake zone. Tianjin's economy rests on its manufacturing industries. It has a diversified industrial basis with heavy industry and an increasing range of light and processing industries. The increase in the role of the service sector marks a return to its historical position when Tianjin was the commercial and financial centre of north China.

The name of Tianjin ('Heavenly Ford') was given to the town of Haijin on the Haihe River to commemorate the crossing of the river by the 'Son of Heaven', the Ming Dynasty Emperor Yongle in 1404. Tianjin was later fortified and became an important transport hub for the capital of Beijing when the Grand Canal from the Yangtze River slowly silted and the grain from the south had to be shipped by sea.[6] In 1860, Tianjin became one of China's open port cities as part of the forced opening of China to foreign trade. Following the opening of rail links, Tianjin's hinterland expanded to include a region covering the present provincial territories of Hebei, Shandong, Henan, Shanxi and parts of Inner Mongolia and the northeast provinces.[7] With the inflow of foreign capital, Tianjin was among China's first industrial cities, starting with flour mills, a textile industry, machine building and marine chemical industries. After the turn of the century, a local Chinese bourgeoisie developed mainly in the light industrial manufacturing sector.[8] By the time Tianjin became a financial centre, it had acquired all the facilities of a modern city of the times with public transport, electricity and water supply and telecommunication, all centred around its port and its flourishing international trade. By the 1930s, Tianjin had become a commercial and financial centre with a national status that was second only to Shanghai.[9]

> Under the Republic of China (1912–1949), Tianjin was a special muni-cipality under the direct administration of the national government. By the early 1930s, Tianjin's export volume of cotton accounted for 47 percent of the nation's total and leather and woolen goods amounted to 60 percent. The major imports were grains, textiles, sugar, paper, and tobacco. The total foreign trade volume in the early 1930s accounted for more than 20 percent of the nation's total.
>
> (Chang, Sen-dou *et al.*, 1992, p. 43)

Under Japanese occupation, Tianjin expanded its industrial base by adding iron and steel, machine building, building materials and other industries.[10] As part of the extensive Japanese economic planning for Tianjin, construction was begun on Tianjin's modern sea port of 'Xingang'.[11]

Like Shanghai, Tianjin also had a middle class and an active workers' movement,[12] and much of Tianjin's history in the early 1950s was influenced by political movements aimed at influencing these two groups.[13] Thus, also in social and political respects, Tianjin had many similarities with Shanghai. However, in one important aspect, Tianjin was different from Shanghai. Tianjin's distance from the capital meant that the city never developed a political and intellectual identity and independence to the degree that it existed in Shanghai; this was in spite of the existence of foreign concessions and a large foreign community. The short intermezzo of Guomindang rule from the southern capital of Nanjing did little to change this.

TIANJIN UNDER CENTRAL PLANNING

Tianjin was the first major city conquered by the Communist Party in early 1949, months before Beijing again became the national capital. During the following period of national reconstruction, Tianjin profited to some degree from the re-establishment of transport links along the coastal region, but at the same time started to loose its commercial advantages when its banks and trading companies were closed.[14] During the period of the First Five Year Plan, Tianjin was disadvantaged in favour of the rapid industrialisation of China's inland provinces when general economic policies and major investment projects were directed towards the hitherto underdeveloped interior provinces. Tianjin shared the same fate as Shanghai, which in 1952 accounted for one-fifth of China's national industrial capacity, and also, like Tianjin, received no national key construction projects under the plan. Beijing and Liaoning were the only province level units in the developed coastal regions to be allocated some of the 156 key construction projects under the First Five Year Plan. Beijing was declared one of the eight key industrial cities and received projects in defence and electronic industries.[15] This changed the industrial and economic balance between Beijing and Tianjin.[16]

In order to develop the economy of the capital, the central government undertook large-scale industrial construction in Beijing. Heavy industry projects ranging from electronic, defence industry and engineering projects among the 156 key construction projects during the First Five Year Plan period to the Shijingshan Steel Plant under the Second Five Year Plan, the Dongfanghong Oilfield under the Third Five Year Plan and the construction of the first 300,000 tonne ethylene plant at Yanshan Petrochemical Factory turned Beijing into one of China's most developed heavy industrial cities. Furthermore, the establishment of a large number of light and textile industrial enterprises, including three cotton mills and one printing and dyeing mill in the eastern outskirts as well as a bicycle plant, sewing machine plant and watch factory also allowed Beijing to achieve partial self-sufficiency in consumer goods markets.

In contrast, the only major project allocated to Tianjin during the 1950s and 1960s, was the Dagang Oilfield in 1964, when Tianjin was part of Hebei Province. However, the refining capacity of the Tianjin Petrochemical Company only amounted to half the capacity of Beijing's Yanshan Petrochemical Factory. Tianjin's light industry suffered from lack of capital and continued to utilise equipment that dated back to the Republican period, if not the Qing Dynasty. Tianjin thus lost its position as the leading industrial centre of north China during the first two decades of the PRC. The surrounding cities of Tangshan and Qinhuangdao were similarly affected by the lack of investment capital and had to rely solely on local funds to maintain their limited industrial base.[17]

Even Tianjin's political status was downgraded. In April 1958, Tianjin lost its status as provincial-level metropolitan city and replaced Baoding as the provincial capital of Hebei Province.[18] It had to support 17 surrounding counties and lost over one hundred enterprises when Hebei's provincial capital moved back to Baoding, before finally moving to Shijiazhuang in 1967/68.[19] However, Tianjin benefited from the discovery of oilfields in the 1960s which remained with the city when the Central Committee resolved in January 1967 to separate Tianjin from Hebei Province and restore its status as a provincial-level municipality.[20]

The following period brought additional sacrifices for Tianjin. Under the 'Third Front' policy, Tianjin had to support the shift of industrial capacities into inaccessible inland regions by financing and supporting investment projects. Tianjin itself received central investment funding to the degree that it was able to maintain its existing industrial basis. Yet, the overall effect of the new investment policies was a relative de-industrialisation of Tianjin compared to Beijing.[21]

During the period 1953–1979, Tianjin's industry grew at 9 percent annually, a rate that was relatively low compared with the national average of 11.1 percent and Beijing's 14.5 percent. From 1950 to 1980, the central government invested a total of 30 billion Yuan for industrial infrastructure construction in the Beijing–Tianjin–Tangshan region. Of this amount, 52.2 percent was allocated for Beijing and 30.5 percent for Tianjin, reflecting the government's inclination toward the capital city.

(Chang, Sen-dou, 1992, p. 44)

Still, compared with other provinces, Tianjin fared reasonably well under central planning. For the total period from 1952 to 1979, its growth of per capita income ranked third after Beijing and Shanghai.[22]

A positive change occurred when, at the beginning of China's opening policies in the early 1970s, 2.3 billion *yuan* of central funds were made available for the construction of port facilities, Tianjin Port was among the beneficiaries with funding allocated for four container berths and nine mixed berths.[23] After the devastating Tangshan earthquake of 1976, which had its epicentre eighty kilometres from Tianjin, the city received more central funding for infrastructure facilities during the Sixth Five Year Plan (1981–1985). But these were likewise allocated to other coastal cities and Tianjin received no project of the importance of the Baoshan Steel Works for Shanghai.

From the early 1980s onwards, the role of the provincial leadership and the intra-provincial political set-up began to play a decisive role in local development. Provincial leaders started to have more say and the strict planning mechanism that defined regional strategies came to an end. Provinces now became recipients of special rights that allowed them to differentiate themselves from other provinces to a much greater extent than had been possible before. For the following period, it will therefore be necessary to examine the role of the provincial leadership.

TIANJIN UNDER LI RUIHUAN

For Tianjin, the beginning of the reform period coincides with the ascendancy of Li Ruihuan, who as the mayor of the city was the driving force behind the formation of Tianjin's political identity and who retained an influential position throughout the 1980s and beyond.

Li Ruihuan, a native of Baodi County in Tianjin, succeeded a weak interim leadership group that had taken over from a group still loyal to the pre-1976 radical leadership. Li Ruihuan was appointed vice-mayor of the city in 1981 and promoted to mayor in 1983. His nomination to the positions of vice-mayor and then mayor of Tianjin was most likely due to his personal style and his background in infrastructure development. His personal style was the hands-on approach which made him famous. He was renowned for taking action once aware of complaints and impressed foreign visitors as a non-bureaucratic, practical personality without the pomp that often still ruled official meetings at the time.

More important for Tianjin was his professional background. He had started as a worker with Beijing No. 3 Construction Company and legend has it that he worked as a carpenter on the building site of the Great Hall of the People during the Great Leap Forward.[24] From 1959 onwards he pursued a party and trade union career in the Beijing construction industry, moving from positions with Beijing Building Materials Supply Company to the Beijing Buildings Materials Bureau. His career there culminated in his positions as a vice-chairman of the Beijing

Municipal Construction Committee and concurrently director-general of the Capital Construction Project Headquarters. At the same time, he held influential positions in the trade union movement as vice-chairman of the Beijing Municipal Federation of Trade Unions and executive member of the All-China Federation of Trade Unions.[25]

It is indicative of his political outlook that he surrounded himself with pragmatic economic leaders as well as trade union representatives. His vice-mayors included prominent reformers, such as Wang Guangying who was general manager of Tianjin Trust and Investment Corporation and later became chairman of Everbright Company Ltd.[26] and the future Deputy Minister for Foreign Trade and Vice-Premier Li Lanqing. The other nationally prominent member of his municipal leadership was a representative of the trade union movement. Ni Zhifu, who was party secretary of the Tianjin Party Committee from 1984 to 1987, had a similar background to Li Ruihuan, having risen from a fitter to chairmanship of the Council of the All-China Federation of Trade Unions and first secretary of its secretariat. Like Li Ruihuan, he weathered the Cultural Revolution in a trade union position, but in a much more exalted one. From chairman of the Beijing Trade Union Council he rose to become deputy chairman of Beijing Revolutionary Committee, and finally gained a seat on the Politbureau. By the time Ni Zhifu joined the Tianjin Party Secretariat, he had already lost his seat as an alternate member of the Politbureau, but retained a seat on the Central Committee until 1992.[27]

As much as Li Ruihuan presented himself as an ardent reformer, his political programme and general strategy also displayed a strong degree of social and economic conservatism. The two main elements of Li Ruihuan's programme for Tianjin were priority for infrastructure development and a preoccupation with social stability. The main features of the city's economic policies during the Li Ruihuan era were a predominance of the state-owned sector with slow growth of the collective and private sectors and a segregation of Chinese–foreign joint ventures from the domestic economic sector. Li Ruihuan's expertise in municipal construction was particularly important for Tianjin, as the city had still not recovered from the huge earthquake of 28 July 1976 which had damaged 60 per cent of all housing in Tianjin, causing an estimated damage of nearly four billion *yuan*.[28] Up to 1979, one million people were still living in small brick-built earthquake shelters that gave little protection from rain and could not be adequately heated in winter. In 1980 the central government allocated 2.6 billion *yuan* of investment funds to Tianjin, to be spent over three years from 1981 to 1983.[29]

Residential construction was one of the first areas of Li Ruihuan's concern. While investment in housing had been increased following the 1976 earthquake, the signs of devastation were still visible everywhere in the early 1980s. During Li Ruihuan's first years in office, from 1981 to 1985, more housing was built than in the preceding 30 years.[30] Among the measures he took in this context were a reform of the urban planning system which allowed more long-term and systematic planning and a change in the investment funding quotas for 'productive' and 'non-productive' investment in favour of third sector and residential construction.[31] By 1983, the area of living space per person had again reached the pre-1976 level and kept steadily rising.[32] Urban planning took a more quality oriented turn with the creation of green spaces and more public amenities, such as eating streets, for residents. Li Ruihuan's immediate brief was to take charge of this reconstruction, but the exclusive attention he devoted to this task was indicative of the overall style of urban management that he was to adopt.

Tianjin's residential gas supply was the next area which attracted Li Ruihuan's attention. After the central State Planning Commission in 1984 had agreed to allocate three hundred million cubic metres of natural gas from Tianjin's Dagang Oilfield to the city, Li Ruihuan promised that within three years all urban households would be linked to the urban gas supply network. In his characteristic fashion, this task was approached with careful planning and a great public mobilisation effort with 'fighting orders' for the 'struggle' to build pipelines and production facilities. As the initial 'fighting targets' were overfulfilled, 'new targets' were propagated in early 1986. When in June 1987, one year ahead of the original schedule, nearly 94 per cent of all households in Tianjin, including all urban households, had been connected to the public gas supply network, this was hailed as a great success for Li Ruihuan.[33]

Li Ruihuan did not confine himself to repairing the damage that had been done by the earthquake, for which he received central funding. He soon moved to change the whole of Tianjin's urban transport infrastructure by means of a number of major road construction projects. Following Beijing's lead, these included three ring roads around the city and 14 arterial roads cutting across them. The major 40km long Middle Ring Road was built within 18 months from January 1985 to June 1986. It was followed by an Outer Ring Road of 70km length which was completed in 1987. This in turn was followed by the construction of a 14km long Inner Ring Road. Other projects under his mayorship included a new railway station, harbour expansion and telecommunications.

Another project bearing the hallmark of Li Ruihuan's rule solved Tianjin's water shortage. Originally, Tianjin had been able to draw water from the Miyun reservoir, but this was closed off when, in the early 1980s, Beijing's supply of drinking water became sparse. The realisation between 1981 and 1983 of the Luan River canal and pipeline system with over 200 kilometres of pipelines and tunnels was largely the responsibility of the then deputy mayor, Li Ruihuan.[34]

Li Ruihuan's emphasis on infrastructure was complemented by his concern for social control and stability. His policies combined welfare and populistic elements. One of his first measures in office was to declare that in future his government would every year do 'ten good things' to improve popular living con- ditions;[35] two years later, he raised the number to 'twenty good things'.[36] Among these 'good things' were residential and urban construction projects, but also the provision of scarce food items, price controls for consumer items, subsidies and better public services. They became part of Tianjin folklore and provided a constant source for anecdotes popularising Li Ruihuan. In 1986, a municipal planning work committee was set up to oversee planning, finance, banking, statistics, auditing material supply, prices, labour and other relevant areas of macro-economic management. In 1987, he promulgated a policy of 'three stabilities'. This slogan stood for price stability during a period of rapidly rising inflation in order to promote social stability, second for balanced development that avoided putting financial burdens on enterprises and consumers, and third for risk minimisation in the market transition of the period.[37]

Li Ruihuan's economic thinking is best characterised by a variant of Chen Yun's famous statement that market forces should be kept like a bird that can fly in a cage. The metaphor used in Tianjin compared the release of market forces to letting a kite fly in the air, but at the same time holding on to it with a string.[38] The tool for maintaining this control was the municipal administration and the way it pursued its tasks is reminiscent of enlightened absolutism. On the one hand strict control was to be maintained over all developments that could be seen as open-ended and leading to unpredictable consequences. On the other hand, the administration was perceived as a service function with a responsibility to enable economic actors to operate in a predictable environment. One year after Li Ruihuan had left his position, a Chinese observer described his administrative style as follows:[39]

> During the reforms, Tianjin always paid attention to preserving the integrity of the administrative system, the unity of government and enterprises and an orderly social life. For one, they emphasised that at no time were administrative means to be abolished or weakened; instead they used strong administrative methods to promote reform measures; what was said counted and what was fixed was realised in a practical, detailed and concrete manner. Second, the improved and strengthened administrative control targeted problems of the presently incomplete new economic mechanism, problems that were neglected or beyond the reach of macro-economic control institutions, and problems resulting from authority meant to be handed down that was not handed down or only handed down insufficiently. Tianjin city emphasised that their grass-root level service was directed at enterprises.
>
> (Ye Limin, 1990, p. 145)

As a result, Tianjin prided itself on an efficient system of municipal government that combined overall social control with promotion of industrial activity, service for enterprises and the provision of welfare services ranging from practical concerns such as better living quarters and food supplies to a clean environment and ideological education.

The down-side effects of Li Ruihuan's policies

While Li Ruihuan's policies showed impressive results in the mid-1980s, they lacked the flexibility to cope with the changing circumstances of the late 1980s. The two areas where this became most obvious were the gradual relative decline of Tianjin's industry, caused by the losses incurred by state enterprises, and the slow growth of foreign investment coming into Tianjin.

As central funding was no longer available for big infrastructure projects, Li Ruihuan had to secure funding from Tianjin's industrial enterprises. The burden on Tianjin's state enterprises during this period increased for two reasons. One was their contribution to the infrastructure projects. The other was the insistence by Li Ruihuan to save loss-making state owned enterprises and their jobs by cross-subsidisation from profitable enterprises.[40] Government support for industries during the Sixth Five Year Plan (1981–85) was channelled into industries which were not sustainable in the long run, such as bicycles, wrist-watches, clothes and textiles.[41]

The industries that suffered most were Tianjin's traditional light and textile industries, while only a few new industries, such as automobiles and electronics, contributed to industrial growth. The ailing traditional industries were, of course, mainly affected by increasing competition from township and village enterprises in surrounding Hebei Province, which had lower labour costs, as well as by the rising prices for raw materials resulting from market liberalisation. Some of the more advanced industrial sectors, such as consumer electronics and white goods, suffered from oversupply after too many provinces had invested in these areas.[42]

By the end of the 1980s, Tianjin had fallen considerably behind the national average in terms of economic growth, increases in assets and living standards. Although one could claim that the figures for 1988 quoted in Table 6.1 are proof of the city's success in controlling excessive growth and inflation, they point to the structural difficulties of Tianjin participating in the economic growth of the late 1980s.

Other economic indicators, such as an average annual GDP growth rate between 1979 and 1992 of only 6.5 per cent put Tianjin in second to last position among all coastal provinces and municipalities and even far behind the corresponding national growth rate of 9.1 per cent.[43] In its traditional market regions in north China where Tianjin products used to hold a market share of 40 per cent, its penetration by 1989 had dropped to 13 per cent.[44] Nearly one-third of Tianjin's industrial products were absorbed by the two provinces of Hebei and Shanxi.[45]

Table 6.1 Tianjin's 1988 economic indicators in national comparison (%)

	Tianjin	National average
Industrial growth rate	10.9	17.7
Increase in state investment in fixed capital assets	8.9	18.8
Increase in local state investment in fixed capital assets	5.0	25.3
Salary increases for workers	19.6	22.1
Increase in cost of living for workers	16.9	20.7
Retail price index	17.7	18.5

Source: Ye Limin, 'Tianjin shinian gaige de huigu' [Tianjin's ten years of reform in retrospect], *Gaige*, No. 1, 1990, pp. 143ff

The overall judgement on Li Ruihuan's industrial policies has therefore been mixed, because in order to finance infrastructure projects he took money from industrial enterprises and by not reinvesting it in the industrial sector, deprived industries of their funds. But then it was not clear whether the ailing industrial sectors could have been saved by additional investment. Instead, it is now argued, the money went into good infrastructure where it had no immediate effect on production, but in the longer run turned out to be a good investment for the city as a whole. The negative example here is industrial development in northeast China, where industrial funding was sunk in state-owned enterprises which later turned out to be beyond salvation.

Tianjin was also not able to make full use of its special status as an open coastal city. Li Ruihuan claimed that foreign investment was one of his priorities and was careful in cultivating a positive reputation in this respect. Tianjin's national reputation at the time and his personal reputation were based on administrative efficiency and support for foreign investors. Tianjin started work on its first economic development zone in 1984 in response to the central government's policy of developing 14 coastal cities by giving them special policy preferences to attract foreign investors with reduced tax rates and land fees. The Tianjin Economic and Technological Development Area (TEDA) had a designated area of 33 square kilometres, situated 45 kilometres from the city centre on the coast with convenient access to the port facilities at Tianjin's Xingang port and to Tianjin airport, rail link and a planned highway link to Beijing. The development area was on state-owned waste land with adjacent areas available for future expansion. Earthquake risk in the area was considered minimal. The area was sub-divided into plots of land which were to be successively developed. The original plan envisaged development in three stages with full utilisation of the whole area by the year 2020.[46] Other smaller and specialised areas have followed since, such as a bonded zone in its port area.

In the early 1980s, Tianjin had already attracted several spectacular and widely publicised joint ventures with partners such as Remy Martin of France for the production of Dynasty wines and the German Wella AG for the production of cosmetic products.[47] By the end of 1985, Tianjin had 55 joint ventures with foreign investment of US$24.16 million. In 1985, 88 joint venture contracts were signed with partners from Hong Kong (39), Japan (21), USA (15), Singapore (3), Great Britain (2) and one each from France, Thailand, Australia, Canada, Malaysia, West Germany, Denmark and the Philippines.[48] Accumulated foreign investment from 1979 to 1990 amounted to US$351.5 million.[49] Annual foreign direct investment during the second half of the 1980s stood at an average US$50million. This development of joint venture investment and actual results during the 1980s were regarded as too limited. The lack of progress was criticised in 1986 by Deng Xiaoping during a visit to Tianjin.[50]

There is so much wasteland lying between the harbour and the city, which is a great advantage and has a great potential. You must be bolder to develop faster. With some infrastructure facilities better than those in Shanghai, you may find it easier to do things. You plan to borrow $10 billion from foreign countries. Do you have a country in mind? You may consider more countries. What do we have to fear when those who lend money to us do not have anything to fear?

(Tianjin Ribao [Tianjin Daily], 21 August 1994)

In spite of the criticism, little changed in the actual running of the development zone. While the Tianjin government continued to state its positive intentions on integrating foreign investment into the domestic economy, it did not put them into practice. In 1993, an article in a Nankai University journal criticised the fact that Tianjin's economic development zone was not linked to Tianjin's domestic economy, that it provided no decent living environment and that it still had not succeeded in attracting large-scale foreign investment.[51]

Foreign investment was not exempt from Li Ruihuan's conservative social policies. When Tianjin was contemplating the plans for its new economic development area, one of the essential decisions was the separation of the area from Tianjin's urban centre and the segregation of foreign and Chinese workers. 'The development area has townships and villages as a back-up and a large area of land. There is no need to build a separate "small society". Industrial and working areas can be kept separated and the living areas of Chinese and foreign can be segregated. This makes administration easier and reduces social conflict.'[52]

This separation has remained a characteristic feature of Tianjin. Compared to Beijing and Shanghai where the employees and hangers-on of foreign joint ventures are noticeable in the streets by dress, public demeanour and consumption, there was little visual impact from the by now considerable foreign investment in the urban landscape.

The more general criticism of Li Ruihuan's industrial policies in the 1980s is that Tianjin did not encourage the spread of the enterprise responsibility system in state-owned enterprises and discouraged the development of the collective sector. Especially in the development of the collective sector, Tianjin lagged far behind the national average. Throughout the 1980s, the contribution of collective enterprises to Tianjin's gross industrial output value never reached 20 per cent, a value much below the national average which by the mid-1980s had already surpassed a level of 30 per cent.

Tianjin's development strategy of the 1980s can be characterised as 'enlightened conservatism'. A policy orientation that presented itself as reformist in the national context was in fact a mixture of conservative economic policies and progressive social policies. The problem was that this mixture cost the city dearly in terms of personal income and overall economic strength and slowly undermined its once advantaged position.

TIANJIN'S DILEMMA OF THE 1990s

In the years following the departure of Li Ruihuan to Beijing at the end of 1989, Tianjin was politically downgraded. Traditionally, it had held a seat on the

Politbureau, which after the death of its interim mayor, Tang Shaowen, in 1993, was not filled with a representative of Tianjin, but with Huang Ju from Shanghai. This was not necessarily meant to slight Tianjin, but rather a step in upgrading the position of Shanghai in its bid to take on the role of Hong Kong after 1997. But the intended or unintended result was that the lobbying power of Tianjin with the central government was further weakened, especially as Li Ruihuan had been moved sideways to the less influential position of chairman of the Chinese Political Consultative Conference.

In Tianjin, the leadership that followed Li Ruihuan is generally perceived as weak in the national context and as imposed on the city in order to reduce its role beside Beijing. What is obvious is that the new leadership tried to continue and even to imitate Li Ruihuan's policies down to details such as continuing to 'do 20 good things' for the people every year.[53] In its urban policies, the new government continued the commitment to infrastructure spending, the maintenance of the state-owned sector and social expenditure. For example, for 1996 the municipal government pledged to spend 2 billion *yuan*, equivalent to the infrastructure spending over the previous five years, on 14 key urban projects, such as highways, bridges and waste water treatment facilities.[54]

There are external and internal reasons for the conservative orientation of the political leadership of Tianjin. An external reason is that Tianjin's geographical proximity to Beijing puts the municipal government under pressure to preserve social peace and avoid unrest which could potentially spill over to the capital. This would explain the strong emphasis on public order and social control. Internal reasons are the commitment to previously successful policies. The municipal leadership tried to imitate what they saw as successful policies under Li Ruihuan and his vision of a socialist society with little income differential, with social security, a clean environment as well as a weak role for collective and private enterprise and a strong coordinating role for the state. This is reflected in public statements by their mayor and other municipal leaders who have continued to extol the virtues of socialism well into the 1990s.[55] In this respect, Tianjin differed considerably from other surrounding provinces and cities which had written economic development as the main item on their agenda and were aware that their progress depended on their competitive strengths. While the conservative approach to planning and social control might have been opportune in the first few years after the post-Tiananmen crackdown when the central leadership was tightening political control, it was out of line after Deng Xiaoping's Southern Tour in early 1992.

In the competitive atmosphere that emerged after 1992, the new mayor, Zhang Lichang, had little standing outside of Tianjin and was easily outmanoeuvred by the mayors from surrounding cities who were better connected in the capital, such as Bo Xilai in Dalian and the mayor of Tangshan. Tianjin in the 1990s was faced with major challenges. In the aftermath of Deng Xiaoping's visit to south China, a conference was held in 1992 on a new strategy for the Bohai Rim region.[56] The Bohai region was to become the third coastal region to be developed after south China around Guangzhou and the Lower Yangtze region with Shanghai at its centre. By virtue of its size, Tianjin was at the centre of this region, but unlike

Guangzhou or Shanghai, the Bohai region did not have a single focal point. Beijing actively competed with Tianjin for domestic and foreign investment projects. Tianjin also faced new competitors in coastal cities that aimed at taking over part of Tianjin's historical role and economic functions. The smaller port cities of Qingdao, Tangshan and Dalian started to make inroads in areas which Tianjin traditionally had regarded as its economic hinterland.

For example, Tianjin was unable to prevent a contract between Beijing city and Hebei Province to construct new enlarged port facilities at Tianjin's neighbouring city of Tangshan which was to make Tangshan instead of Tianjin the major port for the national capital.[57] While the leadership of Tangshan negotiated with Beijing authorities, Tianjin's leadership confined itself to press declarations. Months after the contract between the two had already been signed, the mayor of Tianjin 'extended a warm welcome to Beijing' to join Tianjin in harbour construction and offered Beijing the options of 'carving out an area along the Tianjin coast for Beijing to exploit independently, assigning two berths to Beijing for construction and management or jointly funding the Tianjin port with Tianjin city'.[58] Tangshan by that time had already spent over a year appraising and negotiating its joint project with Beijing and was able to sideline Tianjin in its contract with the capital.

Tianjin's mayor, Zhang Lichang, was faced with more challenges, as the economic performance of Tianjin's state-owned economy was now rapidly deteriorating. Of Tianjin's 20 industrial sectors, only four were profitable by 1996. These four so-called 'pillar sectors' are the automobile industry, electronics, the chemical industry and metallurgy. For 1994, these sectors were reported as having contributed 63.4 per cent of the city's gross industrial output value.[59] The positive state of the pillar sectors is linked to the involvement of foreign investment. The major investors are Daihatsu of the Toyota group in the automobile industry and Motorola in the electronic industry. The two other sectors are linked to large central government investment projects. One is a seamless steel pipe plant which was allocated to Tianjin in the 1980s originally on a repayable basis. After going into operation in 1989, it was defaulting on its repayments until, through the influence of Li Ruihuan, the investment of 10 billion *yuan* was converted into a capital grant in 1994. The ethylene plant which supports the chemical industry was also a matter of controversy. As sources in Tianjin claim, it was only approved by the central government after it was split into two projects, against better economic judgement, one of which went to Beijing.[60]

Tianjin's revenue is mainly derived from these four sectors and from foreign investment in the special areas. According to slightly varying accounts obtained during interviews in Tianjin in 1996, the four pillar sectors employed approximately half the industrial workforce. The problem with this situation is that Tianjin's state-owned sector, which is still the major employer, is making losses in all other departments and industries. This puts serious strains on the municipal budget, as the city receives no more central subsidies.[61] This also means that the actual rate of unemployment is much higher than the official 2 per cent in 1996.

The municipal government has insisted on keeping state enterprises afloat, by paying nominal minimal wages of between 100 and 200 *yuan* to its former employees. Again, this policy seems to result from political commitments as well as outside pressure. Reportedly, when in 1992 Tianjin Watch Factory was laying off workers and a demonstration developed near Nankai University where the main gate of the factory is located, it took only hours before an order from Beijing arrived to stop the unrest and revert the retrenchments. Tianjin was handicapped by the need to preserve political stability. The question of whether this was part of Tianjin's political culture or pressure from Beijing to avoid political unrest near the capital, is difficult to decide. The result of these policies are declining living standards in Tianjin compared to other cities,[62] because of the bad performance of Tianjin's state enterprises and continuing restrictions on collective enterprises.

The total workforce of 600,000 people employed by collective enterprises in 1996 was still far below the number of two million employees of state-owned enterprises. Unlike Shanghai, Tianjin was not pushing the labour force into the social security net, but tried to keep the loss-making enterprises afloat with subsidies. Tianjin in 1994 had an urban labour force of approximately three million people; of these, two-thirds were employed by state-owned enterprises. If the four profitable state industrial sectors account for half of the industrial workforce, as was claimed during interviews in Tianjin, this would mean that one million people work in unprofitable sectors. This is not to say that this workforce is fully dependent on subsidies, as there will be profitable enterprises in those sectors. But these figures indicate that an estimate of half a million people depending on subsidies in one form or another seems to be in the realm of the possible and that the actual unemployment rate is closer to 15 per cent. Thus Tianjin's low social inequality and crime rate are dependent on substantial subsidies and achieved at the cost of declining relative living standards.

Compared with the national ratio of gross value of industrial output by ownership (see Table 6.2), Tianjin displays an irregularity, in that it has a 'conservative' predominance of state-owned enterprises over collective enterprise, but an uncharacteristically high ratio for the foreign-funded economic sector. In this respect, it is closer to Shanghai than to other provinces. The state-owned sector itself has a high proportion of central government-owned enterprises. Though relatively small in number, their share of industrial output value is one-third of the whole state-owned sector.

Tianjin in the 1990s was faced with new challenges and competitors. Similarly to Shanghai, it now felt the disadvantage of being separated by administrative boundaries from its rural hinterland. Collective enterprises in surrounding areas competed for raw material and later for markets. Tianjin with its strong reliance on the state sector could not compete on price. In continuing the policies of the 1980s, the municipal government faced an increasing burden of loss-making state enterprises, but its situation had changed with foreign investors making use of Tianjin's natural and infrastructure advantages. By providing effective municipal services and administration for foreign joint ventures in the Tianjin Economic and Technological Development Area, it has opened up one new area of development.

Table 6.2 Tianjin's 1995 GVIO by ownership (%)

	Tianjin	National average
State owned	42.8	30.9
Collective owned	16.3	42.8
Foreign invested	35.8	13.1
Others	5.2	13.2

Sources: *1996 nian Tianjin tongji nianjian* [Statistical Yearbook of Tianjin 1996], Beijing: Zhongguo tongji chubanshe, 1996, p. 57; Guojia tongjiju (ed.), *Zhongguo tongji zhaiyao 1996* [A Statistical Survey of China 1996], Beijing: Zhongguo tongji chubanshe, 1996, p. 75

Table 6.3 Number and GVIO of local and central SOEs in Tianjin, 1994–1995

	1994 number	1995 number	1994 GVIO	1995 GVIO
Local SOEs	1,553	1,795	47.3bn *yuan*	45.5bn *yuan*
Central SOEs	219	132	18.5bn *yuan*	22.7 bn *yuan*

Sources: *1996 nian Tianjin tongji nianjian* [Statistical Yearbook of Tianjin 1996], Beijing: Zhongguo tongji chubanshe, 1996, pp. 57, 217–218

Dependence on foreign investment

What has allowed Tianjin to maintain public spending and these subsidies is that foreign investors have recognised the unique strategic position that Tianjin occupies in north China and have started to make up for the slack local economy through substantial investment. Foreign investment showed a remarkable increase since 1993 and foreign-invested enterprises now account for one-third of Tianjin's GVIO.[63]

Tianjin has been successful in attracting multinational corporations from Asia, USA and Europe to set up production facilities. These include:

Motorola	USA
Coca Cola	USA
Heinz	USA
Kraft Foods	USA
Toyota	Japan
Yamaha	Japan
Yazaki Auto	Japan
Dunlop	Australia (Britain)
BOC	Britain
Wella	Germany
Chiz Tai	Thailand
Huanmei Corp	Singapore

President Ind.	Taiwan
Goldstar	South Korea
Samsung	South Korea

As a result of increased foreign investment, Tianjin has been able to improve its overall economic performance to the degree that in 1995, for the first time it surpassed the national growth rate for domestic output value with a 4.2 per cent higher growth rate than the national average of 10.3 per cent. More importantly for Tianjin, this growth rate for the first time since 1992 surpassed the respective growth rates of Shanghai by 0.4 per cent and of Beijing by 2.3 per cent. Tianjin's increase in foreign direct investment for 1995 was 49.8 per cent, compared to 36 per cent in Shanghai and 1.5 per cent in Beijing.[64]

Foreign-funded enterprises were major investors and tax contributors (see Figure 6.1). Foreign investment in fixed assets in 1995 amounted to nearly one quarter of total investment (23.1 per cent), while private construction funds contributed 36 per cent, domestic loans 23.6 per cent, government budgetary allocation 2.7 per cent and others 14.6 per cent. Pre-tax profit of foreign funded enterprises accounted for nearly half of the total of all enterprises with 47 per cent, followed by the state-owned sector with 33.6 per cent and the collective sector with 13.4 per cent (see Table 6.4).

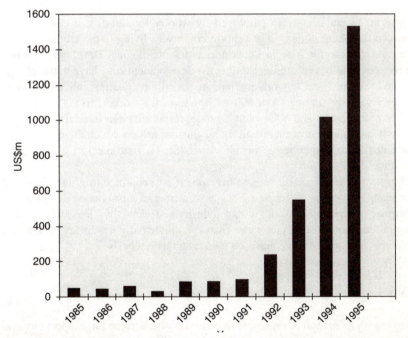

Figure 6.1 Actual foreign direct investment in Tianjin, 1985–1995 (US$ million)
Source: *1996 nian Tianjin tongji nianjian*, p. 52

Table 6.4 Tianjin's GVIO by ownership for enterprises above township level at constant 1980 prices (%)

	1980	1985	1990	1991	1992	1993	1994	1995
State owned	83.1	79.8	74.4	69.7	68.1	58.9	50.1	42.8
Collective owned	16.7	18.4	18.9	19.4	17.9	22.7	17.8	16.3
Foreign invested		0.4	3.6	9.6	10.5	14.0	24.8	35.8
Others		1.4	3.1	16.3	3.5	4.4	7.3	5.2

Sources: Calculated from *1995 nian Tianjin tongji nianjian*, p. 25; *1996 nian Tianjin tongji nianjian*, p. 57; *Zhongguo jingji nianjian*, various years

Employment by foreign-invested enterprises is relatively small compared to their overall economic role. Seen as a group, they have become the largest employer of industrial labour and constituted 80 per cent of companies actively recruiting in the Tianjin labour market in 1996. But their total labour force amounts to only 300,000 people,[65] half the number of people employed by collective enterprises, or 10 per cent of of the total workforce.

In the light of the financial contribution of foreign-funded enterprises to the municipal budget it is questionable how long Tianjin will be able to maintain the segregation between its foreign-funded and its domestic economy. In 1995, of a total workforce of 300,000 employed with foreign-funded enterprises, 140,000 people or 43 per cent were employed by wholly foreign-owned companies.[66] Between 30,000 to 40,000 joint venture employees living in the city are said to commute daily to the Tianjin Economic and Technological Development Area. Employees of joint ventures working in the development zone have to travel over two hours a day to get to work and back to their living quarters in the city. With monthly salaries ranging from 600 to 700 *yuan* for workers to 2000 *yuan* for middle management and 6000 *yuan* for more responsible managerial positions, it can only be a question of time until social tensions arise between those privileged few and the large number of people dependent on state enterprise salaries or subsidies.

Tianjin's dependence on foreign-investment will continue to grow. There are increasing instances of foreign invested enterprises outsourcing to domestic enterprises, especially in the pillar industries. Eventually, they will dictate Tianjin's economic strategies more than the municipal bureaucracy which still maintains its traditional emphasis on a broad industrial basis.

CONCLUSION

Tianjin with its natural advantages, its central position as the largest port city and its factor endowment has longed enjoyed a privileged position as the industrial centre of northern China. Since 1949, Tianjin has gradually lost its focal position, in that it has never been able to again make use of its comparative advantages. As a matter of national policy, these advantages were not fully exploited during the first three decades of the PRC when the development of the country's interior regions took precedence over its coastal areas. But political factors cannot be overlooked, as Tianjin was in intense competition with Beijing for investment funds and other resources during the first three decades of the PRC. When Beijing started to industrialise in the early 1950s, it gradually deprived Tianjin of its leading industrial status in the region. Since the beginning of the reform period, Tianjin not only had to compete with Beijing, but also with other localities for resources and preferential policies. It even faced alliances directed against its interests.

The nearness of Beijing also had its direct political effects on Tianjin. The city had to adopt a political regime that was acceptable to the central government and flexible enough to deal with its close proximity by avoiding any form of political turmoil. Not surprisingly, Tianjin had an overall moderate leadership whose emphasis was on political and social stability. The resulting economic strategy was focused on infrastructure development and income equality to the detriment of enterprise reform and social change. Tianjin thus developed its own specific economic, political and social identity during the reform period. While the municipal leadership and the resulting political culture in the city can be classified as moderate in general terms, a closer look shows a combination of conservative political and progressive social attitudes. Tianjin prided itself on its low income differential, its high social stability and its urban services and infrastructure. The weak link in this equation was the dependence of the municipal economy on state-owned enterprises. At a time when other provinces experienced phenomenal growth in their collective and private sectors of the economy, Tianjin not only tried to maintain a large number of loss-making state-owned enterprises, but even drained them of funds for its urban infrastructure development.

The one factor that brought substantial economic benefit to the city at a time when its domestic economy was sliding deeper and deeper into decline was the inflow of foreign direct investment. Attracted by its traditional advantages, its geographical position, its port, its infrastructure and its proximity to the national capital, foreign investors favoured Tianjin over many other less advantaged areas. Foreign investors now profited from Tianjin's infrastructure projects and disciplined administration. They benefited directly from a well-ordered admin- istration, low labour costs for a highly qualified urban population and a transport infrastructure that enabled them to make use of the city's geographical advan- tages. In the mid-1990s, the volume of foreign investment streaming into Tianjin started to overtake the flow of funds into southern provinces. Tianjin thus has found its niche in concentrating on foreign investment, which finds in Tianjin all the traditional advantages of the 'Gate to North China'.

But Tianjin has not solved the biggest problem of its domestic economy. It has used foreign investment to perpetuate its loss-making state-owned enterprises and is burdened with ever increasing subsidies to maintain social peace. At present, Tianjin is host to two different economies, the state-controlled domestic sector and the foreign-invested sector, both strictly segregated and on very different paths of development. Its leadership is seeking to propagate a socialist society that combines the advantages of one of the cleanest and most orderly cities in China with the living standards that come from international economic integration, while still drawing a borderline between them as far as their own society is concerned.

In the 1980s, Tianjin was falling behind Beijing and Shanghai, the two other provincial-level municipalities advantaged by national policies. The 1980s were not a period of 'quiet achievement' for an urban society which had grown accustomed to wide-ranging social services and a degree of social stability that was incompatible with the free-wheeling entrepreneurialism in less developed provinces. In the 1990s, Tianjin's competitive advantages came to bear fruit. Political conservatism and social stability turned out to be important factors in attracting large foreign investors. As Beijing focuses more on its administrative role and service functions as the national capital, Tianjin has a good chance to re-establish itself as the commercial and manufacturing centre of north China.

ACKNOWLEDGEMENTS

The author would like Professor Wei Hongyun and Associate Professor Dong Rongfeng of Nankai University, Tianjin, for their support in the research for this chapter.

NOTES

1 Dorothy J. Solinger, 'Despite Decentralisation: Disadvantages, Dependence and Ongoing Central Power in the Inland: the Case of Wuhan', *The China Quarterly*, No. 145, March 1996, pp. 1–34.
2 Jae Ho Chung, 'A Recipe of Development in China's Coastal cities: A Comparative Analysis of Qingdao and Dalian', draft paper prepared for presentation at Asian Studies Association of Australia Twentieth Anniversary Conference, La Trobe University, Melbourne, Australia, 1996, pp. 1ff.
3 For example, G. Andrew Walder, 'Economic Reform and Income Distribution in Tianjin, 1976–1986' in Deborah Davis and Ezra F. Vogel (eds), *Chinese Society on the Eve of Tiananmen – The Impact of Reform*, The Council on East Asian Studies/Harvard University, Cambridge, Mass.: Harvard University Press, 1990, pp. 135–156; Yanjie Bian, *Work and Inequality in Urban China*, Albany: State University of New York Press, 1994.
4 See George T. Crane, *The Political Economy of China's Special Economic Zones*, Armonk, New York: M.E.Sharpe, 1990.
5 Sen-dou Chang, Xu Wei-hu, and Jun-jie Sun, 'Tianjin: North China's Reviving Metropolis', in Yeung, Yue-man and Xue-wei Hu (eds), *China's Coastal Cities – Catalysts for Modernisation*, University of Hawaii Press, Honolulu, 1992, pp. 42–68.
6 'Zou xiang shijie de Tianjin' bianji weiyuanhui (ed.), *Zou xiang shijie de Tianjin* [Tianjin Opening to the World], Beijing: The Red Flag Publishing House, 1985, pp. 41ff.

7 Yao Hongzhuo (ed.), *Jindai Tianjin duiwai maoyi 1861–1948* [Modern Foreign Trade of Tianjin 1861 – 1948], Tianjin: Tianjin shehui kexueyuan chubanshe, 1993, pp. 161ff.
8 Lai Xinxia (ed.), *Tianjin jindai shi* [Modern History of Tianjin], Tianjin: Nankai daxue chubanshe, 1987, pp. 209ff.
9 Sen-dou Chang, Xu Wei-hu, and Jun-jie Sun, 'Tianjin: North China's Reviving Metropolis', p.43.
10 Luo Shuwei (ed.), *Jindai Tianjin chengshi shi* [History of the Modern City of Tianjin], Beijing: Shehui kexue chubanshe, 1993, p. 659.
11 Ibid., p. 653.
12 Gail Hershatter, *The Workers of Tianjin, 1900–1949*, Stanford: Stanford University Press, 1986.
13 Kenneth G. Lieberthal, *Revolution and Tradition in Tianjin, 1949–1952*, Stanford: Stanford University Press, 1980.
14 Wu Zhe, *Qingxie de guotu – Zhongguo quyu jingji bu pingheng fazhan de shixian yu qushi* [The Slanted Territory – Reality and Trends of China's Unbalanced Regional Economy], Beijing: Zhongguo jingji chubanshe, 1995, p. 173.
15 Ibid., p. 183.
16 Ibid., p. 173
17 Ibid.
18 Zhu Qihua (ed.), *Tianjin quanshu* [Tianjin Compendium], Tianjin: Tianjin renmin chubanshe, 1991, pp. 3, 783.
19 Ibid., p. 786.
20 Wu Zhe, *Qingxie de guotu – Zhongguo quyu jingji bu pingheng fazhan de shixian yu qushi*, p. 3.
21 See Chang, Sen-dou, Xu Wei-hu, and Jun-jie Sun, 'Tianjin: North China's Reviving Metropolis'.
22 Guowuyuan fazhan zhongxin ketizu, *Zhongguo quyu xietiao fazhan zhanlue* [China's Development Strategy for Regional Coordination], Beijing: Zhongguo jingji chubanshe, 1994, p. 84.
23 Wu Zhe, *Qingxie de guotu – Zhongguo quyu jingji bu pingheng fazhan de shixian yu qushi*, p. 104.
24 Several books have books have been written extolling the legends around Li Ruihuan. See, for example, Liu Zhanggen, *Li Ruihuan zai Tianjin* [Li Ruihuan in Tianjin], Hong Kong: Wenhua jiaoyu chubanshe, 1992; and Zheng Yi, *Li Ruihuan chuanqi* [Legends of Li Ruihuan], Hong Kong: Mingchuang chubanshe, 1991.
25 Editorial Board of Who's Who in China (ed.), *Who's Who in China – Current Leaders 1994 Edition*, Beijing: Foreign Languages Press, 1994, pp. 315ff.
26 Ibid., pp. 624ff.
27 Ibid., pp. 463ff.
28 'Tianjin jianshe 40 nian' weiyuanhui, *Tianjin jianshe 40 nian – 1949–1989* [Tianjin's Construction in the Past Forty Years], Tianjin: Tianjin kexue jishu chubanshe, 1989, p.6.
29 Ibid.
30 Dangdai Zhongguo congshu bianjibu (ed.), *Dangdai Zhongguo de Tianjin* [Tianjin in Contemporary China], Beijing: Zhongguo shehui kexue chubanshe, 1989, Vol. 2, p.101.
31 Dangdai Tianjin chengshi jianshe bianjishi, *Dangdai Tianjin chengshi jianshe* [Urban Construction in Contemporary Tianjin], Tianjin: Tianjin renmin chubanshe, 1987, pp. 259f.
32 *Tianjin jianshe 40 nian – 1949–1989*, p. 120.
33 Ibid., pp. 99ff.
34 Liu Zhanggen, *Li Ruihuan zai Tianjin*, Hong Kong: Wenhua jiaoyu chubanshe, 1992, pp. 10ff.

35   Ibid., p. 97.
36   *Dangdai Tianjin chengshi jianshe*, p. 258.
37   Ye Limin, 'Tianjin shinian gaige de huigu' [Tianjin's Ten Years of Reform in Retrospect], *Gaige*, No. 1, 1990, p. 144.
38   Ibid.
39   Ibid., p. 145.
40   Author's interviews in Tianjin in Summer 1996.
41   Guowuyuan fazhan yanjiu zhongxin UNDP xiangmuzu, *Jingji fazhan gaige yu zhengce* [Reform and Policies of Economic Development], Vol. 3, Beijing: Shehui kexue wenxian chubanshe, 1994, p. 478.
42   Ibid., p. 479.
43   Wu Zhe, 'Lun Zhongguo yanhai diqu jingji fazhan de quyu fenyi' [On the Regional Differentials of Economic Development in China's Coastal Areas], *Nankai Economic Studies*, December 1994, p. 16.
44   *Jingji fazhan gaige yu zhengce*, p. 451.
45   Kong Deyong (ed.), *Huan Huangbohai quyu jingji fazhan yanjiu – Zhong Han jingji zhanwang* [Research into the Bohai Rim Regional Economic Development – Chinese–Korean economic perspectives], Beijing: Zhonggu kexue jishu chubanshe, 1993, p. 261.
46   *Tianjin jianshe 40 nian – 1949–1989*, pp. 175ff.
47   Editorial Board of Tianjin Opening to the World (ed.), *Tianjin Opening to the World*, Beijing: The Red Flag Publishing House, 1985, p. 56.
48   *Dangdai Tianjin chengshi jianshe*, p. 396.
49   Tianjinshi tongjiju (ed.), *1995 Tianjin tongji nianjian* [Tianjin Statistical Yearbook], Beijing: Zhongguo tongji chubanshe, 1996, p. 245.
50   *Tianjin Ribao* (Tianjin Daily), 21/8/1994, FBIS-CHI-94-167.
51   See Ye Limin, 'Tianjin shinian gaige de huigu'.
52   Xie Guangbei, 'Tianjin jingji jishu kaifaqu fazhan moshi yanjiu' [Research into the development model for Tianjin's economic and technological development zones], *Nankai jingji yanjiu*, Tianjin, No. 4, 1993, p. 11.
53   *Tianjin Ribao* (Tianjin Daily), 5/3/1993, FBIS-CHI-93-069.
54   *Xinhua News Agency* (English), 9/4/1996, FBIS-CHI-96-070.
55   *Tianjin Ribao* (Tianjin Daily), 3/2/1996.
56   Li Ning, 'Bohai Rim – Focus of China's 21st Century Economic Upsurge', *Beijing Review*, February 27–March 5, 1995, pp. 11–15.
57   FBIS-CHI-93-136.
58   *Xinhua News Agency* (English), 22/11/1993, FBIS-CHI-93-223.
59   *Xinhua News Agency* (English), 3/12/1995, FBIS-CHI-95-232.
60   Author's interviews in Tianjin in Summer 1996.
61   Author's interviews in Tianjin in Summer 1996.
62   *Jingji Ribao* (Economic Daily), 11/11/1995.
63   Ma Xianlin, '1995 nian Tianjin jingji fazhan de qishi – Jing Jin Lu 3 shi duibi fenxi' [Insights from Tianjin's economic development in 1995 – a comparative analysis of the three cities of Beijing, Tianjin and Shanghai], *Lilun yu xiandaihua*, No. 7, 1996, p. 18.
64   *Tianjin tongji nianjian 1996*.
65   *Zhongguo Xinwenshe*, 6/8/1996, FBIS-CHI-96-153.
66   *Zhongguo Xinwenshe*, 6/8/1996, FBIS-CHI-96-153.

REFERENCES

Beijingshi renkou pucha bangongshi *et al.* (eds), *Jing Jin Hu Sui renkou ziliao duibi* [Beijing/Tianjin/Shanghai/Guangzhou: Comparison of Population Information], Beijing: Zhongguo tongji chubanshe, 1992.

Bian, Yanjie, *Work and Inequality in Urban China*, Albany: State University of New York Press, 1994

Chang, Sen-dou, Xu Wei-hu, and Jun-jie Sun, 'Tianjin: North China's Reviving Metropolis', in Yeung, Yue-man and Xue-wei Hu (eds), *China's Coastal Cities – Catalysts for Modernisation*, Honolulu: University of Hawaii Press, 1992, pp. 42–68

Chung, Jae Ho, 'A Recipe of Development in China's Coastal cities: A Comparative Analysis of Qingdao and Dalian', draft paper prepared for presentation at Asian Studies Association of Australia Twentieth Anniversary Conference, La Trobe University, Melbourne, 1996.

Crane, George T., *The Political Economy of China's Special Economic Zones*, Armonk, New York: M.E.Sharpe, 1990

Dangdai Zhongguo congshu bianjibu (ed.), *Dangdai Zhongguo de Tianjin* [Tianjin in Contemporary China], 2 vols., Beijing: Zhongguo shehui kexue chubanshe, 1989.

Editorial Board of Tianjin Opening to the World (ed.), *Tianjin Opening to the World*, Beijing: The Red Flag Publishing House, 1985.

Gu Shutang (ed.), *Tianjin jingji gaikuang* [Tianjin Economic Overview], Tianjin: Tianjin renmin chubanshe, 1984.

Guowuyuan fazhan zhongxin ketizu, *Zhongguo quyu xietiao fazhan zhanlue* [China's Development Strategy for Regional Coordination], Beijing: Zhongguo jingji chubanshe, 1994.

Guowuyuan fazhan yanjiu zhongxin UNDP xiangmuzu, *Jingji fazhan gaige yu zhengce* [Reform and Policies of Economic Development], Vol. 3, Beijing: Shehui kexue wenxian chubanshe, 1994.

Hershatter, Gail, *The Workers of Tianjin, 1900–1949*, Stanford: Stanford University Press, 1986.

Kong Deyong (ed.), *Huan Huangbohai quyu jingji fazhan yanjiu – Zhong Han jingji zhanwang* [Research into the Bohai Rim Regional Economic Development – Chinese–Korean Economic Perspectives], Beijing: Zhonggu kexue jishu chubanshe, 1993.

Lai Xinxia (ed.), *Tianjin jindai shi* [Modern History of Tianjin], Tianjin: Nankai daxue chubanshe, 1987.

Lieberthal, Kenneth G., *Revolution and Tradition in Tianjin, 1949–1952*, Stanford Stanford: University Press, 1980.

Liu Zhanggen, *Li Ruihuan zai Tianjin* [Li Ruihuan in Tianjin], Hong Kong: Wenhua jiaoyu chubanshe, 1992.

Luo Shuwei (ed.), *Jindai Tianjin chengshi shi* [History of the Modern City of Tianjin], Beijing: Shehui kexue chubanshe, 1993.

Ma Xianlin, '1995 nian Tianjin jingji fazhan de qishi – Jing Jin Lu 3 shi duibi fenxi' [Insights from Tianjin's economic development in 1995 – a comparative analysis of the three cities of Beijing, Tianjin and Shanghai], *Lilun yu xiandaihua*, No. 7, 1996, pp. 16–18, 27.

Quan Yanchi, *Tianjin shizhang* [Mayors of Tianjin], Beijing: Zhonggong zhongyang dangxiao chubanshe, 1993.

Tianjin jianshe 40 nian bianweihui (ed.), *Tianjin jianshe 40 nian* [Forty Years of Tianjin's Construction), Tianjin: Tianjin kexue jishu chubanshe, 1989.

Tianjinshi tongjiju (ed.), *Tianjin tongji nianjian* [Tianjin Statistical Yearbook], Beijing: Zhongguo tongji chubanshe, various years.

Walder, G. Andrew, 'Economic Reform and Income Distribution in Tianjin, 1976–1986', in Deborah Davis and Ezra F. Vogel (eds), *Chinese Society on the Eve of Tiananmen – The Impact of Reform*, The Council on East Asian Studies/Harvard University, Cambridge, Mass.: Harvard University Press, 1990, pp. 135–156.

Wan Hui and Wan Xinping, *Huan Bohai jingjiquan – Tianjin juan* [The Bohai Rim Economic Circle – Tianjin Volume], Beijing: Shehui kexue wenxuan chubanshe, 1996.

Wu Zhe, 'Lun Zhongguo yanhai diqu jingji fazhan de quyu fenyi' [On the Regional Differentials of Economic Development in China's Coastal Areas], *Nankai Economic Studies*, December 1994, pp. 15–20.

Wu Zhe, *Qingxie de guotu – Zhongguo quyu jingji bu pingheng fazhan de shixian yu qushi* [The slanted territory – reality and trends of China's unbalanced regional economy], Beijing: Zhongguo jingji chubanshe, 1995.

Xie Guangbei, 'Tianjin jingji jishu kaifaqu fazhan moshi yanjiu' [Research into the development model for Tianjin's economic and technological development zones], *Nankai jingji yanjiu*, Tianjin, No. 4, 1993, pp. 11–19.

Yao Hongzhuo (ed.), *Jindai Tianjin duiwai maoyi 1861 – 1948* [Modern Foreign Trade of Tianjin 1861 – 1948], Tianjin: Tianjin shehui kexueyuan chubanshe, 1993.

Ye Limin, 'Tianjin shinian gaige de huigu' [Tianjin's ten years of reform in retrospect] , *Gaige*, No. 1, 1990, pp. 143–146.

Zheng Yi, *Li Ruihuan chuanqi* [Legends of Li Ruihuan], Hong Kong: Mingchuang chubanshe, 1991.

Zhu Qihua (ed.), *Tianjin quanshu* (Tianjin Compendium), Tianjin: Tianjin renmin chubanshe, 1991.

Zhu Tong, 'Tianjin fazhan haiwai zhijie touzi de zhanlue chutan' (Enquiry into Tianjin's development of a strategy for foreign direct investment), in Nankai jingji yanjiusuo niankan bianweihui, *Nankai jingji yanjiusuo niankan* (Yearbook of the Nankai Economic Research Institute, 1985), Tianjin: Nankai daxue chubanshe, 1987, pp. 122–134.

Shanxi Province

GENERAL

GDP (billion *yuan*)	130.60
GDP annual growth rate	11.00
as % national average	114.60
GDP per capita	4,199.10
as % national average	74.90
Gross Value Agricultural Output (billion *yuan*)	35.30
Gross Value Industrial Output (billion *yuan*)	205.50

POPULATION

Population (million)	31.09
Natural growth rate (per 1,000)	16.60

WORKFORCE

Total workforce (million)	14.80
Employment by activity (%)	
primary industry	43.30
secondary industry	29.40
tertiary industry	27.20
Employment by sector (%)	
urban	35.14
rural	64.86
Employment by ownership (%)	
state	26.35
collective	35.81
private	10.14
foreign-funded	0.20

WAGES AND INCOME

Average annual wage (*yuan*)   5,183.00
Growth rate in real wage   1.40
Urban disposable income per capita   3,702.69
    as % national average   76.50
Rural per capita income   1,557.19
    as % national average   80.80

PRICES

CPI annual rise (%)   17.90
Service price index rise   14.40
Per capita consumption (*yuan*)   1,589.00
    as % national average   59.40

FOREIGN TRADE AND INVESTMENT

Total foreign trade (US$ billion)   1.20
    as % provincial GDP   7.50
Exports (US$ billion)   0.90
Imports (US$ billion)   0.20
Realised foreign capital (US$ billion)   0.20
    as % provincial GDP   1.30

EDUCATION

University enrolments   68,842.00
    as % national average   89.70
Secondary school enrolments (million)   1.61
    as % national average   110.70
Primary school enrolments (million)   3.35
    as % national average   96.70

Notes: All statistics are for 1996 and all growth rates are for 1996 over 1995 and are adapted from *Zhongguo tongji nianjian 1997* [Statistical Yearbook of China 1997], Zhongguo tongji chubanshe, Beijing, 1997, as reformulated and presented in *Provincial China* no. 5, May 1998, pp. 68ff.

Shanxi Province

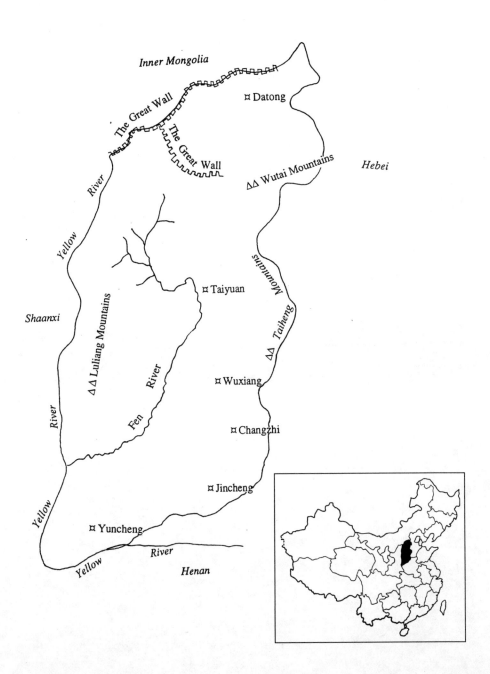

7 King Coal and Secretary Hu

Shanxi's third modernisation

David S.G. Goodman

Shanxi Province is perhaps more usually thought of, both inside as well as outside China, in terms of an undeveloped poor peasant economy rather than as an urbanised, industrialised economy. In part the dominance of the poor peasant perspective on Shanxi in popular consciousness is a function of the province's role in the Sino–Japanese War when it was the location for the three strongest of the Chinese Communist Party's [CCP] front-line base areas – in Jin-Cha-Ji, Jin-Ji-Lu-Yu and Jin-Sui – and the later uses of that history after the establishment of the People's Republic of China [PRC]. Such impressions were undoubtedly assisted during the 1950s to 1970s by the province's support for radical rural policy initiatives, of which the most famous was undoubtedly the national campaign to 'Learn from Dazhai' – the former model production brigade in the Taihang Mountains on the province's eastern border. Though Shanxi undoubtedly does have more than its average share of poor peasants – some 12 per cent of the provincial population are considered to live in rural poverty – none the less Shanxi is, and has been since the 1920s, one of China's more industrialised and urbanised provinces.[1]

Industrialisation came first to Shanxi at a relatively early stage for inland China under the direction of the provincial warlord Yan Xishan. Industrialisation in the 1920s first concentrated on the weapons and military-related industries, but in the 1930s widened out considerably to meet Yan's goals of modernising the province through the introduction of a command economy. Shanxi's second industrialisation came with the establishment of the PRC and the development of heavy industry in the province, especially its coal industry: Shanxi is estimated to contain 30 per cent of national coal reserves, a large proportion of which is high quality anthracite and bituminous varieties.

Shanxi's reform era, effectively its third attempt at modernisation, was somewhat slow to start in comparison to other parts of China. This tardiness was partly due to political problems left over from the period of the Cultural Revolution which combined with the earlier overemphasis on heavy industrial development to create both inflationary pressures and resistance to change. However, the 1990s have seen a dramatic change in the provincial developmental strategy that has begun not only to have a significant impact on Shanxi but also to offer the prospect that the province may not always be bound to fall behind national rates of growth, as had begun to seem to be its fate during the 1980s. The key features of this new strategy have been designed to ensure both Shanxi's greater integration in itself as well as into the national economy. Part of that strategy has been the realisation of the importance of the cultural reconstruction of Shanxi, which has been particularly noticeable since 1992.

Coal and political leadership have played crucial roles in this emerging transformation. Coal is found in 94 of Shanxi's 110 counties and is under 40 per cent of the land. Its extraction is the predominant primary industry in a provincial economy almost exclusively based on primary industry before the 1990s. Since 1992 the modernisation and transformation of the coal industry has been at the forefront of the drive for change in Shanxi as the provincial strategy has moved from almost exclusive reliance on extraction and export of primary produce to the development of provincial processing and manufacturing. In the case of the coal industry this has meant – amongst other developments – the large-scale development of an electricity industry in Shanxi, based on thermal power plants and long-distance power transmission lines to other provinces.

Many of the changes of the 1990s might well have occurred under any provincial leadership, and developments since 1992 certainly continue trends started in the mid-1980s. None the less, in the first half of the 1990s Shanxi had a leadership which was both more than competent and largely home-grown, and so all too aware of the province's strengths and weaknesses. In that context, the arrival of Hu Fuguo in Shanxi in 1992 – first as provincial governor and later CCP secretary – acted as a considerable catalyst to more far-reaching change.

TRADITIONAL SHANXI

Throughout the twentieth century the political leaderships of Shanxi Province and Shanxi people generally have liked to think of themselves as in some sense guardians of the essential 'Chineseness'. While it is easy to see why such an attitude might have been adopted and it is clearly one aspect of provincial political culture, it is also far from a total explanation. Shanxi's political culture has also been shaped by other traditions that are equally as important for understanding its development in the reform era, not the least of which has been a stronger sense of local than provincial identity. In the last half of the nineteenth and first half of the twentieth centuries European influence in Shanxi was quite substantial, particularly for an inland province, largely through missionary activity. Between the end of the Qing Dynasty and Japanese invasion in 1937 Shanxi was ruled by Yan Xishan, who attempted to introduce his own form of conservative modernisation. During the Sino–Japanese War Shanxi was the major location for the CCP's front-line activities and expanding influence. Amongst other things, history bequeathed a tradition of peasant radicalism to Shanxi that persisted right through to the late 1970s. In addition, under the PRC, Shanxi has been a major recipient of state investment and developed as a national industrial base, and that too has influenced Shanxi's political culture.

'Chineseness'

Almost every introduction to Shanxi emphasises that the province is both a major source of Han culture and tradition, and that Shanxi people are both aware and proud of its long history.[2] The length of Shanxi's history is incontestable: a quarter of all Early Stone Age sites in China are located in the province. The traditional single-character signifier of the province – Jin – refers to the principality that was established there in the eigth century BCE, well before the unification of China, and within the province Shanxi is frequently referred to as *San Jin* because of the three separate political entities that succeeded Jin during the Warring States Period.[3] As elsewhere in China current commentary frequently employs both local and provincial historical examples to make a point, even though the definition of 'recent' in Shanxi is more usually to events since the Tang Dynasty rather than to the twentieth century.[4] The reason for such usage is relatively straightforward: the Li family that established the Tang Dynasty originated in Shanxi and its decline as a centre of wealth and political influence started after the fall of that dynasty, though there was a resurgence in the province's economic situation in the late Qing when Shanxi became a national centre for commerce and banking.[5]

Shanxi is, of course, not unique in its sense of history within provincial China. However, under both Yan Xishan and the CCP there have been and remain elements of both exclusivity and superiority in the definition of Shanxi's identity and its place in Chinese culture which do mark the province out as somewhat different. Yan Xishan's brand of Confucian revivalism was based on the presentation of Shanxi as the last bastion of a fast-disappearing 'Chineseness', and for a variety of reasons created the notion of the province as not only conservative but also inward-looking. Gillin in his study of Shanxi during the 1930s referred to 'the unusually conservative outlook' that held 'a profound regard for the ideas and institutions of the past' and an 'intense pride' in Shanxi before anything else.[6] Yan Xishan went to considerable lengths to exclude external influences and foster Shanxi's insularity, most dramatically by his refusal to build the provincial railways using the standard national gauge.[7]

Since 1949 the link between the CCP's history during the Sino–Japanese War and Shanxi as a principal site of Yellow River culture has meant that the province has always been seen by the party-state as a major contributing influence to national identity. In the reform era this use of the idea of Shanxi has grown particularly in the 1990s with the public debates on the meaning of 'Chineseness', and the CCP's increased appeal to feelings of Chinese nationalism. Thus, for example, Hongtong County in the Linfen region of South Shanxi has been promoted as the mythical site of origin of all Han Chinese.[8] A number of recent films and television films have been made on location in Shanxi, making use not so much of its landscapes as its 'traditional' buildings, streetscapes and artefacts. For example, *The East: Anatomy of a Great Civilisation* and *The Peasants* – a couple of television series from the early 1990s dealing with the relevance of Chinese traditions to the present and the future – were both filmed in South Shanxi.

Raise the Red Lantern was filmed for the commerical cinema at Qiaojiadayuan in Qixian, Jinzhong. Though it is debatable whether this and other films are themselves supportive or critical of current politics, none the less the marketing of their 'traditional' locations within Shanxi has been promoted within a distinct conservative discourse that seeks to define 'Chineseness' in specific ways.[9] In similar vein, Shanxi's reputation for traditional values was clearly what attracted the author of *The Third Eye Looks at China* – a conservative critique of the reform era that became a *cause célèbre* not only because of its controversial content but also because the arguments were presented as though they were those of a German and the book first appeared as a translation – to publish with the Shanxi People's Publishing House in Taiyuan.[10]

Filming or making television programmes in Shanxi highlights one of its more obvious contemporary comparative advantages. Given adequate access, Shanxi could be a major tourist centre within China. It has a far greater than average number of temples, pagodas, palaces, buildings, paintings, statues and artefacts that not only offer glimpses into traditional China but that have hardly been opened to tourism. The most spectacular include the Yungang Grottoes near Datong; the walled city of Pingyao; the ceramic life-size funerary figures of Jinci; the Yongle Gong – and particularly its frescoes – in South Shanxi; and Wutaishan – the sacred mountain and first site of Buddhism in China. However, until recently the development of tourism in Shanxi has been hampered by poor transport facilities both within the province and linking Shanxi to the rest of China and the outside world.

Provincial identity and local variety

Shanxi has almost no minority nationalities and there are fairly obvious shared characteristics in the economic geography of all the province's different regions. Most of the province is mountainous, with settlement concentrated in the plains and valleys in-between. Coal is found in every part of the province and there is widespread mining, though there are distinct regional variations in the quality of the coal: the highest quality coal is found in Datong and Yangquan. Agriculturally the staples are produced through dry-cropping and rice is a rarity. In consequence, Shanxi's cuisine centres on grains such as millet, sorghum, oats, wheat, and maize, and is largely flour-based, resulting in noodles, breads and pancakes. Potatoes are both common and popular in much of the province, which is why elsewhere in China Shanxi people are often referred to (and sometimes even affectionately) as 'the potato gang'.[11] Apart from its noodles – which appear in many different forms – the most famous aspect of Shanxi's eating habits is its vinegar. Vinegar is consumed in such large quantities in Shanxi and considered so central to life that its price remains controlled.[12]

Despite shared characteristics, provincial identity has been much less strong in Shanxi than local and regional identity. The province has four distinct regions. The longest-settled region of the province, which consequently makes the greatest claim to essential 'Chineseness', is the southwestern quarter of Shanxi, usually referred to as 'South Shanxi' or *Hedong* (east of the river) because its western and southern borders are the Yellow River. The southeast quarter of the province is *Shangdang* which centres on Changzhi and Jincheng and includes the Changzhi Plain, as well as the mountains and mountain valleys of the Taihang Range. Changzhi is a major central marketing area for neighbouring parts of Henan as well as its region of Shanxi.[13] *Jinzhong* (Central Shanxi) is the region of the provincial capital in Taiyuan, the Taiyuan basin and the Fen River valley down towards Linfen. It is a traditionally rich agricultural area and at least partly in consequence was able to support the development of Shanxi's Exchange Shops – a native banking tradition that emerged in the late Qing.[14]

Hedong, Shangdang and Jinzhong correspond roughly to the *San Jin* of the Warring States era. Contemporarily the fourth region of Shanxi is usually referred to as *Yanbei* and is the land – much of which is plain – north of the mountains that separated Tang Shanxi from the Imperial borderlands and the peoples of Inner Asia. Although this region was the centre of the Northern Wei Dynasty (that dominated North China in the fifth century), it was not incorporated permanently into the Chinese state until after 1300. Datong is the centre of this region, which in the Republican era and under the PRC until 1952 formed part of the separate province of Chahar.

Each of Shanxi's regions has created a relatively strong pattern of identification whose most obvious manifestations are cultural, linguistic and culinary. Such differences are most immediately obvious in Yanbei where Mongolian and Inner Asian influences have been assimilated over the centuries, though not to the extent, as is sometimes suggested, that this region should still be regarded as somehow 'less Chinese'.[15] Even musical traditions vary with Shanxi opera firmly established in South Shanxi, but the Shangdang drama and Shandang folk drama traditions in Southeast Shanxi.[16] Across the province there are strong regional variations in language, so that – quite apart from differences in pronunciation, accent, cadence and grammar – there are major differences in vocabulary.[17]

The point at issue here is not that people in Shanxi's regions do not identify with the province as a whole – that is taken as a given. Rather, they identify more strongly with their village, county and region. There is a distinct hierarchy of identification that starts with the village, and extends with decreasing intensity to encompass county, region and province. This was clearly the case in 1913 and 1917 when South Shanxi rose in rebellion against Yan Xishan, then Shanxi's warlord-in-the-making. These were not movements for separation but protests against what was seen as Yan Xishan's exploitation of South Shanxi to the benefit of Taiyuan and his native Wutai district.[18]

External influences

Twentieth century explanations of Shanxi as the source of 'Chineseness' have tended to portray the province as both conservative and inward-looking, almost completely immune to external influences. They have exaggerated the extent to which it is isolated from the rest of the world by mountains and an impassable terrain. While Shanxi's topography is inescapable, Shanxi was far from completely isolated from external influences and interactions even well before 1949. Shanxi was traditionally a border and trading province: the route into China for many of the Inner Asian people's to the north and a major staging post in the opposite direction. Indeed this was a major source of its wealth in earlier times. It was also regularly the point of entry into China for external religious influences and ideas, including most spectacularly Buddhism.

Quite apart from being on a route of conquest, the north–south passage through Shanxi also became an important trading route. This was one stimulus to Shanxi's banking tradition which developed in the eighteenth and nineteenth centuries when merchants came to Jinzhong on their way from East to West China and required exchange and credit facilities. From Shanxi local bankers used to travel all over China providing rural credit and commerce. In the nineteenth century Shanxi bankers established branch offices in Mongolia, Russia, Korea, Afghanistan and communications with these countries and beyond became quite common.

Shanxi's links with the outside world were further developed in the late nineteenth and early twentieth centuries when the province was a main centre of Christian missionary activity. The China Inland Mission under the English missionary Timothy Richards – who was also later involved in the Reform Movement – established its headquarters in Taiyuan. The Mission was particularly active in education and played a central role in the development of Shanxi University and later the provincial modern school system. The Taiyuan Massacre (of largely foreign Christians) during the Boxer Uprising was an international event of some notoriety that led directly to pressure for the payment of an indemnity. The resultant funds were used to rebuild Shanxi University in full Oxford University style, complete with crenellated roof-line.

In the twentieth century large contingents of both Presbyterians and Methodists followed the Anglicans to Shanxi. Although the relationship between the missionaries and Yan Xishan was often uneasy, missionaries were active in education and public health work and built sizeable churches and congregations. The non-conformist churches in Taiyuan now house government offices and the Shanxi Provincial People's Political Consultative Conference. However, outside Taiyuan, especially in the towns and villages of rural Jinzhong, Christianity has remained active throughout the twentieth century, including the era of the PRC.

Yan Xishan and conservative modernisation

Despite their considerable influence the Christian missionaries in Shanxi were a far less powerful force for the province's modernisation than Yan Xishan, the effective warlord of Shanxi from 1911 to 1937.[19] Yan Xishan's place in history is just about due for revision.[20] As a long-term opponent of both Chiang Kai-shek's Nationalist Party and the CCP, Yan is currently judged more for his failures and the difficulties encountered in his admittedly ambitious reform programme than for what was actually achieved. Reform may not have brought fundamental social, political or economic change, but conflict within both China and the Nationalist Party (particularly before 1930) and the threat of foreign invasion (from 1931 to 1937) meant that there were few years of uninterrupted progress. When stable policies could be implemented – notably from 1920 to 1926 and again from 1931 to 1934 – the preliminary results were impressive and bequeathed to Shanxi a substantial infrastructure of modernisation, including experience of a command economy.

Yan's policies on development and reform were far from constant over the 26 years of his ascendancy. In particular, from 1931 his attitudes became far more urgent and radical. During the 1930s many of Yan Xishan's policies and practices were direct precursors of those to be followed by the CCP, sometimes in quite some detail, as for example in his approach to the politicisation of culture and education in general and the *yangge* in particular. However, on the whole he was essentially a conservative reformer in the mould of Tseng Kuo-fan and the Tung-chih Restoration. A professional soldier, educated in Japan and a member of Sun Yat-sen's Revolutionary Alliance, he wanted to adapt Western technologies and practices but his ultimate goal was a Confucian revivalism based on his own interpretations and writings.

In the 1920s Yan's reform policies were concerned as much with education and value change as with economic modernisation. Universal and free primary education, and the expansion of secondary schooling were introduced alongside dissemination of Yan's own ideas about social progress. To that latter end he established a Heart-washing Society encouraging intense self-criticism and self-cultivation, and developed a Good People's Movement which stressed the importance of cleanliness, diligence, honesty, modesty, obedience and thrift.

At this time attempts at industrialisation were limited though they did include the establishment of the Taiyuan Arsenal, which soon became one of the largest and most productive in the country with a workforce of about 10,000; and the development of a sulphates factory, a machine tool factory, an iron and steel plant and refineries designed to process coal; as well as more light industrial concerns including flour, cotton and paper mills; and a cigarette factory. However, in the expansion of communications during the 1920s Yan's pro-gramme had a permanent impact on Shanxi with the development of road and telecommunications networks – the extended rail network planned at this time had to wait until the 1930s for its introduction. As in the development of the munitions industry, these improvements may well have been occasioned by military considerations but their impact was felt more widely. The 1929 famine in north China was able to be met in Shanxi by the ready provision of relief compared to the starvation of neighbouring provinces.[21]

Yan's determined drive to modernise came after 1931 with a Provincial Ten Year Plan for Economic Reconstruction clearly modelled on the experience of the USSR. Shanxi's development was to be planned, protectionist and achieved without external assistance. By the mid-1930s economic modernisation had become equated with state control to such an extent that almost all industry and commerce was owned by the provincial government. Popular education and propaganda continued as in the 1920s, but now there was a new emphasis on science and technology.

In the 1930s considerable investment and military support was poured into industrial development. New mines were developed and coal production doubled between 1930 and 1934. The Taiyuan Arsenal and associated plants were expanded into a series of capital equipment factories. A chemicals and iron and steel industry were developed in Taiyuan and in East Shanxi, and a modern steel mill established in Taiyuan. The Ten Year Plan also saw the establishment of tanneries, paper mills, a printing plant and a distillery, as well as various heavy-industry supporting factories and plants. The electricity generating power of the province increased out of all comparison with the addition of ten new power stations. A railway was built (largely by the provincial army) from northeast to southwest Shanxi through the centre of the province, and the telephone system was tripled in size.

Peasant radicalism

Yan Xishan's programme for agriculture was equally as radical and as closely modelled on the experience of the USSR, but his plans ran out of time and were forestalled by Japan's invasion in 1937. By that time, Yan Xishan and the CCP were in full alliance which, amongst other things, permitted the latter to establish its base areas, and later its border region governments, in northeast Shanxi (Jin-Cha-Ji), northwest Shanxi (Jin-Sui), and southeast Shanxi (Jin-Ji-Lu-Yu). These three areas played a crucial role in the development of the CCP's drive for national power[22] and bequeathed legacies to the post-1949 era whose influences remain important even into the reform period.

The most obvious consequence of the CCP presence in Shanxi during the Sino–Japanese War was that by 1945 the CCP had developed a significant social base. The Nationalist Party had never been strong in Shanxi largely because of Yan Xishan's relationship with Chiang Kai-shek, and Yan's political support came from urban Shanxi rather than the countryside. With the introduction of land reform during the Civil War that followed, the CCP cemented its community of interest with the peasantry so that even into the 1990s families remain proud to describe themselves as *tubalu* – peasants who had been liberated by the Eighth Route Army, the communist forces of the Sino–Japanese War.

At the same time, the expansion of the CCP presence in Shanxi during the Sino–Japanese War also meant that the CCP recruited large numbers of members from Shanxi, and after 1949 had many leading cadres with direct experience of Shanxi. Where the first generation of CCP revolutionaries came predominantly from Hunan, Hupei and Jiangxi – the areas of early party activity – the generation recruited during the Sino–Japanese War were disproportionately from north China, and particularly Shanxi. This meant that in the post-1949 era there were always Shanxi people able to be appointed by the CCP to the Shanxi provincial leadership, and that concentrations of Shanxi natives were likely to be found in the leaderships of other provinces – as for example in Sichuan before the Cultural

Revolution[23] – and other parts of the political system. An important element in any such calculus of Shanxi's potential political influence is the role played by three senior long-term CCP leaders with roots in Shanxi: Bo Yibo and Peng Zhen, who were both natives, and Deng Xiaoping, the ranking party cadre in Jin-Ji-Lu-Yu during the Sino–Japanese War, whose advisers and supporters during the reform era were disproportionately drawn from that border region.[24]

Perhaps the most obvious way in which Shanxi's political influence was felt nationally after 1949 – apart from through the appointment of personnel – was in the development of rural and agricultural policy. Shanxi's political and physical proximity to Beijing ensured that it became a source for national policies of peasant radicalism. The cooperativisation of agricultural production was already well under way in Shanxi by late 1951, and particularly in the Shangdang region and the areas around Changzhi. In the national debates over collectivisation within the CCP during the 1950s Shanxi was frequently cited approvingly by those attempting a faster and more radical pace of change.[25] This trend culminated in and after 1963 in the national campaigns to 'Learn from Dazhai', the production brigade in the Yangquan area that had been practising 'self-reliance' and became a byword for Mao's radical rural policies.[26]

Whilst Shanxi's policies of peasant radicalism may have brought it much kudos nationally, within the province they led to political tensions. The former base areas came increasingly into conflict with the rest of the province in the 1950s. Contestation initially emerged over resource allocation since it was national policy to ensure privileged treatment for mountain areas and the old base areas. So acute were such tensions that, on grounds of equity, 64 counties (of the 100 counties at the time in Shanxi) were classified as 'mountainous' in order to receive additional funding and support.[27] In the 1960s and again in the 1970s there were new tensions over the appropriateness of the campaign to 'Learn from Dazhai' for the whole province. There were concerns that Dazhai's programme was simply rehearsing the failures of the Great Leap Forward, and whilst the Dazhai model might be a possible solution for mountain regions and drought-stricken areas it was much less useful to development elsewhere.[28]

Heavy industrial development

Yan Xishan's programme of modernisation and Japan's colonialism presented Shanxi with a head-start in its development as a national centre of heavy industry after 1949. The province already had a considerable industrial infrastucture. The coal industry was well established in Datong and Yangquan; Yan's Taiyuan industrial complex had been further developed and technically upgraded; and the Japanese had considerably improved communications within Shanxi, including the conversion of most of Yan Xishan's central railway line to standard gauge track. A second and less obvious advantage of Shanxi's earlier experience of modernisation was that most of the provincial industry and commerce was already state owned by the early 1950s and the process of socialisation was less traumatic than might otherwise have been the case.[29]

A start was made in realising Shanxi's potential during the period of the First Five Year Plan through the receipt of considerable central investment. Total central investment 1952–7 was about 1.625 billion *yuan*, which was equivalent to about 56 per cent of GDP in 1957.[30] Investment had two particular focuses: Taiyuan and the coal industry. Taiyuan received a quarter of all investment in the province during the First Five Year Plan, for amongst other projects, the development of the Taiyuan Iron and Steel Plant as China's major specialist steel centre; the Taiyuan Thermal Power Plant; chemical and fertiliser plants; and the expansion of the machinery industry, especially mining machinery. Coal industry development centred on bituminous seams in Datong – where some 30 mines were either refurbished or newly opened – and anthracite in Yangquan.

Shanxi's industrial growth was impressive during the 1950s: the average annual growth rate of industry's share of GDP was 34 per cent a year from 1952 to 1959.[31] At the same time, the specific conditions of Shanxi and the way growth was generated created problems for both the short term and of longer-term significance. In the short term there was a lack of the necessary social infrastructure to support the rapid expansion of the industrial workforce and Shanxi's increased urbanisation.[32] In the longer term Shanxi was faced by inadequate water supplies, poor communications with the rest of China, and little or no development of consumer goods or light industry .

In addition, Shanxi's close political relationship with Beijing resulted in quite a tight economic dependancy. A high proportion of Shanxi's economy was effectively under Beijing's direct control. By 1957, 30 per cent of provincial gross value of industrial output (GVIO) was produced by central government enterprises. Whilst Beijing was willing or able to support Shanxi's industrial development, a dependant relationship posed few problems to the province. However, this relationship changed to Shanxi's disadvantage with the introduction of Mao Zedong's 'Third Front' Project during the late 1960s and early 1970s which diverted resources further west and into China's interior. Although, the Cultural Revolution and factional politics clearly had an adverse impact on Shanxi's economic development, and particularly industrial output, during 1965–1975, the introduction of the 'Third Front' Project reinforced this trend and denied Shanxi the support it required for its continued development. Industrial growth was on average less than 1 per cent a year from 1965 to 1976 as the number of central enterprises in Shanxi fell from 238 to 49, and overall economic growth was similarly if not as severely muted.[33]

ECONOMIC REFORM

Shanxi's economic development in the reform era has been characterised both by its relatively slow start and its resonances with earlier attempts at modernisation in the province. Most inland provinces were almost inevitably slower off the marks of reform than those in the coastal regions, and particularly compared to those in the south of China. In addition, Shanxi suffered from the severe dislocations in its political economy during the previous decade. A significant turning point in provincial development appears to have been 1992. During 1982–1984 a renewed emphasis nationally on the development of Shanxi's primary industries resulted in double digit general economic growth. However, from 1985–1989 and into the early 1990s growth rates dropped dramatically and growth in GDP fell behind inflation[34] largely because of the effects of a national development strategy focused on the coastal areas and the need for new provincial perspectives. Since 1992 Shanxi's reform programme has faced the need for a redirection and has been radically revitalised through the introduction of a new 'Overtaking Strategy' which has already proved successful.

Catching up and falling behind

Shanxi's role in the history of the CCP – and particularly the Sino–Japanese War – seems somewhat paradoxically to have been a principal reason for its disfavour during the decade of Cultural Revolution. Peng Zhen and Bo Yibo were both major targets for criticism and attack by the radical forces of the Cultural Revolution, and their connections in Shanxi clearly suffered through association. Unlike many other provinces, Shanxi had not been dominated by 'outsiders' during the first two decades of the PRC but had been led by Shanxi natives and cadres who had lived and worked in the province for some time. All the pre-Cultural Revolution governors of Shanxi – Cheng Zihua, Lai Ruoyu, Pei Lisheng, Wang Shiying, Wei Heng and Wang Qian – and most of the provincial first CCP secretaries at the same time – Cheng Zihua, Lai Ruoyu, Gao Kelin, Tao Lujia and Wei Heng – were Shanxi natives. The only exceptions were Gao Kelin and Tao Lujia. Gao was a native of Shaanxi who had long served in Suiyuan. Tao, although originally from Jiangsu, had been in Shanxi since the start of the Sino–Japanese War where he had served in the Taihang base area and by any standard could not really be regarded as an 'outsider'. The nativism of Shanxi's leadership changed somewhat during 1965–75 when its ranking cadres came from outside the province.

However, the leadership changes of the Cultural Revolution – now regarded as 'leftist mistakes'[35] – had not been achieved without cost. Shanxi was the first province to undertake a 'seizure of power' based on the alliance of provincial 'revolutionary rebels', PLA troops and representatives of mass organisations.[36] In January 1967, shortly after the Shanghai Commune was announced, the authority of the CCP Shanxi Committee was overthrown, if not from below, then at least largely from outside the structures – informal as well as formal – of provincial political power. This 'revolutionary three-in-one combination' was heralded nationally as the model 'seizure of power' in the Cultural Revolution, with Mao Zedong even going on record to tell Shanghai's leadership that it should follow the Shanxi example.[37]

One particular reason the 'revolutionary three-in-one combination' had been used in Shanxi to achieve the Central Cultural Revolution Group's ends was the hardly surprising strength – given the CCP's history in the province – of the entrenched local establishment. A necessary corollary was that such processes left deep divisions within the province that could not quickly be remedied, not least because politics in the late 1960s and into the 1970s were not simply polarised between Shanxi natives and those from outside the province, or localist interests as against national concerns. There were Shanxi natives and even senior cadres from before the Cultural Revolution who sided with the radical forces. Moreover, there were clearly a number of underlying issues of regional inequality within Shanxi with tensions between urban and rural areas; mountain regions on the one hand, and the plains and river valleys on the other; and even to some extent the north and the south of the province, given that the technological benefits of industrialisation had tended to move south from Taiyuan along the valley of the Fenhe. These and similar problems concerned the post-Cultural Revolution leadership of Shanxi and were not fully resolved until the Fourth Session of the Sixth Provincial People's Congress in May 1986.

Apart from the effects on personnel and appointments, divisions within the leadership of Shanxi meant that the 'leftism' of the Cultural Revolution and the period since 1957 was slow to be removed in areas of policy. For example, decollectivisation emerged far slower in Shanxi than in many other provinces. Though the Dazhai Work Management Method was abandoned by the province in 1979 after the Third Plenum, none the less the first stage of decollectivisation, the substitution of collective work by household contracts, was not achieved until the end of 1983.[38]

At the same time, the end of the politics of Cultural Revolution and the national changes in policy settings had a more immediate impact on some aspects of Shanxi's development. This was noticeably the case with national support and increased central investment for the development of Shanxi's heavy industry during the Sixth Five Year Plan which led to a rapid recovery in the early 1980s. The number of enterprises, the extent of activities and the size of output all increased dramatically, not least as the reductions and changes of the Cultural Revolution were simply reversed. In 1984 industrial output increased by 19 per cent over the previous year and GDP grew by 21 per cent.

The number of large-scale central government enterprises in Shanxi doubled from 1980 to 1984. The development of the coal industry led the way, with the refurbishment of some mines and the establishment of others, including the Pingshuo Mine, which is the world's largest open-cast coal mine. In addition Shanxi developed new thermal power stations (for the transmission of electricity to other provinces), the Taiyuan Iron and Steel Plant's specialist steel production, and the start of an aluminium industry to exploit Shanxi's bauxite reserves, estimated to be 42 per cent of the national total. These and other projects were all relatively successful. By the 1990s Shanxi had become the aluminium as well as the coal capital of China, and had developed the country's largest aluminium smelter. Seventy-eight per cent of transported coal in China emanated from Shanxi; and 40 per cent of China's stainless steel was being produced at the Taiyuan Iron and Steel Plant, as was 33 per cent of all silicon steel.

On the other hand, the restoration and further development of the status quo ante did nothing to assist in the resolution of Shanxi's longer-term problems. When the Seventh Five Year Plan diverted national resources elsewhere once again – in the second half of the 1980s and to the development of the coastal regions – Shanxi's economic growth slowed in tandem. The distinct prospect for Shanxi became one of inevitably falling increasingly behind national average growth rates.

Structural imbalances

In the late 1980s the long-term problems facing Shanxi were by no means new and some even dated back to the 1920s. A fundamental problem in a number of different ways has been the role of the state in economic development and the subsequent structure of the provincial economy. Since the 1920s almost all Shanxi's industry has been state owned, and the emphasis in industrial development has been overwhelmingly on large-scale heavy industry. Even in the mid-1990s some 78 per cent of Shanxi's industrial economy is heavy industry. A substantial proportion of Shanxi's economy remains not only state owned but under the direction of central government, despite the decentralisations of the 1980s. There are one hundred central government enterprises – all of them large scale – in Shanxi in the coal, power, post and telecommunications, railway, nonferrous metals and munitions industries, including the relatively newly developed satellite and missile launching site in Kelan County. Central government's share of these provincial industries ranges from a complete monopoly in munitions and railway concerns to about a third of mined coal, through seven very large coal mines. Central government enterprises in Shanxi are estimated to be responsible for about 25 per cent of the total value of provincial production, which it is also estimated – by officials in the province – to be likely to be amongst the largest proportionate share of a provincial economy.[39]

Shanxi's dependency on central government and state industry has brought clear advantages but it has also posed structural challenges, quite apart from the obvious difficulties caused when, as in the Cultural Revolution and second half of the 1980s, resources and investment were not available to support its continued development. As elsewhere in China, a large part of Shanxi's industry uses outdated technology and is woefully inefficient. Remarkably, of the 340 large and medium-sized state-owned industrial enterprises in the province in the early 1990s more than 200 had been built before the mid-1950s, and some dated from the 1920s and 1930s.[40]

One set of problems results from tensions between the planned and marketised economies, and problems of transition between the two. Shanxi is at the core of the planned economy, and a substantial part of the provincial economy is planned, yet competitiveness and success are now determined by the market and state pricing policy sometimes struggles to keep up with the pace of change. An obvious example in Shanxi is not in heavy industry but in vinegar production. The price of vinegar remains controlled and has not been allowed to rise with inflation and market forces. Prices are set at the county level effectively by Qingxu County, which dominates vinegar production. However, the costs of vinegar production have now increased so much that every vinegar factory in Shanxi knows it will make a loss every year.[41] Much of Shanxi's heavy industrial output remains subject to price controls and there is a persistent lobby for higher prices, especially for coal and energy. Price reform is probably inevitable but so too are changes in the province's investment structure which will mean less investment by central government.

The more long-term consequences of central government dependence have been that apart from heavy industry Shanxi's infrastructural development has been fairly limited. Shanxi has perennially faced problems with an inadequate water supply and restricted transport and communications links with the rest of China and indeed the world. Furthermore, there has been relatively little processing and manufacturing in Shanxi, and almost no consumer goods industry.

The lack of water has been a major problem for both agricultural and industrial development. Shanxi's agricultural production has never been stable and reliable, largely because of the frequency of droughts and floods, and the absence of remedial measures, such as irrigation. This was the context from which the Dazhai model emerged, offering an apparently small-scale and manageable alternative to large-scale water- and conservation-works, even though in the 1960s the debate became (perhaps unneccessarily) polarised. With economic growth and heavy industry's demand for water the supply situation worsened, leading to environmental degradation. The situation was already at crisis point in the mid-1950s when provincial leaders floated the idea of diverting the Yellow River to provide water to Shanxi.[42] By the late 1970s overuse of water began to have a noticeable effect, not least in the centre of Taiyuan where the Fen River started to shrink. Several bridges cross a very broad, but by the 1990s almost completely dry, river bed. Though the water supply is marginally better in Yanbei, this picture is repeated throughout the province. It is estimated that Shanxi has water capacity of 5.6 billion litres, but that the province's central government enterprises alone require 7.1 billion litres a year. In Shanxi's 11 largest cities demand for water outstrips supply by more than 7 billion litres a year.[43]

Transport and communications have also been perennial problems for Shanxi. Yan Xishan's development of roads, rail and telecommunications provided an excellent foundation for the later internal development of the province. However, Yan's policies seem to have been deliberately designed to exacerbate Shanxi's isolation from the rest of the country, already considerable because of the mountains that separate it from the rest of China in the north, east and south. Land links were particularly important if Shanxi's primary products and especially coal were to be exported.

Yet paradoxically, after 1949 central government investment in developing Shanxi's transport links was not as forthcoming as investment for heavy industrial enterprises. The paradox was bizarre – although central government saw (over)-production of Shanxi's coal as a necessary part of its various national developmental strategies, it consistently failed to ensure the delivery of that coal to the rest of the country. The result in the coal industry has been considerable stockpiling and loss of output. Processing within the province offered one possible alternative, but this too has been limited and only marginally improved in the 1980s with the first thermal power plants established to supply electricity to north China. Some additional relief was provided in the 1980s with the construction of China's first double track electrified railway between Taiyuan and Shijiazhuang.

In general, one consequence of the central government's emphasis on the development of Shanxi's heavy industry has been that there was little development of processing, light industry or a consumer goods industry. Even Shanxi's cotton – grown in south Shanxi and approximately 7 per cent of national production – was by no means all processed in the province. The lack of a consumer goods industry is not a new situation for Shanxi but mirrors the late Qing and Republican era economies, which exported primary products and services, and imported manufactures. Yan Xishan had discussed the need for a second stage of industrialisation which focused on consumer goods and light industry, but was never able to take his ideas any further.[44] Quite apart from its other consequences, this structural imbalance in Shanxi's industrial structure, and the difficulties attending its economic integration with the rest of the country, has almost invariably led to excessive inflation at times of economic growth.[45]

The 'Overtaking Strategy'

Faced by these strategic considerations, the poor economic performance again during the second half of the 1980s, and the prospect of permanent underdevelopment, the provincial leadership developed a 15 year 'Overtaking Strategy' in 1992 for introduction from 1996. The strategy has three stages: the period of the Ninth Five Year Plan, to be followed by a ten year provincial developmental plan in two equal parts. In broad terms the province plans to become the economic leader of the mid-western provinces in the first stage (1996–2000), to catch up with national average economic performance in the second stage (2001–2005) and to exceed the national average during the third five years (2006–2010.)[46]

The relationship between each stage of the Overtaking Strategy has been quantified. In the first stage Shanxi's GDP is set to rise at an average annual growth rate of 12 per cent to reach 240 billion *yuan* by 2000, and GDP per capita will increase to 7,500 *yuan*, three times that of 1980. In the second stage the aim is that Shanxi's GDP will continue to rise at an annual average rate of about 11.8 per cent, but in any case it is calculated that the provincial economy can grow at a rate about 4 per cent greater than the national average. In the third stage there is an expectation that steady growth will continue so that GDP per capita will be twice that of 2000.

The starting point for developing the Overtaking Strategy was to take a hard look at Shanxi's circumstances and achievements. In reflecting on the process of policy-making, Provincial CCP Secretary Hu Fuguo emphasised that 'Shanxi is an isolated, inland province with a low market growth rate, poor investment environment, a shortage of capital and human resources, and a definite tension between the drive for development and environmental concerns.'[47] In general the provincial leadership has regularly highlighted the need to tackle a series of problems: the unstable agricultural production and its low capacity to meet natural disasters, the inefficiencies of enterprises in the state sector, environmental pollution and degradation, conservatism in leadership and corruption among members of the CCP.

The essence of the Overtaking Strategy is not simply to achieve economic growth but also to transform the structure and practice of the provincial economy. The strategy has been summarised in terms of 'The three foundations, the four key projects and the four campaigns' which have become part of the discourse of politics in Shanxi during the 1990s. The three foundations are a stable agricultural production, infrastructural development and support for key industries. The four key projects are 'mining coal' (coal extraction and processing), 'building roads' (developing the infrastructure of transport and communications for land, sea, air and telecommunications), 'channelling water' (harnessing the Yellow River for Shanxi's interior) and 'generating electricity' (for commercial production.) The four campaigns are those to control inflation, develop agriculture, reform state-owned enterprises and to increase Shanxi's financial income.

Although the Overtaking Strategy is presented as being implemented from 1996, in practice its principles have underlain the actions of the provincial leadership since 1992. A range of policies have already been developed to support the goals of the strategy including provision of support for agricultural development, the market determination of industrial restructuring and economic demand, the reform of state enterprises, increased interaction with the outside world and a policy of sustainable development. Particular emphasis has been placed on the development of science and education not least in order to ensure technological innovation in traditional industries and the development of a better qualified workforce. Given its earlier development Shanxi's investment efficiency ratio is low, requiring relatively high levels of investment to sustain growth. However, rather than continue dependence on central government as the sole source of investment funds, Shanxi has diversified, seeking investment additionally not only from foreign investors but also from within the province and to a considerable extent from elsewhere in China.

During 1994–6 the new provincial strategy started to have a noticeable impact on Shanxi's development. In 1994 the province's rate of growth equalled the national average and in 1995 it surpassed it for the first time – provincial GDP grew by 11.4 per cent over 1994. In 1995 Shanxi's GDP was 108.89 billion *yuan*, 3,557 *yuan* per capita. Foreign trade grew from US$0.2 billion in 1993, to US$0.8 billion in 1994, to US$1.37 billion in 1995. Perhaps more gratifyingly for the provincial leadership, in 1995, for the first time in a decade provincial revenue met provincial expenditure. Amongst a whole host of substantial achievements, 12.4 million *mu* of land were treated for soil erosion and and additional 2.3 million *mu* brought into cultivation. So many new roads were developed during 1993 to 1995 – 3.6 times the amount of road developed in the whole decade to 1993 – that Shanxi CCP Secretary Hu was frequently, if colloquially, referred to as 'the road-building secretary'. In the remote mountain areas of the province 40,000 children who had left school prematurely were provided with the opportunity to return, and the supply of drinking water to 8,826 villages was ensured.

Although coal still dominates the economy – approximately 20 per cent of the provincial economy is derived from extraction and processing and a further 10–13 per cent from coal-related industry[48] – it has become more diversified. In heavy industry Shanxi has concentrated on new products and materials with advanced technology, high added value and strong market demand. This has meant increased production of specialised steels and aluminium, heavy duty lorries and trucks, fertilisers and refined chemicals, concrete, glass and ceramics and newly developed construction materials. However, the diversification of the economy has been most apparent in the town and village enterprises that have concentrated on the development of a processing and consumer goods industry, particularly in coal-derived and coal industry-supporting activities, foodstuffs and textiles. By 1996 this sector accounted for about 33 per cent of provincial GDP.[49]

At a grander level, there were several very large-scale projects that started to come to fruition during 1994–6, all concerned with infrastructure development. Perhaps the most ambitious is the attempt (with echoes of suggestions from the mid-1950s) to solve Shanxi's water shortage through four large-scale water conservancy projects. The largest of these is the project to channel water from the Yellow River at Wanjiazhai into Shanxi, which is the largest such project ever attempted in the PRC. Necessarily this is a national project not least since it involves more than one province, but interestingly the Inner Mongolia Autonomous Region was the only one of Shanxi's neighbours to express any concern.

Coal may dominate Shanxi's economy but the national utility of Shanxi's coal has been hindered, as already indicated, through weak transport infrastructure. A major plank in the Overtaking Strategy has been the development of Shanxi as a long-distance provider of electricity. In addition to exporting coal to other provinces – one coal train leaves Shanxi every four minutes – Shanxi is using the coal locally in thermal power plants to produce electricity which is then transmitted to other parts of the country. This development had already started to some extent in the 1980s with Shanxi rapidly becoming the major supplier of electricity to Beijing (where it supplies about a quarter of electricity), Hebei and Tianjin from the Shentou Power Plants in Shuozhou. The development of new thermal power plants and Shanxi's electricity industry to supply other parts of China, including the north and east is now well under way, and Shanxi is the largest national producer of electricity. New power stations and more long-distance electricity transmission are now being planned or already underway, with for example the new 210 million kWh capacity Yangcheng Power Plant scheduled to supply Jiangsu Province.

Coal may require transport, but Shanxi's other interactions with the rest of China and the world also require good communications. Several major achievements were signalled by 1996 to improve the circulation of people as well as goods. There were improvements in the railway service and to the main Taiyuan Railway Station. Taiyuan Airport was redeveloped in 1994–5, with improvements including the laying of adequate runway facilities for large international jet aeroplanes and the development of terminal facilities. In May 1996 Taiyuan's first international air route opened to Hong Kong.

More spectacularly still, a new four-lane expressway was driven through the Taihang Mountains from Taiyuan to the provincial border with Hebei on the way to Shijiazhuang. Opened on 25 July 1996, the Tai–Jiu (from Taiyuan to Jiuguan) Expressway already threatens to revolutionise certain aspects of Shanxi's development. Beijing is currently less than six hours and 240 *yuan* away by bus (compared to the more than ten hours by train) and the Shanxi market has conversely suddenly become readily accessible to those outside. Funding for this project, which took less than three years to complete, exemplifies the extent to which Shanxi's economy has embarked on reform. Some 40 per cent of the needed investment was still provided by the central government. However, the remainder came from the Shanxi Provincial Government and from within the province, largely through 'voluntary' contributions levied on those working in the party-state system and the various parts of the public service.

SOCIAL CHANGE

Although the Overtaking Strategy only started to come into effect after 1992, other aspects of the reform era had already started to lead to social change during the 1980s. This was particularly the case in Shanxi's rural areas where de-collectivisation started to effect rural society in the mid-1980s. The impact of economic reform on social change has been complex, reflecting not only considerable change in structures and values but also maintenance of some of the traditions and conservatism to which Shanxi people often claim adherence. The mix of change and continuity is particularly evident in the process of economic restructuring and consequent changes in the political economy. At the same time, alongside the transformation of the social base of the party-state has been the emergence of new consumer values and activities, as well as other more usually post-materialist values, some of which also have resonances with earlier periods in Shanxi's history.

The party-state in transformation

Both Shanxi's pre-1949 experience and the development of the province after the establishment of the PRC as a national centre of heavy industry emphasise the leading social position of the CCP. While the reform era has undoubtedly altered the province's political economy, it has done little to alter the centrality of the party-state. On the contrary, in both urban and rural Shanxi the party-state in its various forms has been the major driving force leading change.

As in other provinces, economic restructuring and growth has come with the expansion of the local government or collective sector of the economy.[50] Since the mid-1980s the collective sector of industry in Shanxi has been growing at an average annual rate of about 20–25 per cent. By 1995 in Shanxi the collective and state sectors were approximately equal in size with each contributing about 40 per cent of GVIO. On the other hand, where in other provinces the collective sector has grown in a number of ways – including the development of local industry, private and individual ownership, joint ventures with foreign investors, and the rationalisation and restructuring of state enterprises – and been driven essentially by market forces,[51] in Shanxi the party-state and its connections has played the main role.

Shanxi's rural collective sector enterprises (the town and village enterprises) are to be found largely in 15 suburban counties.[52] Their development in the reform era mirrors the general tendencies in the provincial economy. Those that were established in the1980s were mainly concerned with heavy industry or support activities for heavy industry, and include such activities as the production of construction materials, glass and ceramic manufacturing, and various coal industry and coal by-product enterprises. For example, the suburban areas of Taiyuan, Datong and Yangquan now include coking plants and chemical factories of this kind. In the 1990s there has been a move away from heavy industry towards textiles, processing and consumer goods production.

These activities are unplanned in the conventional sense of being outside the formal state plan; equally their management and operations are subject to market pressures. However, the party-state and particularly the provincial authorities have played key roles in the development of the rural collective sector just as they have generally in the development of new industries in Shanxi and the re-structuring of the provincial economy. The available evidence on Shanxi's collective sector is fairly limited but would seem to suggest that the initiative for the development of collective sector enterprises has usually come from either provincial or local party-state agencies rather than from individual entrepreneurs. The provincial government has established all kinds of development programmes, including those for bringing technological innovation through local government and agencies to medium and small-scale enterprises in Shanxi's cities, towns, rural and suburban areas.[53] Moreover, most of the entrepreneurs and managers seem to have been CCP members from well before their involvement in the developing collective sector. This is in complete contrast to the situation in Zhejiang where a large proportion of collective sector entrepreneurs were recruited to the CCP only after they became successful.[54]

The development of urban collective enterprises bears the mark of party-state involvement even more clearly. The typical route of formation for the estab-lishment of an urban collective sector enterprise is that an already established state sector enterprise, party-state institution or social entity (for example, a school, hospital or university) decides to either commercialise part of its activities or to establish a commercial venture. Unsurprisingly, the range of activities covered by such collectives is much larger than for suburban industry and in addition to heavy-industry support enterprises includes a large number of textile factories and a sizeable number of service organisations including financial institutions.

The continued social centrality of the party-state in the reform era is reflected in the above average membership levels of the CCP in Shanxi. During the reform era CCP membership has grown both in real terms and as a proportion of the population. By the end of 1995 there were 1.6 million members of the CCP in Shanxi – 5.3 per cent of the 30 million total population. During the mid-1950s Shanxi had 450,000 CCP members or approximately 3 per cent of its population which in proportionate terms already made the provincial organisation one of the largest in the country.[55] Nationally in 1994 CCP membership was approximately 4.5 per cent of the population.

Consumerism

As elsewhere in China, the most obvious impact of the reform era on Shanxi has been in the emergence of a consumer society. The streets of the province's cities and towns have become noticeably commercialised, not only through the growth of the retail sector but also through changes in streetscapes. Quite apart from an increase in the number of shops and the construction of several new multi-storey large department stores in the bigger cities – the Tianlong Building in central Taiyuan is a noted example – these changes include improved road and footpath access and street lighting, both of the road and of buildings and shops. In Datong, the Exhibition Centre, originally built during the Cultural Revolution, has been almost completely commercialised. The building now houses the Datong People's Department Store and other shops, with only a few areas left in use for exhibition purposes.

Part and parcel of the consumer revolution has been the increased contact with the rest of China which has brought investment and trade from other provinces into Shanxi. Though it is hard to estimate the extent of inter-provincial trade[56] the number of businesspeople on the streets and in the hotels of Shanxi's cities has increased visibly, particularly since the opening of the Tai–Jiu Expressway. At the same time, migrant workers have also come to Shanxi in large numbers. The official figure for urban unemployment in Shanxi is 1.4 per cent of the population (compared to a national figure of 2.9 per cent) and the 'unofficial' figure is 4 per cent (compared to a national estimate of about 10 per cent) which perhaps explains why by 1996 there were some 800,000 non-resident migrant workers to be found in Shanxi, mainly engaged as labourers of various kinds.[57]

In addition to travel for business, it is also clear that tourism has increased dramatically, both from within Shanxi and from other provinces, as well as from different overseas countries. The tourist industry in Shanxi is by no means new – Datong, Dazhai and Wutaishan have long been on major tourist routes of various kinds – but access, particularly in large numbers, has been limited by lack of transport and accommodation. The case of Wutaishan is instructive. Wutaishan is the original centre of Buddhism in China and contains a series of pagodas, temples and sacred sites stretching along the Wutai Plain and rising 3,000 metres into the mountains on the provincial border with Hebei in the northern part of the Taihang Mountains, northeast of Taiyuan. Taihuai, the main centre of tourism is about five hours by fast car from Taiyuan and two or three hours (depending on the time of year and road conditions) from the nearest railway at Wutai. The first hotel was not built in Taihuai until 1980, and there was no commercialised accommodation there until 1988. However, in the 1990s the situation has dramatically changed. There is a well-maintained direct road to Taiyuan, well served by both a regular bus service and several companies of tourist mini-buses operating out of Shanxi's larger cities. Accommodation in Taihuai has also improved. Many party-state institutions have built holiday accommodation which also accept paying guests, there are a number of tourist hotels, and a vigorous bed and breakfast industry has developed.

Tourism within the province by Shanxi people is one manifestation of the increased real disposable income that economic reform and growth have brought to some sections of the population. As throughout China, increased wealth for Shanxi's new rich has brought demand for consumer goods, greater expenditure on weddings, and the development of new housing, on new housing estates in urban areas as well as in rural and suburban districts. However, the growth of private schooling and the entertainment industry in Taiyuan appear to have particular characteristics.

In the 1990s there has been a sudden explosion in the number of non-government primary and secondary schools in Shanxi. By the end of 1995 there were about 40 such schools in Taiyuan, and another 18 elsewhere, with a total school population of about 15,000.[58] Though these are all fee-paying it would be misleading to regard them as a completely private sector of education since most have a strong organisational relationship with the party-state, often institutional as well as associational. The curriculum of all schools is controlled by the provincial government, which also monitors their operation. The schools effectively have a licensing arrangement with the provincial government.[59] Colleges and universities are often either joint venture partners in the development of a school or have provided teaching staff. For example, the South Ocean International School was founded in 1994. It has purpose-built buildings in its own compound, and will eventually grow to about 1,800 students and 200 teachers. It has recruited its head teacher and many of its staff from Shanxi University, and was provided with a publicly displayed inscription on its establishment by the CCP Provincial Secretary Hu Fuguo.[60]

Taiyuan has also seen a boom in 'karaoke bars' and 'song halls'. Popular music in very large and garish discotheques has become a significant part of the entertainment industry in Taiyuan, Datong and Yangquan, modelled no doubt on Guangzhou, Shanghai and Beijing. However, the number of karaoke bars in Taiyuan has grown quite remarkably during the 1990s, so that by 1995 it had roughly about ten to 12 times as many per capita as Beijing. There were no karaoke bars in Taiyuan before 1993 but by September 1995 there were more than 1,000. At the same time Beijing – which has about 10 million inhabitants compared to the 2.7 million in Taiyuan – only had about 300 song and dance halls, cafes and bars.[61]

Post-materialism

The development of consumerism and economic-rationalist values in Shanxi during the reform era has also been accompanied by other concerns often, at least in Western societies, regarded as more post-materialist in outlook. These include the growth of environmentalism and Christianity. Though there may be individuals whose interests in these issues follow from personal affluence, in general their emergence is more likely to be a function of other materialist concerns or a simple conservatism.

Sustainable development has become a major topic of discussion not least because pollution and environmental degradation even before the 1990s have left Shanxi facing serious problems. As a result of Shanxi's heavy industrial development and agricultural policies since 1949 the quality and supply of land, air and water have all deteriorated. Cultivated land has decreased from 4.8 *mu* to 1.8 *mu* per person as a result of population growth coupled with the loss of cultivated land to industry and through over-use. By 1996 some 10 per cent of Shanxi's total land area had been lost through mine use. The air over Shanxi's cities has become badly polluted with coal dust and waste gasses: lung cancer has a higher incidence in Shanxi than anywhere else in China. Datong and Taiyuan have air suspensions in excess of 1,000 milligrams per cubic metre, about 15 times the maximum recommended safety level set by the WHO.[62] As already indicated, Shanxi's water problems are equally as severe with shortages, pollution and land slips resulting.

Reactions to Shanxi's environmental problems are interesting. Though every commentator, and the province's leadership, argues the case for sustainable development there appears to be a difference in emphasis between two views: one that focuses on the need for sustainable development policies to support continued economic growth, and another view that more generally highlights the importance of the quality of life in Shanxi's future. Thus, for example, a newspaper article on water shortage in Datong emphasises the costs: the need for deeper wells and more expensive pumping; the costs of dealing with polluted instead of clear water; and the need to rebuild when land slips.[63] One magazine article on the Taiyuan and Iron Steel Plant emphasises how the utilisation of waste residue at the plant can be commercially profitable. In discussing Li Suangliang's recycling of waste to produce cement and fertiliser it concludes: 'environmental protection is really a profitable industry and we can even conclude that it is an industry with a high return on its investment'.[64] In contrast, another article (in a different journal) in its comments on Taiyuan is implicitly critical of the location of the Iron and Steel Plant within Taiyuan, and of large chemical plants upwind of the city. It lists numerous examples of severe environmental degradation, and reports that in the mid-1980s USA observers using satellites mistook the flames and smog generated by peasant-operated local coking plants for a forest fire in

Xiaoyi, Shanxi. It concludes with an exhortation to remember that: 'A beautiful life depends on nature and even more on awakening the human conscience about that nature!'[65]

Christianity has grown substantially in Shanxi during the reform era. The precise number of practising Christians is difficult to ascertain, but there were estimated to be about 360,000 officially recognised Christians – in the Protestant and Catholic Churches organised by the party-state – in Shanxi at the end of 1996. In certain parts of Shanxi – the south and Jinzhong – churches are very much in evidence. However, there would appear to be a difference between rural and urban Shanxi in the adherence to various forms of Christianity. In parts of rural South Shanxi and Jinzhong, Christianity has relatively deep social roots and adherence is traditional. In Taiyuan, adherence seems to have come from those who are attracted to Christianity as a form of Westernisation and by its association with modernisation.

In general there is more than a hint of Shanxi's conservatism to be found in responses to both the rest of the world and modernisation. Since 1984 Shanxi Provincial Government has established its own scholarship fund of US$1.5 million a year to send students and scholars abroad. To 1996 about 1,100 people have taken advantage of the scheme to study in the USA, Canada, England, Germany, France, Japan and Australia. Similar schemes exist nationally but remarkably the return rate for scholarship holders from Shanxi appears to be significantly higher than for other Chinese, even though some have also stayed abroad.[66] In a completely different area of activity, one of the frequent complaints of provincial leadership has been that Shanxi entrepreneurs are too restrained in their attitudes to advertising and marketing. Although both *Fenjiu* (a white spirit made from sorghum) and Shanxi vinegar are well-established industries (the Fenjiu Factory was one of the first modernised plants in the province) there seems to be an unwillingness to promote them outside Shanxi. Their producers are said to still believe they will sell on their excellence without new packaging or an adequate advertising budget.[67]

NEGOTIATING SHANXI

Despite the suggestion of an element of anti-nativism in Shanxi politics during the Cultural Revolution, in general there has been little conflict between 'insiders' and 'outsiders' in this province. Unsurprisingly, given the history of the CCP, Shanxi natives have dominated the party-state system in the province and its leadership. Since the introduction of reform in 1978, 70 per cent of all those who have served as either governor or deputy governor of the Shanxi Provincial Government (or the equivalent in 1978–80), or secretary or deputy secretary of the Shanxi CCP Committee (39 out of a total 56 individuals) have been natives of Shanxi.[68]

At the highest levels of leadership since 1978 there have been five separate appointments as Shanxi CCP provincial secretary and four as governor of the

Shanxi Provincial People's Government. Of the five people who have been provincial secretary – Wang Qian, Huo Shilian, Li Ligong, Wang Maolin and Hu Fuguo – only Wang Maolin was not a Shanxi native. In contrast, of the four who have been governor – Luo Guibo, Wang Senhao, Hu Fuguo and Sun Wensheng – only Hu Fuguo was a Shanxi native. Moreover, of these eight individuals all but Sun Wensheng had considerable experience of the province before appointment.[69]

None the less, since 1992, coinciding with Hu Fuguo's return to the province as (acting) Governor[70] and the start of discussions and the policy process which led to the adoption of the Overtaking Strategy, there has been a distinct change in the style of politics in Shanxi. Particularly under Hu Fuguo's guidance as provincial secretary since 1993, politics has become both more popular and populist. The Shanxi leadership and the party-state have gone out of their way to project a high profile – both for themselves and the province – and to address issues of public concern. Provincial leaders no longer limit their public appearances to statements to the CCP newspapers or set speeches. In the course of a day there may be, as for politicians outside China, many photo-opportunities, and appearances on the full range of television channels – in both news and other programmes – are considered desirable.

Hu Fuguo has led the way in raising the provincial leadership's profile and popularity through public exposure. A native of Changzi in Shangdang and originally a miner, he is a good public performer and presents himself as a 'man of the people'. In June 1996 he even played the traditional peasant drums of his native Shangdang region as part of the opening ceremony for the Tai–Jiu Expressway.[71] Secretary Hu is frequently in the public eye through the print and electronic media and it is almost impossible to travel in Shanxi without coming across examples of his calligraphy gracing a wide range of economic and social enterprises including for example schools, housing estates and trucking companies. In part this popularity may be because he has a particularity auspicious name – *fuguo* can mean 'making the country rich' – but there can also be no doubt that his attempt to reinvigorate the party-state's relationship with society has sucessfully struck resonances during the mid-1990s. For all that ordinary people in Shanxi are disinclined to trust political leaders any longer there is a more than grudging respect afforded Secretary Hu and he seems to have become genuinely popular. Someone even opened a Fuguo Restaurant (on Pingyang Road) in Taiyuan named after him, though he had absolutely no connection with its management or operation.[72]

However, this search for profile and popularity is less personal than instrumental and is allied to a strong populism. The aim was summarised in a four-character phrase originally coined in 1993 for the province's new strategy as it was emerging: *xing Jin fu min* – 'A Prosperous Shanxi and a Wealthy People'. It is a populist message that recurs throughout the selling of the Overtaking Strategy since 1992 regardless of whether the audience is Shanxi at large, central government, potential foreign investors, economic managers or party cadres, and the approach needs to be tailored accordingly. The flavour of its appeal can be seen, for example, in Secretary Hu's speech to the Seventh Shanxi CCP Provincial Congress in January 1996:

> It has been nearly half-a-century since the Liberation. What reason do we have to see our people live such a poor life? Shanxi enjoys rich natural resources and our people are kind-hearted and hard-working. How can we continue to let them live in poverty? Shanxi people made enormous contributions to the nation during the revolutionary war and subsequent socialist construction. How can we reward them with such poverty? How can we allow our people to enter the twenty-first century in the shackles of poverty?[73]
>
> (Hu Fuguo, 1996, p. 10)

The project is little less than the reconstruction of the notion of Shanxi, essentially the creation of cultural capital for the development of the province. It is designed not simply to improve Shanxi's economic development and quality of life but also, in the process, to unite the province and reinvigorate the authority of the CCP, particularly after the factional conflicts and divisions engendered by the Cultural Revolution. In that context, the timing of the stylistic change in politics may have less to do with the arrival of Hu Fuguo and simply reflect the generational change which saw Shanxi's revolutionary era cadres largely pass from the provincial scene with the 1980s.

Secretary Hu himself has been active in promoting a more positive and inclusive notion of Shanxi. This is the cultural unification of the province that matches and parallels the emphasis on the physical integration of Shanxi through the extensive road-building programme and improvement of internal transportation. Though Shanxi's Overtaking Strategy does not include explicit blueprints for or discussion of the creation of a 'new' provincial culture and the bringing together in a single identity of its sub-provincial regions – as has been the case elsewhere – this has certainly been one corollary and intended result of its promotion. In this context, the emphasis on a unifying provincial (and presumably national) history is particularly intense. Throughout Shanxi the provincial dimensions of sites of historical interest have been highlighted, in many cases graced by Hu Fuguo's inscriptions. His calligraphy serves such functions in widely diverse settings including a revived museum and a new theme park. The museum is that in Qixian, dedicated to the history of local banking and trade, which has now become the Shanxi Museum of Commerce. The theme park is in Qingxu County, and is a purpose-built tourist attraction dedicated to the historical novel *The Romance of the Three Kingdoms* whose supposed author-compiler Luo Guanzhong was a native of that county. The theme park takes the form of a model 'traditional' city which also contains a Shanxi Hall of Fame, as well as a temple to Guan Yu, one of Liu Bei's generals from *The Romance of the Three Kingdoms* and a native of Haizhou (now in Yuncheng) in south Shanxi.

Hu Fuguo and his colleagues in the provincial leadership emphatically talk about Shanxi and provincial identity rather than earlier, more prevalent (and conflictual) identifications based on sub-provincial regions or base areas of the Sino–Japanese War. Thus, for example, he is commonly held to have criticised the lack of a specifically Shanxi cuisine, as opposed to the well-established traditional cuisines and dishes of Shanxi's constituent regions, and to have encouraged the development of Shanxi restaurants. Certainly, one feature of restaurant life in the 1990s is the birth of large numbers of Shanxi restaurants which specialise in noodles, breads and pancakes, in general the common element of food throughout the province.

At the same time, this emphasis on the greater integration of Shanxi and its cultural construction does not appear to have been attempted through the domination of any one tradition or part of the province, in contrast to earlier politics. On the contrary, and in contrast for example to the agricultural development policies of the Mao-dominated years, the Overtaking Strategy of the 1990s makes explicit the need for a range of policies to apply to the different parts of the province according to their varying circumstances. An important part of the new strategy is a regional development policy which on a county-by-county basis differentiates between Shanxi's rural mountain areas, rural plains communities, suburban districts and industrial and mining centres.[74]

Moreover, a recognition of diversity that extends well beyond questions of regional difference has generally become much more the order of the day than the reactive conformity that characterised the earlier political status quo. The result has not been political pluralism, but it has been the deliberate introduction of a much more open system, even though this may lead to more complex political problems for the provincial leadership. To quote the head of a department in the provincial government: 'The difficult point in reform is to solve the problem of the re-allocation of power to meet the demands of different interest groups.'

ACKNOWLEDGEMENTS

This chapter results from a research project supported by the Australian Research Council into Shanxi's social and economic development. In addition to documentary analyses of various kinds, the project centres on interviews with 120 cadres, entrepreneurs and managers throughout the province. Access to Shanxi has been provided through the Shanxi History and Archive Institute, and particularly its Institute for Research on Contemporary Shanxi. Considerable advice and assistance in Shanxi has been provided by Professor Tian Youru of the Institute for Research on Contemporary Shanxi and Li Xueqian of Shanxi University. Although references to specific interviews are provided in footnotes where appropriate, acknowledgement should also be made to all those who have given freely and so helpfully of their time and assistance in research for this project, particularly Hu Fuguo, Secretary of the Shanxi CCP Provincial Committee; Cao Zhonghou, Mayor of Taiyuan; Du Yulin, Mayor of Datong; Wei Deqing, Mayor of Yangquan; Cai Peiyi, Shanxi Association for International Education Exchange; Li Tianrui, Director of Shanxi's Economic Commission; Li Zhenxi,

Director of Shanxi's Scientific and Technological Commission; Ma Jiajun, Deputy Director of Shanxi's Economic and Trade Commission; and Zhang Kui, Director of Shanxi's Planning Commission. None of those individuals are responsible for any of the comments and observations expressed in this chapter.

NOTES

1 Historical data on Shanxi (and other provinces) may be found in State Statistical Bureau, *Quanguo gesheng, zizhiqu, zhixiashi lishi tongji ziliao huibian 1949–1989* [Collection of Historical Statistical Material for all Provinces, Autonomous Regions and Municipalities 1949–1989], Beijing: Zhongguo tongji chubanshe, 1990, pp. 153–183, especially p. 153 on urbanisation and p. 159 on industrialisation, for the period 1949–1989. Data on selected years back to 1884 may be found in *Shanxi nianjian 1986* [Shanxi Yearbook 1986], Taiyuan: Shanxi renmin chubanshe, 1987, p. 410. Comparative contemporary data for China's provinces derived from State Statistical Bureau, *Zhongguo tongji nianjian 1995* [China Statistical Yearbook 1995], Beijing: Zhongguo tongji chubanshe, 1995, may be found in *Provincial China* 1, 1996, pp. 39–41.

2 For example: Hua Shilin (ed.), *Zhongguo renkou – Shanxi fence* [China's Population – Shanxi volume], Beijing: Zhonguo caizheng jingji chubanshe, 1989, pp.1ff and 31ff; Bai Suyu (ed.), *Dangdai Zhongguo de Shanxi* [Shanxi Today], Beijing: Zhongguo shehui kexue chubanshe, 1991, vol.1, p. 17. In English, Gillin's study of Yan Xishan observes, 'The people of Shansi are distinguished by the pride they take in the antiquity of their civilization', in Donald G Gillin, *Warlord Yen Hsi-shan in Shansi Province 1911–1949*, Princeton, New Jersey: Princeton University Press, 1967, p. 6.

3 The name *Shanxi* was not applied until the Ming Dynasty. See Zhang Jizhong, *Shanxi lishi zhengqu dili* [Historical Geography of Shanxi's Administrative Regions], Taiyuan: Shanxi renmin chubanshe, 1992.

4 See, for example, a story against corruption, and particularly extravagant dining at public expense, which drew parallels with the end of the Jin, in 'Yiyannanjin Shanxiren' [Some comments on Shanxi people] in *Linfen ribao* [Linfen Daily] 19 January 1996, p. 2; and 'Shuo chi' in *Shanxi ribao* [Shanxi Daily] 22 January 1996, p. 8.

5 A useful indicator of provincial political influence and wealth in the Empire was the number of graduates and senior ministers. Until the Ming, Shanxi had been one of the leading provinces in these terms, producing 201 chief ministers, but thereafter no chief minister came from the province and Shanxi was replaced in national standing by Jiangsu, Zhejiang and Jiangxi.

6 Donald G Gillin, *Warlord Yen Hsi-shan in Shansi Province 1911–1949*, Princeton, New Jersey: Princeton University Press, 1967, pp. 6–8.

7 Jiang Shunxing and Li Liangyu (eds), *Shanxi wang Yan Xishan* [Yan Xishan, King of Shanxi], Zhengzhou: Henan renmin chubanshe, 1990, p. 95.

8 See, for example: 'The Spirit of People in Hongtong County' in *Shenghuo chenbao* [Morning News] 22 March 1996, p. 6; Lu Kun *et al.* (eds), *Shanxi shixian jianzhi* [An Introduction to Shanxi's Cities and Counties], Taiyuan: Shanxi renmin chubanshe, 1990, p. 796.

9 See, for example: Zhao Xuejun, 'Shanxi dayuan shubuqing' [Shanxi has many courtyards], in *Shanxi gongrenbao* [Shanxi Worker News] 26 May 1996, p. 2.

10 Wang Shan, *Disanzhi yanjing kan Zhongguo* [The Third Eye Looks at China], Taiyuan: Shanxi renmin chubanshe, 1994. Interview with Ma Jian, deputy general editor, Shanxi People's Publishing House, 25 January 1996.

238 David S.G. Goodman

11 See, for example: Zhu Shaojin, *'Shanyaodangpai' yu Sanjin wenhua* [The Potato Gang and Shanxi Culture], Changsha: Hunan jiaoyu chubanshe, 1995.

12 Shanxi has the highest per capita consumption of vinegar. In 1978 average consumption in Taiyuan was three and a half times greater than consumption of vinegar in Tianjin and almost three times greater than Beijing. 'Shanxi, Shanxi's People and Shanxi's Vinegar', in *Yanjiu yu Fudao* no. 2 1990, p. 44.

13 The most famous book in English on agriculture in the Changzhi region is William Hinton, *Fanshen: A Documentary of Revolution in a Chinese Village*, Harmondsworth: Penguin, 1966.

14 On local banking traditions, see amongst other sources: Wang Yeh-chien, *The Development of Money and Banking in China, 1644–1937*, Taipei: Institute of Economics, Academica Sinica, Studies of Modern Economy Series, 1981; *Shanxi piaohao shiliao* [Source materials on Shanxi Exchange Shops] Taiyuan: Shanxi jingji chubanshe, 1990; and 'Shanxi piaohao yu gupiao' [Shanxi's Exchange Shops and Shares] in *Taiyuan wanbao* [Taiyuan Evening News] 9 February 1996, p. 8.

15 Wang Huguo (ed.), *Datongshi qing chu tan* [Investigations about Datong], Taiyuan: Shanxi renmin chubanshe, 1992, pp. 8ff suggests that the Yanbei culture is not that of Shanxi and that the inhabitants of the region are not really Shanxi people at all but largely the descendants of Mongolians and other Inner Asian peoples.

16 Shandang *laozi* was originally known as Licheng *laozi* after the name of one of the richest counties in the Taihang range, but its name was officially changed in 1954: 'Shangdang laozi' [Shangdang folk drama] in *Shenghuo chenbao* [Morning News] 15 March 1996, p. 6.

17 For example, 'head' in Taiyuan is *naodai*, in Changzhi is *ganao*, in Yuci is *dalao dazi*. Since 1993 the *Taiyuan wanbao* [Taiyuan Evening News] runs a regular column on language matters across the province.

18 Donald G. Gillin, *Warlord Yen Hsi-shan in Shansi Province 1911–1949*, Princeton, New Jersey: Princeton University Press, 1967, p. 43.

19 Yan was first the military governor of the province after the 1911 Revolution, and then from 1917 the civil governor until defeated by Chiang Kai-shek and forced to flee the province (for Dalian) in December 1930. He returned to Shanxi and power in September 1931 as pacification commissioner of both Shanxi and Suiyuan, taking advantage of Chiang Kai-shek's political difficulties elsewhere and local opposition to 'outsiders'.

20 Some standard sources on Yan Xishan are: Jiang Shunxing and Li Liangyu (eds), *Shanxi wang Yan Xishan* [Yan Xishan, King of Shanxi], Zhengzhou: Henan renmin chubanshe, 1990; Donald G. Gillin, *Warlord Yen Hsi-shan in Shansi Province 1911–1949*, Princeton, New Jersey: Princeton University Press, 1967; and the selections of articles from *Shanxi wenshiziliao* [Shanxi Culture and History] reprinted in Shanxi wenshi ziliao bianjibu (ed.), *Shanxi wenshi jingxuan: Yan Xishan longduan jingji* [Selections from *Shanxi Wenshi Ziliao*: Yan Xishan's monopoly economy], Taiyuan: Shanxi gaoxiao lianhe chubanshe, nd; Shanxi wenshi ziliao bianjibu (ed.), *Shanxi wenshi jingxuan: Yan Xishan qiren qishi* [Selections from *Shanxi Wenshi Ziliao*: About Yan Xishan], Taiyuan: Shanxi gaoxiao lianhe chubanshe, nd.

21 Donald G. Gillin, *Warlord Yen Hsi-shan in Shansi Province 1911–1949*, Princeton, New Jersey: Princeton University Press, 1967, p. 91.

22 Lyman van Slyke, 'The Chinese Communist Movement during the Sino–Japanese War, 1937–45' in *The Cambridge History of China*, Vol. 13, Republican China, 1912–1949, Part II, Cambridge University Press, 1986, Chapter 12, p. 609.

23 Lijian Hong, 'Sichuan: disadvantage and mismanagement in the Heavenly Kingdom' in David S. G. Goodman (ed.), *China's Provinces in Reform: Class, Community and Political Culture*, London: Routledge, 1997.

24 David S. G. Goodman, *Deng Xiaoping and the Chinese Revolution*, London: Routledge, 1994, pp. 44ff.

25 Wang Jian, 'Shanxisheng de nongye gaige wunian yilai' [Five Years of Agricultural Reform in Shanxi] in *Renmin ribao* [People's Daily] 11 November 1951 – letter from Wang Jian, secretary of Changzhi CCP to Bo Yibo; also Tao Lujia, 'Zhonggong Shanxi shengwei dui sixiang gongzuo de lingdao' [Shanxi Provincial CCP Committee on leadership of ideological work] in *Xuexi* [Study] vol. 5, No. 1, 1 November 1951. Meng Hsien-chun, 'The Question of Rightist Opportunism in the Agricultural Cooperativization Movement of China' from *New Construction* no.12, December 1955, translated in US Consulate General (Hong Kong), *Extracts from China Mainland Magazines* no. 26, p. 1.

26 Dazhai refused state aid from 1953 on and became a provincial model for emulation during the 1950s. In the summer of 1963 it was struck by severe floods that destroyed most of the terracing and retaining walls that had been painstakingly developed, as well as homes and crops. Surrounding areas applied for and received state relief aid. Dazhai continued with its policies of self-reliance and after a successful harvest in 1964 its story came to Mao's attention.

27 Wei Heng, 'Guanyu kaizhan zengchan jieyue yundong wancheng he chaoe wancheng diyige wunian jihua de baogao' [Report on developing a movement to increase production and practise economy, and to fulfil and overfulfil the First Five Year Plan] in *Shanxi ribao* [Shanxi Daily], 8 December 1956: Report to the 1956 Provincial People's Congress.

28 The comments of the CCP secretary of Yuxian who had difficulties in promoting Dazhai among county and commune cadres during the 1960s are interesting. He reported their hesitant responses to the Dazhai model – 'We erred in our work a few years ago because we aimed too high and did not keep to our own lot. It is with great difficulty that we have returned to normal. . . . Never commit such recklessness again' – in *Renmin ribao* [People's Daily], 18 October 1965. Resistance during the 1970s is reflected in, for example: a report of the 21 February 1973 provincial symposium on 'Learn from Dazhai' which admitted frankly that in this regard Shanxi had fallen behind national benchmarks, in *Renmin ribao* [People's Daily], 31 March 1973; and an editorial in *Shanxi ribao* [Shanxi Daily], 1 November 1973 that indicated many counties were unclear about the precise message to be learnt from Dazhai.

29 Yang Xiaochi (ed.), *Zhongguo ziben zhuyi gongshangye de shehui zhuyi gaizao – Shanxi tao* [The Socialist Transformation of Capitalist Industry and Commerce in China – Shanxi volume], Beijing: Zhonggong dangshi chubanshe, 1992, pp. 30ff.

30 Details on investment in Shanxi may be found in *Shanxi ribao* [Shanxi Daily], 12 May 1958, p.2. Shanxi's GDP since 1949 may be found in *Shanxi tongji nianjian 1995* [Statistical Yearbook of Shanxi 1995], Beijing: Zhongguo tongji chubanshe, 1995, p. 20.

31 *Shanxi tongji nianjian 1995* [Statistical Yearbook of Shanxi 1995], Beijing: Zhongguo tongji chubanshe, 1995, p. 23.

32 Tao Lujia, in his speech to the Second Session of the First National People's Congress, 26 July 1955, deals at length with the social problems, in *Xinhua yuebao* [New China Monthly] no. 8 (General 70), 28 August 1955.

33 *Shanxi tongji nianjian 1995* [Statistical Yearbook of Shanxi 1995], Beijing: Zhongguo tongji chubanshe, 1995, p. 265.

34 *Shanxi tongji nianjian 1995* [Statistical Yearbook of Shanxi 1995], Beijing: Zhongguo tongji chubanshe, 1995, p. 23 and p. 186.

35 Bai Suyu (ed.), *Dangdai Zhongguo de Shanxi* [Shanxi Today], Beijing: Zhongguo shehui kexue chubanshe, 1991, vol. 1, pp.151ff.

36 Zhonggong Shanxi shengwei zuzhibu, Zhonggong Shanxi shengwei dangshi yanjiushi, Shanxisheng danganbu (ed.), *Zhongguo gongchandang Shanxisheng zuzhi shi ziliao 1949.10–1987.10* [CCP Shanxi Organisational and Historical Materials October 1949 – October 1987], Taiyuan: Shanxi renmin chubanshe, 1994, p. 12. A first-hand account of the 'seizure of power' by one of the leaders may be found in

Zhang Riqing, 'Steadfastly Support the Proletarian Revolutionaries in their Struggle to Seize Power' in *Hongqi* [Red Flag] No. 4, 1 March 1967, translated in JPRS [Joint Publications Research Services] 40471, 31 March 1967, p. 33.

37 Shanxi's experience and the 'revolutionary three-in-one combination' were the subject of editorials in *Renmin ribao* [People's Daily] on 24 and 25 January 1967. Mao Zedong's exhortation to Shanghai that 'it should follow the Shanxi example' may be found in 'Dui Shanghai wenhua dageming de zhishi' ['Directive on the Great Proletarian Cultural Revolution in Shanghai'], 12 February 1967 in *Mao Zedong sixiang wansui* [Long Live Mao Zedong Thought!], August 1969, nd, np, p. 668.

38 Bai Suyu (ed.), *Dangdai Zhongguo de Shanxi* [Shanxi Today], Beijing: Zhongguo shehui kexue chubanshe, 1991, vol. 1, pp. 185ff.

39 Interview with Ma Jiajun, deputy director of Shanxi Provincial Economic and Trade Commission, Taiyuan, 12 July 1996. While the proportion of the provincial economy sourced by central government is undoubtedly high it may not be the highest. Evidence in this volume from Shaanxi suggests that 34 per cent of that province's economy is sourced from central government.

40 'Shanxi qiye que shenmo' [The defects of Shanxi enterprises] in *Guangming ribao* [Guangming Daily], 1 January 1996, p. 1.

41 'Laochencu de ganga' [Laochen Vinegar falls into dire straits] in *Shanxi qingnian bao* [Shanxi Youth News], 26 March 1996, p. 4.

42 Tao Lujia, speech of 26 July 1955 to Second Session, First National People's Congress, in *Xinhua yuebao* [New China Monthly] no. 8 (General number 70), 28 August 1955, pp. 140 ff.

43 'Factors of restraint in Shanxi's economic development' in *Shanxi fazhan daobao* [Shanxi Development Report], 12 April 1996 p. 2.

44 Ji Shengfang (ed.), *Sanjin jingji lunheng* [A Discussion of the Economy of Shanxi], Beijing: Zhongguo shangye chubanshe, 1993, pp. 21 ff.

45 Li Yuying and Zhang Chuanchun, 'Shanxi tonghuo pengzhang de zoushi yu duice' [Suffering and dealing with inflation in Shanxi] in *Zhanlue yu guanli* [Strategy and Management] No. 6, 1995, p.115.

46 An overview of the Overtaking Strategy is contained in the speeches to the Seventh Shanxi Provincial CCP Congress in January 1996 by Provincial CCP Secretary Hu Fuguo and Provincial Governor Sun Wenshen. Texts may be found in Hu Fuguo, 'Quanmian guanche dang de jiben lilun he jiben luxian wei shixian xingJin fumin de kuashijie mubiao er fendou' [Fight to ensure the global goal of *A Prosperous Shanxi and a Wealthy People* through thoroughly implementing the CCP's basic theories and policies] in *Qianjin* [Forward !] No. 2 1996, p. 4, and Sun Wenshen, 'Guanyu zhiding quansheng guomin jingji he shehui fazhan dijiuge wunian jihua he 2010 nian yuanjing mubiao jianyi (caoan) de shuoming' [Explanatory Notes on Draft Proposals for Provincial Goals and Objectives in Social and Economic Development during the Ninth Five Year Plan and to 2010] in *Qianjin* [Forward !] No. 2 1996, p. 26. Greater detail on the change in strategy, and particularly the thinking behind its evolution may be found in a number of preparatory research reports published as Li Zhenxi (ed.), *Xing Jin Fu Min: shida keti yanjiu* [A Prosperous Shanxi and a Wealthy People: Ten important questions for research], Taiyuan: Shanxi renmin chubanshe, 1994. A useful commentary is also contained in Lu Rizhou, 'Shanxi sheng gaige kaifeng fenxi' [The analysis of Shanxi's reform and openness] in *Shanxi ribao* [Shanxi Daily], 2 May 1996, pp. 1 and 3.

47 Interview, 25 January 1996, Taiyuan.

48 Interview with Ma Jiajun, deputy director of Shanxi Provincial Economic and Trade Commission, Taiyuan, 12 July 1996.

49 A useful survey of early 1990s industrial development in Shanxi is contained in 'Shanxi Jianhang xindai zhanlue he zhizhu chanye xuanze [The Shanxi Construction

Bank's credit strategy and selection of pillar industries] in *Touzi daokan* [Investment Guide] No. 1 1996, 1 February 1996, p. 9.

50 See, for example: Jean Oi, 'The role of the local state in China's transitional economy' in *The China Quarterly*, No. 144, December 1995, p. 1132.

51 The experiences of Zhejiang, Jiangsu and Guangdong present contrasting and different cases. See, for example: Keith Forster, 'Zhejiang: paradoxes of restoration, reinvigoration and renewal' in David S. G. Goodman (ed.), *China's Provinces in Reform: Class, Community and Political Culture*, London: Routledge, 1997; Junhua Wu, 'Economic Growth and Regional Development Strategy in China' in *Japan Research Quarterly* Vol. 2, No. 3, Summer 1993, p. 31 (on Jiangsu); and Ezra F. Vogel, *One Step Ahead in China: Guangdong under Reform*, Cambridge: Harvard University Press, 1989, especially p. 313.

52 An analysis of these 15 counties may be found in Li Zhenxi (ed.), *Xing Jin Fu Min: shida keti yanjiu* [A Prosperous Shanxi and a Wealthy People: Ten important questions for research], Taiyuan: Shanxi renmin chubanshe, 1994, pp. 142 ff.

53 Interview with Li Zhenxi, director, Shanxi Science and Technology Commission, Taiyuan, 13 July 1996.

54 David S. G. Goodman, 'The People's Republic of China: the party-state, capitalist revolution, and new entrepreneurs' in Richard Robison and David S. G. Goodman (eds), *The New Rich in Asia: Mobile Phones, McDonald's and Middle-class Revolution*, London: Routledge, 1994, p. 225.

55 Frederick C. Teiwes, 'Provincial Politics in China: Themes and Variations' in John M. H. Lindbeck (ed.), *China: Management of a Revolutionary Society*, London: Allen and Unwin, 1972, Table 9 – Party Membership by Province, p. 165.

56 The most thorough and recent investigation of inter-provincial trade is Anjali Kumar, 'China: Internal Trade, Output and Marketing', paper presented to the Workshop on East Asia: Politics, Economy and Society, Department of Political Science, University of Chicago, 1994.

57 Official figures on urban unemployment are from *Zhongguo tongji nianjian 1996* [Statistical Yearbook of China, 1996], Beijing: Zhongguo tongji chubanshe, 1996, p. 114. Interview with Zhang Kui, director, Shanxi Provincial Planning Commission, Taiyuan, 14 July 1996.

58 Jia Baiguo, 'Shehui liliang banxue' [Social-force run schools] in *Shanxi chengren jiaoyu* [Shanxi Adult Education] no. 1, 1996, p. 17.

59 Interview with Professor Cai Peiyi, former director, Shanxi Provincial Education Commissiom, Taiyuan, 23 January 1996.

60 Interview with Shu Yi, director, and Yao Li Yun, principal, Shanxi South Ocean International School, Taiyuan, 22 January 1996.

61 Chen Yu, '"Kala" shi fou "OK" – Taiyuan geting shichang sanmiao' [Is Karaoke ok? – an investigation of Taiyuan's song halls] in *Beiyue Feng* [The Beiyue Scene] no. 1, 1996, p. 41.

62 [Laws to protect the land] in *Jinyang xuekan* [The Taiyuan Academic Journal] no. 2, 1996, p. 1.

63 [Over-pumping underground water threatens Datong City] in *Datong kejibao* [Datong Science and Technology News], 23 March 1996, p. 4.

64 Zhang Huaguo, 'TaiGang "Huanbao chanyehua" de qishi' [Enlightenment from environmental protection at the Taiyuan Iron and Steel Plant] in *Jizhe guancha* [Reporters Notes] no. 3, 1996, p. 11.

65 Ah Ji, 'Youtian – daqi wuran yousilu' [Anxiety – concerns about pollution] in *Zhengfu fazhi* [Government Legislation] no. 1, 1996, p. 11.

66 Interviews with Professor Cai Peiyi, former director, Shanxi Provincial Education Commissiom, Taiyuan, 23 January 1996; and Yang Shuguo, deputy director, Shanxi Provincial Education Commission, Taiyuan, 13 July 1996.

67 Interview with Li Tianrui, director, Shanxi Economic Commission, Taiyuan, 23 January 1996.

68 Since many individuals served as leading cadres of both party and government simultanously, the following lists provide details in alphabetical order:

Shanxi natives: Bai Qiucai, Chen Yonggui, Du Wuan, Guo Fenglian, Guo Qinan, Guo Yuhuai, Hu Fuguo, Huo Fan, Huo Shilian, Jia Jun, Jiao Guonai, Li Ligong, Li Xiuren, Liu Zemin, Lu Gongxun, Pan Ruizheng, Ren Yinglong, Shi Huaibei, Shi Jiyan, Wang Daren, Wang Kewen, Wang Qian, Wang Dingtong, Wang Wenxue, Wang Xi, Wang Xin, Wang Yunlong, Wang Zhongqing, Wei Fengqi, Wu Guangtang, Xue Jun, Yan Wuhong, Yue Weifan, Zhang Jianyi, Zhang Weiqing, Zhao Jun, Zhao Lizhi, Zhao Yuting, Zheng Shikui.

Non-natives: Feng Zhimao (Tianjin), Ji Xinfang (Liaoning), Jia Chongzhi (Hebei), Jia Yunbiao (Hebei), Liang Guoying (Hebei), Liu Zhenhua (Shandong), Luo Guibo (Jiangxi), Ma Guishu (Hebei), Peng Zhigui (Gansu), Sun Wensheng (Shandong), Wang Jiangong (Hebei), Wang Maolin (Jiangsu), Wang Senhao (Zhejiang), Wu Dacai (Jiangsu), Wu Jie (Inner Mongolia), Wu Junzhou (Hebei), Zhang Jianmin (Hebei).

69 The work experience in Shanxi of the Shanxi natives is: Hu Fuguo worked in the Datong Mining Administration from the 1960s to 1980; Li Ligong served in Shanxi during and immediately after the Sino–Japanese War; Wang Qian served in the Taihang Base Area and after 1949 was CCP secretary of Changzhi. The work experience in Shanxi of the non-natives is: Luo Guibo served in Northwest Shanxi during the Sino–Japanese War; Wang Maolin had been in Shanxi since 1964 and had become deputy head of the Shanxi Provincial Revolutionary Committee in 1977 and mayor of Taiyuan in 1979; Wang Senhao had worked in the Datong Mining Administration after the mid-1950s; Sun Wensheng had worked in Hunan from 1981 to 1993 before arriving in Shanxi as acting governor.

70 Hu Fuguo is originally a miner from Changzi who worked in the Datong Mining Administration from 1964 to 1980. In 1982 he became vice-minister of the Coal Industry, returning to Shanxi as acting governor and deputy secretary of the Shanxi CCP Provincial Committee in 1992.

71 The story and pictures appear in *Shanxi ribao* [Shanxi Daily], 26 June 1996.

72 After a few months it was suggested to the restaurant owners that a change might be in order – it became the Guofu Restaurant with an overnight character exchange in its neon sign.

73 Hu Fuguo, 'Quanmian guanche dang de jiben lilun he jiben luxian wei shixian xingJin fumin de kuashijie mubiao er fendou' [Fight to ensure the global goal of *A Prosperous Shanxi and a Wealthy People* through thoroughly implementing the CCP's basic theories and policies] in *Qianjin* [Forward!] No. 2 1996, p. 10.

74 Details are presented in 'Keti zhisan: Jiushi niandai wosheng quyu zonghe kaizhan yanjiu' [Question 3: A synthesis of developing research on Shanxi's regions in the 1990s] in Li Zhenxi (ed.), *Xing Jin Fu Min: shida keti yanjiu* [A Prosperous Shanxi and a Wealthy People: Ten important questions for research] Taiyuan: Shanxi renmin chubanshe, 1994, pp. 141ff.

REFERENCES

Bai Qingcai (ed.), *Shanxi sishi nian 1949–1989* [Forty Years of Shanxi 1949–1989], Taiyuan: Zhongguo tongji chubanshe, 1989.

Bai Suyu (ed.), *Dangdai Zhongguo de Shanxi* [Shanxi Today], Beijing: Zhongguo shehui kexue chubanshe, 1991, 2 vols.

Donald G Gillin, *Warlord Yen Hsi-shan in Shansi Province 1911–1949*, Princeton, New Jersey: Princeton University Press, 1967.

Chen Guoliang (ed.), *Shanxi jishi* [Shanxi Markets], Taiyuan: Shanxi jingji chubanshe, 1990.

Guo Yuhuai (ed.), *Zhongguo xian (shi) gaige zongheng – Shanxi juan* [Strategies of Reform in China's Counties and Cities – Shanxi], Beijing: Renmin chubanshe, 1994.

Hu Fuguo, *Jiang zhenhua, ban shishi, zuo biaoshuai: zaichuang Sanjin huihuang* [Tell the truth, make things happen and set an example: Reconstructing Shanxi's glory], Beijing: Zhonggong zhongyang dangxiao chubanshe, 1996.

Hua Shilin (ed.), *Zhongguo renkou – Shanxi fence* [China's Population – Shanxi volume] , Beijing: Zhongguo caizheng jingji chubanshe, 1989.

Ji Shengfang (ed.), *Sanjin jingji lunheng* [A Discussion of the Economy of Shanxi], Beijing: Zhongguo shangye chubanshe, 1993.

Jing Yinqiang (ed.) *Shanxi shichang* [The Shanxi Market], Taiyuan: Shanxi renmin chubanshe, 1990.

Li Xiuren (ed.), *Shanxi dashiji 1840–1985* [Chronicle of Shanxi 1840–1985], Taiyuan: Shanxi renmin chubanhse, 1987.

Li Zhenxi (ed.), *Xing Jin Fu Min: shida keti yanjiu* [A Prosperous Shanxi and a Wealthy People: Ten important questions for research], Taiyuan: Shanxi renmin chubanshe, 1994.

Liu Liping *et al.* (eds), *Zhongguo dangdai qiyejia mingdian – Shanxi tao* [Contemporary Entrepreneurs in China – Shanxi volume], Beijing: Gongren chubanshe, 1989.

Lu Kun *et al.* (eds), *Shanxi shixian jianzhi* [Introductory Record to Shanxi's Cities and Counties], Taiyuan: Shanxi renmin chubanshe, 1990.

Lu Rizhou, *Shanxi sheng gaige kaifang fenxi* [The Analysis of Reform and Openness in Shanxi], Taiyuan: Shanxi jingji chubanshe, 1996.

Shanxi sheng shizhi yanjiuyuan (ed.), *Zhongguo gongchandang Shanxi lishi dashijisu (1976.10 – 1992.12)* [CCP Historical Record of Events in Shanxi, October 1976–December 1992], Taiyuan: Shanxi renmin chubanshe, 1995.

Wu Houzhou (ed.), *'Qiwu' mingjian Shanxi sheng jiben jian chengjiu* [Capital Construction Achievements of Shanxi Province during the Seventh Five-year Plan], Taiyuan: Shanxi renmin chubanshe, 1992.

Xu Guosheng and Chen Ninghua (eds), *Shanxi xian qu jingji fazhan shilue* [Historical outline of the economic development of counties and regions in Shanxi], Taiyuan: Shanxi jingji chubanshe, 1992.

Yan Wuhong (ed.), *Shanxi jingji* [Shanxi's Economy], Taiyuan: Shanxi renmin chubanshe, 1985.

Yang Xiaochi (ed.), *Zhongguo ziben zhuyi gongshangye de shehui zhuyi gaizao – Shanxi juan* [The Socialist Transformation of Capitalist Industry and Commerce in China – Shanxi volume], Beijing: Zhonggong dangshi chubanshe, 1992.

Zhang Dengyi (ed.), *Keji yu Jin* [Science, Technology and Shanxi], Beijing: Zhongguo kexue jishu chubanshe, 1994.

Zhang Weiqing (ed.), *Shanxi sheng qing yu gaige fazhan yanjiu* [Research on reform and development in Shanxi], Taiyuan: Shanxi renmin chubanshe, 1989.

Zhonggong Shanxi shengwei dangshi yanjiushi (ed.), *Zhongguo gongchandang Shanxi lishi gangyao* [Outline History of the CCP in Shanxi], Beijing: Zhonggong dangshi chubanshe, 1991.

Zhonggong Shanxi shengwei zuzhibu, Zhonggong Shanxi shengwei dangshi yanjiushi, Shanxisheng danganbu (ed.), *Zhongguo gongchandang Shanxisheng zuzhi shi ziliao*

1949.10–1987.10 [CCP Shanxi Organisational and Historical Materials October 1949 – October 1987], Taiyuan: Shanxi renmin chubanshe, 1994.

—— , *Shanxisheng danganbu (ed.), Shanxisheng zhengquan, difang junshi, tongyi zhanxian, qunzhong tuanti xitong zuzhi shi ziliao 1949.10–1987.10* [Organisational and Historical Materials on the Systems of Political Power, Local Armed Affairs, United Front Work, and Mass Organisations in Shanxi Province October 1949 – October 1987], Taiyuan: Shanxi renmin chubanshe, 1994.

Jiangxi Province

GENERAL

GDP (billion *yuan*)	151.70
GDP annual growth rate	13.40
as % national average	139.60
GDP per capita	3,696.10
as % national average	65.90
Gross Value Agricultural Output (billion *yuan*)	73.30
Gross Value Industrial Output (billion *yuan*)	133.60

POPULATION

Population (million)	41.05
Natural growth rate (per 1,000)	10.50

WORKFORCE

Total workforce (million)	20.60
Employment by activity (%)	
primary industry	54.90
secondary industry	17.90
tertiary industry	27.20
Employment by sector (%)	
urban	25.24
rural	74.76
Employment by ownership (%)	
state	16.99
collective	18.45
private	16.02
foreign-funded	0.19

WAGES AND INCOME

Average annual wage (*yuan*)	4,852.00
Growth rate in real wage	6.60
Urban disposable income per capita	3,780.20
as % national average	75.10
Rural per capita income	1,869.63
as % national average	97.10

PRICES

CPI annual rise (%)	8.40
Service price index rise	17.40
Per capita consumption (*yuan*)	1,559.00
as % national average	58.20

FOREIGN TRADE AND INVESTMENT

Total foreign trade (US$ billion)	1.20
as % provincial GDP	6.10
Exports (US$ billion)	0.90
Imports (US$ billion)	0.30
Realised foreign capital (US$ billion)	0.32
as % provincial GDP	1.80

EDUCATION

University enrolments	84,592.00
as % national average	83.50
Secondary school enrolments (million)	2.09
as % national average	108.40
Primary school enrolments (million)	4.44
as % national average	97.30

Notes: All statistics are for 1996 and all growth rates are for 1996 over 1995 and are adapted from *Zhongguo tongji nianjian 1997* [Statistical Yearbook of China 1997], Zhongguo tongji chubanshe, Beijing, 1997, as reformulated and presented in *Provincial China* no. 5, May 1998, pp. 68ff.

Jiangxi Province

8 Jiangxi in reform

The fear of exclusion and the search for a new identity

Feng Chongyi

Broadly speaking, there are three factors determining the trajectories of economic development of China's provinces in the reform era: natural endowment, including geographical position, accessibility and natural resources; relations between the province in question and the centre, particularly as reflected in the latter's changing policies towards different provinces at different times; and economic culture, including a range of dominant beliefs and the behaviour of local governments and the public in solving their economic problems.

This chapter is an attempt to understand the interaction of these three factors in shaping the development of Jiangxi Province, with special emphasis on the cultural determinants. In spite of the controversies surrounding the use of cultural factors to explain economic development, cultural explanations have had a strong academic legitimacy ever since Max Weber traced the connections between capitalist development in Western Europe and the precepts of seventeenth-century Protestantism. One flourishing area of academic studies in China since the 1980s has been precisely a discussion of the importance of regional cultures, each covering one or more provinces.[1] Without accepting for a moment any simple causal relationship, it seems reasonable to draw on the existing literature and explore the role of economic culture and its propagation in China's recent provincial development.

In any consideration of Jiangxi Province there would seem to be a number of clear reasons for targeting cultural factors, not the least of which has been the province's woeful feeling of exclusion in the reform era. Reform has not been universally welcomed in Jiangxi since the late 1970s, in large part because of the actual practice of central government policy during the 1980s quite as much as adherence to earlier traditions. Anti-commercialism has been an important factor deterring Jiangxi from achieving economic modernisation since the 1840s, if not earlier, and was certainly reinforced in many ways during the Mao-dominated years of China's politics. Jiangxi's role in the history of the CCP and the consequences for the post-1949 period merely were to reinforce such latent tendencies. More recently, the construction of a new 'Gan' (the classical term for Jiangxi) culture since the 1990s has been promoted with a missionary zeal and is designed to combat earlier reluctance to reform and to forge a new, commercially and economically oriented, identity for the province.

A GLORIOUS PAST

Rich resources

The name Jiangxi is misleading because, taken literally, it means west of the Yangtze River, whereas Jiangxi Province is located south of the river. The name Jiangxi is the abbreviation for 'Jiangnan Xidao', one of the 15 administrative units at provincial level established in the reign of Emperor Kaiyuan of the Tang Dynasty. As the Gan River runs from north to south along the length of Jiangxi, the province is also known as Gan for short. Although Jiangxi is inland it is located not far from the coast – about 450 miles upstream on the south bank of the Yangtze from Shanghai – and is surrounded by the coastal provinces of Zhejiang and Fujian to the east and Guangdong to the south. However, its lack of direct access to the sea means that Jiangxi does not belong to the coastal provinces selected by the central government to enjoy preferential treatment in reform and opening by 'getting rich first'. While its eastern and southern neighbours have been in the forefront of economic development, Jiangxi in the early 1990s woke up to the fact that it had been left far behind its coastal neighbours. By 1994 Jiangxi's per capita GDP was only 2570 *yuan*, less than half that of Fujian and less than 44 per cent that of Guangdong and Zhejiang.[2]

This outcome of the reform era has been an obvious embarrassment to Jiangxi, a province of rich resources, famed as the cradle of the Chinese revolution. Jiangxi has deposits of rare minerals and is a key producer of nonferrous metals in China. Of the 151 types of minerals discovered in the province, 89 have proved reserves for industrial use. Thirteen of these minerals, including uranium, copper, silver and tantalum-niobium, are the largest reserves in China, 19 of them are the second largest, and 33 are to be found among China's five largest reserves. Jiangxi also produces significant amounts of coal and iron; there is a significant coal mine in Pingxiang and a sizeable iron mine in Xinyu. There are 89 large or very large mines, 157 medium-sized mines and 322 associated or symbiotic mines in operation in Jiangxi. Daji Mountain, Yichun and Dexing are the largest producers of tungsten, tantalum and copper respectively in China. Gan'an is even known as 'the world capital of tungsten'.

An important forest area in China, Jiangxi has more than 100 million *mu* (6.67 million ha) of forest. Of its land area 41 per cent is forest coverage, which is much higher than the world average, and ranks Jiangxi second among China's provinces. More than 650 varieties of trees are suitable for wood processing, 170 for producing oil and nearly 3,000 for producing medicine, fruit or perfume. The province has a timber reserve of 250 million cubic metres, producing 1 million cubic metres of timber and 5 million cubic metres of bamboo per annum.

Jiangxi is also rich in water resources. Its 25 million *mu* of area covered by freshwater account for 9.3 per cent of the national total, the third highest of all provinces. Boyang Lake, located in north Jiangxi, is the largest freshwater lake in China, with an area of 3,841 square kilometres, or 4,700 square kilometres during flood seasons. A famous 'fish reservoir', Boyang Lake produces 171 varieties of fish, including more than 30 of high economic value, such as red carp, grass carp and stonefish. The Gan, Xin, Fu and Rao rivers flow across the province, with a total length 2,012 kilometres. The Gan River, 751 kilometres in length, is the longest in the province and the second largest tributary of the Yangtze River, with an annual water drainage close to the total of the Yellow River Valley. The climate of Jiangxi is quite favourable for agriculture. It has a mild subtropical monsoon climate with four distinct seasons. Its annual average temperature is between 16.2–19.7 degrees Celsius, with annual sunshine of 1,400–2,000 hours and an annual rainfall of 1,341–1,934mm.

The birthplace of Neo-Confucianism

Southeast China began to overtake Northwest China – 'the birth-place of China's civilisation' – in terms of economic activities from the period of the Northern and Southern Dynasties (420–681) when North China suffered from successive wars and a great proportion of the better-off population migrated to settle in the south. Jiangxi emerged as a national economic centre no later than the Tang Dynasty, and benefited particularly from the development of the Grand Canal which linked Luoyang with the Lower Yangtze Valley. In the period of the Song Dynasty (960–1279) Jiangxi was a leading province in terms of its population, grain production, tea production, mining, ceramic industry, ship making, textile industry and trade.[3]

With rapid economic development, Jiangxi became one of the most populous areas in China during the late Tang Dynasty, when there were more than 290,000 registered households, 12 per cent of China's total. By the late Southern Song Dynasty, there were more than 2.2 million households in Jiangxi, with a population of nearly 5 million, accounting for more than 17 per cent of the total in China. Also during the Tang Dynasty, Jiangxi became one of the major producers of food grains in China. Its position in grain production was so important that during the Northern Song Dynasty, Jiangxi contributed 1.2 million *dan* of grain transported to the capital annually, accounting for one-fifth of the total. During the Southern Song Dynasty, the contribution of grain to the capital from Jiangxi increased further to 2 million *dan* (220 million pounds) annually, accounting for one-third of the total.[4] Tea was probably the second most important agriculture produce next to grain in traditional China. Jiangxi was considered one the most important tea centres in China after the Song Dynasty. Among the 15 prefectures or counties identified the Northern Song Dynasty as key producers of tea in China, ten were located in Jiangxi. During the period of the Southern Song Dynasty, the annual output of tea in Jiangxi amounted to more than 4.6 million *jin* (pounds), which made it the largest provincial producer.[5]

Jiangxi fared equally well in industry during the same period. The most remarkable achievement was that Jingdezhen became 'the world capital of ceramic production'. Extraordinarily high quality ceramics had been produced at Shangnan, Jiangxi, since the Eastern Han Dynasty (25–220). During the reign of the Zhensong Emperor in the Southern Song Dynasty, he ordered Shangnan to produce ceramics for use in his court, with the title of his reign, 'Jingde', under the glaze. From then on, ceramics made in Shangnan were known as 'Jingde ceramics' all over China and the town also changed its name to Jingdezhen.[6]

In the meantime, Jiangxi took the lead in both silver and copper mining and smelting. Denggongchang Silver Mine at Leping in northeast Jiangxi produced more than 100 thousand tael annually during the Tang Dynasty. The nearby Xianshan Copper Mine at Dexing was the largest in China during the Northern Song Dynasty, with an annual output of 38,000 Chinese ounces of pure copper and over 100,000 workers at its height. The production of copper in Jiangxi was so important to China during this period that the coins made at Yongpingjian in Northeast Jiangxi accounted for half of the national total during the Southern Song Dynasty.[7] Based on their higher level of economic and technological development, Ganzhou and Nanchang emerged as two of the most important cities for ship building during the Tang Dynasty. By the Northern Song Dynasty, these two cities were able to build ships 40 metres long and 9 metres wide, with a cargo tonnage of 10,000 *dan*[8] and this capacity increased several more times during the Southern Song Dynasty.[9]

More importantly, trade and production complemented each other in Jiangxi. To quote a poem by Wang Anshi – a Jiangxi native and prime minister during the Northern Song Dynasty – on flourishing trade in Jiangxi at that time: 'thousands of merchants are carrying with them all sorts of treasure, and ships as big as mountains are busy transporting goods to other parts of China.'[10] Many cities in Jiangxi, such as Jiujiang, Ganzhou, Nanchang, Linjiang, Zhangshu, Wucheng and Hekou, were commercial centres of national importance during the Ming Dynasty (1369–1644), when merchants of Jiangxi origin were known as the 'Jiangyou Merchant Clique', active all over the country and as famous as both the Anhui and Shanxi merchants.[11]

The development of trade in Jiangxi was facilitated by its geographical advantage as a thoroughfare for north and south China, a position beyond any contemporary imagination. In the early imperial period, Hanshui and Xiangjiang formed the only communication link between the Lingnan region and north China. After Ganjiang was linked to the Great Canal during the Tang Dynasty, together with the road between Jiangxi and Guangdong built through Dayuling, the Great Canal–Ganjiang-Dayuling Road became the most important communication link from north China and east China to Guangdong and Guangxi, with the circulation of migrants, traders and goods.

However, Jiangxi's rapid industrial and commercial growth did not last. After the Ming gave way to the Qing Dynasty, Jiangxi lost its momentum in industrial and commercial development, although its position as a centre of grain production has remained intact up to the present. To put it another way, Jiangxi since the end of the Ming Dynasty has purposely developed agriculture, and grain production in particular, at the expense of industrial and commercial development. This was certainly the intention of the conservative Neo-Confucian scholar-officials who eventually came to dominate Jiangxi in the late imperial period.

Historically, Jiangxi natives have been very proud of their Neo-Confucian heritage. Neo-Confucianism took shape in Jiangxi during the Song Dynasty, to become the most important ideology and living faith among educated Chinese in the late imperial era. Spreading from China, it became one of the most influential systems of ethics in the Oriental world. All five founders of this system of thought, Zhou Dunyi, Cheng Yi, Cheng Hao, Zhu Xi and Lu Jiuyuan, elaborated and taught Confucianism at different locations in Jiangxi.[12] The mountains in Jiangxi, Lushan in particular, accommodated many well-known academies of Neo-Confucianism, the best known being Bailudong Shuyuan, a school where Zhu Xi and Lu Jiuyuan taught for a long period.[13]

The development of Chan Buddhism in Jiangxi after the Tang Dynasty contributed a great deal to the creation of Neo-Confucianism, which borrowed heavily from elements of Buddhist transcendentalism. Again during the Ming Dynasty, when Wang Yangming came to Jiangxi as a scholar-official and general to suppress peasant rebellions, he pursued the ideas of both Zhu Xi and Lu Jiuyuan in developing Neo-Confucianism to a new stage. One striking feature of Neo-Confucianism, an idea put forward by Lu Jiuyuan and Wang Yangming in particular, is its stress on moral principles, putting moral training over practical learning, self-cultivation over worldly success, righteousness over profit, and agriculture production over trade. In a word, among other things, orthodox Neo-Confucianism is an ideology of anti-commercialism which fits perfectly a self-sufficient agrarian economy.[14]

After the Opium War in 1840–1842, modern industrial and commercial enterprises were established in Jiangxi's neighbouring provinces, schools of Western thought developed, and groups of liberal politicians and scholars started to emerge. In Jiangxi itself, however, the province's political and spiritual leadership turned its back on modernisation and fought to consolidate the province as a self-sufficient small peasant economy and a stronghold of orthodox Neo-Confucianism. They became very proud of not being involved in 'disgraceful commercial activities', and were convinced that 'the supply of grains and domestic animals is sufficient within the boundary of the province, with extremely few merchants needing to go out to do business elsewhere'.[15]

Of course, the rise of Neo-Confucianism was not the sole factor responsible for the decline of trade in Jiangxi. Changes to the transportation system in the modern era had a major impact on Jiangxi. The designation of Jiujiang, the northern gateway to the province, as a treaty port in 1861, by virtue of the Anglo–Chinese Treaty of Tianjin, enabled Jiujiang and Nanchang to maintain their role as important trans-shipment points and regional commercial centres. However, the importance of the Gan River as a major national communication line disappeared with the development of ocean shipping along the coast and the completion of the Nanjing–Hankou and Canton–Hankou railways at the turn of the century, resulting in the decline of commercial activities along the Gan River, in particular its southern part.

The province suffered further when, in 1854, for the purpose of supporting his troops in fighting against the Taiping Rebellion, Zeng Guofan imposed the likin, a new kind of tax on goods in transit which was imposed at check-points set up along major communication lines in Jiangxi. After the Taiping Rebellion was suppressed, the likin was institutionalised nationally by the Qing regime to strengthen its revenue, but its impact remained most severe in Jiangxi. Originally, more than 70 posts had been set up throughout Jiangxi, collecting tax on all goods at the rate of 2 to 5 per cent (the announced rate was 1 per cent), totalling more than one million tael of silver annually, equal to the tax on arable land from the province. In 1860, Zeng Guofan further increased Jiangxi's rate of likin to a level of 9 per cent, the highest in the nation. In practice, the rate of likin could be as high as 30 to 40 per cent. The total amount of likin collected in the province amounted to 2.5 million tael of silver per annum at its peak, more than 160,000 tael at the outpost at Hukou alone in 1866. Even in the 1890s, when most of the outposts established to collect likin in other provinces had been demolished through the pressure of local merchants, more than 70 of them remained in Jiangxi, more than anywhere else in China.[16]

By the end of the nineteenth century, all Jiangxi's neighbouring provinces had established their modern munitions industry and modern mining industry, while Pingxiang Coal Mine, the first modern enterprise in Jiangxi, was established only in 1902.[17] The establishment of Pingxiang Coal Mine has an interesting background. When in the 1880s, Wen Tingchi, a famous reformist official from Pingxiang, tried to introduce modern machinery for excavating coal to his home town, he was driven out by all the degree holders of the county. Pingxiang Coal Mine was later established by the Qing government as a support enterprise for the Hanyang Ironworks. In 1949, when the Communists took over Jiangxi, modern industry hardly existed in the province, which had an industrial output value at that time of only 192 million *yuan*.[18]

'The Cradle of the Chinese Revolution'

The Chinese Communist revolution is usually characterised as an agrarian or peasant revolution. Viewed from this perspective, it is not surprising that the Chinese Communist Party [CCP] secured its support predominantly in more agriculture-oriented provinces such as Jiangxi. The development of the revolutionary bases in Jiangxi is certainly an important factor shaping the course of economic development in that province in the history of the People's Republic of China, during both the Maoist period and the reform era.

In April 1928 Mao Zedong, who had taken his peasant army to Jiangxi's Jinggang Mountains in September 1927, and Zhu De, who had joined Zhou Enlai and others to stage an uprising on 1 August 1927 (later the official 'birthday' of the PLA), combined their armed forces at Jinggang to create the Chinese Red Army of Workers and Peasants and the first revolutionary base of the CCP. The Jinggang Base Area became the Central Revolutionary Base in early 1929, with its headquarters at Ruijin, where the Chinese Soviet Republic was proclaimed in November 1931. The Chinese Red Army fought to expand and defend the Jinggang Base Area for six years until it was defeated by the KMT forces in 1934 and embarked on the Long March to northwest China. During these years, thousands of Jiangxi natives joined the CCP and the Red Army, and many of them came to know Mao personally.

When the CCP finally rose to power in 1949, many Jiangxi natives who had been active in the period of the Chinese Soviet Republic in the Jinggang Mountains Base Area were put in charge of Jiangxi Province. Their personal links to the central party leadership dated back to the Jiangxi Soviet period when Mao had been particularly happy with the growth and development of northeast Jiangxi under the direction of Fang Zhichun's brother Fang Zhimin and Shao Chiping. Back in 1931, as a member of both the Central Executive Committee and the Central Revolutionary Council of the Soviet Republic, Shao Chiping had already worked closely with Mao Zedong and Zhu De. When the CCP conquered Jiangxi and established the Nanchang Military Commission to run provincial affairs on 6 June 1949, the Commission was led by Chen Zhengren, Chen Qihan and Shao Shiping, all of whom were Jiangxi natives and had been active in the revolutionary movement in Jianggang Mountain during the late 1920s and early 1930s. They were joined by Fang Zhichun and Yang Shangkui, two other Jiangxi natives to form the top leadership of the province. Shao Shiping was appointed chairman of the provincial government, and Chen Zhengren the party secretary. Among their four deputies, only Fan Chiren was not a Jiangxi native. Shao Shiping held the position of governor of the Jiangxi People's Government until his death in 1965, with Fang Zhichun serving as his deputy and successor. When Chen Zhengren was transferred to Beijing to head the Ministry of Construction, Yang Shangkui succeeded him as the party secretary and remained in the position until 1967.[19] As Frederick C. Teiwes has observed, it is an extraordinary state of affairs that this group of Jiangxi elites dominated Jiangxi politics in the 1950s and early 1960s and provided one of the most stable provincial leaderships in China during that period.[20]

In the 1950s and early 1960s Jiangxi was a model province for the implementation of Maoist policies, such as land reclamation, downward transfer of cadres and educational revolution. There was no particular land shortage in Jiangxi during the 1950s and 1960s. Jiangxi in 1957 had a cultivated area of 42.2 million *mu* (2.8 million ha), accounting for more than 17 per cent of the total area of the province. Per capita, the farming population in Jiangxi had an average of 2.6 *mu* of farm land, higher than the national average. However, in order to produce more grain and demonstrate the revolutionary zeal of the people in the old revolutionary bases, the provincial leadership in the late 1950s worked out an ambitious land reclamation programme, creating the well-known slogan of 'conquering the red soil'. During the period from 1956–1958, more than 3 million *mu* of waste land, mostly in the hilly and mountainous regions, were reclaimed, more than twice the original estimate of 1.4 million *mu*. This extraordinary effort was publicised nationwide, including an article entitled 'Raising the Red Flag and Conquering the Red Soil' in the 1959 New Year issue of *Red Flag*.[21]

Jiangxi's contribution to the Maoist educational revolution was the Jiangxi Communist Labour University, which was portrayed as the model of educational revolution for other provinces to emulate. It was established in Nanchang on 1 August 1958, at the beginning of the Great Leap Forward, in response to Mao's call for the 'Great Educational Revolution'. Its teaching programme was based on the principles of 'part-work and part-study', 'the combination of study and productive labour' and 'the combination of political and professional studies'. In the first year, it established more than 30 campuses on state farms all over Jiangxi, with an enrolment of 11,000 from Jiangxi as well as other parts of China. By the end of 1961, the Jiangxi Communist University had expanded to 103 campuses, with 46,000 students. Mao Zedong was so pleased with the development of the Jiangxi Communist University that, on the occasion of its third anniversary, he wrote a letter to the university praising its achievement and instructing the staff and students to be more vigilant in the struggle between the two classes, the two roads, and the two lines.[22] In 1975, a political film, *Rupture*, based on the story of the Jiangxi Communist University, was made by the more Maoist elements in China's politics to attack Deng Xiaoping's 'Right deviation of reversing correct verdicts'.

Throughout the 1950s and 1960s, the leadership maintained a close political association and personal ties with top leaders in Beijing and worked closely with the central government to secure preferential treatment and resources for their province. The position of Jiangxi as 'the Cradle of the Chinese Revolution' served as their justification when, for example, Yang Shangkui, the first secretary of the CCP Jiangxi Provincial Committee, argued in 1956 in his report at the Eighth Party Congress that Jiangxi deserved special attention and more resource allocation, because its economic backwardness had much to do with the cost of the revolution to the province.[23]

Jiangxi clearly fared well in economic development during the Mao Era, in spite of complaints in the 1980s by academics in Jiangxi that 'Jiangxi never became a focus for state investment and construction after liberation',[24] because it had not been included among priority areas in the early 1950s and under the Third Front policy from 1965–1975.[25] Indications are that the Jiangxi leadership was very effective in pressuring the central government and soliciting its support, particularly for badly needed financial and technological assistance. Despite the fact that, due to its poor industrial base, Jiangxi had no strategic importance for the central government, six key national projects were allocated to Jiangxi during the period of the First Five Year Plan (1952–1957). Among these six projects, the Shangraojiang Hydroelectric Station and the Nanchang Bayi Bridge were meant to lay down the infrastructure for industrial development in Jiangxi, and the Hongdu Engineering Factory in Nachang was to build the first aircraft of the People's Republic of China in 1954. With the support of the central government, 169 local key projects were also initiated during the same period, including the Jiangxi Textile Factory, the Jiangxi Paper Mill, the Jiangxi Tractor Factory, the Jiangxi First Sugar Refinery and the Pingxiang Steelworks. As a result, the value of industrial output in Jiangxi increased from 192 million *yuan* in 1949 to 1.25 billion *yuan* in 1957, with an annual growth rate of 16.5 per cent during the period from 1952–1957.[26]

During the period of the Second Five Year Plan (1958–1962), when the priority of development in China shifted from the development of heavy industry to a simultaneous development of agriculture and light industry, Jiangxi was able to attract more support from the central government because of its importance in agricultural production. Jiangxi was selected as one of the major provinces to mechanise its agricultural operations, improve transport facilities and the supply of chemical fertilisers and electricity.[27] The investment in state sector capital construction in Jiangxi during the 'Great Leap Forward' amounted to 2.1 billion *yuan*, 2.4 times the total investment in Jiangxi during the period of the First Five Year Plan. From 1958–1960 63,000 reservoirs were built in Jiangxi, 70 of them with a capacity of 10 million cubic metres or more, bringing 90 per cent of the arable land under irrigation.[28]

At the initiative of the central government, several thousand technicians, university graduates and skilled workers, as well as many factories from Shanghai, Zhejiang and other more developed areas, were transferred to help develop industry in Jiangxi. In 1957 and 1958 257,000 and 327,000 personnel settled in Jiangxi respectively in this way.[29] As a key recipient of central government support, Jiangxi was not hit very badly by the disaster of 1958–1960. An estimated 30 million people starved to death in China during the famine, but statistical figures for Jiangxi still show a population increase of 1.1 million during the three years 1958–1961, even though the natural growth of the population in the period was exceptionally low.[30] People in south Jiangxi today retain a proud memory of the fact that they were able to provide food for refugees from Guangdong during the 'three years of hardship'.[31] Moreover, during the following 'recovery' period, Jiangxi was able to sell 1.2 million tons of grain to other provinces according to the state plan from 1961–1963.[32]

The situation for Jiangxi changed when the provincial leadership, at that time headed by Fang Zhixun and Yang Shangkui, fell out of Mao's favour at the very beginning of the Cultural Revolution. The reason was precisely their concentration on economic development during the 'recovery' period which was then said to have been dominated by Liu Shaoqi's 'revisionist line'. Governor Fang Zhixun and First Party Secretary Yang Shangkui were removed from their positions in early 1967, and the 'Decision on handling problems in Jiangxi' issued by the Central Committee of the CCP on 10 August 1967 accused Fang of being 'the most senior capitalist roader in Jiangxi'. The power struggle between the faction in support of the former provincial leadership, which was assisted by the Jiangxi Military District Commander Wu Duanshan, and the various rebel groups was remarkably intense, and resulted in numerous armed skirmishes with several thousand casualties.[33]

The situation in Jiangxi during Autumn 1967 was so chaotic that the Centre sent troops from Guangzhou and Jinan Military Regions, led by Cheng Shiqing (the 60th Army Commander and Lin Biao's protege) and Yang Dongliang (Commander of the 203rd Division, 68th Army) to restore political order.[34] In January 1968, when the Jiangxi Provincial Revolutionary Committee was established, its senior leaders were Cheng Shiqing, Yang Dongliang, Chen Changfeng and Wen Daohong, four professional military commanders of troops dispatched to Jiangxi in 1967. There was continuous friction between these military commanders (who came from outside the province) and the local rebel leaders. Power struggles, purges and factional strife in the province continued during the Cultural

Revolution and proved to be disastrous for the Jiangxi economy. The provincial gross output value of industry and agriculture fell by 8.7 per cent, 7.7 per cent and 7.7 per cent respectively over the years 1967, 1974 and 1976.[35]

CHALLENGE AND OPPORTUNITY

In the era of reform and opening Jiangxi has fallen behind its neighbouring provinces, particularly Guangdong, Fujian and Zhejiang. This can be partly explained by the coastal strategy of the central government and the inaccessibility of Jiangxi Province. Nevertheless, self-inflicted suffering deserves at least equal attention. Jiangxi's economic development since the early 1980s seems to have been conditioned greatly by the province's economic culture, although a purely cultural explanation cannot by any means provide a total analysis. One legacy of Jiangxi's success during the Maoist Era is the stronger attachment to Maoist notions of egalitarianism and a strong antagonism towards commercialism and capitalism. The local governments and public in Jiangxi have proved to be more resistant to reform policies than their counterparts in neighbouring coastal provinces. Some Jiangxi academics and government officials have asserted categorically that 'there are many reasons for the low level of economic development in Jiangxi, but the root cause is the poor quality of its people'.[36]

Recent traditions of Maoist revolutionary ideology have played a significant role in retarding marketisation and market-oriented economic growth in Jiangxi. Several features of cultural beliefs and behaviour patterns in Jiangxi can be identified as obstacles to the development of a market economy: the lack of social approval (or even acceptance) for commercial activities, especially the profession of merchants engaged in private trade; conservative thinking; a wait-and-see attitude; and a mentality of dependence on others for economic initiatives and development. In the 1980s when local governments and the public in Guangdong and Fujian were vying with each other to involve themselves in commercial activities, the public in general and government officials in particular in Jiangxi still stuck to the Maoist revolutionary tradition. According to one Jiangxi academic, the general trend in the province at that time was to 'equate the commodity economy with capitalism' and to 'long for wealth but without any courage in its pursuit'.[37] Local government supressed rather than encouraged commercial activities. During the worst period in the early 1980s, there were 1,594 check-posts set up by public security organs, the traffic control organs, the administrative office of industry and commerce, and the tax office on highways throughout Jiangxi to control the circulation of goods – one outpost for every 30 kilometres on average. As a result, 'check-posts stood like trees in a forest, separating the markets, blocking each other, and hindering the circulation of goods and the opening to the outside world'.[38] Control was so strict that peasants in southern Jiangxi could only smuggle their agricultural produce to Guangdong and Fujian during the night by taking meandering footpaths through mountains or sending them by river.[39]

Conservative thinking and a wait-and-see attitude by the government and public of Jiangxi have been best manifested in their passive reaction to the initial waves of reform. The process of dismantling the commune system in Jiangxi was extraordinarily long and tortuous. In mid-1981, when household responsibility systems had emerged in most provinces, there were even difficulties in Jiangxi in reaching a consensus to employ the new system to 'change the face of some notably poor and backward communes and production teams', let alone in agreeing to universal implementation. By the end of 1982, 60 per cent of production teams in Jiangxi still managed to maintain collective farming.[40] To make things worse, peasants were required to plant more ideologically acceptable crops rather than more profitable ones. Jiangxi fell far behind other provinces in expanding the area of cash crops during two key periods in the 1980s. From 1980–1982 when the area for cash crops in China increased more than 60 million *mu*, it only increased 930,000 *mu* in Jiangxi, accounting for 1.5 per cent of the total; again in 1985 when the area for cash crops increased more than 46 million *mu*, it only increased 659,000 *mu* in Jiangxi, accounting for less than 1.4 per cent of the total.[41]

For the same reason, in the 1980s, the local governments of Jiangxi were reluctant to develop the domestic private economy or encourage foreign-funded enterprises, none of which had been favoured by Maoism. In the words of the party secretary of Jiangxi in 1992,

> some of our comrades have often been confused by the problem of capitalism and socialism. They have always been nervous whenever mentioning the lease of state property or annexation of enterprises. They have always been worrying that our direction is wrong whenever mentioning the development of 'three capital' entreprises: private economy, joint-stock enterprises or the stock exchange.[42]
>
> (Mao Zhiyong, 1992, p. 15)

The private sector in Jiangxi was negligible throughout the 1980s. Up to 1994, there were only 77,789 people working in private enterprises and 523,719 self-employed, whereas the figures for the two categories for neighbouring Hunan with a population half as large were 269,200 and about 2.7 million respectively.[43] One government official argued that there was strong discrimination against the private economy in Jiangxi, as expressed in the phenomena of 'suspicion', 'exclusion' and 'squeeze'.[44]

One secret of economic success in the coastal provinces of China has been the use of foreign capital and technology to upgrade production. Scarcity of capital has always been a fundamental obstacle to the development of the Jiangxi economy. Due to its inaccessibility and the unfavourable central policies for interior provinces, Jiangxi has been in a weak position in terms of opening to the outside world. However, the situation was aggravated further by the passive and reluctant attitudes towards foreign investment adopted by the government and the public in Jiangxi. The provincial government only approved its first joint-venture project in March 1984.[45] From 1987 to 1990, there were only 128 foreign-funded enterprises established in the province, with a total investment of US$71 million, less than 5 per cent of the direct foreign investment in Guangdong for the single year of 1990.[46] Jiangxi also lagged far behind its western neighbour Hunan in attracting foreign investment. From 1984–1992, US$2.68 billion of foreign capital was utilised in Hunan, compared to US$567 million in Jiangxi.[47]

In observing the underdevelopment of the foreign-funded sector in Jiangxi and painting a picture in distinct contrast to the situation of foreign investment in the coastal provinces, one provincial scholar complained that

> we have lagged behind in our understanding of the new situation of utilising foreign investment. Initially, some comrades believed that foreign invest-ment was dispensable and needed no attention, because it was foreign investors who would make money. They treated foreign-funded enterprises in Jiangxi as harshly as possible, for fear that foreigners would gain the extra advantage. In particular, they could not tolerate a foreign investor becoming a director or holding more than 51% of shares in a joint venture.[48]
>
> (Huang Zhigang, p. 29)

In the early 1980s, Jiangxi was also characteristically slow in developing the non-state sectors of its economy, although it enjoyed exceptional advantages for the development of the collective sector, with an abundant agricultural surplus, cheap labour and a solid rural industrial base. Jiangxi had a good starting base for developing town and village enterprises at the beginning of the reform era. Compared to other provinces, its commune and production brigade enterprise sector had developed well during the 1960s and 1970s. In 1975 Jiangxi had more than 24,000 enterprises of this kind, with assets of 310 million *yuan*, an output value of 463 million *yuan*, and 390,000 workers.[49] However, in the early 1980s, when the neighbouring provinces of Zhejiang, Guangdong and Fujian concentrated on developing their non-state sectors (which led them to become the key dynamos in economic growth), Jiangxi chose to rely on the state sector for its development. During 1982–1988 the growth rate of the industrial output value of the state sector in Jiangxi surpassed all neighbouring provinces except Guangdong with its special circumstances, but its overall industrial output value was falling behind.[50] It was the development of town and village enterprises that made the difference between the level of economic development in Jiangxi and its coastal neighbours, as shown by Table 8.1.[51] In 1992, Jiangxi's state sector still accounted for 59.3 per cent of industrial output value of Jiangxi, compared to 33.8 per cent in Guangdong, 35.4 per cent in Fujian and the national average of 48.1 per cent.[52]

While Jiangxi in its reform policies was thus lagging behind central government initiatives, the latter did certainly continue the policy of 'vigorously giving aid to and exercising leadership in the economic and cultural development of the old revolutionary bases'. This policy favoured revolutionary centres such as Jiangxi, where between half[53] and two thirds[54] of the population were considered

Table 8.1 Gross output value and industrial output value of the town and village enterprises in Jiangxi and neighbouring provinces, 1987

Province	Zhejiang	Guangdong	Hubei	Hunan	Anhui	Fujian	Jiangxi
GOV (billion yuan)	45.5	34.3	18.7	16.2	16.1	11.3	7.0
Per capita GOV (*yuan*)	996	447	375	—	287	352	244
IOV (billion yuan)	40.3	21.6	10.7	8.5	8.2	6.8	4.2

Source: see note 51

as living in 'old revolutionary bases', by providing aid to develop infrastructure and industry, albeit on a much smaller scale than in the pre-reform period.[55] For example, during the period from 1980–1985, the central government allocated a special grant of 20 million *yuan* annually to Jiangxi for the economic development of the 'old revolutionary bases' in the province.[56] The significance of such an amount of money to the development of the Jiangxi economy was limited, yet it helped to sustain the mentality of dependency among local governments and the province in general, characterised by academics as 'wait, be dependent on others, and beg'.[57] Jiangxi, in short, continued to rely almost exclusively on the financial aid of the party-state, and the state sector of the economy until the late 1980s.

The 'Old revolutionary area mentality' was widely blamed for the prevailing dependency mentality in Jiangxi during the 1980s. As condemned by a Jiangxi native scholar,

> the old revolutionary area mentality has long paradoxically fostered laziness and sluggishness, the opposite of the revolutionary martyrs' eagerness to make progress. If we accept the concept of 'Jiangxi as an old revolutionary area' by habit, consciously or unconsciously tolerating the condition of poverty, consciously or unconsciously expecting support and charity from other people, the glory of the 'old areas' turns out to be a negative mental obstacle, damaging our own creative powers and destroying our own vitality.[58]
>
> (Jiang Bing, 1995, p. 21)

It took a new generation of political leaders before these attitudes started to change.

In search of a new identity

The first provincial leadership of the reform era – headed by Jiang Weiqing and Bai Dongcai, who were both over 70 when they became party secretary and governor of Jiangxi respectively – was dominated by a group of old revolutionaries preoccupied with the factional struggle of the past and extremely cautious about reform and opening. There was minor excitement in Jiangxi in 1985 when two relatively young cadres, Wan Shaofen and Ni Xiance, both of them Jiangxi natives, were appointed to the positions of party secretary and governor respectively. However, both were unable to hold on to their positions for long enough to make their impact felt. Wan was the first female provincial party secretary in China and she had been chosen for this position by Hu Yaobang. Apart from being affected by the rumour that she was Hu Yaobang's secret lover (an almost inevitable rumour, unfortunately, for the first woman to hold such a position in the CCP), her earlier experience as a cadre of the Communist League and director of the Provincial Women's Federation seems to have provided little experience for the management of political and economic affairs of the province. Ni Xiance was widely expected to be a young leader of boldness and resolution, qualities badly needed to move Jiangxi ahead. Unfortunately, he rapidly became involved in a scandal and was sentenced to prison 16 months after his appointment.[59]

In October 1986, Wu Guanzheng became the new governor of his home province. Born in Yugan County, Jiangxi in 1938, Wu Guanzheng had graduated in mechanical engineering from Qinghua University in 1968. His career can be characterised as that of a typical technocrat. He served first as an engineer at a chemical plant in Wuhan and eventually rose to the positions of party secretary and mayor of that city. Eighteen months after his appointment, Wan Shaofen, who still retained her position as party secretary, was replaced by Mao Zhiyong, who was transferred to Jiangxi from his position as party secretary of Hunan province. With a reputation as a conservative official left behind in Hunan, Mao in his new position was reluctant to take any initiatives or a high political profile and gave Wu a free hand in persuing his policies. Wu Guanzheng's ascendance marked the overdue emergence of a stable reform leadership in Jiangxi and he remained in his position until 1995, when he became party secretary of the province.[60]

Wu had a very strong sense of mission to put an end to the backwardness of his province. The strategy he adopted for Jiangxi in 1987 was to open the province to the coastal areas according to the principles of 'Support, catch-up, replace'. The establishment of the 'Southern Jiangxi Reform Experimental Area' in December 1987 was probably the first important move he took in this direction. The experimental area, adjoining Guangdong and Fujian and centring around Ganzhou, had 17 counties and one city with a population of more than seven million under its jurisdiction. The area was encouraged to make use of economic policies available in Guangdong and Fujian and was additionally assigned provincial-level powers in foreign trade, price reform and infrastructure construction in addition to the administration of industrial and commercial affairs. The original idea was to fully integrate this area with the economies of Guangdong and Fujian. The additional cultural significance of the undertaking lies in the fact that this area was the heart of the Central Soviet Area in the late 1920s and early 1930s. Precisely for that reason, the event was reported on the front page of *Renmin Ribao* [People's Daily] in an article entitled 'Red Soviet Area in the past, Special Economic Zone today'.[61] It was obviously a shock to the public of Jiangxi that an old revolutionary base area could be turned into a Special Economic Zone, and some Jiangxi academics, not without some justice, regarded the event as a breakthrough in the reform and opening of the province.[62] Of course, due to its poor infrastructure, the achievements of the zone in boosting foreign economic activities have only been modest.[63]

Wu put great effort into building a consensus for his reform programme among officials and intellectuals in Jiangxi. He twice solicited essays on strategies for the development of the province from officials and intellectuals, first in 1988 and again in 1994. Drawing an analogy with the famous story of Liu Bei seeking advice from Zhuge Liang during the period of the Three Kingdoms, Wu Guanzheng called the arrangement 'Discourse on revitalising Jiangxi at Longzhong'. Wu's twofold objectives were to collect good proposals from local intellectuals on the one hand, and uncover talented individuals on the other.[64] The second time around the process lasted seven months and was widely publicised by provincial media. Of the 250 essays received, 19 were rewarded with publication in an edited volume.

The establishment of Nanchang University was another important step taken by Wu Guanzheng to motivate Jiangxi academics and secure their support. By 1993 academics in Jiangxi had been embarrassed by their own particular 'three nos' – no members on the State Academic Council, no key universities designated by the state, no PhD student programmes. To change this situation the provincial government spent RMB 130 million *yuan* to establish Nanchang University through the merger of Jiangxi University with Jiangxi Engineering University in 1993, a model later followed by other provinces.

Gan culture fever

A major initiative was Wu Guanzheng's personal involvement in the promotion of Gan culture in an effort to create a provincial identity for Jiangxi. The notion of 'Gan culture' was first put forward by a famous Jiangxi historian during the high tide of national 'culture fever' that struck in China during the mid-1980s. At that time, however, there was no immediate response within Jiangxi, neither from the public in general nor from academic circles. The only significant event for cultural development in Jiangxi at that time was the (re)construction of Tengwang Pavilion on the riverbank at Nanchang in 1985.

The Tengwang Pavilion was originally built in 653 during the Tang Dynasty by Li Yuanying, governor of Hongzhou (now Nanchang). *Tengwang* [Lord Teng] was the title conferred on Li by the emperor, hence the name Tengwang Pavilion. Part of its lasting fame was a beautiful prose poem composed by Tang Dynasty scholar Wang Bo, who praised the province as 'a treasured land of many great men'. In 1985 a huge sum of money was spent to rebuild the Tengwang Pavilion according to its description in Wang Bo's poem but, in fact, not to its original design nor at its original location. The contribution of Tengwang Pavilion to Jiangxi's identity was that it housed the huge 'Picture of Great Men', with portraits of all Jiangxi natives who had achieved fame in the history of Imperial

China. These included the poet and recluse Tao Yanming of the Eastern Jin Dynasty, the reformer Wan Anshi of the Northern Song Dynasty, the founder of Neo-Confucianism Zhu Xi of the Southern Song Dynasty, the Ming Dynasty playwright Tang Xianzhu and the Ming Dynasty scientist Song Yingxing. It even included some negative figures who rose to prominence, such as Yan Song, a notorious official of the Ming Dynasty.

However, apart from this there was little public awareness of Jiangxi culture and identity. It was noted that as late as 1990 the editors of the *Knowledge of Literature and History* in Beijing were unable to solicit enough contributions for a special issue on Gan culture.[65] When a group of young scholars wrote and published *Jiangxi Culture* in 1993, their book only contained an outline of religions, philosophy, literature, art, and science and technology in Jiangxi, but no attempt to delineate a more specific and distinguished culture for the province.[66] A change occurred when Governor Wu Guanzheng took a personal role in the promotion of Gan culture.

Backed by the provincial government, the Institute of Gan Culture Studies was established at Nanchang University in February 1994. The Institute organised a series of seminars on Gan culture in conjunction with the *Jiangxi Daily*, the Jiangxi Broadcasting Station and Jiangxi Television, all of which provided wide publicity to their activities. Two notable slogans put forward by the Institute were 'construct Gan culture' and 're-vitalise the splendour of Gan culture'. Governor Wu and one of his deputies granted an interview to members of the Institute in July 1994. During the interview, Wu praised their endeavours in exploring Gan culture and mentioned the historical achievements of famous Jiangxi natives as an encouragement for the staff of the Institute to 'accomplish great tasks' and 'become outstanding figures' themselves. His talk was later revised and published under the title 'Gan culture: its splendid past, current prosperity, and magnificent prospects.'[67]

In responding to the governor's call, academics and officials at all levels of the province have been keen on talking about Gan culture, amounting to a veritable 'Gan culture fever'. Within a year after the publication of Wu Guanzheng's talk, another two centres for the study of Gan culture were established at Jiangxi Normal University and Jiangxi Academy of Social Sciences. The Jiangxi Provincial Society of Gan Culture Studies was established in Nanchang. More than one hundred articles on Gan culture were published in journals and newspapers, both inside and outside Jiangxi, and a series of seminars and an exhibition on Gan culture were organised. Local city and county governments organised forums on Gan culture.[68] For university students, courses on Jiangxi Culture and *An Outline of Jiangxi: past, present and future* were added to Jiangxi's tertiary education curricula. *An Outline of Jiangxi: past, present and future* was written at the direction of the provincial government, which provided the outline, with Governor Wu as the editor.[69]

However, the construction of a Jiangxi identity has proved to be a daunting task. Unlike many regional or provincial cultures in China, Gan culture is by no means readily defined. First of all, there is no dominant language or dialect in

Jiangxi. While more than 99.9 per cent of Jiangxi's population are Han, they speak several different dialects.[70] The Gan dialect covers only a small area around Nanchang; Hakka is spoken in south Jiangxi; Minnanhua in east Jiangxi; Wu language in northeast Jiangxi; Anhui and Jianghuai dialects in north Jiangxi; and Hunanese and the Hubei dialect are spoken in north-west Jiangxi. All of these linguistic groups have a natural tendency to identify themselves with people speaking the same language or dialect and sharing many other customs across the provincial borders. Second, Jiangxi can not be traced back to any independent political entities in the remote past, as can other provinces.[71] Third, in modern times there has been no Jiangxi school of philosophy, literature or art comparable to those giving a local identity to other provinces and regions.

Nevertheless, this state of affairs to some extent made the advocates of Gan culture only more eager and determined in their endeavour. They warned that Gan culture was in the process of 'dismemberment' and 'submerging'. By 'dismemberment' they referred to divisive, centrifugal forces tearing Jiangxi apart. 'In terms of economic and cultural exchange', they complained, 'people in the south of Jiangxi are fascinated by Guangzhou and Shenzhen; those in Shangrao (the north-east) by Shanghai, Jiangsu and Zhejiang; those in Yintan (the east) by Xiamen and Fuzhou; those in Pingxiang (the west) by Changsha and Zhuzhou; those in Jiujiang (the north) by Wuhan, Shanghai and Nanjing; leaving no room for a 'cultural centre' in Nanchang, the provincial capital'.[72] 'Submerging' referred to people losing interest in things related to Jiangxi and only wondering whether they should follow the fashions of Shanghai, Guangdong or Beijing; to provincial intellectuals who were looking for outside opportunities and leaving without hesitation; and generally to the apparent popular loss of confidence in Jiangxi.[73]

To some extent, this kind of language and argument was deliberately alarmist, designed to serve the purpose of cultural construction. In any case, the construction of Gan culture was certainly an ideological exercise, a reinterpretation of history that selectively negates the undesirable values and patterns of behaviour and creates something new and useful for current economic development. The advocates of Gan culture never hid their intention to serve the province's drive for economic development. According to Zheng Xiaojiang, founder of the Institute for Gan Culture, the priority in constructing Gan culture was to meet the demands of a modernising Jiangxi economy.[74] With this purpose in mind, their cultural construction has focused on three interrelated themes: the negation of the revolutionary traditions, an attack on parochialism and the promotion of commercialism.

'Revolutionary culture' or 'Soviet Area culture' had long been regarded in Jiangxi as its most important asset. From 1949 to the late 1980s the symbols of Jiangxi's local identity used to be the Ruijin Revolutionary Museum, the 'Centre for the Study of Mao Zedong Thought' in Jinggangshan, the Communist Labour University, the '1st August Nanchang Uprising Monument and Memorial Hall', and thousands of revolutionary relics throughout the province. Repudiation of these symbols became a priority for the advocates of Gan culture. 'It is not enough' a scholar from Nanchang University told Governor Wu Guanzheng 'to categorise Jiangxi culture as Soviet Area culture or revolutionary culture.'[75] Another author went as far as to totally negate Jiangxi's exceptional contribution to the revolution, and characterised the identification of 'Jiangxi culture' with 'revolutionary culture' as a false consciousness. Purportedly, this consciousness had severely affected leading cadres and educated people in Jiangxi and greatly hampered economic and cultural development in the province. In this view, 'the battles on Jinggangshan lasted less than two years and the Nanchang Uprising only several days. Furthermore, most of the leaders of these events were Marxist youth from other provinces.'[76]

Jiangxi's parochialism was seen as one element in the province's isolation, as well as a reason for its rejection of commercial activities. It was variously attributed to the province's geographical position, its long history as a small peasant economy and the negative legacy of the command economy.[77] The geographical position of Jiangxi as a basin surrounded by mountains was said to have nurtured an inward-looking mentality among its inhabitants; and the relatively fertile land of the province was said to keep people from working harder for outward-looking development. One Jiangxi scholar elaborated that the province's parochialism was a 'basin mentality', as well as a 'periphery mentality' and a 'self-satisfaction complex'.[78] In short, parochialism in the province was interpreted as small peasant consciousness rooted in a self-sufficient economy reinforced by the command economy of the Mao era.

Reference to the historical past, especially to Neo-Confucian traditions, was another way to attack conservative economic attitudes and to support the claim that Jiangxi once had been home to a successful commercial culture. With its discrimination against merchants and trade, the rise of Neo-Confucianism in Jiangxi was seen as the cause of serious economic setbacks for the province. Thus, during the Ming and the Qing Dynasties, while Jiangxi scholars accounted for one-tenth of all successful candidates in the highest imperial examinations based on Neo-Confucianism, Jiangxi's merchants were under tremendous pressure to divert much of their capital to buying degrees, official titles and land, as well as the support of lineage activities, such as the publication of family books, construction of ancestral temples and the provision of donations for charity. The decline of trade in Jiangxi was directly related to the spread of Neo-Confucianism and the rising status of the rural Confucianist scholar-gentry.[79]

In this view, the blow from which Jiangxi merchants never recovered was dealt by Zeng Guofan, the Neo-Confucian scholar-official and general equally famous as Wang Yangming, with his introduction of the likin tax in 1854. As masters of Neo-Confucianism, Zeng Guofan and his followers in Jiangxi were deeply suspicious of merchants because they did not produce things but only moved them around in search of profit, it was argued. After the suppression of the Taiping Rebellion, they were punished by imposition of the new levy on their activities. Jiangxi scholars depicted their province as one of the most miserable victims of this new levy and claimed that it essentially ensured that production and trade in a variety of goods, ceramics and tea in particular remained profitless in Jiangxi.[80]

With the overt aims of strengthening provincial self-confidence and creating a common purpose in developing an open market economy, the advocates of Gan culture uncovered many valuable properties of that culture. Quite apart from its revolutionary traditions and backwardness, they recreated a Jiangxi with a glorious past and, particularly, an advanced commercial culture from the Tang Dynasty to the Ming Dynasty. This culture had supported the famous 'merchant clique from the right side of the river', one of the three famous merchant groups in imperial China. In addition, people in Jiangxi in ancient times were said to be always ready to learn new things from other provinces and, on that ground 'a readiness to absorb new and diverse things' was even regarded as a characteristic feature of Gan culture. It was argued that this commercial culture, with its spirit of enterprise and openness, had been too long overwhelmed by the 'literati culture' and 'revolutionary culture'. It was now time to set it free and let Jiangxi resume its central role on the national stage.[81] The economic development in Jiangxi in the 1990s indicates that the Gan culture campaign is both a reflection of the awakening of the province to market consciousness as well as a stimulus to the development of a new, commercially oriented mentality.

A new strategy for an industrial and commercial Jiangxi

In spite of the differences between China's east and west, it seems wrong to speak of a dual economy, consisting of a dynamic modern sector located along the coastal areas and a large, stagnant, subsistence sector located in the rural hinterland. There has been relatively equal diffusion of industrialisation and modernisation throughout China since the 1950s, except for Tibet and Xinjiang. Regional autarky in the Mao era meant that each province developed its own industrial base, which in Jiangxi's case was by no means weaker than in neighbouring provinces. As claimed by some Jiangxi economists, Jiangxi was not only a leader in the mining industry in China during the Mao era, but also in some manufacturing industries, such as agricultural machinery and armaments.[82]

Jiangxi currently is in a weak position to compete with coastal provinces because it missed the wave of modernisation and the economic boom of the early 1980s. However, Jiangxi can mobilise advantages in some areas and there is a possibility for the province to catch up, declared Wu Guanzheng, who in 1995 became party secretary of the province. 'Jiangxi does not fall behind in every aspect. As a matter of fact, rapid progress has been made and great change has taken place in Jiangxi since a decade ago. There are very bright prospects for Jiangxi, where much can be accomplished.'[83]

Due partly to the central government's strategic shift of priorities to inland provinces and partly to the rise of market consciousness in the province, Jiangxi has been speeding up its reform and development, and Jiangxi economists point to some key indicators to prove that the face of the province has greatly changed in the 1990s. The industrial output value in Jiangxi exceeded that of agriculture for the first time in 1993.[84] More importantly, the economic growth rate in Jiangxi has been higher than the national average since 1991, a remarkable achievement

Table 8.2 Average annual growth rate of major economic items in Jiangxi and China,
           1991–1995 (%)

Items	Jiangxi	China
GNP	14.5	11.6
Investment in fixed assets	34	34.7
Government revenue	21	16.3
GVIO (industry)	33.6	22.2
GVAO (agriculture)	7.1	6.7

Source: Huang Qiyi, *et al.*, (eds), *'96 Jiangxi tongji nianjian* [Jiangxi Statistical Year Book 1996], Beijing: Zhongguo tongji chubanshe, 1996, pp.14–18; Ye Zheng, *et al.*, (eds), *Zhongguo tongji nianjian* [China Statistical Year Book 1996], Beijing: Zhongguo tongji chubanshe, 1996, pp. 22–24

for an under-developed province. The per capita GDP of Jiangxi surpassed that of Shaanxi in 1992 and the province ranked nineteenth nationally, bringing to an end its long-term status as one of the ten backward provinces and placing it in the category of middle-ranking provinces (see Table 8.2).

The central element of Jiangxi's growth strategy for the 1990s is the construction of the Changjiu (Nanchang–Jiujiang) Industrial Corridor. The decision to establish the Changjiu Industrial Corridor was made by the provincial government in February 1992, at the time of Deng Xiaoping's famous inspection tour to southern China which gave a boost to the national economy. According to the original plan, over the next 30 years a new industrial belt would be constructed for a length of 150 kilometres along the highway between Nanchang and Jiujiang, with an industrial core and parallel development of agriculture and commerce. Over three stages the project is to proceed from individual industrial centres to an integrated area by 'linking points to a line and expanding the line to an area'. The first stage of creating 'points' was from 1992 to 1995, the second stage of linking up these 'points' to a 'line' from 1996 to 2000, and the final expansion into a corridor in the third stage is expected to last from 2001 to 2020. The designated area has advanced land and water communication, with the Nanchang–Jiujiang Railway, the Beijing–Jiujiang–Kowloon Railway, the Nanchang–Jiujiang Express Highway, Jiujiang Harbour open to international shipping, and two airports with regular connections to major Chinese cities.

There are already a number of established enterprises in this area, including the Jiangling Automobile Group, the Gongqing Down Group, the Sanhai Enterprise Group and the Xinghuo Chemical Plant. More significantly, in order to attract foreign investment and Sino–foreign joint ventures, the provincial government has formulated preferential policies for overseas investors – the *Regulations Encouraging Development of Changjiu Industrial Corridor* – and set up several development zones. These are the Changbei Open Development Zone with a focus on machinery, electronics, new material industries and foodstuffs; the Gongqing Open Development Zone concentrating on food processing, building materials, brewery, and textiles; the Jiujiang Open Development Zone for power generation, a petrochemical and sulfur and phosphorus-based chemical industry;

the Sanhai Economic and Technological Development Zone for down products, pharmaceuticals, fine chemicals, machinery and light industries; the Yunshan Economic and Technological Development Zone concentrating on light industries, textiles, fine chemicals and foodstuffs; the Xinghuo High and New Technology Development Zone concentrating on a series of organisilicon products; and the Jinniu Open Development Zone concentrating on soft drinks, foodstuffs and animal husbandry.[85] So far, these areas have not been particularly successful in attracting foreign investment.[86]

It should be noted that the development of the Changjiu Industrial Corridor will aggravate economic imbalance in the province. Modern industrial development in Jiangxi has been concentrated along two major railways in the north of the province, with Nanchang and Jiujiang as the most important industrial and commercial centres. Agriculture was dominant in the southern, eastern and western 'peripheries' of the province. This situation has not changed in the reform era. Table 8.3 shows that the level of economic development in general and industrial development in particular are much higher in the industrial belt consisting of Jingdezhen, Nanchang, Xinyu, Yichun and Pingxiang in north and central Jiangxi than in other regions of the province.

To the advocates of Gan culture the construction of the Changjiu Industrial Corridor confirms the break with Jiangxi's traditional 'inland mentality', as it demonstrates the determination of the provincial leadership to integrate Jiangxi into the coastal and international economy. They claim that people in Jiangxi have come to the conclusion that 'the inland geographical position inland does not matter as long as the mind of the people is liberated'.[87] An often cited example of the opening of the provincial economy is the sharp increase in labour migration to the coastal provinces. In the mid-1980s, when millions of peasants from Sichuan, Hunan, Zhejiang and other provinces went to Guangdong to look for work,

Table 8.3 GDP and GVIO per capita of prefectural-level units in Jiangxi, 1994

Location	GDP per capita (yuan)	GVIO per capita (yuan)
Nanchang	4,481	6,787
Xinyu	4,168	5,961
Pingxiang	2,388	5,581
Jingdezhen	3,005	5,375
Yichun	2,375	4,113
Yingtan	2,498	3,835
Jiujiang*	2,579	3,498
Fuzhou	1,800	2,672
Shangrao	1,789	2,566
Ji'an	1,775	2,246
Ganzhou	1,788	1,968

Note: *The explanation for Jiujiang's relatively low per capita GDP figures is that it includes a large rural area in north-west Jiangxi

Source: Calculated from You Huilong, *et al.*, (eds), *'95 Jiangxi tongji nianjian* [Statistical Year Book of Jiangxi 1995], Beijing: Zhongguo tongji chubanshe, 1995, pp. 27, 37 and 282

peasants from Jiangxi were reluctant to join them. According to one anecdote, some tried their luck in Guangdong, only to return after a couple of months complaining they could not adapt to the lifestyle in Guangdong and taking a bath three times a day. However, in the 1990s millions of peasants from Jiangxi went to work in the coastal provinces. Some of them even earned enough money and learned enough skills to set up enterprises back home. This has been hailed as a big change in the thinking and behaviour of Jiangxi peasants.[88]

The opening of the Beijing–Kowloon Railway in July 1996 also aroused excitement in Jiangxi, where both the government and the public see it as a golden opportunity for areas along the line to improve their economic vitality. The Jiangxi section of the Beijing–Kowloon Railway is more than 700 kilometres long, accounting for one-third of the total length and running through 22 cities and counties of the province, particularly in the south. Nanchang is the only provincial capital and Jiujiang an important harbour on the route of the railway. Jiangxi is now directly linked to Hong Kong by both the Beijing–Kowloon Railway and a shipping link between Hong Kong and Jiujiang.

Jiangxi's history of inaccessibility seems over and there are expectations that the Beijing–Kowloon Railway will bring an economic miracle, as did the Grand Canal–Ganjiang–Dayuling Road in history. Every contributor to the essays in the *Collection of Essays on Strategies for the Development of Jiangxi Advancing Toward the Twenty-First Century* solicited by Governor Wu, mentioned the opening of the Beijing–Kowloon Railway as the golden opportunity for Jiangxi. One author even praised it as a 'lifeline' and 'hope-line' for Jiangxi, as it would completely change the geographical position of Jiangxi and turn the province into a communications hub for China.[89] However, these writers fail to mention that, judging from similar situations in Hunan, Hubei and Henan, the locational advantage of a communications hub in itself is not a sufficient condition for economic progress.

CONCLUSION

In the course of ideological transformation in Jiangxi from revolutionary traditions and the parochialism of small peasants towards acceptance of a market economy and international economic integration, local culture has purposefully been used as a tool to overcome ideological resistance to reforms. Jiangxi's leadership set out to create a new identity for Jiangxi which gave the province a tradition of commercialism and successful entrepreneurs. Neo-Confucianism, side by side with radical Maoist ideas, were among the factors that had led Jiangxi to lose its historic role in the late Ming and Qing Dynasties and fall behind its neighbouring provinces in the 1980s. Encompassing aspects of Jiangxi's history and culture from the neolithic period to the present, this effort represented a cultural construction that gave provincial intellectuals self-awareness and a common purpose. In return, they lent their voices and powers of persuasion to the reformist leadership of the province. People in the province today tend to identify with an industrial, commercial and urban Jiangxi rather than an agricultural and revolutionary Jiangxi, and the economy is likely to benefit further from these changes in ideology and cultural construction.

The ambition of the advocates of Gan culture to construct a new Jiangxi culture centred around Nanchang might, however, prove to be little more than their own wishful thinking. For one thing, the natural links among linguistic communities and historical ties of people across the Jiangxi borders can be expected to be strengthened in the process of modernisation and opening, especially when the local economies in Jiangxi's south, east, north-east and north-west become increasingly integrated with the more advanced economies centred around Guangdong– Shenzhen, Fuzhou–Xiamen, Suzhou–Hongzhou–Shanghai and Wuhan respectively, possibly at a faster rate than even their integration within the province will happen. In other words, while people in Jiangxi are embracing new cultural ideas conforming with a market economy, Gan culture, if it ever existed, is becoming more diverse rather than otherwise.

It should also be noted that, although it might appear to be pursuing a provincial agenda, the propagation of Gan culture was meant to bring Jiangxi in line with national policies. The advocates of Gan culture made it absolutely clear that they were not in favour of 'cultural localism' in any form. Instead, they argued that 'Gan culture will exhibit Jiangxi's local features as an eye-catching component in the splendour of Chinese culture'.[90] The hierarchy of identities in China has changed and continues to change constantly with individuals shifting the priority of their loyalty to their local communities, provinces and the nation in different periods, but these identities are certainly not mutually exclusive, and may even be complementary. Regional cultures have emerged in China's current cultural construction as a function of localised economic modernisation, hence regional cultures are competing with each other for a more salient role in the country, rather than with the national culture for hegemony.

ACKNOWLEDGEMENTS

The author would like to gratefully acknowledge the financial support of a UTS Large Internal Research Grant and thank David S. G. Goodman, Mark Selden, Hans Hendrischke and the participants of the Hangzhou Workshop, 20–24 October 1996 for their helpful comments and suggestions on an earlier draft of the chapter, as well as Wen Rui and Shao Hong for the collection of materials.

NOTES

1 Several series of monograph have been published on this subject, for example, Liaoning jiaoyu chubanshe published *The Series of Regional Cultures in China* covering 18 cultures, such as such *Yanzhao, Qilu, Xiyu, Zhongzhou, Wuyue, Bashu, Jingshu, Lianghui, Sanjin, Sanqin, Guandong, Qinzhang* and *Lingnan*.

2 *Provincial China*, 1 (March 1996), p. 37.
3 Wu Guanzheng, ed., *Jiangxi sheng qing gailun: lishi, xianshi, yu weilai* [An Outline of Jiangxi: Its Past, Present and Future], Nanchang: Jiangxi renmin chubanshe, 1995, pp. 37–39.
4 Wu Guanzheng, *Jiangxi sheng qing gailun*, p. 38.
5 Ibid.
6 Fang Yan *et al.*, eds, *Jiangxi xue* [Jiangxi Studies], Tongji University Press, 1989, p. 34.
7 Wu Guanzheng, *Jiangxi sheng qing gailun*, pp. 39–39.
8 1 *dan*= 110.2 pounds.
9 Fang Yan *et al.*, *Jiangxi xue*, p. 35.
10 Quoted in Wu Guanzheng, *Jiangxi sheng qing gailun*, p. 39.
11 Xu Huailin, *Jiangxi shigao* [A History of Jiangxi], Nanchang: Jiangxi gaoxiao chubanshe, 1991, pp. 539–540.
12 Zhou Dunyi was born in Hunan but his major career was in Jiangxi; Cheng Yi and Cheng Hao were born in Henan but received their early education from Zhou Dunyi in Jiangxi; Zhu Xi was from Wuyuan, which used to belong to Anhui but was incorporated into Jiangxi in 1934; and Lu Jiuyuan was born in Fuzhou, Jiangxi. See Zhou Wenying, *Jiangxi Wenhua* [Jiangxi Culture], Shenyang: Liaoning jiaoyu chubanshe, 1993, pp. 152–153.
13 Wu Guanzheng, *Jiangxi sheng qing gailun*, pp. 41–42.
14 For detailed analysis of Song and Ming Neo-Confucianism, see Thomas A. Metzger, *Escape from Predicament: Neo-Confucianism and China's Evolving Political Culture*, New York: Columbia University Press, 1990; and William Theodore de Bary, *The Message of the Mind in Neo-Confucian Thought*, New York: Columbia University Press, 1989.
15 Quoted in Wan Zhenfan, 'Jindai Gan wenhua de shuailuo jiqi yuanyin' [The decline of the Gan culture in modern times], *Gan Wenhu Yanjiu* [Studies on Gan Culture], 1 (1994), p. 242.
16 Wu Guanzheng, *Jiangxi sheng qing gailun*, pp. 58–60.
17 Wan Zhenfan, 'Jindai Gan wenhua de shuailuo jiqi yuanyin' [The decline of the Gan culture in modern times], *Gan Wenhu Yanjiu* [Studies on Gan Culture], 1 (1994), pp. 242–243.
18 Wu Guanzheng, *Jiangxi sheng qing gailun*, p. 118.
19 For their biographies, see Donald W. Klein and Ann B. Clark, *Biographical Dictionary of Chinese Communism, 1921–1965*, Cambridge, Mass.: Harvard University Press, 1971; and Union Research Institute, *Who's Who in Communist China*, Hong Kong: Union Press, 1969.
20 Frederick C. Teiwes, 'Provincial Party Personnel in Mainland China, 1956–1966', *Occasional Papers of the East Asian Institute*, New York: Columbia University, 1967, and 'Provincial Leadership in China: The Cultural Revolution and Its Aftermath', *East Asia Papers*, Ithaca: Cornell University, No. 4, 1974.
21 Fu Yutian *et al.* (eds), *Dangdai Zhongguo de Jiangxi* [China Today: Jiangxi], Beijing: Dangdai Zhongguo chubanshe, Vol. 1, pp.187–188.
22 Fu Yutian *et al.* (eds), *Dangdai Zhongguo de Jiangxi*, Vol. 2, p.10.
23 Yang Shangkui, 'Jiaqiang geming lao genjudi de gongzuo' [Strengthen work in the old revolutionary bases], *Xinhua Ban Yue Tan*, No. 21, 6 November 1957.
24 Fan Shengsi, 'Dui Jiangxi sheng jingji fazhan de huigu he fansi' [Economic development in Jiangxi: a retrospective]', in *Jiangxi Shehui Kexue* [Social Sciences in Jiangxi], 6 (1991), p. 27; see also Wu Guanzheng, *Jiangxi sheng qing gailun*, p. 180.
25 Han Guang, *et al.*, eds, *Dangdai Zhongguo de jiben jianshe* [China Today: Capital Construction], Beijing: Zhongguo shehui kexue chubanshe, 1989, Vol.1, pp. 24–25, 157–162.
26 Fu Yutian *et al.*, *Dangdai Zhongguo de Jiangxi*, Vol. 1, p. 47.

27 Ibid., p. 317.
28 Ibid., pp. 55–60.
29 Ma Juxian *et al.* (eds), *Zhongguo renkou: Jiangxi fence* [Chinese Population: Volume of Jiangxi], Beijing: Zhongguo caizheng jingji chubanshe, 1989, p. 75.
30 Ibid., pp. 61, 71 and 74–75.
31 Liu Fangren, 'Zhuazhu jihui jiasu fazhan Jiangxi' [Seize the opportunity to speed up the development of Jiangxi], Sao Zehua, ed., *Jiangxi kua shiji gouxiang* [Blueprint for Jiangxi beyond the century], Jiangxi renmin chubanshe,1992, p. 45; Interviews with Jiangxi academic and government officials in Nanchang, April 1995.
32 Fu Yutian *et al.*, *Dangdai Zhongguo de Jiangxi*, Vol.1, p. 72.
33 'Jiangxi duoquan douzheng jingwei' [Ramifications of power struggle in Jiangxi], *Jinri Dalu* [Mainland Today], January 1968, pp. 7–13.
34 Fu Yutian *et al.*, *Dangdai Zhongguo de Jiangxi*, Vol.1, p. 75.
35 Ibid., pp. 73–77.
36 Fang Yan *et al.*, *Jiangxi xue*, p. 259. According to their list, the manifestations of the 'poor quality' include the weak impulse to do pioneering work, the low expectations for change and new things, the dependent mentality, the lack of initiatives, and the strong tendency to stick to old ways. This viewpoint was repeatedly confirmed by Jiangxi academic and government officials interviewed by the author in April 1995.
37 Wu Guangzheng, *Jiangxi sheng qing gailun*, p. 141.
38 Ibid., p. 149.
39 Ibid., p. 172.
40 Fu Yutian *et al.*, *Dangdai Zhongguo de Jiangxi*, Vol.1, pp. 95–96.
41 Fan Shengsi, 'Dui Jiangxi sheng jingji fazhan de huigu he fansi' [Economic development in Jiangxi: a retrospective]', in *Jiangxi Social Sciences*, 6 (1991), p. 28.
42 Mao Zhiyong, 'Ba jiefang sixiang tong zheng zhua shigan jiehe qilai, cheng gaige kaifang dashao shi jingji dengshang yige xin taijie' [Combine ideological liberation with solid work and develop our economy to a new level], Sao Zehua, ed., *Jiangxi kua shiji gouxiang* [Blueprint for Jiangxi beyond the century], Nanchang: Jiangxi renmin chubanshe, 1992, p.15.
43 You Huilong *et al.* (eds), '*Jiangxi tongji nianjian,1995* [Jiangxi Statistical Yearbook, 1995], Zhongguo tongji chubanshe, 1995, p. 45; Yu Boqing *et al.* (eds), *Hunan tongji nianjian,* [Hunan Statistical Yearbook], Beijing: Zhongguo tongji chubanshe, 1995, p. 40.
44 Liu Shutian, 'Suggestions for speeding up development of private economy', *Neibu Luntan* [Internal Forum], No. 279, February 1995, p. 8.
45 Wu Guanzheng, *Jiangxi sheng qing gailun*, p.181.
46 You Huilong, *et al.*, p. 459; Zhang Zhizheng and Shi Zupei, eds, *Gaige kaifang zhong de Guangdong jingji* [Guangdong economy in reform and opening], Guangzhou: Zhongshan University Press, 1992, p.140.
47 Liu Yao, 'Jiangxi yu yanhai diqu waixiangxing jingji fazhan bijiao ji zhanwang' [Development and prospect of foreign trade and foreign-funded sector in Jiangxi and coastal regions: a comparison], *Qiye Jingji* [Enterprises and Economy] , 3 (1994), p. 9.
48 Huang Zhigang, 'Attracting foreign investment to Jiangxi: problems and solutions', *Jiangxi Shehui Kexue* [Social Sciences in Jiangxi], 5 (1995), p. 29.
49 Fang Yan *et al.*, *Jiangxi xue*, p.185.
50 Fan Shengsi, 'Dui Jiangxi sheng jingji fazhan de huigu he fansi [Economic development in Jiangxi: a retrospective]', in *Jiangxi Shehui Kexue*, 6 (1991), p. 29; see also Fang Yan *et al.*, *Jinagxi xue*, p. 97.
51 Fang Yan *et al.*, *Jiangxi xue*, p. 189.
52 Shi Liangzhong, *et al.*, 'Speed up market economy in Jiangxi', in Zhong Qihuang *et al.* (eds), *Zouxiang 21 shiji xing Gan 'longzhongdui' wenji* [Collection of Essays on

Strategies for the Development of Jiangxi Advancing Toward the Twenty-First Century], Nanchang: Jiangxi renmin chubanshe, 1995, p. 43.

53 Hen Xing, *et al.*, *Jianxi tongguan* [A Survey of Jiangxi], Beijing: Renmin Ribao chubanshe, 1985, p. 107.

54 Fu Yutian *et al.*, *Dangdai Zhongguo de Jiangxi*, Vol.1, p. 233.

55 Ibid., p. 236.

56 Ibid., pp. 237–240.   .

57 Xiao Guiquan, 'Cong ba hu nongmin jiating bianhua kan jianshe you Zhongguo tese shehui zhuyi lilun de weili' [The change of eight peasant households and its significance in proving the power of the theory of building socialism with Chinese characteristics] , *Qiushi* [Seeking Truth], 3 (1996), p. 9; Interviews with Jiangxi academics in Nanchang, April 1995.

58 Jiang Bing, '*Gan wenhua miaoshu lun* [On description of Gan culture]', *Journal of Nanchang University*, Special Issue on Gan Culture Studies, October 1995, p. 21.

59 For details of the accusations of adultery and graft against Ni Xiance, see 'Zhongjiwei guanyu kaichu Ni Xiance dangji de jueding' [The CCP Central Discipline Committee's decision to dismiss Ni Xiance', *People's Daily*, 29 May 1987. For details of the case, see also Zhao Xiangru, 'Ni Xiance Waizhuan' [Ni Xiance: an unauthorised biography], *Fazhi Wenxue* [Legal Literature], 11 (1987), pp. 32–45.

60 In October 1995 when Mao Zhiyong retired, Wu Guanzheng became the party secretary of Jiangxi and nominated Shu Shengyou, one of his deputies and a Jiangxi native to succeed him as the governor. In early 1997 when Wu was appointed the party secretary of Shandong Province, he was succeeded by his deputy Shu Huiguo, another Jiangxi native.

61 *Renmin Ribao* [People's Daily], 20 December 1987. The event was also reported six days later by Hong Kong *Wenhui Bao* with the same title.

62 Wu Guanzheng, *Jiangxi sheng qing gailun*, p.175.

63 For details of economic development in the zone, see Huang Mingjian, 'Banhao chiyan qu, jianshe xin Gannan' [Successfully manage the experimental zone and build a new south Jiangxi], in Sao Zehua, ed., *Jiangxi kua shiji gouxiang* [Blueprint for Jiangxi Beyond the Century], Nanchang: Jiangxi renmin chubanshe, 1992, pp. 253–263.

64 Wu Guanzheng, 'Speech at the opening ceremony of the activity of soliciting essays on strategies for the development of Jiangxi advancing toward the twenty-first century', in Zhong Qihuang, *et al.*, eds, *Zouxiang 21 shiji xing Gan 'longzhongdui' wenji* [Collection of Essays on Strategies for the Development of Jiangxi Advancing Toward the Twenty-First Century], Nanchang: Jiangxi renmin chubanshe, 1995, pp. 7–12.

65 Jiang Bing, '*Miaoshu Gan wenhua, zengqiang zixinxin* [Describe the Gan culture to strengthen confidence]', *Gan Wenhua Yanjiu* [Gan Culture Studies], 1 (1994), p. 25.

66 Zhou Wenyin, *et al.*, *Jiangxi Wenhua* [Jiangxi Culture], Shenyang: Liaoning jiaoyu chubanshe, 1993.

67 *Gan Wenhua Yanjiu* [Gan Culture Studies], 1 (1994), pp. 3–7.

68 Zhen Keqiang, 'Gan wenhua re de lilun shensi' [A theoretical reflection on 'fever of the Gan culture'], *Journal of Nanchang University*, Special Issue on Gan Culture Studies, October 1995, p. 9.

69 Wu Guanzheng, 'postscript', pp. 289–290. According to a speech of Deputy Governor Huang Wuheng, the original title of the book was *Wo ai Jiangxi* [I Love Jiangxi]. See Huang Wuheng, 'Heavy responsibilities of the Gan culture studies', *Gan Wenhua Yanjiu* [Gan Culture Studies], 1 (1994), 11.

70 Han accounted for 99.98 per cent of the population in Jiangxi in 1952 and 99.93 per cent in 1982, the total population of 37 minority nationalities in 1982 amounted to 22,000 people. Ma Juxian *et al.*, *Zhongguo renkou: Jiangxi fence*, p. 298.

71 For example: *Xilu* for Shandong, *Yanzhao* for Beijing and Hebei, *Bashu* for Sichuan, *Wuyue* for Zhejiang and Jiangsu, *Jingchu* for Hubei, and *Yue* for Guangdong.

72 Hu Ping, Zheng Xiaojiang and Hen Dongyou, 'Qian hu wan huan Gan wenhua' [Calling ten thousand times for the Gan culture], *Gan Wenhua Yanjiu* [Gan Culture Studies], 1 (1994), p. 56.

73 Ibid., p. 56.

74 'Summary of the forum on 'strategy for developing the Gan culture', *Gan Wenhua Yanjiu* [Gan Culture Studies], 1 (1994), p. 37.

75 Wu Guanzheng, *Jiangxi sheng qing gailun*, p. 21.

76 Hu Ping, Zheng Xiaojiang and Hen Dongyou, 'Qian hu wan huan Gan wenhua' [Calling ten thousand times for the Gan culture], *Gan Wenhua Yanjiu* [Gan Culture Studies], 1 (1994), p. 59.

77 Ibid., p. 58.

78 Yao Yaping, Fu Xiuyan, Hu Xin and Zheng Xiaojiang, 'Haohao "Ganjun" neng fou jueqi' [Can 'the Gan Army' suddenly appear on the horizon]? *Gan Wenhua Yanjiu* [Gan Culture Studies], 1 (1994), pp. 100–101.

79 Wu Guanzheng, *Jiangxi sheng qing gailun*, p. 49.

80 Ibid., pp. 58–60.

81 Shao Hong and Jiang Bing, 'Ganren, Gantu, Ganhun: Gan wenhua shuoyuan yu zhanwang' [The Gan people, the Gan land and the Gan spirit: origin of and prospect for the Gan culture], *Gan Wenhua Yanjiu* [Gan Culture Studies], 1 (1994), pp. 70–93.

82 Zheng Keqiang, Wang Yuqi and Li Jiande, 'Jingji fanzhan yu Gan wenhua zai su' [Reconstruction of the Gan culture and economic development], *Gan Wenhua Yanjiu* [Gan Culture Studies], 1 (1994), p. 118.

83 *Gan Wenhua Yanjiu* [Gan Culture Studies], 1 (1994), p. 3.

84 You Huilong *et al.* (eds), '95 Jiangxi tongji nianjian [Statistical Year Book of Jiangxi 1995], Beijing: Zhongguo tongji chubanshe, 1995, p. 24.

85 Zhong Qihuang and Zhou Zheping (eds), *Zhongguo Jiangxi* [China's Jiangxi], Nanchang: Jiangxi meishu chubanshe, 1993, pp. 55–63.

86 See Chen Saiwen, 'Jingjiu zhaoshang "re" Jiangxi' [Jiangxi as a hot spot in attracting investment along the Jingjiu Railway], *Jiangxi Daily*, 1 July 1996.

87 Wu Guanzheng, *Jiangxi sheng qing gailun*, p. 170.

88 Zheng Keqiang, Wang Yuqi and Li Jiande, 'Jingji fazhan yu Gan wenhua zai su' [Reconstruction of the Gan culture and economic development', *Gan Wenhua Yanjiu* [Gan Culture Studies], 1 (1994), p. 113; see also Zhong Shiyin, 'Gannan dagong renyuan fanxiang xingye jishi' [An account of labourers of south Jiangxi origin setting up business back home], *Jiangxi Daily*, 8 October 1995. One author put the numbers of Jiangxi peasants working in coastal provinces in 1994 as three million, Wu Guanzheng, *Jiangxi sheng qing gailun*, p. 176.

89 Liu Feng, 'The overall arrangement of productive force in Jiangxi', Zhong Qihuang, *et al.*, eds, *Zouxiang 21 shiji xing Gan 'longzhongdui' wenji* [Collection of Essays on Strategies for the Development of Jiangxi Advancing Toward the Twenty-First Century], Nanchang: Jiangxi renmin chubanshe, p. 19.

90 Hu Ping, Zheng Xiaojiang and Hen Dongyou, 'Qian hu wan huan Gan wenhua [Calling ten thousand times for the Gan culture]', *Gan Wenhua Yanjiu* [Gan Culture Studies], 1 (1994), p. 65.

REFERENCES

Fang Yan *et al.* (eds), *Jiangxi Xue* [Jiangxi Studies], Shanghai: Tongji University Press, 1989.

Fu Yutian *et al.* (eds), *Dangdai Zhongguo de Jiangxi* [China Today: Jiangxi], Beijing: Dangdai Zhongguo chubanshe, Vol. 1, pp. 187–188.

Ma Juxian *et al.* (eds), *Zhongguo renkou: Jiangxi fence* [Chinese Population: Volume of Jiangxi], Beijing: Zhongguo caizheng jingji chubanshe, 1989.

Sao Zehua (ed.), *Jiangxi kua shiji gouxiang* [Blueprint for Jiangxi Beyond the Century], Nanchang: Jiangxi renmin chubanshe, 1992.

Wu Guanzheng (ed.), *Jiangxi sheng qing gailun: lishi, xianshi, yu weilai* [An Outline of Jiangxi: Its Past, Present and Future], Nanchang: Jiangxi renmin chubanshe, 1995.

Xu Huailin, *Jiangxi shigao* [A History of Jiangxi], Nanchang: Jiangxi gaoxiao chubanshe, 1991.

You Huilong *et al.* (eds), *'95 Jiangxi tongji nianjian* [Jiangxi Statistical Year Book, 1995], Beijing: Zhongguo tongji chubanshe, 1995.

Zhong Qihuang *et al.* (eds), *Zou xiang 21 shiji Xing Gan 'Longzhongdui' wenji* [Collection of Essays on Strategies for the Development of Jiangxi Advancing Toward the Twenty-First Century], Nanchang: Jiangxi renmin chubanshe, 1995.

Zhong Qihuang and Zhou Zheping (eds), *Zhongguo Jiangxi* [China's Jiangxi], Nanchang: Jiangxi meishu chubanshe, 1993.

Zhou Wenyin *et al.*, *Jiangxi wenhua* [Jiangxi Culture], Shenyang: Liaoning jiaoyu chubanshe, 1993.

Index